POST-PANDEMIC ECONOMY, TECHNOLOGY, AND INNOVATION

Global Outlook and Context

POST-PANDEMIC ECONOMY, TECHNOLOGY, AND INNOVATION

Global Outlook and Context

Edited by

Samina Yaqoob

Arwa Abdulkreem AL-Huqail

Fakhra Aziz

AAP | APPLE ACADEMIC PRESS

First edition published 2024

Apple Academic Press Inc.
1265 Goldenrod Circle, NE,
Palm Bay, FL 32905 USA

760 Laurentian Drive, Unit 19,
Burlington, ON L7N 0A4, CANADA

CRC Press
2385 NW Executive Center Drive,
Suite 320, Boca Raton FL 33431

4 Park Square, Milton Park,
Abingdon, Oxon, OX14 4RN UK

Library and Archives Canada Cataloguing in Publication

CIP data on file with Canada Library and Archives

Library of Congress Cataloging-in-Publication Data

CIP data on file with US Library of Congress

ISBN: 978-1-77491-410-6 (hbk)
ISBN: 978-1-77491-411-3 (pbk)
ISBN: 978-1-00341-407-0 (ebk)

About the Editors

Samina Yaqoob

Samina Yaqoob is a PhD Researcher of Management Sciences at the Dr. Hasan Murad School of Management (HSM), University of Management and Technology, Lahore, Pakistan. She graduated from Government College University, Faisalabad, and earned an MS in Management Sciences from International Islamic University, Islamabad, Pakistan. She has published three book chapters with Springer and Elsevier and has many articles in journals indexed in Scopus.

Arwa Abdulkreem AL-Huqail, PhD

Arwa Abdulkreem AL-Huqail, PhD, is a Distinguished Associate Professor in Ecology (since 2021) in the Department of Biology, College of Science at Princess Nourah bint Abdulrahman University, Riyadh, Saudi Arabia. She is an environmental and community service activist having more than 60 publications in journals indexed in Web of Science (Core Collection). She has more than 26 years of experience in university teaching and research and has organized, participated in, and attended many workshops and scientific meetings at the national level. She was the Vice Dean of the College of Science for Community Service and Environmental Development for three consecutive years, Vice Dean of Development and Quality at the Community College for a year, and Adviser to the Saudi Ministry of Environment, Water and Agriculture and the National Center for the Development of Vegetation Cover and Combating Desertification for 2 years.

Fakhra Aziz, PhD

Fakhra Aziz, PhD, is a tenured Associate Professor and Head of STEM Education at the Lahore College for Women University, Pakistan. She has a decade of experience in teaching and research. She earned her master's degree in Science Education with a biology major. Dr. Aziz later specialized in Educational Leadership and Management, doing her postdoctorate at Dicle University in Diyarbakir, Turkey. She regularly presents at national and international conferences, webinars, and training sessions to share her research and provide exposure to others. A strong believer in the power of positive thinking in the workplace and in the empowerment of women, she has a number of publications focusing on gender-based issues related to leadership, new trends in educational leadership, and technology assistance for leadership in national and international journals. Dr. Aziz is Editor of the Journal of Arts and Social Sciences and a member of editorial boards of many national and international journals.

Contents

Contributors

Izaz Ahmad
Materials Chemistry Laboratory, Department of Chemistry, GC University, Lahore, Pakistan

Shakeel Ahmad
Department of Agronomy, Bahauddin Zakariya University, Multan, Pakistan

Rahat Ajmal
Department of Arabic, Lahore College for Women University, Lahore, Pakistan

Sana Arshad
Materials Chemistry Laboratory, Department of Chemistry, GC University, Lahore, Pakistan

Farkhanda Asad
Department of Zoology, Government College University, Faisalabad, Pakistan

Asma Ashraf
Department of Zoology, Government College University, Faisalabad, Pakistan

Sidrah Azam
Government Associate College for Women, Eminabad, Gujranwala, Pakistan

Fakhra Aziz
STEM Education Department, Lahore College for Women University, Lahore, Pakistan

Naheed Bano
Faculty of Veterinary and Animal Sciences, MNS-University of Agriculture, Multan, Pakistan

Ayoub Rasid Chaudhary
Department of Chemistry, GC University, Lahore, Pakistan

Birra Dar
Materials Chemistry Laboratory, Department of Chemistry, GC University, Lahore, Pakistan

Catalina Georgeta Dinu
Faculty of Law, Transilvania University of Brasov, Romania

Aiman Elahi
Department of Biochemistry, Government College University, Faisalabad, Pakistan

Sidra Farid
Materials Chemistry Laboratory, Department of Chemistry, GC University Lahore, Lahore, Pakistan

M. Zia-Ul-Haq
Office of Research, Innovation and Commercialization (ORIC), Lahore College for Women University, Lahore, Pakistan

Arshad H. Hashmi
Office of Research, Innovation and Commercialization (ORIC), Virtual University of Pakistan, M.A. Jinnah Campus, Lahore, Pakistan

Arwa Abdulkreem AL-Huqail
Department of Biology, College of Science, Princess Nourah bint Abdulrahman University, Riyadh, Saudi Arabia

Iram Iqbal
Department of Pharmacology, Faculty of Pharmacy, Bahauddin Zakariya University, Multan, Pakistan
Drug Testing Laboratory, Health Department, Government of Punjab, Lahore, Pakistan

Marius Irimie
Faculty of Medicine, Transilvania University of Brasov, Brasov, Romania

Sadia Javed
Department of Biochemistry, Government College University, Faisalabad, Pakistan

Nimra Kanwal
Materials Chemistry Laboratory, Department of Chemistry, GC University, Lahore, Pakistan

Muhammad Ayaz Khan
Department of Agriculture Extension and Adoptive Research, Punjab, Pakistan

Muhammad Mehroz Khan
Department of Biochemistry, Government College University, Faisalabad, Pakistan

Abia Mahboob
Materials Chemistry Laboratory, Department of Chemistry, GC University, Lahore, Pakistan

Ghulam Mujtaba
Intellectual Property Organization of Pakistan, NTC-HQs Building, Islamabad, Pakistan

Tehmina Fiaz Qazi
Hailey College of Banking and Finance, Punjab University, Lahore, Pakistan

Uzma Qureshi
The Women University, Multan, Pakistan

Maham Saeed
Materials Chemistry Laboratory, Department of Chemistry, GC University, Lahore, Pakistan

Ramsha Saleem
Lahore College for Women University, Lahore, Pakistan

Fatima Saqib
Department of Pharmacology, Faculty of Pharmacy, Bahauddin Zakariya University, Multan, Pakistan

Rahma Shafaat
Institute of Business & Management, University of Engineering and Technology, Lahore, Pakistan

Javed Hussain Shah
Materials Chemistry Laboratory, Department of Chemistry, GC University, Lahore, Pakistan

Muhammad Shahbaz
Materials Chemistry Laboratory, Department of Chemistry, GC University, Lahore, Pakistan

Zunaira Shaheen
Department of Zoology, Government College University Faisalabad, Faisalabad, Punjab, Pakistan

Shahzad Sharif
Materials Chemistry Laboratory, Department of Chemistry, GC University, Lahore, Pakistan

Laraib Shoukat
Department of Biochemistry, Government College University, Faisalabad, Pakistan

Muhammad Tariq
Central Cotton Research Institute, Multan, Pakistan

Muqeet Wahid
Department of Pharmacology, Faculty of Pharmacy, Bahauddin Zakariya University, Multan, Pakistan

Samina Yaqoob
Dr Hasan Murad School of Management (HSM), University of Management and Technology, Lahore, Pakistan

Abbreviations

ADB	Asian Development Bank
AI	artificial intelligence
AR	augmented reality
ARDS	acute respiratory distress syndrome
BAs	business angels
CCRT	Catastrophe Containment and Relief Trust
CEPI	Coalition for Epidemic Preparedness
COA	Chinese Council of Agriculture
CODA	Commission on Dental Accreditation
CI	computational intelligence
CT	computed tomography
DSSI	initiative of debt service suspension
EEA	European Economic Area
EMEs	emerging market economies
F.Is	financial institutions
GEN	generative adversarial networks
GFC	global financial crisis
GHS	Global Health System
GIS	geographic information system
GISAID	Global Initiative on Sharing All Influenza Data
HCW	healthcare worker
ICT	information and communication technology
IEA	International Energy Agency
IIF	International Institute for Finance
ILO	International Labor Organization
IMF	International Monetary Fund
IoMT	Internet of Medical Things
ISM	International Student Mobility
MDRI	Multilateral Debt Relief Initiative
ML	machine learning
NIC	nature-inspired computing
NIH	National Institute of Health
NLP	natural language processing
OECD	Organization for Economic Cooperation and Development

OPD	outpatient division
PPE	personal protective equipment
PRGT	Poverty Reduction and Growth Trust
PSS	psychosocial support
PTDC	Pakistan Tourism Development Corporation
RCF	rapid credit facility
RFI	Rapid Financing Instrument
SARS-CoV-2	Severe Acute Respiratory Syndrome Coronavirus 2
SDGs	sustainable development goals
SEN	special educational needs
SIRD	susceptible-infected-recovered-dead
SMEs	small and medium enterprises
SOPs	standard operating procedures
STI	science, technology, and innovation
TAP	Tech Access Partnership
UAVs	unmanned aerial vehicles
VCs	venture capitalists
WB	World Bank

Preface

Coronavirus has changed the world's focus as it has changed the economy and health of the world community. Researchers, health care providers, administrators, and policymakers have been trying their best to manage the pandemic at their levels. Researchers, writers, and publishers have been playing their part in giving timely information to cope up with the effects of this unforeseen pandemic.

Feeling the need for comprehensive coverage of the COVID-19 pandemic in an organized way for researchers in all fields of life, we have thoroughly overviewed the current situation in this book titled "Post-Pandemic Economy, Technology, and Innovation: Global Outlook and Context." This book is themed with key objectives to provide a state-of-the-art and systematic review about the impact of COVID-19 on various fields of life. The book consists of 10 chapters.

Chapters 1 and 2 provide detailed information about impact of pandemic on economy and entrepreneurship, respectively. Chapter 3 describes how COVID-19 impacted the agriculture sector. In Chapter 4, the authors have discussed the role of health professionals before, during, and after COVID-19.

Chapter 5 discusses in detail how COVID-19 has revolutionalized the teaching methodologies and introduced virtual classrooms while Chapter 6 comprehensively describes how COVID-19 has impacted the innovation cycle, the resulting technologies, and relaxed IPR laws. Chapter 7 and 8 discuss the marketing strategies during COVID-19 and banking mechanisms during the pandemic. Chapter 9 describes the impact of COVID-19 on science and technology while Chapter 10 discusses the issues, challenges, and lessons faced by travel and tourism during and after pandemic.

We hope that researchers from all walks of life will find this book valuable and exciting. This book is written in an easy-to-understand style, keeping in mind the general public, so we hope that the layman will be interested in this book as it presents existing literature in simple language.

We want to thank each of the authors for their contributions and dedicated efforts to provide prepared chapters according to the instructions of the AAP. The editors aim that this book is of benefit and a reference source to anyone researching how COVID-19 impacted various fields of life. We tried to include existing pertinent literature in the book; however, we might have missed some essential papers due to the massive literature on this topic. Our apologies to the authors whose articles we could not include. We are obligated to the staff at Apple Academic Publishers for their support in assembling this work and their efforts in keeping this book on schedule.

—Samina Yaqoob
Dr. Arwa Abdulkreem AL-Huqail
Dr. Fakhra Aziz

CHAPTER 1

COVID-19 and Its Global Economic Effects: Erstwhile and Afterwards

RAMSHA SALEEM[1], SIDRAH AZAM[2], and ARSHAD H. HASHMI[3]

[1]*Department of Economics, Lahore College for Women University, Lahore, Pakistan*

[2]*Department of Economics, Government Associate College for Women, Eminabad, Gujranwala, Pakistan*

[3]*Office of Research, Innovation and Commercialization (ORIC), Virtual University of Pakistan, M.A. Jinnah Campus, Lahore, Pakistan*

ABSTRACT

Pandemic COVID-19 is much more than a health shock as it has deteriorated various aspects of lives. These aspects include social, economic, and political setups, leaving deep damages. Concerning the economic aspects, the pandemic has caused a severe crash in crude oil and petroleum markets both on the demand and supply sides, deviated the pattern of external resource influxes (FDI, remittances, external debt, and foreign aid) from developed to underdeveloped economies. Furthermore, World Bank, IMF, and other international financial institutions have launched many debt relief programs for poor countries to offset the adverse impact of virus. . Public debt in developing and emerging markets has reached to levels not seen in the last five decades. COVID-19 has inevitably affected international trade due to the wide term closure of borders and airlines. The current pandemic has restricted the movement and trade to prevent the spread of the disease. As an example, social distancing disrupted the labor supply, travel, and

Post-Pandemic Economy, Technology, and Innovation: Global Outlook and Context.
Samina Yaqoob, Arwa Abdulkreem AL-Huqail, and Fakhra Aziz (Eds.)

transport directly. Evidently, the medical equipment trade has been very high since the second quarter of 2020. The equipments specifically related to COVID-19 are traded most till the present date. In addition, global GDP has declined at the start of this decade. Home quarantine and the lockdowns have jammed construction, manufacturing, production, and service supply chains both locally and globally, which resulted in a significant rise in unemployment. World GDP shrunk by an unparalleled amount in 2020. However, the magnitude of the recovery is uncertain because the pandemic shock has brought severe value chain disruption. COVID-19 has embodied the greatest risk to the Global Health System (GHS) and economies in the 21st century. Overall, it is observed that no country was sufficiently prepared to confront the pandemic socially and economically. The outbreak of COVID-19 has awakened most of the world's population to the broken and insufficient health and economic setups. The pandemic provided food for thought to policy-makers, governments, health institutions, such as WHO, financial institutions, employers, and individuals to step necessary actions to combat the spread of the virus and economic losses to mitigate the economic and health damages due to the outbreak of COVID-19.

1.1 INTRODUCTION

Coronavirus is much more than a health issue. It has serious effects on all the continents except Antarctica, having the potential to deteriorate social, economic, and political setups which probably will leave deep scars.

The prominent consequences of such a pandemic include immense destruction of economic systems through the reduction in employment, increase in cost of production, transaction costs, and unavailability of raw materials to be readily used which either was imported or purchased domestically. Furthermore, governments halted international flights and widespread outskirt closures have also been observed. The lockdown trials that have been executed by almost all the countries affected businesses and essential services.[1]

1.2 GLOBAL CRUDE OIL PRICES AND PANDEMIC

The outline of economic activities is vulnerable to not only the economic principles of demand and supply, macroeconomic fluctuations, and political actions but also to pandemic aspects.[2] Production of goods and services necessarily demands various kinds of fuel or energy, such as coal, petroleum, electricity, natural gas, and renewable energy. The energy industry is inevitably not immune to the influences of this pandemic. The international energy agency (IEA) claimed that the shock to the energy demand caused by COVID-19 is the biggest in the last 70 years and this demand, on average, fell by 6% as compared with demand in 2019. The demand for electricity also followed a huge shock after experiencing a boost in 2019. On average, the total electricity demand by the European economies has dropped by 9%, whereas the demand for fossil energy has decreased by 28% globally in April 2020. In addition to these, nuclear energy consumption has fallen by 14% at the global level. On the contrary, demand for renewable energy has increased by 15%.[3] Among the various energy requirements, oil fulfills a significant share. This section focuses on the crude oil demand during and post-pandemic period in detail. The pandemic (COVID-19) generates uncertainty, plunges the global economy, and intensifies the financial markets' volatility. The oil price response to COVID-19 was steadily accommodated until March 9, 2020, and 49 days later, after the announcement of the first coronavirus monitoring report by the WHO, Saudi Arabia made excess supply and flooded the market with oil. Quite considerably, during this oil price response, global oil prices drop more than 20% in a single day called the "Black Monday."[4] Oil per barrel prices dropped to US $32.01 from US $55.66 in February 2020. However, the demand for oil has dried up as the worldwide lockdowns have confined people inside their homes. In April 2020, crude oil prices experienced a remarkable reduction (US $18.38 per barrel)[1] as the rapid increase in infected cases obligated several countries of the world to re-tighten measures and impose fresh lockdowns. Evidently, the global uncertainty due to this outbreak has extensively disturbed the price dynamics of the oil industry.

1.2.1 DEMAND AND SUPPLY-SIDE CONSIDERATIONS

Economic disruptions related to the COVID-19 occurrence have slowed down production and mobility globally, causing a significant slump in demand for oil. In April 2020, the demand for crude oil was 30% lesser as compared with previous year, estimated by the IEA. The demand reached such a level not observed since 1995. With such a significant fall in demand, oil producers were wondering about facilities to store excess crude oil.

Eventually, stocks reached their highest level in June 2020. Since then, producers focused to reduce production to ease the pressure on storage capacity.[3] According to Stewart Glickman, an energy equity expert, "The demand shock was so massive that it overwhelmed anything that people could have expected."

BBC news on 20th April published that OPEC and its associates settled on a deal to slash global oil production by about 10%. The deal involved reducing the collective daily production of OPEC members by almost one quarter for the next 2 months.[5] This agreement was the largest reduction in oil output ever established. But many analysts argued that this cut was not enough to recover the price as before the pandemic.[6]

1.2.2 EFFECT OF OIL PRICES SLASH ON THE GDP

Most of the oil-producing countries are nondiversified economies, that is, sector-dependent, which means that a significant proportion of their GDP is gained from oil export revenues. The fall in oil prices during the pandemic confined the ability of these countries to respond to the multiphase domestic pressures produced by COVID-19. IEA estimated that key oil-producing countries would likely see a drop in their GDP of 50–85% in comparison with the GDP of 2019.[3] The estimated plunge in their income is the highest in over two decades. Furthermore, if the pandemic continues over the coming year, IEA has alerted that revenues could slash further, based on future market conditions.[7]

World Bank has released its report on commodity outlook 2020, which stated that *"The impact of COVID-19 on commodities has been uneven and could have lasting effects for energy markets."* This report also contains a valuable recommendation for oil-producing countries, that is, these countries need to be necessarily aggressive in developing and implementing such policy structure that aims to reduce their dependence on oil revenues to avoid a further economic slump in the coming years.[8]

1.2.3 CRUDE OIL PRICES: TOWARD RECOVERY

Widespread lockdown during this pandemic slowed down economic activities all over the world and so dampened the fuel demand which in turn brought downward pressure on the prices per barrel. It is evident from the data of 2020 that worst hit months of this year are March till July. Later, various countries considered smart lockdown strategies but somehow the production and firms woke up. According to Longley and Blas,[9] situations are not back to normal yet, but the optimistic signals are thriving ahead. The huge excessive stock of fuel that accumulated in 2020 is being gradually depleted with the new normal. However, airports and border prohibitions are also getting ease which will enhance the fuel demand and thus prices.

Although this (corona) epidemic is worse than ever in the US, hitherto demand in Europe is vigorously back as the second wave of lockdown eases, but Asian states continued to wrench into a huge volume of crude oil. However, some nations completely recovered the demands.[10] For instance, the largest refiner in India narrated that on the one hand, the plants of India are processing at their full volume, and on the other hand, India is expecting a V-shaped reflection in its fuel use. Amrita Sen, co-founder of London-based consultant Energy Aspects, stated that *"With vaccines slowly rolling out, we expect investors to start returning to the oil sector and for prices to continue firming."*

As the government relaxed the lockdown in European states, the vehicle drivers of France, the UK, and Spain started hitting the roads. According to an index of road usage and traffic compiled by Bloomberg News, the demand of fuel started recovering after the lockdown and the corporations of the petroleum exporting industries started squeezing their limits on production, and crude oil surpassed US $50-barrel in the last week of December for the first time since the second quarter of 2020.[9]

After disintegrating the remarkable slumps in the early 2020s, the prices of fuel, and crude oil ought to recover at a jerky pace. However, different analysts provided various comments for returning to the pre-pandemic levels, by the end of 2021.[10] A group of 10 investment banks forecast that the international benchmark for Brent crude oil will be around the average of US $53.50/per barrel in the fourth quarter of 2021. This benchmark will be around the average of US $50.31 in the United States in the same quarter.[11] However, oil price recovery needs effective oil demand. A substantial increase in the demand for oil is improbable to happen before the second quarter of 2021 when the vaccines of this pandemic are most probable to be available globally.

Besides the oil market, the demand for renewable energy has increased in 2019 and new energy resources installed took the share of 72% among the total energy resources. However, this demand further increased by 14% in April 2020. According to many environmental scholars, renewable energy will be the only way forward in the post-pandemic period.[6]

1.3 JET OIL DEMAND AND PRICE SLASH

COVID-19 halted the mobility of people, both nationally and internationally causing the closure of airports for extended periods. Governments prohibited the movement across the border to avoid imported infected cases, thus the demand for flights declined to the lowest and so did the demand for jet fuel. The airline industry has been effectively hit by COVID-19 and recovery seems muted in almost all the markets due to travel restrictions to avoid human contact which can facilitate the virus spread.[12]

Arguably, it might take years to recover the demand for flights and jet fuel prices that are distorted by the health and economic crisis created by COVID-19, whereas airlines kept striving for survival in their worst slump. The slump has been further accompanied by possible alterations in the habits of various kinds of travelers, that is, business people, tourists, and students.[13] Businesses and education get used to online meetings and classes. Furthermore, it revealed that the increasing international travel restrictions viciously affected the level of economic activities.[14]

The International Air Transport Association (IATA) has foretold about a slower recovery for jet fuel prices than in past crises. The Association also estimated a revenue loss of over 25% for the year 2020, which is equivalent to US $314 billion. However, Richard Gorry, JBC Energy Asia's managing director said that recovery would be evident by the second quarter of 2021, after the 70% fall in jet fuel demand during the second and third quarters of 2020. Moreover, some analysts believe that progress in online working during lockdowns might not vanish completely even though the disease vanishes. For instance, finance directors who would prefer to reduce travel costs would choose the option of online meetings.[13]

Given the reduced demand for flights and jet fuel, IATA forecast that industry fuel bill will decline by 15% of the average operating cost. Furthermore, the decline in the jet fuel price is even more than oil prices. Figure 1.1 shows the deterioration of jet fuel prices due to the pandemic in 2020. The price crash is even more than the world financial crisis in 2008. Hence, the airline industry is among the hard-hit industries in a dual manner, that is, revenue loss due to lack of its demand and oil price slash.

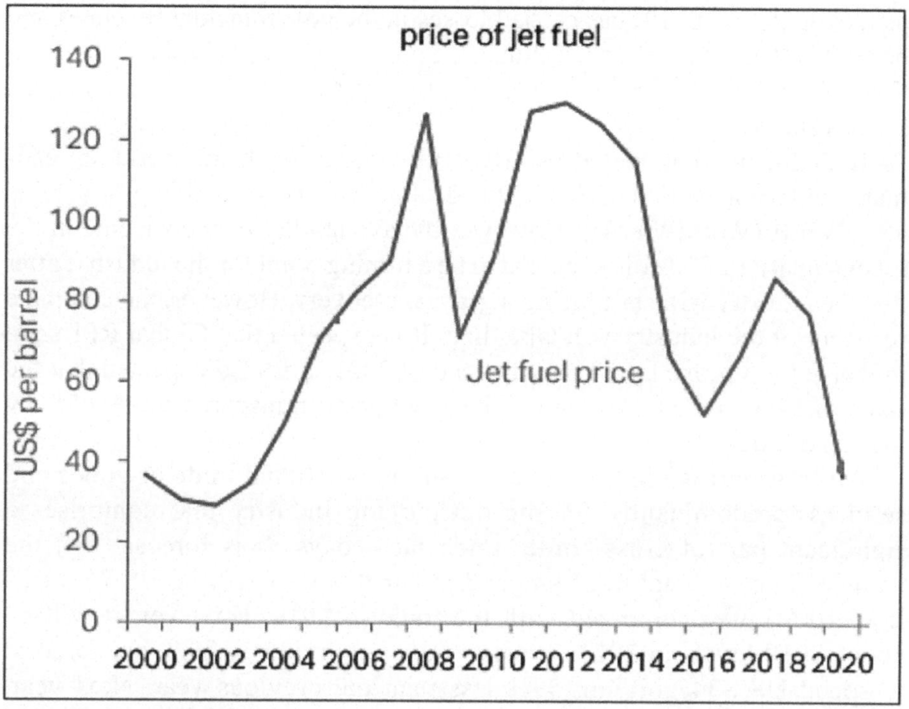

FIGURE 1.1 Jet fuel price.

Source: Modified with permission from Ref. [12]. [Economic Per formance of the Airline Industry. *Semi Annual Report* **2020**.].

In the real term, travelers will be benefited because of lower real travel charges as airlines are discounting ticket prices to enhance the demand significantly. It is expected that the average fare would be 68% lower than that in 1998 after adjusting for inflation.[12]

1.3.1 GDP AND GOVERNMENT REVENUE LOSS DUE TO FALL IN DEMAND OF AIR FLIGHTS AND JET FUEL DEMAND

Air transport is a significant driving factor in economic development. This economic benefit is reinforced by both (national and international direct connections)

During the last decade, the governments profited from the dense performance of the airlines industry as their customers generated a tax revenue of around US $111 billion/per year. However, the emergence of global pandemic (COVID-19) has caused losses in the governmental revenues and become a threat to the airline failures. Spotting the importance of the aviation industry, the government strode top to help the industry to overcome this serious shock.[12]

In 2020, International RPKs (Revenue Passenger Kilometers) are estimated to face a decline of 66%. This decline was the second largest decline after WWII (World War II). However, the availability of the vaccine in the second quarter of 2021 is expected to be a turning point for the industry, after that the industry will start facing a gradual recovery. However, the complete recovery of the industry will take time. It is expected that Global RPKs are probable to improve by 50% by the end of 2021. It is also expected that the share of the world's GDP that will be spent on air transport will be 0.5% by the end of 2021.[13]

Air transport is vital for national and international trade of goods and services, predominantly for the outsourcing industry that comprises a significant part of cross-border trade these days. It is forecast that the value of international trade shipped by air this year will be US $5.8 trillion, 10% lower compared with the trade in 2019. However, it will be above 2019 levels in 2021. Tourists traveling by air in 2020 are forecast to spend US $347 billion, 59% less than the previous year. Next year, tourists traveling by air are forecast to spend US $559 billion, equivalent to the level last seen in 2012. Another adverse impact of the crisis will be on jobs. Globally, total employment supported (directly and indirectly) by the air transport sector has declined to 42.8 million people in 2020; a 51% reduction relative to 2019.[12]

1.4 DEVIATED PATTERN OF INFLOW OF EXTERNAL RESOURCES DUE TO THE SHOCK OF COVID-19

The world economy has been construed as almost standstill, making COVID-19 a global issue.[15] Among the various economic impacts brought by the pandemic, one ought not to be get ignored, that is, the inflow of external resources from developed to developing countries which halt significantly. This matter is food for thought because developing nations depend upon these resources to fill various domestic gaps like the expenditure–revenue gap, saving–investment, and technological gap between developed and developing economies.[16] The financing gap is also among one of the limitations to achieve the LR (long run) sustainable EG (economic growth), which is also handled with external funds.[20] Governments of developing countries finance budget deficits through foreign loans and grants. These influxes can act as a supplement in domestic resources.[23] Foreign resource influxes take several forms, for instance, external debt, FDI (foreign direct investment), remittances, and foreign aid.[17] Undoubtedly, COVID-19 deviated the pattern of inflows of these resources from the trend.

1.4.1 DROP IN THE GLOBAL FDI

Most of the developed nations have withdrawn their FDI from developing economies when the Corona virus was at its peak, that is, during the second quarter of 2020. This contraction in FDI hit developing economies adversely because inflows of FDI fell even more than the expected level globally, and severely influenced those sectors that account for a larger share of FDI influxes in the developing countries.[18] Infected developing nations have become more contingent on FDI in the last few decades, and so the prevailing scenario will harshly affect their GDP. This fact can be observed from the significant rise in FDI toward developing countries between 1985 and 2017, that is, from 25 to 46%. Henceforth, the reduction in global FDI is directly related to the disturbances in the global supply chains which have been clearly witnessed due to the COVID-19 pandemic.[19] According to the UN Conference on Trade and Development (UNCTAD), worldwide FDI influxes are expected to drop between 30 and 40% during 2020/21.[20] This is because uncertainty around the world and negative growth are discouragements to foreign investors. Henceforth, given the simultaneous decline in crude oil prices and slash in the health system, the inflow of FDI is also adversely affected.[21] More so, an empirical investigation revealed a positive association between COVID-19-related confirmed deaths and outflows of FDI.[22] Meaningful to say, the health crisis induced multinational firms to relocate their investments.

Global investment trends released a report, according to which, the rate of decline in developing countries is expected to flatten in 2020 as some economic and investment activities appeared to jump.[22]

Somehow, East Asia was showing signs of economic recovery signals that FDI flows toward developing economies are expected to stabilize. Despite a significant drop in FDI influxes in the year 2020, it is still an overt fact that FDI remained a chief source of finance for developing economies, during this year.[23]

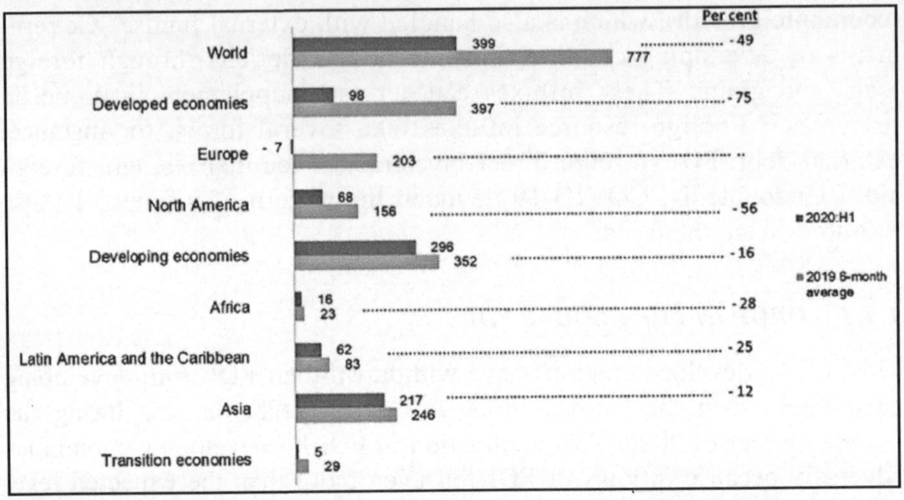

FIGURE 1.2 FDI inflows by region.

Source: Reprinted from Ref. [23]. https://unctad.org/news/global-foreign-direct-investment-falls-49-first-half-2020

Figure 1.2 reveals the FDI drop by an unprecedented ratio in the first half (H1) of 2020 as compared with the previous year's ratio, around the globe. Thus, the pandemic distorted the inflows of FDI in a recordable manner.

1.4.1.1 WHO WILL BE AFFECTED MOST?

The quality and quantity of FDI inflows toward the developing countries are not identical. Fast-growing economies of Asia particularly India, China, Cambodia, and Malaysia have been experiencing economic surges over the past three decades. The injection of FDI in these countries is mostly concentrated in the manufacturing and services sectors. However, if the continent of Africa is considered, foreign investment more often takes place in extractive industries, such as mining and oil. These countries faced more volatility in FDI influx during the pandemic specifically due to a lack of energy demand caused by the widespread shutdown of economic activities.[19]

1.4.1.2 CONSEQUENCES OF FDI CONTRACTION RELEVANT TO SUPPLY CHAINS IN THE LONG TERM

In the long term, COVID-19 may affect foreign investors and developing economies, contingent on continental context and investment motivations.

For example, if there will be speedy projected growth in the healthcare sectors, FDI inflows would have direct relation, that is, FDI may estimate to recover symmetrically. Subsequently, problems experienced by firms functioning in the energy sector that have faced the collapse in demand may bring adverse consequences for economies depending on resource-seeking investment. However, for efficiency-seeking FDI, future trends are still undefined. Global distortions brought by coronavirus may lead to volte-face for some MNEs with respect to the geographic and sectoral spread of their economic activities and cut their supply chains.[18] Hence, further deteriorating the client and investor relationship. Consequently, Other MNEs may command to increase resilience toward regional-specific shocks by diversifying the supplier networks. This diversification may involve disinvestments from some locations but expansions from some others.[24]

1.4.1.3 STRANDS FOR THE RECOVERY OF FDI AND ECONOMIC GROWTH

The impact of COVID-19 on FDI influxes in the coming period will vary among the countries and sectors. However, there are three strands explained by a report revealed by the Organization for Economic Cooperation and Development (OECD) related to the conditions of foreign investments by the end of 2021.[18] First, the optimistic strand illustrates that economies shall recover by the end of 2021 and earnings are expected to return to the pre-crisis levels. Consequently, the FDI inflows are also anticipated to recover toward historic levels. However, there might be a fall (between 30 and 40%) in the medium term, that is, the second quarter of 2021. Second, the middle strand moderately describes that economies will recover, but this recovery will be uneven, that is, some sectors will recover while others will remain below the pre-pandemic levels. This view predicted that FDI inflows will show a recovery of about one-third of pre-pandemic levels. Third, the pessimistic strand displays a bleak picture of economic recovery and investment earnings. According to this view, most of the sectors will experience a depression and a consequent tumble in earnings. The FDI influxes shall begin to improve only after the availability of vaccines which will expectedly normalize the social setup.

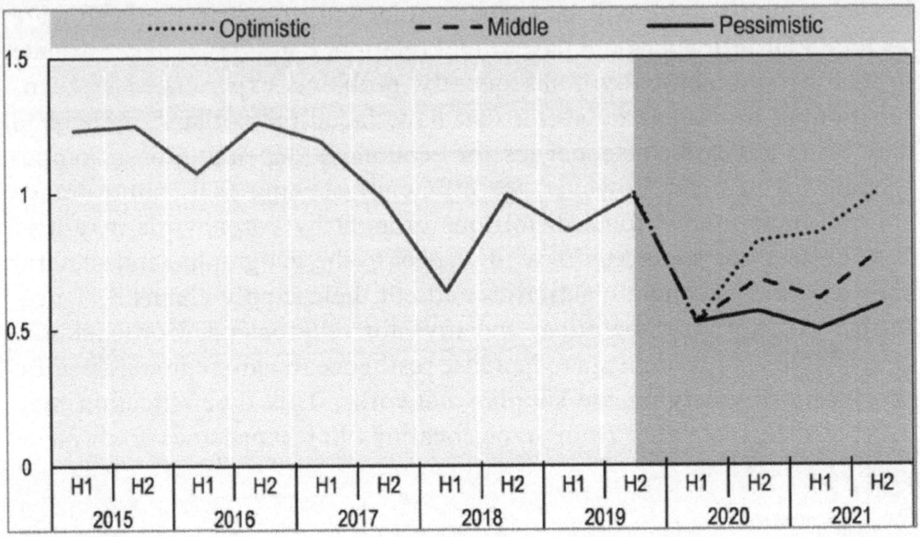

FIGURE 1.3 Recovery of FDI and economic growth.
Source: Reprinted from Ref. [18]. © 2020 OECD.

1.4.2 *EXTERNAL DEBT*

Developing economies are contingent on external debt for development funding because it has capacity to accelerate governmental resources.[25] External debt is usually transferred from the developed to the developing world officially either in cash or other forms of assets in order to provide assistance to finance development or income distribution obstinacies.[26] Also, foreign debt is used by the government to reduce the budget deficits.

The pandemic is flaring-up enormous challenges globally. The bug is highly contagious as it is causing a significant loss of world population. Countries are struggling for mitigation in lockdown rules which are presumably applied for limiting interactions to hinder the disease spread. These lockdown policies are associated with considerable economic costs in the form of shutdowns and likely unemployment. The governments even opt to impose lockdowns to save human lives at the cost of a reduction in output and thus fall in GDP.[27] Meanwhile, governments attempted the narrow tax base which further intensified their need to borrow internationally. Generally, debts smooth consumption during curfews and lockdowns, but limit fiscal revenues for supporting the pattern of consumption. Default risks also enhance the cost of social distancing, because along with depressing production of income, they also lessen the prospects for debt refund, increasing the possibility of a long-lasting, and expensive debt disaster. Consequently, developing economies are facing the epidemic with debt challenges.[25] This pandemic is a great external shock for emerging and developing markets with crumpling export demand, capital flows, remittances, and tourism.[28] Additionally, developing countries have limited fiscal budgets, which has made governments unable to extend support to their people. However, an impediment for these nations is their long-lasting issue with external debt and high vulnerability to debt overhang.[29] Considering debt during the time of Coronavirus is important because it changes the outcome of pandemic as it alters the costs of lockdowns. Subsequent health crises and sharp downturns in global financial markets have brought the developing world into the wave of a hard time. Imagine a highly indebted country, with an imminent debt crisis that selects a less strict lockdown due to its inadequate ability to utilize international financial markets to support consumption. Accordingly, the highly indebted country will end with a higher death rate resulting from the virus spread. So, health economists find that countries that begin with high debt and virus outbreaks will experience more severe health and debt crises, that is, a higher number of fatalities and more extended defaults. Factually, lockdowns are attempted to save future lives.[27] It is revealed that high foreign debt and default criticize lockdowns with the base related to the debt overhang.[30] It means COVID-19 is an adverse shock to an already fragile world economic position.

It is the fastest and most broad-based upsurge in debt in developing economies which has been observed in the past 50 years. Since 2010, the total foreign debt of the developing world boosted by 60 percentage points of GDP to a notable peak of about 170% of GDP in 2019 and attained another peak in 2020 as displayed in Figure 1.4.

Subsequently, the present global recession is uncommon in its severity. However, the pandemic and economic recession are testing the resilience of severely indebted economies and firms, institutions, and policies to be developed to cope with the situation. They are experiencing a recession with a much likelihood vulnerable position than the 2009 crisis. Furthermore, it is predicted that there are high chances for extended debt distress in highly indebted poor countries of the world which is displayed in Figure 1.5.[31]

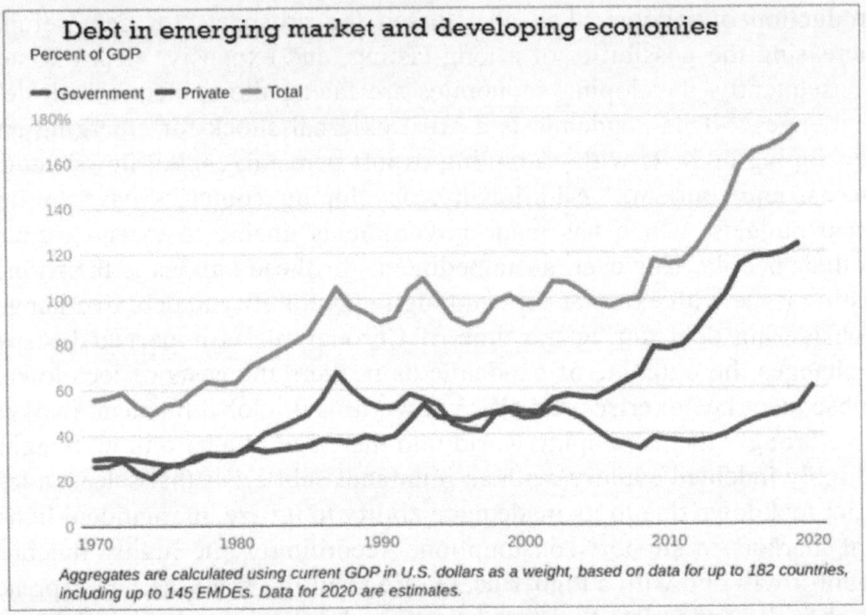

FIGURE 1.4 Debt in emerging and developing economies.

Source: Reprinted with permission from Ref. [31]. © 2021 IMF; World Bank.

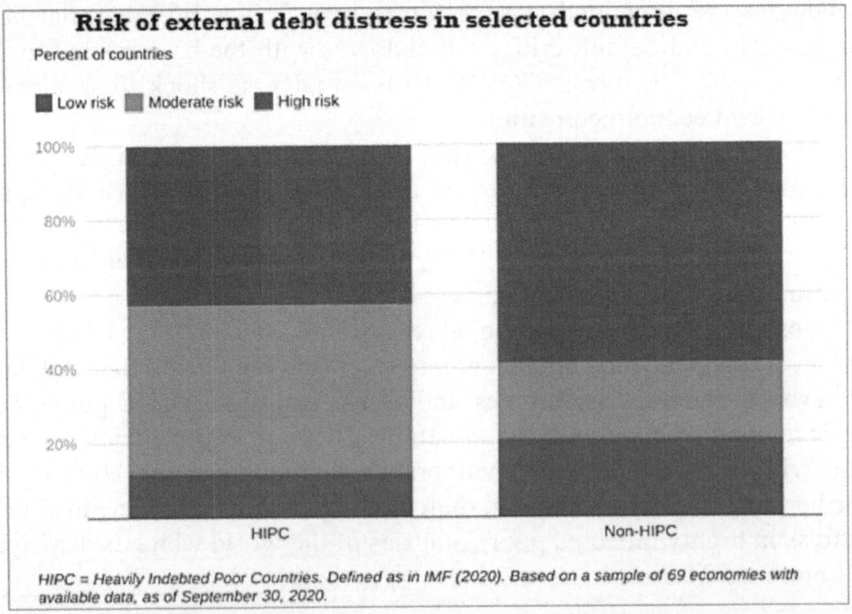

FIGURE 1.5 Debt distress.

Source: Reprinted with permission from Ref. [31]. © 2021 IMF; World Bank.

1.4.2.1 LOW INTEREST RATE AND THE MITIGATION OF UNPRECEDENTED DEBT LEVELS

In order to overcome the unprecedented debt levels, the possible and most probable response is lowering the rate of interest.[32] Economists predicted that debt levels could have further intensified but the plausible answer of low policy rates may revive the business and investment mood. According to IMF, there are visible downturns in policy rates during the pandemic in 2020. This fall is uncommon and prominent enough to consider the strategic outlook of all the economies to avoid the overwhelmed debt distress.[21]

1.4.3 REMITTANCES INFLUXES DURING PANDEMIC

Remittances are an important source of income proceeds for developing economies. These are private income transmissions by the migrants to their families in order to support and smooth their consumption patterns. Additionally, remittances also help the governments to finance trade balances as they are a source of tax income for them in these countries.[33]

The present pandemic is hamstringing the global economy. However, for many poor and fragile countries, this global shock will be exaggerated by the loss of remittance.[34] As mentioned earlier, Coronavirus provokes the social distancing and lockdowns which confine people to their homes and thus shut down the economic units. Migrant workforce who lose their jobs are likely to cut remittances to their home. Consequently, recipient economies lose a significant source of personal and tax income at the time when they need it most.[35] "The impact of COVID-19 is pervasive when viewed through a migration lens as it affects migrants and their families who rely on remittances," said Mamta Murthi, Vice President for Human Development and Chair of the Migration Steering Group of the World Bank.

1.4.3.1 GLOBAL IMPACT

In a comparing scenario with the historic economic and health crisis, it has been claimed by the World Bank that, this pandemic posits a much greater threat to the world economy. Among these threats, the drying of remittances is a serious one for countries that are heavily contingent on remittance income. [[34] According to the World Bank, remittance streams are dropped approximately by 20% from their 2019 level. As the COVID-19 and economic crisis stays, it is predicted by the World Bank that the amount of remittances by migrant workers is projected to fall by 14% by 2021 as compared with the pre-COVID-19 heights in 2019 (World Bank's Migration and Development Brief). Subsequently, fiscal and trade deficits would be exaggerated, and in turn, the ability to finance and service the debt would be contracted.[35] The global nature of the pandemic crisis illustrates that impression is not confined with remittances to dry up, but will instantaneously confront outflows of foreign capital, and maybe a deduction in aid from foreign donors and boost up in loans and services is realized (see Fig. 1.6). The World Bank Group President David Malpass argued "The ongoing economic recession caused by COVID-19 is taking a severe toll on the ability to send money to home and makes it all the more vital that we shorten the time to recovery for advanced economies."

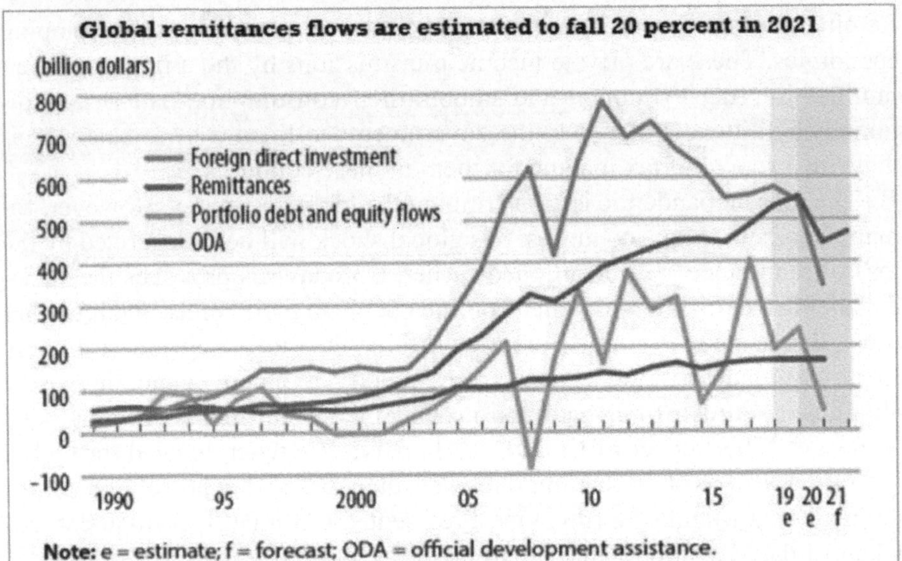

FIGURE 1.6 The flow of global remittances.

Source: Reprinted with permission Ref. [36]. © 2020 International Monetary Fund.

Fundamentally, when capital flew from an economy due to a macroeconomic shock, remittance influxes lessen the impact of such capital flight. Notwithstanding, in the present crisis, poor economies are victimized in a dual manner, that is, capital outflows along with a drop in remittance inflows.[36] It happened for the first time in the recent history that the number of international immigrants is likely to fall because new migration has reduced cum banned, and backward migration has increased. Backward migration has been informed in all parts of the world. Growing unemployment in the face of strict visa limitations on migrants would likely result in a further rise in backward migration.

The issue of coping with the further adverse impacts due to a fall in remittances calls for an emergency answer not just on behalf of the poor economies, but from the developed world as well. Purposefully, the global community ought to consider the benefits to retain migrants in the host states as much as can be achievable. This strategy will bring dual benefits. Firstly, it will help the host economies to restart core services in their countries as soon as possible, and secondly will facilitate remittances to be received in recipient economies. Regardless of the decisions at the local or regional level, international financial institutions must also take initiatives to assist migrant-source states not only to combat the worse effects but also to cushion the loss of remittances.

1.5 DEBT RELIEF

Since the time of the pandemic, all the economies are experiencing an unprecedented economic crisis and are making meanwhile attempts to overcome the impact of COVID-19. An economic downturn of such a significant magnitude can bring tremendous long-term destruction in terms of critical economic associations among employees and businesses, government, and revenues which could further compel budget deficits and loans.[37] COVID-19 has led to an abrupt collapse in capital influxes toward developing and emerging economies.

In addition to the economic impact on billions of people, the pandemic took more than a million lives globally.[38] According to IMF, the current pandemic is a disaster like no other previously observed or suffered pandemic. Truthfully, this pandemic carries substantial uncertainty regarding its overall impact. Furthermore, many economies now experience multiple crises out of this crisis like a prominent fall in tourism and travel, health crisis, financial crisis along with the collapse in commodity prices. Although policymakers are supporting the financial markets through their valuable suggestions, making the platform convenient for firms and households, yet, there is much to be done for substantial economic prospects. Nonetheless, the COVID-19 pandemic has a significant influence on the working of the financial sector.[39]

1.5.1 G-20 RESPONSE TO PANDEMIC

Public debt in developing and emerging markets has reached to levels not seen in the last five decades. Many developing economies have taken non-concessional term debts from various financial institutions and private lenders to compromise with the pandemic. Somehow, COVID-19 is continuously wreaking destruction at the global level but poorer economies are hardest hit by this disease and are facing great difficulty to confront the debt crisis. Subsequently, developing nations that are already suffering in-depth economic crises and debt burdens are in dire need of some debt relief to handle the endangered risks related to both economic and health scenarios.[39]

Debt relief can take many forms. For instance, a debt annulment is a form of debt when a portion or a debt is fully written off, debt rescheduling means, the terms like rate of interest or maturity period are renegotiated and discounts in the face value of principal amounts which is formally called "haircuts," whereas refinancing means, to allot new loan to pay off a previously taken loan or may be an extension in time allotted to pay off debt possibly with discounted interest rates.[40]

In response to these crises, the G-20 leading countries agreed to a provisional debt service cessation on bilateral official loan refunds from the so-called IDA countries, a group of 76 of the poorest economies (including Angola) of the world.[41] The G-20 was established in 1999 to provide a medium for a small group of economies representing much of the global economy to efficiently collaborate in addressing emergent financial crises. When the pandemic was at its peak and the world economy was confronting in-depth crises, on April 15, 2020, G-20 responded by allotting a debt moratorium until the end of 2020 on official consensual creditor debt service (for a group of 77 least developed economies as defined by the World Bank and the United Nations). However, there were no discounts on the principal amount, that is, no "haircuts." Postponed payments would be refunded over the coming 3 years.[40]

The debt service suspension initiative (DSSI) is an optimistic powerful tool that is expected to bring real assistances to people in these poor economies which do not acquire such financial resources to respond to the current crisis.[38] Moreover, IDA identifies that debt sustainability is a major concern for many poorer countries. Therefore, when economies are facing difficulties in servicing their foreign debt, as is the case of this pandemic, IDA adjusts the terms of its support so that economies can continue accessing additional funds without increasing their servicing burden.[41] From April till the end of

2020, the World Bank provided US $19.5 billion for financing IDA countries participating in the G-20 DSSI. This huge amount included US $3.8 billion in grants. The total distributed amount is about eight times the debt service repayments (US $1.5 billion) received from DSSI economies.[39] This ingenuity will do much in protecting the lives and livelihoods of people who are currently facing vulnerabilities.[40]

1.5.2 WORLD BANK AND IMF INITIATIVES

The IMF and World Bank have answered to the coronavirus crisis with extraordinary speed and magnitude of monetary assistance to help economies, particularly to safeguard the most vulnerable. IMF Managing Director Kristalina Georgieva noted "The IMF is striving to support countries by providing policy advice, financial support, capacity development, and debt relief for the poorest."[42]

The IMF's relief trust which is formally called "Catastrophe Containment and Relief Trust" (CCRT) allowed it to deliver debt service relief for the most vulnerable and poorest economies hit by natural or public health disasters. The trust is financed by various resources which primarily include donor aid; it assists to pay for debt service to the financial institutions for a limited time. The latest feature in the CCRT relief initiative is to give a grant-based loan relief in tranches so that funds can be instantly available to eligible countries, hardest hit by COVID-19, without requiring to wait until the trust collects enough resources. Till April 2021, the upfront grants have been disbursed coupling with the decision that additional tranches to encompass the service relief to cover another year would be provided in April 2022.[38] This form of debt relief provides benefits to poorer countries for channelizing their scarce resources to facilitate their emergency health conditions. These members are also struggling by themselves to combat with the influence of COVID-19, but the critical effects of the disease still need more assistance, exclusively as the economic effect of the pandemic continues. The IMF stands ready against such requests with its further lending tools, possessing a longer duration of return along with its ability to grant larger total amounts. For instance, in March 2020, the International Monetary Fund passed an "Extended Fund Facility" to Jordan keeping in view its increasing needs in relevance of pandemic effects.

Debt relief was formerly provided under the "Multilateral Debt Relief Initiative" (MDRI), which accompanied the HIPC Initiative (HIPC) to help deserving economies in order to attain the United Nations Millennium Development Goals. Moreover, "Poverty Reduction and Growth Trust" (PRGT) borrows funds from IMF associates and lends these borrowed funds to low-income economies at discounted rates in tough times. The International Institute for Finance (IIF) also responded to the initiatives of IDA, DSSI, and PRGT during the pandemic situation by endorsing that the private sector could similarly provide debt payment forbearance.[27]

Meanwhile, the IMF and World Bank, have expressed their support for a further extension of the DSSI until the end of 2021. The G20 also agreed to examine the need for a further extension by the time of the IMF–World Bank Spring Meetings in April 2021. Furthermore, the IMF is also responding to several emergencies for more than 100 economies. The "Rapid Credit Facility" (RCF) and "Rapid Financing Instrument" (RFI) also permit IMF and World Bank to meet emergencies for financing the health and economic crises specifically arising during this pandemic.[38,40,41]

1.5.3 SMART LOOK UP OF DEBT RELIEF

Supporting developing and emerging economies is a vital priority. These economies are already economically vulnerable in comparison to the developed world. Therefore, developing economies are currently hard hit by a shortage of medical supplies. There is a sudden cessation of the global economy along with difficulties in accessing international capital markets.[42] Multilateral institutions like the World Bank and several other multilateral development banks constructed a central credit facility, permitting poorer countries for putting request of temporary debt relief in financing emergencies to hinder the adverse impacts of the pandemic.

Empirical evidence revealed that the IMF, the World Bank, Inter-Development Bank, and other international financial institutions are funding debt relief assistance to support poorer and highly indebted countries of the world at the time of the COVID-19 pandemic. Financial assistance programs are also embedding great positive social values in curtailing debt crises and attempting to assist in hammering out mitigation policies for saving lives and livelihoods.[27]

1.6 GLOBAL ECONOMY SLASH: BASELINE COVID-19

The outbreak of the COVID-19 has brought uncertainties worldwide and is brutally influencing the global economy. It is evident from historical events that such diseases create many thoughtful challenges at not only regional and national but also at global levels. During the pandemic, most people remained isolated and confined as the world populace has been advised cum ordered not to leave homes for staying safe. Likewise, most businesses and industries remained shut for months, worldwide. It is not the end, the subsequent ceasing of the aviation, hospitality industries, and shutdown of small and medium enterprises (SMEs) has created significant threats to revenue declines. In the early stage of the pandemic, some states were following partial lockdown but all this eventually led to a complete lockdown and a comprehensive global economic fall happened during the pandemic COVID-19.

COVID-19 has noteworthy short-term and long-term economic consequences.[43] It vibrantly influenced macroeconomic variables, such as exchange rates, investments, production, travel, growth, cross-border cooperation, supply chain, trade, finances, and banking.[44] Since, the start of COVID-19, abrupt falls in worldwide commodity prices, governmental revenues, FDI, and foreign financial influxes have been witnessed. Frozen labor markets also remained evident.[45] However, there is great ambiguity about what exact effects on global economic conditions will take place in the coming years because of many unknown relevant factors, such as the severity of the disease spread, length of the pandemic, economic disruption, health crises, and impact of government policies to deal with the coming situations ahead.

1.6.1 ECONOMIC GIANTS AND PANDEMIC

From February 2020, global crises prominently began when the manufacturing and service sectors experienced an intense decline in China.[46] Then COVID-19 has adversely affected the industrial giants, that is, developed countries, such as Germany, Japan, China, the USA, the UK, Italy, France, Brazil, Spain, Russia, and India. These economies supply finished products as well as raw materials globally. Global supply has fallen due to the closing outskirts, but for some goods, demand has remained unaffected. It is estimated that COVID-19 would reduce the GDP of China, Japan, the UK, and the USA by 6.2, 9.9 6.0, and 8.4%, respectively.[43] China exports a huge number of industrial commodities worldwide. Meanwhile, the demand for several new vital goods, such as hand sanitizers, masks, soaps, gloves, personal protection gears, surface cleaners, and bleaching powder have increased; consequently, the prices of numerous commodities have amplified. As a result, global economy became sluggish. States are associated globally by flows of goods, services, financial capital, foreign direct investment, international banking, and exchange rates through the outskirts. Therefore, some of these states suffered serious economic shocks.[47]

It is argued that a month lockdown in Tokyo has led to a loss of total production of 27 trillion yen in Japan, which is about 5.3% of its yearly GDP and this loss is much greater than the earthquakes and tsunamis that took place in the previous decade.[48] The COVID-19 pandemic has instigated disorder in the giant US economy, thus, there is boundless uncertainty about the length and depth of the disruption.[4] Consequently, there would have been a significant rise in the need for global expenditures to guard vulnerable populaces from the economic and health disasters.

1.6.2 GLOBAL GDP, OUTPUT, POVERTY, AND UNEMPLOYMENT: A SUMMARY

There is no doubt that COVID-19 has brought substantial human suffering and threatened the global economy. According to IMF, the virus will cost the global economy up to US $9 trillion, which is almost equivalent to the collective national income (GDP) of Germany, Japan, or almost half of the USA's GDP. Similarly, it is also estimated that the total loss could be about 18% of the usual global output.[49] Normally, Japan, the EU, and the USA comprise half of the global GDP, while the Chinese economy accounts for almost 16% of global income. Infect, these states are based on industries, trade, and services.

When the direct economic impressions of COVID-19 are considered, these incorporate a rise in the global unemployment rate, a fall in future economic growth, investment, consumption, weakening FDI, and assets price. Additionally, it affected fuel demand and prices, supply chains, travel and tourism, businesses, fiscal events, governmental budgets, and sports events. Moreover, the global market value has been destroyed by about US $23 trillion since its outbreak.[50] United Nations Conference on Trade and Development (UNCTAD) made a forecast that FDI influxes could drop by 30–40% amid 2020–2021.[51] Saudi Arabia suspended incoming pilgrims to the holy cities due to fear of imported infections of COVID-19 in the kingdom which caused huge losses in revenues to the government.[52]

Home quarantine and the lockdowns have jammed construction, manufacturing, production, and service supply chains both nationally and globally, which resulted in a significant rise in unemployment.[53] International Labor Organization (ILO) has forecast that global unemployment may rise from 5.3 million (optimistic) to 24.7 million (pessimistic scenario) people. Global loss in the labor sector is anticipated to be US $860–3,440 billion, contingent on the length of virus control.[54]

Overall, it is estimated that world GDP would fall significantly. Global GDP may drop 2–8%.[55] As a result, an economy on average will suffer a 6% reduction in consumption and concurrently an 8% decline in GDP due to the pandemic spread.[56] Expectedly, government tax revenue will fall, and meanwhile, foreign currency assets will be influenced adversely.[4] However, the developing world might suffer much more than expected. Inevitably, the global economic loss would be huge. Regarding poverty, it is estimated that approximately 2 billion people in excess (addition of new half a billion) would become extremely poor globally (living on US $1.90 a day). Population vulnerable to poverty, living on US $5.50 a day or less would become approximately 4 billion. Henceforth, the situation will even get worse if the pandemic prevails longer.[55]

1.7 GLOBAL TRADE AND PANDEMIC

Globally, the number of new infections of COVID-19 is increasing up to an alarming end, and in many economies, second and third waves are an undesirable reality. The grim consequences of the pandemic COVID-19 reflect the enormous challenges and sufferings. The virus exposed the global economy weaknesses and brutally set back the phase of development and growth.

This pandemic continuously affected every sphere of life and is still creating socioeconomic woes. This section focuses on the vast consequences of global trade. According to WTO Director General Roberto Azevêdo *"The unavoidable declines in trade and output will have painful consequences for households and businesses, on top of the human suffering caused by the disease itself. The immediate goal is to bring the pandemic under control and mitigate the economic damage to people, companies, and countries. But policymakers must start planning for the aftermath of the pandemic."*

The pandemic has had an inevitable and strong immediate effect on international trade. The foremost signs of the trade slump were evident in January 2020 when most of the major economies verified negative trends.[32]

The overall current crises inevitably invited comparison with the financial crises (2008–2009). Both have common consequences in some respects whereas several different are also to be owed. For instance, governments intervened in the instruments of fiscal and monetary policies during the financial crises (2008–2009) to overcome the adverse impacts and to support businesses and households. Contrarily, the current pandemic prevented the movement and trade to limit the spread of the disease. Such a social distancing policy halted the labor supply, travel, and transport directly which were not observed during the financial crises of 2008.[57] Furthermore, global trade never returned to its previous levels after the financial crisis of 2008–2009.

1.7.1 TRADE IN VALUE ADDED DATABASE

Similarly, the disruption of value chains is also a salient feature of COVID-19 crisis which was not part of financial crises previously faced globally. Social distancing largely helped the imports of key production inputs which led to a temporary closure of factories in China, North America, Europe, and several other regions. Managing such disruptions in the supply chain is a challenge for all enterprises locally and globally. According to the OECD trade in value-added database, electronic and automotive products constitute a significant proportion of foreign value added in exports, specifically USA, China, Korea, Singapore, Mexico, Malaysia, and Vietnam.[58]

1.7.2 SERVICES TRADE

Services trade assumes an important component of world trade which has been severely affected due to social distancing, restrictions on mobility of labor, closure of airports, and so on. Certainly, most of the trades of goods are not possible without services trade which primarily involves transport as services trade related to air transport and transport through the outskirts. Despite all these, demand for information technology services reached a peak as it enabled employees and workers to work from home and ensure social distancing remotely.

Trade in services was exposed to be highly resilient during the financial crises of 2008, as compared with the merchandise trade because of its low sensitivity to demand shocks and supply finance.[59,60] However, the present crises brought by the pandemic have shown an instant supply shock which is ultimately shadowed by a demand shock. This time, social distancing and fear of virus spread limited the services transactions due to physical contact between buyers and sellers which cannot be replaced by online services.[61]

According to WTO intuitively, services are traded among the outskirts in four ways, and three of those needed the proximity between buyer and seller. Mode 1 includes a variety of services transactions that can be operated online and can be continued even from home. Mode 2 illustrates the consumption of services abroad like tourisms. Mode 3 comprises FDI services and Mode 4 constitutes the movements of IT professionals.[61] Hence, Modes 2, 3, and 4 require physical proximity among buyers and sellers.

The antagonistic impact of social distancing due to COVID-19 largely hit services performed through Modes 2, 3, and 4. This idea can be explained with the estimates (shown in Fig. 1.8) of the year 2017 during which globally, the commercial trade in services was US $13.3 trillion, among them more than half the services transactions were performed via Mode 3. Around 12% of services transactions were done through Mode 2 and 4% were catered through Mode 4.[62] The estimates suggest that the pandemic stalled services trade via Mode 3 (more than half of global services trade) completely. Not to end with this, the pandemic also caused visible disruptions for the other half also. Shortly, at least 50% of global services trade (equivalent to US $7 trillion) would be compromised by virus.[61]

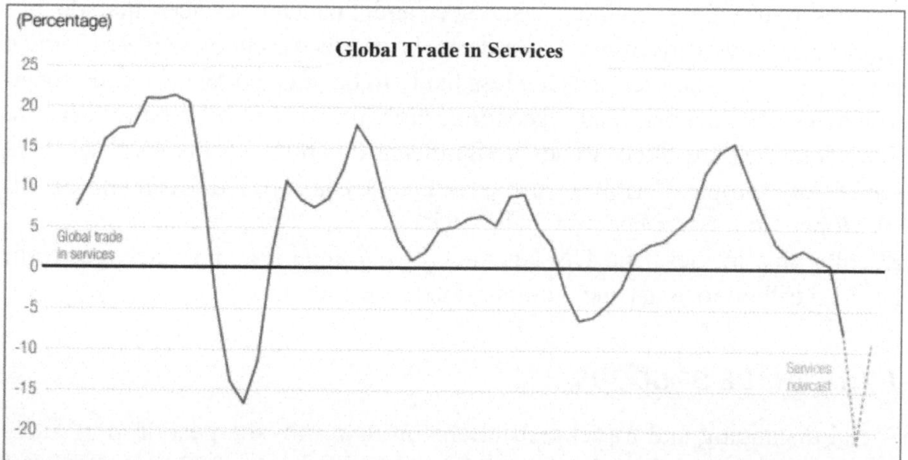

FIGURE 1.7 Global trade in services.

Source: Reprinted from Ref. [65]. © 2020, United Nations. https://unctad.org/system/files/official-document/osg2020d1_en.pdf.

Figure 1.7 shows the trends followed by services in trade globally. The value of total services trade showed an instant negative trend in the first quarter of the year 2020 (fell by 7.6%). Travel services were specifically hard hit which fell by more than 24%. Alarmingly, it would take sufficient time to recover globally.

Intuitively, several services sectors (like education, tourism, travel, and restaurant) are severely affected and are also expected to take significant time to recover. These sub-sectors accounted for about 70% of Mode 2 services the work of exports. However, air transport services are related to merchandise trade and are disturbed significantly and belong to Mode 1. Pandemic also affected services such as construction and other services that demand the mobility of labor across the outskirts. The decline in such services accounted for about a quarter, the comparison of which was observed through 2nd, 3rd, and 4th modes in 2017.[61] In comparison to services like insurance, other services including telecoms and online-related services are less affected by pandemic because such services remained transacted online via the internet. Conclusively, the effects of the pandemic on services trade sector have implications for services trading economies. The intensiveness of these economies related to the share of services trade, share in total exports, GDP, and modes of services transaction will determine their speed of recovery. For instance, in Switzerland, 43% of the Swiss labor force can work via Mode 1 (work from home) by involving services transactions online, insurance, and financial services that do not require the movement of labor. Similarly, IT services comprise 40% of India's export services. Such services are less likely to be affected by pandemic social distancing.. In contrast, many economies rely on tourism hospitality services. Such countries are likely to see a significant downturn in the services trade sector (for example, Caribbean and small Pacific islands). These economies will take longer to recover because their services export sector demands proximity. Keeping this in view, the UN has aimed to arrange a global package worth US $2.5 trillion to assist such tourism-intensive countries.[63]

1.7.3 TRADE OF GOODS

Social distancing and travel restrictions brought the sharpest drop in international goods trade in the second quarter of the year 2020 when global merchandise trade fell by even more than 20% as compared with the second quarter of the previous year (2019). Although, the highly visible fall in global trade during 2020 has been widespread yet it is more pronounced in developed economies, specifically in the exports sector.[64]

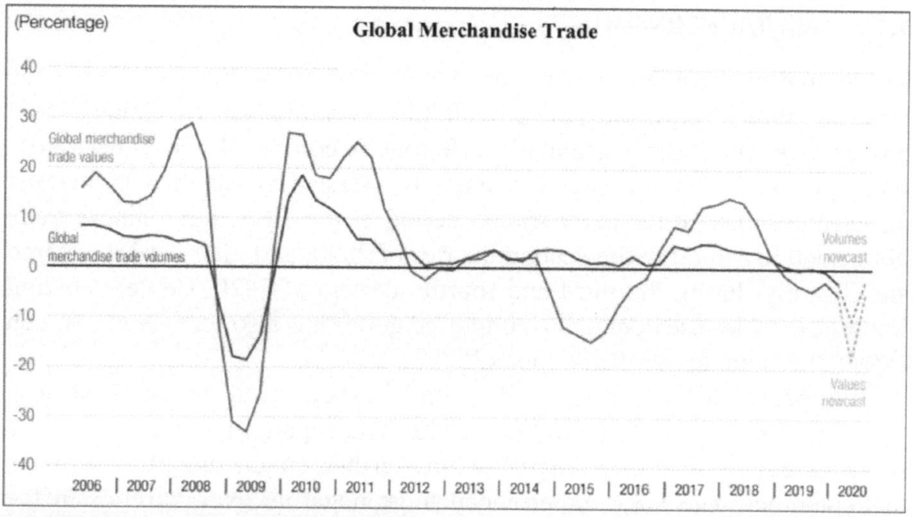

FIGURE 1.8 Global merchandise trade.

Source: Reprinted from Ref. [65]. © © 2020, United Nations. https://unctad.org/system/files/official-document/osg2020d1_en.pdf

Figure 1.8 illustrates the trends followed by trade in goods. Merchandise trade fell significantly in the first quarter of 2020 as soon as the primary pandemic effects began. Trade in goods detected a greater dramatic decline in the second quarter. Based on the data availability at the time of writing, the trends for the third quarter showed improvement. The trends for the fourth quarter, though still negative, are seemingly better than the beginning of the year 2020. However, optimistic experts strongly believe that global trade trends would show meaningful recovery as the vaccines will become available all around.[64]

1.7.4 DEVELOPING ECONOMIES

All the economies in the developing world face severity of trade declines and none of them have been spared from the adverse effects of pandemic. But the trends in East Asian countries are relatively found better. Because of trade resilience capacity, these economies faced a relatively lower drop in the year 2020. Furthermore, this trend turned out positive in the third quarter of 2020. Despite this fact, oil exporting economies faced a huge downfall in oil exports because of low or negative demand for oil globally. However, transition economies, the West Asian and North African economies faced a huge decline in the third quarter of 2020 as compared with the trend observed in 2019.[64]

1.7.5 *MAJOR ECONOMIES*

Major trading economies also faced a vast deterioration in their trade trends. Figure 1.9 illustrates the downfall in several industries. China's trade movements have been particularly different as compared with other major trading economies. China was the first to be affected by the virus. China was affected severely in the early spread period of the virus, but Chinese trade got a soothing trend in the second quarter of 2020, and afterward recovered significantly during the third and fourth quarters of 2020. Contextualizing imports, the Chinese demand for imported goods has also recovered to much extent, but quite lesser than exports.[65]

European Union and the United States experienced the sharpest drop in trade trends in April and May 2020. Trade pattern got recovered to some extent in July and August while further enhancement took place in September. The USA experienced huge negative export trends in the industries of automotive, chemicals, and communication equipment, whereas trade drop in the textile and apparel sector was much lower. European Union faced a significant decline in the trade of textile and office machinery and a limited decline in the exports of chemicals, apparel, and communication equipment.

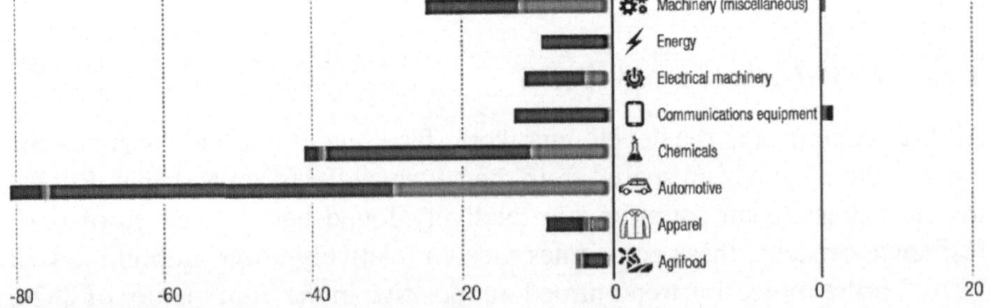

FIGURE 1.9 Major economies trade decline.

Source: Reprinted from Ref. [65]. © 2020, United Nations. https://unctad.org/system/files/official-document/osg2020d1_en.pdf

1.7.6 MEDICAL PRODUCTS TRADE

Medical equipment trade has been very high since the second quarter of 2020. The equipment specifically related to COVID-19 are traded most till the present date. These medical products include ventilators, disposable masks, personal protective equipment, thermometers, sanitizers, and surface cleaners. In May 2020, trade of such products experienced 186% increase as compared with the same month in 2019. Other nonmedical goods related to COVID-19, including Wi-Fi routers, internet, laptops, portable, etc. enjoyed significant growth in the second and third quarters of 2020 as shown in Figure 1.11.[65]

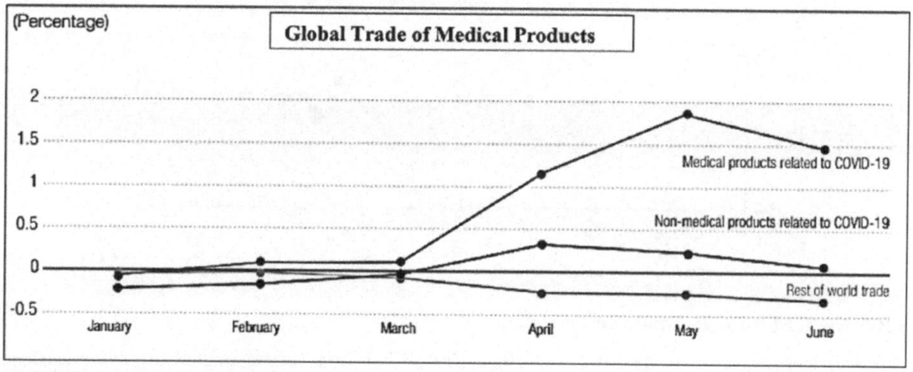

FIGURE 1.10 Global trade of medical products.

Source: Reprinted from Ref. [65]. © 2020, United Nations. https://unctad.org/system/files/official-document/osg2020d1_en.pdf

1.7.7 TRADE AND GLOBAL OUTPUT

The current pandemic has deteriorated the global economy. It has shaken almost all spheres of life and socioeconomic conditions. Alarmingly, the global GDP shrunk by an unprecedented extent in 2020, that is, 5%.[66]

According to the World Bank, the value of global trade is likely to fall by 8%. If the pandemic is brought under control, pessimistic economists anticipated that these negative trends would show rebound in 2021 to much extent about 2019 levels. The pandemic has reinforced the volatility of the value of international trade which was observed during the previous decade. During the past several years, it has been observed that the world economy is becoming less dependent on trade, indicated by the share of global trade in the total global output. This ratio touched its peak in 2008 at even higher than 30%. The share of trade in the global output has fallen below 26% in

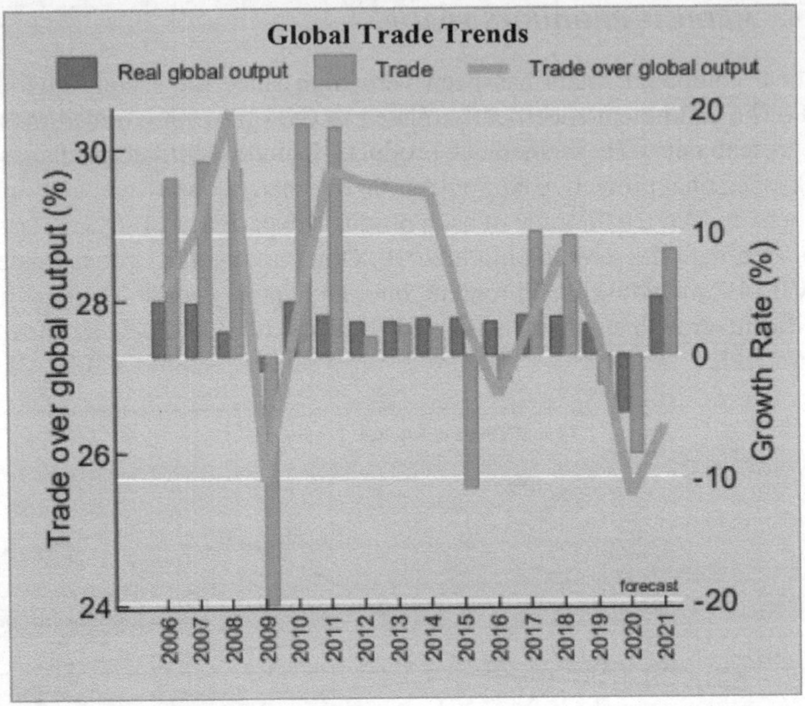

FIGURE 1.11 Global trade and growth.

Source: Reprinted from Ref. [64]. © 2021 United Nations. https://unctad.org/system/files/official-document/ditctab2020d4_en.pdf

2009, indicating the effects of world financial crises. Afterward, this ratio experienced ups and downs till the world met the COVID-19 crisis. The value of trade in the total output dropped by 25% in the year 2020, touching the lowest level since the last decade. There has been a loss of trade value in terms of goods and services because of limitations across the borders and due to social distancing. In 2021, and beyond, predictors expect the recovery of these trends. However, the magnitude of the recovery is uncertain because the pandemic brought severe value chain disruptions.[64]

1.8 GLOBAL HEALTH SYSTEM AND PANDEMIC

This decade has begun with one of the biggest pandemics ever suffered. The present situation is walled by several uncertainties; no region or nation has been spared. The crisis has created deep-rooted weaknesses in every economy's healthcare system. It has been witnessed, within and between economies, how vulnerable and marginalized sections are experiencing the uneven burden of pandemic virus.[67] Though the effects of the pandemic are ultimately devastating, they bring novel challenges to healthcare systems globally. Globally, billions of people have been confined to their homes as a result of lockdowns, to date, even then 3,278,187 people have died due to the virus spread, while 157,329,411 people have suffered the infection.[68]

The current pandemic has continued and dominated life losses globally, and its impressions in comparison to other historic pandemics are also leading.[69] This section aims to highlight the effect of COVID-19 on the global health system (henceforth GHS) by elaborating on the current situations, efforts, provision, and needs of GHS.

COVID-19 has had a significant impact on the health systems and limited the delivery of crucial health services. While GHS is being challenged by rising infections and thus demands for the care of patients, it remained pivotal to sustain preventive and medicinal services, especially for highly vulnerable populations, such as children, older people with chronic conditions, and people with disabilities.[70]

1.8.1 GLOBAL HEALTH SYSTEM: HISTORY AND WHAT HAS BEEN DONE

Historically, the center of focus for global health efforts has remained narrow, that is, disease-specific interventions are repeatedly conducted by private establishments or public–private associations. These associations kept promising to support and build stronger healthcare institutions but their performance remained mostly unsatisfied.[71] During the late 1970s, although international medical units made memorable efforts for the eradication of smallpox, yet, the meager investment in the health sector kept countries unable to deliver medical care for other diseases.[72]

Despite many positive intentions, neither the Alma Ata (an initiative to promote good health for all) announcement in 1978 nor the selective Primary Health Care reinforced health organizations to deliver good quality medical care globally.[73] In a similar vein, the World Bank and IMF promoted some healthcare policies to ultimately provide health facilities which were not need-based, rather the facilities were provided to those who had the affordability to get them.[74] At this juncture, the efforts of HIV movement should not go unnoticed that painted a rosy picture because campaigners offered equivalent services for poor countries, and regimes responded with initiatives that distributed care based on need.[75] Still, the efforts are lesser than enough in bringing the collective and widespread action to strengthen the healthcare systems. These efforts with little outcome have deep-rooted impressions on the history of GHS. The World Health Organization (WHO) has largely engrossed in inadequate vertical progress of programs. Additionally, the human capital extraction in the form of "brain drain" of researchers, scientists, and medical experts from South to North created discrepancies in health systems across the South.[76] The global research on health and diseases fronts is funded by several major agencies (WHO, World Bank, USAID, the Bill and Melinda Gates Foundation, CDC, and so on) each agency has its own specific aims and interests.[71] Almost all of these institutions are led by specialists from the Global North and the share of middle- and low-income economies practitioners remained at just 19%.[77]

These considerations matter a lot at this point because such discrepancies lead to inequalities in recruitment and equipment allotment eventually creating an imbalanced health system with the major deficiencies observed in lower and middle-income countries. Despite the efforts of collaboration, capacity edifice and horizontal association between the North and South provided unequal structures which prevented the fair and alike distribution of medical services across the regions globally and led to ineffective systems in the developing world.[78] The current crisis shows that the rhetoric of equity and cooperation among the North and the South, which is usually employed by the world health institutions and bilateral and multilateral contributors, is hollow. This has influenced the capacity of numerous health institutions to respond to COVID-19 repercussions.

This pandemic required health infrastructure including laboratories for the provision of community-wide testing, contact tracing systems, medical practitioners, and medical care instruments enough to treat people when sick. The African CDC (Africa Centers for Disease Control and Prevention), has put valuable efforts to respond to COVID19,[79] but major needs remain unfulfilled in terms of laboratories, medical workforce, essential medicines, and apparatus like ventilators in order to fight against the pandemic. For instance, Haiti invested a million dollars for the development, but this economy with a population of 11 million has only 62 ventilators for critical care.[80] Another example is Sierra Leone which has only one ventilator. Despite the urgencies ordered by the WHO for strengthening the health systems after the 2014 Ebola disaster, none of these economies possessed the capacity to screen the population for COVID-19 infections. Moreover, more than 20,000 health professionals migrated from Africa toward the global north to do the needful.[81] Meanwhile, global differentials in strengthening the health system are observed as medical practitioners in the global south called for protest due to the lack of protective measures and medical tools required to respond to the pandemic.[82]

1.8.2 PANDEMIC AND PRESENT SITUATION OF GLOBAL HEALTH SYSTEM

COVID-19 embodies the greatest risk to GHS and economies in the 21st century.[83] In December 2019, since the emergence of COVID-19 from China, the virus has spread over to 210 economies and territories globally by infecting about 157,329,411 people and causing 3,278,187 casualties (World Health Organization).[84] Before this virus, about half of the global population did not have access to vital healthcare services, and the pandemic has even increased in such vulnerable populations. The year 2020 gave a prominent indication that healthcare systems all over the world need to be more accessible and prepared for future pandemic events so that every country in the world is able to provide medical care to its population during emergencies.[68]

The year 2020 has shown that the pandemic is striking massive pressure on healthcare services all over the world. The overcrowded situation at the hospitals, exhausted doctors and assistant staff, insufficient protective equipment, and scarce treatment tools and mediations illustrate that this time, the pandemic has pushed all the healthcare units to its limits even in high-income countries. By the end of March 2020, the global demand for ventilators was 10 times more than the available number.[85]

Unfortunately, the scarcity is not only in material resources but also in human beings in the form of frontline medical practitioners.

1.8.2.1 *WORST HIT COUNTRIES*

The virus wreaked havoc in Europe after China. In Europe, the total infections and death toll due to this virus are notably 45,297,334 and 1,030,734, respectively (World Health Organization). The plague engulfed the United States after striking Europe. Currently, the USA is the worst hit with 33,376,109 people infected and more than 594,135 people have died. Then the situation in India became worst. This shows that countries like India have not learned much from the devastation of Europe and America. The present situation is walled by several uncertainties; no region or nation has been spared. The total infectious population in India reached 21,874,777 and 238,081 deaths, to date of writing.[86]

A valuable empirical analysis demonstrated that at the height of the first wave of epidemics in April in the United States and the European Economic Area (EEA), the burden on hospital resources far exceeded existing hospital capacity.[87]

In order to cope with the severe shortage of manpower as a result of the epidemic, EEA countries have recruited staff, including medical students, retired, inactive and untrained health professionals, and even volunteers to increase the strength of health professionals. The pandemic has pushed the entire health system to its limits, highlighting the huge gap in public health infrastructure, even in the high-income developed countries.[88,89]

1.8.2.2 DEVELOPING WORLD

COVID-19 is a health challenge that has affected dramatically the population living in low- and middle-income countries. Health systems in these countries are already plagued by a double burden of infections like malaria and schizophrenia coupled with an increasing frequency of noninfectious diseases, such as hypertension, depression, and diabetes. The further pressure of COVID-19 has overwhelmed these health systems that are already fragile.[90] According to the WHO, half of the world's population does not have access to health-related services in these countries. The poorest countries will be most affected by COVID-19.

The current epidemic shook the world and the world has realized how important it is to have a strong and collaborative health-related system to deal with such emergencies. A valuable analysis revealed that most of the least prepared countries are located in Southeast Asia, West Asia, and Central and West Africa.[91] "*Health care access and quality index*" measures the performance of the health system of a country from 0 to 100. Most Central and Western African and Asian countries score less than 31. Such countries are sharing a significant burden of the pandemic because they already suffered fragile health systems due to the least investment in education and health, that is, human capital. However, these economies also face acute shortages of paramedical staff, healthcare units, and personal protective equipment.[82]

1.8.2.3 HIGH-INCOME COUNTRIES

Based on the available data, from the year 2020, it is evident that developed countries are also excessively affected in the initial months of the pandemic.

"*Health care access and quality index*" measures the performance of the health system of a country from 0 to 100, the US scores 88. Despite the US ranking first for pandemic readiness in the "*Global Health Security Index,*" it has, to date, informed the highest COVID-19 cases and deaths in the world. Although the USA has an impressive arrangement of public and private laboratories, technology companies, pharmaceuticals, and a national public health foundation with wide capacity, yet, the country eventually had to depend upon a highly fragmented health system to confront the brutal attack of the pandemic.[92] The socioeconomic impact also remained challenging and growing. In the US alone, the total cost of the pandemic is estimated more than US $16 trillion, which is approximately 90% of the US GDP.[69]

Several countries from the EEA with high scores in the health quality index, for example, Spain 91.9, Italy 94.9 also remained worst hit during the first wave of COVID-19. China scored 77.9 before the pandemic. Inevitably numerous factors can also severely damage the healthcare system in high-income countries, one of those could be the apparent aging of their population, which is another risk factor for deaths in COVID-19. Factually, noncommunicable diseases are more prevalent in rich countries, which seem positively and strongly associated with mortality and severity of COVID-19.[93]

More importantly, the severity and mortality due to COVID-19 are also strongly correlated with old age. More so, it is observed that during COVID-19 spread, the process of diagnosing and preventing the disease, isolating, testing, and tracing has remained delayed in the European Union countries relative to Asia, with the exception of Germany.[94] Furthermore, in several European nations, such as Spain and Italy, the implementation of austerity measures since decades has weakened the healthcare system.[95]

Despite decades of efforts done by numerous multilateral and international organizations, governments, and NGOs, the COVID-19 pandemic unleashed the weaknesses of global public health systems.[96]

1.8.2.4 FRONT HEALTH WORKFORCE

Paramedical staff is on the front line to fight all kinds of challenges that the COVID-19 is throwing forward. So, they are the foremost workforce in controlling the spread of the virus.[97]

Quite considerably, the patients' crowd exceeded the available capacity of healthcare units and intensive care units globally. However, the fear of illness, exhaustion, and fear of transmission to family, healthcare workforce provided uneased services to the patients. Additionally, paramedical staff facing the scarcity of personal protective tools also further enhances the chances of being infected.[98] The life of doctors was also in great danger. Doctors in every country kept their lives at risk to save patients. Only in the United States, the number of doctors who have died due to the virus is 3600, who aged less than 60.[99] At the global level, at least the death toll of healthcare force is more than 17,000.[100] The figurative framework shows the loss of a valuable workforce, which is demanded immensely amid present emergencies. The global shortage of personal protective tools has led to the emergence of an editorial body in the Lancet, which is being immensely asked to provide maximum protection to the healthcare workers.[101]

The world is experiencing an acute shortage of doctors, medical advisors, nurses, and allied staff. As mentioned earlier, there is an uneven distribution of paramedical workforce globally, and the global north is quite rich on this platform. Developing world specifically facing scarcity of doctors and healthcare units in rural areas remained vulnerable. All the countries have focused on the prevention and spread of the virus. Globally, the number of health practitioners in governmental and private health institutions is still insufficient to meet the upcoming rising number of patients suffering from COVID-19. In the EEA and the USA, several organizations have begun a series of training sessions for youth and the clinical workforce on prevention and how to deal with this infection.

1.8.3 GRANULARITY OF THE SUBJECT MATTER

Overall, it is observed that no country was sufficiently prepared to confront pandemic socially and economically. The current pandemic has challenged the GHS brutally. COVID-19 made the world realize the importance of government and its policies to restrict the spread of epidemics in a well-deserved manner. However, an additional lesson that can be learned from this pandemic is the significant role of frontline paramedical staff which deals directly with such emergencies which are equivalently important. The outbreak of COVID-19 has awakened most of the world's population to the broken and insufficient health setups.

The crisis has also provided an exclusive opportunity to rethink and reemphasize worldwide health setups so that future diseases and viruses do not become so devastating and the health benefits remain, permanent and sustainable.[68]

In a similar vein, COVID-19 offers a chance for a reset. Governments now should focus on strengthening social setups and infrastructures by uniting together all sectors of society like workforce and human capital development, education, food security, water, sanitation, and the environment in community contexts. Meanwhile, it is of utmost importance to ensure the resilience of health institutions and supply chains.

In other words, there is a need of global stand in solidarity to build effective and resilient health setups all around. For vigilance in the coming future, there is a dire need to re-evaluate the current indices that determine the efficiency and performance of national health institutions. This can be done by learning from the current situations and crises. It will help the world to assess the preparations for future pandemics accurately.[91]

1.9 THE NEW NORMAL: BEFORE AND AFTER

The COVID-19 pandemic caused the most severe global health crisis confronted by the world over a century, which resulted in disturbances of the daily activities of the entire populace.[102] As the COVID-19 cases are continuing to grow till the date of writing, various ideas and concepts will evolve that would aim to help and control or adapt the new situations to tackle the occurrences. Possibly, these ideas to hinder the pandemic, will bring in a new normal state, and governments might have to introduce various standards to control the growing infections and to continue with minimum risk for paramedical staff and patients.[103]

As a result, newer and wider social and economic standards are being implemented across the world. These standards include the closures of multiple facilities, such as educational institutions, restaurants, and grocery stores. Putting differently, such standards kept promoting social distancing orders. The world is going toward the new normal. The pandemic stresses the breakdown of ordinary functions into principal components to control and then eliminate the spread of virus by using personal protective equipment, masks, and social distancing.[104]

It is clearly stated that there is no return to "old normal" and we are going toward "new normal" that is being constructed on the ashes of our old lives.[105] This "new normal" that we are running toward, what will it be like? What changes will it take? What is the difference between this life and the old life? Some of these questions can be answered now.

1.9.1 MASKS AND PERSONAL PROTECTIVE EQUIPMENT

Several countries have already introduced guidelines and strict instructions regarding the use of masks for all and personal protective equipment for front-line paramedical forces. In many countries, the general public has also realized the severity of disease and fatality so they remained legally bound to follow the usage of masks at crowded places to minimize the widespread. Consequently, wearing masks at public places is among one of the scientifically proven ways to control the spread of COVID-19 in a large population.[106] This change is already visible in the world. This will become part of our daily routine before we leave home. Thus, the usage of masks can become a new normal once the virus leaves the world.

1.9.2 MODE OF STUDY

Continuing the previous discussion, another aspect of the new normal is the expected digitalization in educational and learning institutes. This forces education to move toward technological advancement, a new form of development that is already ongoing, driven by the commercialism and market ideology of governance. It is worthwhile to say that many institutions intended to make more use of technology in teaching.[107] This plan might have taken years to practically realize, but for the pandemic, it was a matter of a few months to change the mode of study.

Today countries have different rates of COVID-19 impressions in various walks of life. There are more than 1.2 billion children in 186 countries worldwide affected by the closure of educational institutes. With the sudden departure from the classroom in many parts of the world, some are wondering whether the epidemic will continue after the adoption of online learning, and how such a change will affect the global education market.[108]

The pandemic is altering the ways of teaching from physical presence to online across the globe. Due to governmental restrictions, educational institutions continue to prefer online modes, and teachers and faculty are trying their best to deliver education and skills digitally through their utmost efficiency.[109] Physical presence is almost negligible in educational institutes around the globe because many countries imposed strict restrictions against physical presence to avoid the further embark of disease. The circumstances emphasized the increased usage of the internet and relevant apparatuses which could help in online studies. Online learning activity has led to an increased usage of several softwares, such as Zoom, Google classroom,

Microsoft teams, Lark.[110] It is worth mentioning, that in new normal, students' educational activities will usually be online.

However, there are challenges to overcome, that is, without reliable internet access and/or devices, some pupils suffer and hardly participate in digital learning. This difference has been observed worldwide and across income groups. According to OECD estimates, 95% of students from Switzerland, Austria, and Norway have computers for schoolwork, and comparatively only 34% of students in Indonesia acquire this facility. Contextualizing the USA, there is a significant difference between people from privileged and disadvantaged societies. Virtually, all the students (15 years old) from privileged backgrounds have computers to conduct online classes, whereas 25% of students from backward backgrounds did not have these necessary ingredients. Furthermore, the situation is even worse in poor nations where a large population is vulnerable to poverty, and digitalization is considered a luxury for them. However, some educational institutions and governments are arranging digital devices for pupils indeed, for instance, in "New South Wales," Australia can be exemplified for it. Still, there are many apprehensions that disease will further expand the digitalization become inevitable.[108]

1.9.3 RESTAURANTS AND FOOD DELIVERY SERVICES

In many parts of the world, restaurants are not as vibrant as they used to be. The government has restricted restaurant services to avoid the virus spread and the restaurant business income has dropped dramatically around the globe. Ordering food at home is indeed among one of the significant characteristics of "new normal" along with other kinds of business services that can be done cum served online.[111]

1.9.4 PUBLIC TRANSPORT

In developing countries, public transportation is the preferred mode of travel, specifically for day-to-day activities. Henceforth, crowded public transport is a particular risk factor for transmitting this deadly infection. On the other hand, affording private transport has increased traffic crowds and deteriorated the overall atmosphere quality in urban societies. Besides this fact, those who cannot afford private vehicles are becoming vulnerable because a shortage of public transport is affecting their economic activities.[112] Despite a dramatic reduction in rides, government restrictions, public health concerns, public transport service, service providers around the world have continued to limit their services which specifically involves the cancellation of certain activities, and shutting down selected stations in order to improve their services through the governmental guidance and follow SOPs.

Transit Moovit application global survey was proposed to see the effect of COVID-19 on the use of public transport. This analysis stated that up to 34% of people have avoided the usage of public transport. Whether these riders will ever return to the previous level of using public transport is impossible to predict, but another study into people's travel behaviors in 104 countries districts stated that imposition of lockdowns raised the remote work from home opportunity and reduced the commuting of people.[113]_Preliminary estimates from the COVID-19 epidemic show that in major cities in China, Iran, and the United States, riding during lockdown periods has been reduced from 80 to 90%.[114]

In the poor and developing economies, informal transport services are principally out of the government's order, and it is now extremely hard for government officials to turn to them and demand to follow the pandemic measures. For instance, in South Africa, several hundreds of informal mini-vehicle operators have rejected government efforts to impose capacity restrictions, complaining that it will make it difficult for them to win bread for a living. However, forcing operators to suspend or lessen their services can also keep them out of business endangering a chief means of communication as a result of COVID-19.[115]

On a different note, but still linked to travel and inequality, air travel has been condemned and airport remained closed for several months around the world. Still, many economies have imposed restrictions on air travel to avoid the greater spread of the virus. If the same situation persists after the departure of the virus (through vaccination) worldwide, it will not only reduce air travel vain but may also disrupt the economic activities and growth.[116]

1.9.5 CONCLUDING REMARKS AND POLICY IMPLICATIONS

COVID-19 emergency has slashed the world economy by a number of perspectives, such as deterioration of demand and supply, fuel price slash at the global level, increasing poverty, rising unemployment, governmental revenue losses, policy destructions, outflows of FDI, GHS slash, altering the mode of education and leaning, shutting down the business, mitigating travel, lessening exports. As estimated by Oxfam's (2020) empirical analysis, due to business destruction and lack of investment, unemployment will surge to an unprecedented level which will compel more than half a billion people in the world (most of them live in Africa and Asia) to the poverty who were prominently above the poverty line before the outbreak of the virus.[55] Keeping in view the scenario, Governments and international institutions should focus to enhance the capacity of debt compassion, should generate additional international reserves by the IMF, and should adopt the progressive nature of the tax system and massive injections of aid to compensate the poorer world.[55]

At the household and the society level, timely checkups, quarantine, and reduced traveling could be proven effective to reduce infections and deaths. Government should impose heavy penalties for discouraging and not following the standard operating procedures (SOPs). Furthermore, vaccine availability around the globe can prevent the spread in the future, and meanwhile, the developed world should take bold steps and concessions toward the developing world.

Governments, employers, and individuals ought to take necessary actions to combat the spread of virus and economic losses to mitigate the economic and health damages due to the outbreak of COVID-19.

It has challenged and altered the way we worked, the way we played and entertained, and certainly the way we learned. Keeping the discussion lane in that manner, with the evolution of the new normal, we will educate ourselves in a variety of ways and will adapt the chainrings in our lives accordingly. The world will definitely go through the current difficult times and would be better prepared to face such future challenges with the evolution of new ways to live.

KEYWORDS

- **agriculture**
- **COVID-19**
- **economic impact**
- **inflation**
- **oil prices**
- **restaurants**
- **transport**

REFERENCES

1. Sharif, A.; Aloui, C.; Yarovaya, L., COVID-19 Pandemic, Oil Prices, Stock Market, Geopolitical Risk and Policy Uncertainty Nexus in the US Economy: Fresh Evidence from the Wavelet -Based Approach. *Int. Rev. Financial Analy.* **2020,** *55* (2), 443–465.
2. Ichev, R.; Marinc, M. Stock Prices and Geographic Proximity of Information: Evidence from the Ebola Outbreak. *Int. Rev. Financial Analy.* **2017,** *89* (9), 168–211.
3. Andreson, C.; Engebretsen, R. The Impact of Coronavirus (COVID-19)and the Global Oil Price Shock on the Fiscal Position of Oil-Exporting Developing Countries, 2020. https://read.oecd-ilibrary.org/view/?ref=136_136801-aw9nps8afk&title=The-impact-of-Coronavirus-COVID-19-and-the-global-oil-price-shock-on-the-fiscal-position-of-oil-exporting-developing-countries.
4. Hewings, G. J. D. et al. *Illinois Government Faces Revenue Losses of Billions If Not Tens of Billions Due to COVID-19*. E. F. I. G. Report, Editor. University of Illinois, 2020.
5. Brower, D. Why the Record Opec Cut Is No Match for Coronavirus Hit to Demand. In *Financial Times*. US Energy Editor, 2020.
6. Walker, A. US Oil Prices Turn Negative as Demand Dries Up. *BBC News* **2020,** 6–9.
7. Petroleum Economists Covid-19 Puts African Energy on Pause. *Petroleum Economists* 2020.
8. WTI Crude Oil Prices—10 Year Daily Chart, 2020. https://www.macrotrends.net/2516/wti-crude-oil-prices-10-year-daily-chart
9. Longley, A.; Blas, J. Oil Prices Find New Strength as Financial Markets Prep for a 2021 Recovery. *World Oil* 2020.
10. Shafto, J.; Luhavalja, A. Oil Prices Could See Choppy Recovery Through 2021 as World Wrestles Pandemic. *S and P Global Market Intelligence* **2020**.
11. Hodari, D. Oil's Recovery Set to Drag On Beyond Next Year. *Wall Street J.* **2020**
12. IATA. Economic Per formance of the Airline Industry. *Semi Annual Report* **2020**. https://www.iata.org/en/iata-repository/publications/economic-reports/airline-industry-economic-performance---november-2020---report/
13. Sharafedin, B.; Hepher, T.; Samanta, K. Jet Fuel Demand to Remain Low as Airlines Buckle Up for Tough Ride. *Reuters News* **2020**.
14. Ozili, P. K.; Arun, T. Spillover of COVID-19: Impact on the Global Economy. *SSRN Electron. J. Ser.* **2020,** 29.
15. Acikgoz, Ö.; Gunay, A. The Early Impact of the Covid-19 Pandemic on the Global and Turkish Economy. *Turk. J. Med. Sci.* **2020,** *50*, 520–526.
16. Sothan, S. Foreign Aid and Economic Growth: Evidence from Cambodia. *Int. Compar. Rev.* **2017,** *27* (2).
17. Hayat, A. Foreign Direct Investments, Institutional Quality, and Economic Growth. *J. Int. Trade Econ. Dev.* **2019,** *28* (5), 561–579.
18. OECD. Foreign Direct Investment Flows in the Time of COVID-19. 2020. https://read.oecd-ilibrary.org/view/?ref=132_132646-g8as4msdp9&title=Foreign-direct-investment-flows-in-the-time-of-COVID-19 (accessed 4 Jan 2021).
19. Seric, A.; Hauge, J. COVID-19 and the Global Contraction in FDI. 2020. https://oecd-development-matters.org/2020/06/29/covid-19-and-the-global-contraction-in-foreign-direct investment/#:~:text=COVID%2D19%20and%20the%20global%20contraction%20in%20foreign20direct%20investment,29%20June%202020&text=According%20

to%20the%20UN%20Conference,hard%2C%20mainl%20for%20two%20reasons (accessed 29 Jan 2021).
20. IMF. The Great Lockdown: Worst Economic Downturn Since the Great Depression. 2020.
21. Nwosa, P. I. Oil Price, Exchange Rate and Stock Market Performance During the COVID-19 Pandemic: Implications for TNCs and FDI Inflow in Nigeria. *Transnational Corp. Rev.* **2020,** *4*, 14.
22. Ajide, F. M.; Osinubi, T. T. COVID-19 Pandemic and Outward Foreign Direct Investment: A Preliminary Note. *Global Econ.* **2020,** *8* (2), 2303–5005.
23. UNCTAD2. Global Foreign Direct Investment Falls 49% in First Half of 2020, 2020. https://unctad.org/news/global-foreign-direct-investment-falls-49-first-half-2020
24. OECD. Multinational Enterprises in the Global Economy Heavily Debated But Hardly Measured, 2018. https://www.oecd.org/industry/ind/MNEs-in-the-global-economy-policy-note.pdf (accessed 12 Dec 2020).
25. Sareen, S. COVID19 and Pakistan: The Economic Fallout. Observer Research Foundation Working Papers 2020 (251).
26. Todaro, P. *Economic Development*, 9th ed.; 1998.
27. Arellano, C.; Bai, Y.; Mihalache, G. P. Deadly Debt Crises: COVID-19 in Emerging Markets. Nber Working Paper Series, 2020.
28. Hevia, C.; Neumeyer, A. A Conceptual Framework for Analyzing the Economic Impact of COVID-19 and Its Policy Implications. COVID19 | Policy Documents Series, 2020.
29. Gourinchas, P.-O.; Hsieh, C.-T. The COVID-19 Default Time Bomb, 2020. https://www.project-syndicate.org/commentary/covid19-sovereign-default-time-bomb-by-pierre-olivier-gourinchas-and-chang-tai-hsieh-2020–04?barrier=accesspaylog (accessed 1 Jan 2020).
30. Aguiar, M.; Amador, M. Growth in the Shadow of Expropriation. *Quart. J. Econ.* **2011,** *126* (2), 651–697.
31. Nagle, P.; Sugawara, N. What the Pandemic Means for Government Debt, in Five Charts. *World Bank Blogs* **2021.**
32. Mensia, W. et al. Impact of COVID-19 Outbreak on Asymmetric Multifractality of Gold and Oil Prices. *Resour. Policy* **2020,** *69*, 280–291.
33. Barajas, A. et al. What's Different About Monetary Policy Transmission in Remittance-Dependent Countries? *J. Dev. Econ.* **2018,** *134*, 272–288.
34. Chami, R. Umbilical Cord of Remittances Under Threat. *Finance Dev.* **2020.**
35. Abdih, Y. et al. Remittances Channel and Fiscal Impact in the Middle East, North Africa, and Central Asia. *IMF Working Papers* **2012,** *12* (104), 40.
36. WorldBank, P. COVID-19: Remittance Flows to Shrink 14% by 2021, 2020.
37. Bolton, P.; et al. Born Out of Necessity: A Debt Standstill for COVID-19. *Center Econ. Policy* **2020,** *103*, 1–11.
38. W.Goodell, J.; Goutte, S. Co-Movement of COVID-19 and Bitcoin: Evidence from Wavelet Coherence Analysis. *Finance Res. Lett.* **2021,** *38* (101625).
39. Yarovaya, L. et al. Rethinking Financial Contagion: Information Transmission Mechanism During the COVID-19 Pandemic. *Infect. Dis. eJ.* **2020,** *34* (9).
40. Acker, K.; Brautigam, D.; Huang, Y. Debt Relief with Chinese Characteristics, 2020.
41. WorldBank, P. Debt Service Suspension and COVID-19. *How the World Bank is Helping* 2021.

42. IMF. The IMF's Response to COVID-19, 2021. https://www.imf.org/en/About/FAQ/imf-response-to-covid-19 (accessed 2 Feb 2021).
43. McKibbin, W. J.; Fernando, R. The Global Macroeconomic Impacts of COVID-19: Seven Scenarios. *Centre Appl. Macroecon. Analy.* **2020,** *19* (20).
44. Baldwin, R.; Mauro, B. W.d. *Mitigating the COVID Economic Crisis: Act Fast and Do Whatever It Takes*; Centre for Economic Policy Research: CEPR Press, 2020.
45. AfricanEconomy. Impact of the Coronavirus (COVID 19) on the African Economy. *Afican Union* **2020**.
46. Gopinath, G. *Limiting the Economic Fallout of the Coronavirus with Large Targeted Policies*; IMF: Editor, 2020.
47. Baldwin, R.; Mauro, B. W.d. *Economics in the Time of COVID-19*; Centre for Economic Policy Research: CEPR Press, 2020.
48. Inoue, H.; Todo, Y. The Propagation of Economic Impacts Through Supply Chains: The Case of a Mega-City Lockdown to Prevent the Spread of COVID-19. The Research Institute of Economy, Trade and Industry (RIETI) Discussion Paper, 2020, E-037 (20).
49. Yang, C. et al. *Quantifying Projected Impact of Social Distancing Policies on COVID-19 Outcomes in the US*; University of Illinois, 2020.
50. Morath, E.; Coronavirus Risk Rises for US, Global Economies. *Wall Street J.* **2020**.
51. UNCTAD. *Coronavirus Could Cut Global Investment by 40%.* New Estimates: Geneva, 2020.
52. Arezki, R.; Nguyen, H. Novel Coronavirus Hurts the Middle East and North Africa Through Many Channels. *J. Int. Econ.* **2020**, *53*.
53. OECD. Turning Hope Into Reality-OECD Economic Outlook. *Interim Report*, 2020.
54. ILO. COVID-19 and the World of Work: Impact and Policy Responses. 2020; pp 1–15.
55. Oxfam, I. Half a Billion People Could Be Pushed Into Poverty by Coronavirus. Oxfam, W., Ratcliff, A., Thériault, A., Eds., 2020.
56. Barro, R. J.; Ursúa, J. F.; Weng, J. The Coronavirus and the Great Influenza Pandemic: Lessons from the "Spanish Flu" for the Coronavirus's Potential Effects on Mortality and Economic Activity NBER Working Paper Series, 2020 (26866).
57. WTO. Trade Shows Signs of Rebound from COVID-19, Recovery Still Uncertain, C. M. E. (CME), Ed., 2020.
58. Miroudot, S. B. Reshaping the Policy Debate on the Implications of COVID-19 for Global Supply Chains. *J. Int. Busi. Policy* **2020,** *3*, 430–442.
59. Ariu, A.; Crisis-Proof Services: Why Trade in Services Did Not Suffer During the 2008–2009 Collapse. *J. Int. Econ.* **2016,** *98*, 138–149. .
60. Borchert, I.; A. Mattoo, The crisis-resilience of services trade. The Service Industries Journal **2010,** 30: p. 2115–2136
61. Shingal, A.; The Impact of COVID-19 on Commonwealth Services Trade. CW International Trade Working Paper, 2020.
62. UNCTAD. UN Calls for $2.5 Trillion Coronavirus Crisis Package for Developing Countries. 2020. https://unctad.org/news/un-calls-25-trillion-coronavirus-crisis-package-developing-countries.
63. ILO. Teleworking During the COVID-19 Pandemic and Beyond A Practical Guide, 2020.
64. UNCTAD. Key Statistics and Trade Trends Under the COVID-19 Pandemic United Nations Conference in Trade and Development, 2020. https://unctad.org/system/files/official-document/ditctab2020d4_en.pdf

65. UNCTAD. Impact of the Pandemic on Trade and Development: Transitioning to a New Normal. in United Nations Conference on Trade and Development, 2020. https://unctad.org/system/files/official-document/osg2020d1_en.pdf
66. WorldBank. The Global Economic Outlook During the COVID-19 Pandemic: A Changed World. 2020. https://www.worldbank.org/en/news/feature/2020/06/08/the-global-economic-outlook-during-the-covid-19-pandemic-a-changed-world.
67. WorldBank. The Human Capital Index 2020 Update: Human Capital in the Time of COVID-19, 2020.
68. Cuffari, B.; Coveney, S. How Has the COVID-19 Pandemic Impacted Global Health?, 2020. https://www.news-medical.net/health/How-has-the-COVID-19-Pandemic-Impacted-Global-Health.aspx (accessed 24 May 2021).
69. Cutler, D. M.; L. H. Summers, The COVID-19 Pandemic and the US $16 Trillion Virus. JAMA, **2020,** 324 (15), 1495–6.
70. WHO. Maintaining Essential Health Services During the COVID-19 Outbreak, 2021. https://www.who.int/emergencies/diseases/novel-coronavirus-2019/related-health-issues (accessed 6 May 2021).
71. Birn, A.-E. Philanthrocapitalism, Past and Present: The Rockefeller Foundation, the Gates Foundation, and the Setting (s) of the International/Global Health Agenda. *Hypothesis* **2014,** *12* (1).
72. Greenough, P. Intimidation, Coercion and Resistance in the Final Stages of the South Asian Smallpox Eradication Campaign, 1973–1975. *Soc. Sci. Med.* **1995,** *41* (5), 633–645.
73. Cueto, M. The ORIGINS of Primary Health Care and SELECTIVE Primary Health Care. *Am. J. Public Health* **2004,** *94* (11), 1864–1874.
74. WHO. Beyond Ebola, Keeping Patients and Health Workers Safe, 2016. https://www.who.int/en/news-room/feature-stories/detail/beyond-ebola-keeping-patients-and-health-workers-safe (accessed 16 Feb 2021).
75. Webster, P. PEPFAR at 15 years. *Lancet* **2018,** *392* (10143).
76. Yeboah, I. E. A. Capitalism and Sub-Saharan African Human Capital. *Afr. Identities* **2018,** *6* (1), 67–86.
77. Zicker, F.; Fonseca, B., Albuquerque, P. Global Health: A Review of Concepts. Players, and Publications. *Int. J. Travel Med. Global Health* **2019,** *7* (1), 4–9.
78. Gautier, L.; Sieleunou, I.; Kalolo, A. Deconstructing the Notion of "Global Health Research Partnerships" Across Northern and African Contexts. *BMC Med. Ethics* **2018,** *19* (1).
79. C. D. C., A. Novel Coronavirus (2019-nCoV) Global Epidemic, 2020. https://africacdc.org/disease-outbreak/novel-coronavirus-2019-ncov-global-epidemic-31-march-2020/ (accessed 2 Feb 2021).
80. Losonczy, L. I. et al. Critical Care Capacity in Haiti: A Nationwide Cross-Sectional Survey. *PLoS ONE* **2019,** *14* (6).
81. Pang, T.; Lansang, M. A.; Haines, A. Brain Drain and Health Professionals. *Br. Med. J.* **2002,** *324* (7336), 499–500.
82. A.Williams, G. et al. What Strategies Are Countries Using to Expand Health WorkforceSurge Capacity During the Covid-19 Pandemic? *Eurohealth* **2020,** *26* (2).
83. Schlegel, J. CCP Helps Johns Hopkins Protect Itself from COVID-19, 2021. https://ccp.jhu.edu/2020/08/24/ccp-helps-johns-hopkins-covid-19-campaign/?gclid=Cj0KC

Qjwna2FBhDPARIsACAEc_XRKcAzNH0WhZuAqsLRsyjHw3ugYeM4xfXqLaZ-v3lsBOswCoWav84aAkZHEALw_wcB (accessed 4 Apr 2021).
84. WHO. WHO Coronavirus (COVID-19) Dashboard: Situation by Region, Country, Territory & Area, 2021. https://covid19.who.int/table.
85. Hong, J.; Lyu, D. World Ventilator Demand Now 10 Times What's Available. *Bloomberg* **2020**.
86. Worldometer. COVID-19 CoronaVirus Pandemic, 2021. https://www.worldometers.info/coronavirus/ (accessed 24 May 2021).
87. Murray, C. J. Forecasting the Impact of the First Wave of the COVID-19 Pandemic on Hospital Demand and Deaths for the USA and European Economic Area Countries. *BMJ* **2020**.
88. Dalglish, S. L. COVID-19 Gives the Lie to Global Health Expertise. *Lancent* **2020**.
89. Razavi, A.; Erondu, N.; Okereke, E. The Global Health Security Index: What Value Does It Add? *BMJ Glob Health* **2020,** *5* (10).
90. Both, R.; Schrimpf, G. A Global Challenge, 2021. https://www.merckgroup.com/en/company/press/press-kits/corona-pandemic/global-health-in-times-of-covid-19.html (accessed 3 May 2021).
91. Bcheraoui, C. E. et al. Assessing COVID-19 Through the Lens of Health Systems' Preparedness: Time for a Change. *Globalization Health* **2020**.
92. Tromberg, B. J. et al. Rapid Scaling Up of Covid-19 Diagnostic Testing in the United States—The NIH RADx Initiative. *N. Engl. J. Med.* **2020,** *38* (11), 1071–1077.
93. Ruan, Q. et al. Clinical Predictors of Mortality Due to COVID-19 Based on an Analysis of Data of 150 Patients from Wuhan, China. *Intens. Care Med.* **2020,** *46* (5).
94. Han, E. et al. Lessons Learnt from Easing COVID-19 Restrictions: An Analysis of Countries and Regions in Asia Pacific and Europe. *Lancent* **2020,** *396* (10261), 1525–1534.
95. Stuckler, D. et al. Austerity and Health: The Impact in the UK and Europe. *Eur. J. Public Health* **2017,** *27* (4).
96. Shamasunder, S. et al. COVID-19 Reveals Weak Health Systems by Design: Why We Must Re-Make Global Health in This Historic Moment. *Global Public Health* **2020,** *15* (7), 1083–1089.
97. Arshid, M. A.; Mumtaz, M.; Nazir, R.Unforeseen Challenges to Global Health System, in Particular Context to COVID-19 Pandemic and Health Care Personnel. *Arab J. Basic Appl. Sci.* 2020.
98. Gault, A. COVID-19: A Heavy Toll on Health-Care Workers. *Lancent* **2021,** *09*.
99. Guardian, T. Lost on the Frontline US Healthcare, T. G.o. Years, Editor, 2021.
100. Melimopoulos, E. At Least 17,000 Health Workers Have Died from COVID: Amnesty. *Aljazeera* **2021**.
101. Lancent. COVID-19: Protecting Health-Care Workers. *PMC* **2021,** *395*.
102. Gelfand, J. M.; Hefele, B. E. Clinical Research After COVID-19: Embracing a New Normal. *J. Investig. Dermatol.* **2021,** *141*, 481–483.
103. Pragholapati, A. New Normal " Indeonesia" After COVID-19 Pandemic Nursing Department, Faculty of Sport Education and Health Science, Universitas Pendidikan Indonesia, 2020.
104. Luker, G. D. Transitioning to a New Normal After COVID-19: Preparing to Get Back on Track for Cancer Imaging U.o.M. Department of Radiology, Editor, 2020.
105. Žižek, S. Pandemic!: COVID-19 Shakes the World, 1st ed.; 2020.

106. Rab, S.; Javaid, M.; Haleem, A. Face Masks Are New Normal After COVID-19 Pandemic. *Diab. Metabol. Syndr. Clin. Res. Rev.* **2020,** *14*, 1871–4021.
107. Daniel, S. J. Education and the COVID-19 Pandemic. *Prospects* **2020,** *39*, 91–96.
108. Li, C.; Lalani, F. The COVID-19 Pandemic Has Changed Education Forever. This Is How, 2020. https://www.weforum.org/agenda/2020/04/coronavirus-education-global-covid19-online-digital-learning/ (accessed 28 Apr 2021).
109. M, L. Why Hybrid Teaching Might Be The Future Of Online Courses, 2021. https://www.topuniversities.com/student-info/videos/why-hybrid-teaching-might-be-future-online-courses (accessed 5 May 2021).
110. Koeze, E.; Popper, N. The Virus Changed the Way We Internet. *NewYork Times* **2020**.
111. Brouder, P.; Teoh, S.; Salazar, N. B. Reflections and Discussions: Tourism Matters in the New Normal Post COVID-19. *Tour. Geogr.* **2020,** *22* (3), 735–746.
112. Bandyopadhyay, S.; Public Transport During Pandemic. *Clean Technol. Environ. Policy* **2020,** *22*, 1755–1756.
113. Fleming, S. COVID Made Many of Us Avoid Public Transport—What Will It Take to Get Us Back on the Bus? 2021. https://www.weforum.org/agenda/2021/02/public-transport-covid-data/ (accessed 2 May 2021).
114. UTTP. Public Transport Authorities and Covid-19 Impact and Response to a Pandemic. Australia, 2020.
115. Bird, J.; Kriticos, S.; Tsivanidis, N. *Impact of COVID-19 on Public Transport.* International Growth Centre, 2020.
116. Gkiotsalitis, K.; Cats, O. Public Transport Planning Adaption Under the COVID-19 Pandemic Crisis: Literature Review of Research Needs and Directions. *Transp. Rev.* **2021,** *41* (3), 374–392.

CHAPTER 2

Global Aftermath of COVID-19 on Entrepreneurship

TEHMINA FIAZ QAZI[1], RAHMA SHAFAAT[2], and UZMA QURESHI[3]

[1]*Hailey College of Banking and Finance, Punjab University, Lahore, Pakistan*

[2]*Institute of Business & Management, University of Engineering and Technology, Lahore, Pakistan*

[3]*The Women University Multan, Punjab, Pakistan*

ABSTRACT

Severe acute respiratory syndrome coronavirus 2 (SARS-CoV-2) has globally emerged as a pandemic that resulted in the halt of all activities worldwide. As a result, all the government and private institutions and organizations were entirely shut, countries went into lockdown situations globally. Keeping view of its disastrous effects, the World Health Organization (WHO) declared the coronavirus (COVID-19) outbreak to be a pandemic on March 11, 2020. The devastating effects of COVID-19 have posed serious threats to the economic condition worldwide. The increasing effects of the pandemic on local and global economies were parallel to the humanitarian tragedy. The top economies of the world are already influenced to a great deal by the fears of unforeseeable impacts of the pandemic, whereas the recession is being forecasted by several economies. In doing so, the issue of resuming the economy has fueled controversy, as there is no certainty about when and how this will happen due to the unpredictability of COVID-19's sustainability and resilience. Due to its negative economic impact, the pandemic has become an entrepreneur's response to declining market

Post-Pandemic Economy, Technology, and Innovation: Global Outlook and Context.
Samina Yaqoob, Arwa Abdulkreem AL-Huqail, and Fakhra Aziz (Eds.)

demand, difficulty reconciling with resources, and/or entrepreneurial failure due to strict measures to secure social distance. Therefore, referring to this overview, it is expected that the start of entrepreneurial projects will be significantly reduced. Dealing with such disasters caused by the coronavirus requires changes in entrepreneurship and the environment. Entrepreneurship requires rational decision-making to seize opportunities in markets where decisions must be made by assessing opportunities and recognizing the need to identify market gaps.

2.1 INTRODUCTION

Wuhan, a city in China, reported a new coronavirus in December 2019. Being extremely contagious, the virus affected a huge number of individuals in Wuhan.[1] The live animal markets of Wuhan were initially believed the source from where the virus evolved, but later, the exact origin of the virus became controversial. Consequently, the government of China locked down the city of Wuhan, making the residents of the city to be at home and prevented them from leaving their houses except for essential needs. After the announcement of a complete lockdown of Wuhan city by the Chinese government, more than five million residents of Wuhan left the city on January 23rd, 2020.[2] The virus affected the world socially and economically. Change in the working and living conditions brought about social impacts. Reliance on digital communication has increased due to social distancing. Digitalization was already making its way when the virus emerged, but it accelerated when it became known that the virus can be transmitted. There was a collapse of several healthcare systems as the number of casualties overwhelmed the healthcare systems. As the virus spread its dreadfulness, several initiatives took place, for example, “Clap for Carers,” in order to show support with healthcare systems in treating virus patients. Non-pharmaceutical strategies were introduced and promoted, such as washing hands, personal hygiene, and social distancing, as the virus had no pharmaceutical treatment. Although the strategies positively worked in stopping the spread of the virus, several consequences also came forward that included drastic mobility and social restrictions as well as the closure of academic institutions and playgrounds.[3]

The virus came forward as a global calamity with its social and economic consequences throughout the world. Coronavirus was declared a pandemic on 11th March 2020 by World Health Organization due to its dreadful effects.[4] The year 2020 will be remembered for the COVID-19 pandemic. With its devastating effects, the outspread of the pandemic has been so quick that it caused turmoil, overshadowing all other events that occurred. Within no time, it propagated from country to country, including emerging, developing, and developed ones.[5] The SARS-CoV-2 (severe acute respiratory syndrome coronavirus 2) globally emerged as an unprecedented bolt from the blue, especially in referring to the economy.[6] Although it was unsurprising for Virologists that the pandemic was caused by a new virus, the measures, such as social distancing taken to downturn the spread of the pandemic employed colossal pressure on the economy worldwide.[7] The institutions that significantly shape the economy have metaphorically referred to this pandemic as a "black swan event" having a paramount importance.[8] The intensity and unpredictability of this pandemic caused severe effects that turned the political and economic scenarios drastically.[9] Where COVID-19 has been viewed as an opportunity, it has marked the current scenario as a dreadful plight with unusual societal lockdowns. The pandemic has equally posed serious consequences on the world economy. Considerably greater than the recent financial crisis of 2008–2012,[10] the initial forecasts have assumed that COVID-19 has brought the most dreadful economic crisis even since World War II, whereas it is feared that its influence on startup activities and entrepreneurship is even worse.[11] With economists predicting economic decline and depression, there has been a notable decrease in economic activities.[12,13] Along with human tragedy, the local and global economies have been hugely affected by the pandemic. The worlds top economies are already heavily impacted by fears of the unpredictable effects of pandemics, but some economies are forecasting recessions.[14] The estimated effects of this pandemic on the worldwide economy are widely varied and sketchy, but research on this effect has suggested an estimation of US $90 trillion of the economy affected globally. Such a consequence has not been experienced in almost a century.[15] Furthermore, it has been suggested that the unpredictability of this pandemic has led a huge fraction of the labor force to lose their jobs, whereas, working in an informal economy, 1.6 billion people are said to have faced colossal damage in terms of earning a living.[16] As a calamity affecting the health of the masses globally, COVID-19 has caused individuals to stay at home for months and the cessation of businesses. The number of individuals losing their jobs and/or being laid off with no certainty to return to work is in the millions. Thereby, the question of restarting economies has enkindled the argument because there is no certainty about when and how it will be possible due to the unpredictability of COVID-19 persistence and resilience.[17] The pandemic has given rise to a double-edged crisis worldwide:

first by burdening health systems and secondly, the economic activities have enormously gone into a sudden halt due to the control measures being taken. Therefore, the prevention of the spread of this pandemic amid masses with ensured, smooth, and untroubled economic operations is the biggest challenge posed to the decision-makers by such socioeconomic scenario.[18]

Well ahead of the appearance of COVID-19, a debate initiated on the status of newborn companies and the future of globalization in the current state of world order that is in continuous emergence.[19] Several queries have been raised by anti-globalization movements, populist and nationalist, having different ideas and doctrines, regarding the place of international institutions and the beneficiaries of internationalization.[20] At odds with this political turbulence running in the backcloth, COVID-19 appeared as a worsening factor, giving rise to concerns regarding the role of small, large, and multinational firms as well as the future of global business. When considering the worldwide business climate and what it means for global endeavors, evidently the pandemic has effectively achieved significant changes that will considerably affect these organizations for quite a long time to come. Pandemics affect people in terms of individuals changing their lifestyles, way of thinking, executing, and organizing their social orders accordingly.[21] Most significant changes caused by this pandemic till now include re-structuring supply chains globally, disturbing individual networks and existing firms, damaging well-established organizations, as well as sabotaging the outflow of knowledge, thoughts, and people and technological capital beyond global boundaries. Although the business activities of ventures can be handicapped due to each of the aforementioned changes, their mutual impact is probably to be more pulverizing because these changes are interlinked.

2.2 ENTREPRENEURSHIP AND COVID-19

To manage the catastrophe caused by the coronavirus, it is required to adopt an entrepreneurial orientation and change in the environment. The behavioral aspects on the organizational level of encouraging innovative behavior as well as pioneering innovative proactiveness, the commencement of risky startups, and being engaged in product-market innovation are referred to as entrepreneurial orientation.[22] Thus, it can be comprehended that in order to deal with the crisis brought about by the pandemic, the key aspects of entrepreneurship are needed that comprise risk-taking, resilience, skills, innovation, and marketplace practice. It has now become an immediate need for individuals and organizations to engage in entrepreneurial activities signifying that a more contemporaneous approach to entrepreneurial orientation is required. It depends on the ability of entrepreneurs to seize opportunities by utilizing their social networks as social interactions are at the core of entrepreneurship. Social ties signify the degree to which entrepreneurs hold networks depending upon social interactions that enable them to utilize an extensive array of social resources for their entrepreneurial activities. These resources can be different in nature, for example, the members of these social networks can offer suggestions and advice for business. Such aspects of social entrepreneurship may help in contributing toward the development of methods and strategies to combat the crisis caused by the current pandemic.[23]

Evaluating the probability of the occurrence of particular events is paramount to getting insights about the environment. As some environments undergo continuous actions, they are expected to be less vulnerable to such crises than others. Thus, how a business is affected by such an environmental crisis could be judged easily. However, some environmental conditions may be dynamically based on political activities, therefore, it is important to assess possible business prospects with vigilance. On the other hand, the environments that are more vulnerable to turbulence can be profoundly changed because of unpredictability. This implies that various recommended directions can be inferred regarding the planning of situations about how to manage the novel coronavirus that may enable a more careful strategy to be developed about what measures to be taken to downturn possible consequences.

Entrepreneurship requires rational decision-making in order to acquire opportunities in the market where the decisions are to be made by evaluating opportunities and recognizing that it is needed to identify gaps in the market. The need to perform activities with innovation is enclosed in the decisions concerning entrepreneurship. A study denotes that actions taken to carry out entrepreneurial activities are essentially paramount in the subject of entrepreneurship which means that the intention to bring about a change results in entrepreneurial aspirations.[24] Hence, it can be apprehended, the behavior that is exhibited in response to a decision (that can be judged) under unpredictability regarding prospective earning opportunity can be referred to as entrepreneurial action.[25] Focusing on the phenomenon of entrepreneurship in terms of actions emphasize the perception that a particular behavior results in entrepreneurial intention.

A person who utilizes an opportunity to make profits through innovation is referred to as an entrepreneur. Such individuals recognize a market gap and try to fill it through a new business venture. To reach financial profits, the creation of some sort of service, process, or product is required. Entrepreneurs emphasize on involving in innovation-based business activities that can earn them profits by capturing new market opportunities effectively. Identifying and recognizing new ideas and opportunities are the key characteristics of entrepreneurship that can be achieved through creativity as the development of new ideas requires diverse thinking patterns. Producing new and profitable ideas can be referred to as creativity.[26] On the other hand, in order to deal with COVID-19 aftereffects, it is imperative to exhibit creativity as it may provide a competitive advantage in the market worldwide.

2.3 ENTREPRENEURSHIP AND COVID-19 AFTERMATHS

The pandemic not only influenced human lives but also caused greater effects on entrepreneurial businesses worldwide.[27] With its negative economic effects, the pandemic has augmented the fears of entrepreneurs about the failure of new ventures and startups due to a decrease in market demand, difficulty in approaching resources and/or strict actions to ensure social distancing. Therefore, concerning this overview, a notable decline has been expected, in the commencement of entrepreneurial ventures. Moreover, entrepreneurs are facing additional hurdles in entrepreneurial activities due to this pandemic as startups are found to be already hit by the economic havoc created by COVID-19.[28] The entrepreneurial activities of the developed countries were greatly affected by the financial crisis earlier as well as the economies of emerging countries were also influenced.[29] A research work showed that during the beginning of the 2008 crisis, a huge decline was noted in the investments of venture capital. Hence, the pandemic is feared to create a similar situation as seen in the old times of crises. Nonetheless, as the economic upshots are expected to be more grave, entrepreneurial activities are expected to fall even to a larger extent and one can presume that the consequences will be global, regardless of the development level of countries.

The process and action of designing and initiating a new business venture or running a business that already existed but on a small level is referred to as "Entrepreneurship" by a researcher in her research article on entrepreneurship.[3] Entrepreneurship is significant in the economic growth of a region and hence viewed as one of its fundamental drivers. On the other hand, entrepreneurs are signified as the building blocks of new ventures and businesses, creating and driving innovation; accelerating structural changes; introducing competition and hence contributing toward the economy.[30] Taking up a crisis overview, the research on entrepreneurship is well suited for the purpose that may provide development in the literature of further streams such as sociology and business. Although the concept of crisis is not new, COVID-19 has caused ravaging effects. Moreover, as entrepreneurship and innovation are evidently sustaining and sparking factors in the international business actions of organizations, usual queries are being made as to how COVID-19 will be looked after and its effects on global business, significantly, global entrepreneurship. Among the new businesses, 40% have been estimated to be red-zoned.[31] The pandemic compelled several businesses to cease contracts with its full-time workers. On the contrary, an increase was observed in entrepreneurial activities in a few businesses,[32] for example, high demands experienced by automotive industries for new product lines like ventilators.[33] In order to deal with the crisis, certain measures have been taken on individual as well as organizational level worldwide. A great number of startups, small-scale companies, and entrepreneurs have been most vulnerable to the effects posed by the preventive measures employed by governments worldwide during this crisis.

2.3.1 ENTREPRENEURIAL FUNDING AND COVID-19

Although, it has been strongly proposed by studies that during the time of crisis in the past, innovative companies have faced more problems in terms of accessing financial capital from banks, for example, during the GFC (Global Financial Crisis).[34] However, the impacts of such crises on the access to financial markets, such as Venture Capitalists (VCs) and Business Angels (BAs), for entrepreneurship is still understudied.[35] VC is extremely unpredictable which makes this type of funding profoundly vulnerable to the ambivalence brought about by such crises,[36] although, it is being suggested that COVID-19 has influenced entrepreneurial investment specifically.[37] Equity capital is emphatically established on the close personal association among entrepreneurs and investors as a prerequisite that is contrary to debt capital.[38] Oral "pitch" is a vital characteristic of the personal interface that is undertaken by entrepreneurs to acquire funding from investors. Further significant personal interfaces suggested by researchers among entrepreneurs and investors are improvised gatherings that accentuate key elements of the decision-making process of the investment. Investors are aware that each entrepreneur holds weaknesses and strengths and so informational opaqueness related to startups is decreased through exclusive information and thorough evaluation of persons concerned to produce delicate knowledge. To identify, evaluate, and monitor the opportunities for investment, equity investors signify such close relations since they greatly depend on individual links and direct acquaintances

Provided that such relations are significant in the market of entrepreneurial investment sources, it is feared that this type of finance may be disrupted by the situation created by recent pandemic.[40] A study suggests a momentous decline in the stages of entrepreneurial investment deals in the first quarter of 2020 as compared with the 2019 first quarter of 31%.[41] In a country like the UK, the months of April and May of the year 2020 have observed a striking decline when compared to the preceding years (i.e., 134 new entrepreneurial financial agreements compared with April and May 2018 with 286 and April and May 2019 with 245 agreements). The results indicate that the volume of entrepreneurial investment agreements has declined to half of which it was in the previous years, signifying that the second quarter of 2020 has seen a greater fall as compared with the first quarter of 2020. A 39% decline has been seen in seed finance for entrepreneurial activities since the first quarter of 2019 compared with the first quarter of 2020 which makes it the type of deal that the pandemic most vigorously affected in the United Kingdom. Along these lines, the results of the study also suggested that the first quarter of 2019 and 2020 has seen an increase in late-stage deals signifying that the current crisis has comparatively augmented the greater deals. Subsequently, where the pandemic caused serious damage to seed finance, the slight increase in the late-stage category of finance has counterbalanced the damage. The results also demonstrate that there was a huge decline in equity capital value and volumes in China through the year 2020 first quarter. On the whole, China has seen a 60% decline in the volume of entrepreneurial investment deals compared with the year 2019 first quarter. Thus, COVID-19 has damaged emerging startups the most, regardless of the geographical location of countries.

2.3.2 ELECTRONICS INDUSTRY AND COVID-19

The community of commerce is typically linked around the world, but it became a dreadful problem when they were unable to connect with vendors in the red zone.[42] Out of 1,000 firms, 94% were connected to China in terms of their supply chain systems, with China being the center of the coronavirus as stated in a whitepaper published by Dun & Bradstreet. Technology and healthcare were challenged by such issues in the supply chain.[43] In China, there was a temporary closure of a number of electronic centers in order to restrict the spread of the pandemic that affected the supply chain worldwide due to which a notable decline was seen in the production of automobiles and electronics as there was a shortage of goods and materials.[44] The pandemic has caused the electronic industry to work only 30–50% as compared with its full capacity.[45] On the other hand, the pandemic has caused a marked decline of 30–40% in entrepreneurial activities in the electronic industry. Consequently, the electronic industry reported a loss of 2.2 billion dollars.[46]

2.3.3 EDUCATIONAL ENTREPRENEURSHIP AND COVID-19

Likewise, several queries were brought to the front with regard to the threats posed to higher education. Educational entrepreneurship has been certainly affected by the current pandemic.[47] The cancellation of public events and conferences as well as the transition from face-to-face to online lectures bound the universities to modify their methods and strategies.[48] Institutions like Florida State University, New York University, and Harvard switched to e-learning during the current pandemic.[49]

2.3.4 FOOD INDUSTRY AND COVID-19

The entrepreneurial activities in the food industry have also happened to be disrupted by the COVID-19 crisis. According to a survey conducted by World Food Programme[50] nearly 98% of the small and medium-sized businesses and startups were to be affected by the virus and steps taken to control it. The main effects to be quoted by 75% are a decline in sales; 53% reported problems in the access of inputs and 47% reported hindrances in the access to finance. About 42% of these SMEs and startups referred to the effects of the pandemic as moderate and controllable, 44% indicated it as substantial and hard to recover, and 11% have stated the effects to be severe that may lead to the shutdown of their business activities. Moreover, the startups have been referred to owe colossal debts to the farmers as a result of the closure of their businesses.[51]

2.3.5 THE EFFECTS OF COVID-19 ON TRAVEL AND TOURISM INDUSTRY

The industry of travel and tourism contributes 10.4% to the global GDP, topping the global economy growth for eight consecutive years as stated by WTTC (World Travel & Tourism Council). A recent research has shown that more than 75 million jobs have been put to immediate risk, causing US $2.1 trillion loss to the worldwide economy in 2020 with Asia-Pacific being the most affected with 48.7 million jobs at risk (Pakistan Tourism Development Corporation-PTDC).[52] World Tourism Organization situated in the United Nations (UNWTO) has notified that the current pandemic may result in a loss of US $900 billion to US $1.2 trillion in the tourism industry worldwide. The economic outlook report by Organization for Economic Cooperation and Development (OECD) has stated that the pandemic and the steps taken to reduce its outspread has affected small and medium enterprises (SMEs) working in this industry to a larger extent.[53] McKinsey & Company conducted a study signifying that the sector of Tourism and Hospitality is at significant risk as the effects of COVID-19 are feared to remain for the longest period as compared with any other sector[54]. A study revealed that in the upcoming 9 months since August 2020, the people operating in the tourism industry are feared to lose US $25 billion in roaming income owing to COVID-19. Since March 2020, 90% of tourists were affected by these traveling constraints.[55] The entrepreneurial startups in the industry of travel and tourism also received the aftermaths of the current pandemic. The entrepreneurs running their startups in the industry faced the cancellation of tours and refunding the booking amounts of their respective clients, suspension of operations, cost-cutting measures as well as salary cuts.[56] Like other countries, the travel and tourism industry of Pakistan is also suffering the consequences of the current pandemic. The industry is expecting extensive losses in the time to come. The industry embraces SMEs and startups with their income sources relying on tourism. According to PTDC, a substantial number of these ventures and businesses are feared to go bankrupt. A study shows that 83% of travel and tourism ventures have deferred their services for the time being, 67% have carried out downsizing and pay cuts, whereas a large number of startups have postponed their plans to expand their businesses.[57]

2.3.6 ENTERTAINMENT INDUSTRY AND COVID-19

The pandemic has caused a striking level of ambivalence in the industry of media and entertainment globally. Gaming, advertising as well as television and film industries are paralyzed and continue to halt lacking a clear insight into when they will return to normal due to the economic recession worldwide and change in customers' behavior. It is feared that cinemas will not be able to witness the pre-pandemic level of audience till 2022 as people will refrain from outdoor entertainment venues as a safety measure.[58] The shutdown of cinemas has caused major setbacks to the shopping centers and mall owners who are already facing bankruptcies.[59] The turbulence caused by the pandemic resulted in the delay in releasing of some new movies and for some, the release was even postponed. Major events in the industry were either delayed, postponed, canceled, or changed their formats to virtual events.[60] While witnessing such conditions, an alert has been sent out by the Events and Entertainment Management Association to businesses and entrepreneurs of the industry as the industry employing 60 million individuals has come to a halt. The cancellation of public and private events, concerts, exhibitions, award shows, film festivals, and many other events have choked the lifeline of the events industry, with both established businesses as well as entrepreneurial startups being affected. Even at a lower level, entrepreneurs operating in the events industry had to face the consequences of lockdown situations with their events delayed or canceled, making them return huge amounts of finance to their clients. According to the Events and Entertainment Management Association, 10 million out of 60 million individuals working in the events industry have been directly influenced due to the pandemic, with entrepreneurs being most vulnerable to the impacts.[61] Moreover, several events of sports were also postponed or canceled. The events that were canceled or those being conducted without the audience also influenced entrepreneurship worldwide as it comprises several other sectors.[62] In Tokyo, the cancellation of the Olympics affected the industry of sports and entertainment as well as the entrepreneurs associated with it. On the other hand, due to the pandemic, people were restricted to their homes with the television set being the only source to connect with the world outside, making this industry to observe a significant increase in its viewership[63] whereas, the online streaming platforms witnessed massive revenues. The platforms, such as Netflix, Amazon Prime, and Disney+ witnessed tremendous increases in their memberships, with each acquiring millions of new subscribers. This provided increased income to the entrepreneurs associated.[64]

2.3.7 COVID-19 WORLDWIDE UPSHOTS ON SMALL-SCALE ENTREPRENEURSHIP

A huge number of entrepreneurs all through the world have fallen prey to the economic upshots brought about by the pandemic.[65] A number of entrepreneurs working at a small level have been bound to terminate their business activities, whereas others have been working precariously and putting great effort to their businesses. Such small-scale ventures have a vital role to play in generating jobs and providing services and products that are significantly required.[66] A policy had to be enacted by Youth Business International to help entrepreneurship in nearly 50 countries through the identification of problems and furnishing resolutions.[67] SOS meeting and response/recovery program are the two initiatives that have been launched globally that hold the capacity to support more than 200,000 small-scale businesses and ventures in 32 countries during COVID-19, making it possible to help young entrepreneurs to grow their businesses and ventures.[68]

2.3.7.1 IMPACTS ON EARNINGS

Although 29% of startups were already going through difficult period, the pandemic has led 41% of startups toward the red zone with almost no cash left in hand for 3 months. It signifies that a further 40% threat has been caused by the virus to these small-scale businesses.[69] According to the evaluation of a study,[70] investors pulled their term sheets from startups after the pandemic; mainly 20% of startups were affected in this way; 53% of startups witnessed stoppage in their work, while there were only 28% of small-scale startups being able to conduct their working normally as well as continued receiving financial capital.

2.3.7.2 IMPACTS ON JOBS

About 74% of startups conducted layoffs by terminating their employees with the inception of the pandemic. Later on, it was observed that 20% of employees were further terminated by 39% of these small-scale startups. The situation appeared to be worsened for the entrepreneurs as a plunge in the share values of startups was observed. Furthermore, a few startups were left with no other option than terminating all their workers at the cruelty of the pandemic. A huge downsizing has been witnessed in continents with 84% employee-layoffs by startups with which North America is at the top, 67% of employee termination in Europe, whereas Asia has seen the least employee terminations by startups with 59%.[71]

2.3.7.3 IMPACTS ON OPERATIONS AND MANAGEMENT

With the onset of the virus, startups have seen myriad fluctuations in terms of conducting their business activities. It has been observed that nearly two-thirds of small-scale startups lowered their expenditures. It was noted that a few firms aggressively reduced their costs. About 60% of cost depletion was witnessed in more than 10 firms, while a few startups reduced their costs up to 76%. COVID-19 has posed the most dreadful threats to the operations and management of small-scale ventures. According to the sources (World Health Organization, 2020), the figures mentioned above are the direct consequences of the crisis brought about by the current pandemic. Studies have shown the reasons behind the hindrances caused by COVID-19 in entrepreneurship.

2.4 WOMEN ENTREPRENEURSHIP AND COVID-19

The pandemic has adversely affected the societies altogether, particularly those groups that were already at risk even prior to the crisis brought about by the pandemic. An emergency and lockdown were declared in several countries with the inception of the coronavirus first wave in March 2020. Consequently, the business activities of 56% of the medium-sized entrepreneurial ventures were influenced, 22% of entrepreneurial ventures were expected to be negatively affected within 2–5 months, while 11% were not affected or expected to have negative effects in the time to come.[73] It has been signified by UNWOMEN in their research that women have been predominantly influenced by the crisis caused by the pandemic. Where the female entrepreneurs had to handle the hitches created by the pandemic equally on family and economic grounds, the females doing jobs confronted different scenarios in their work, for example, hurdles in maintaining a balance between family and work as well as the stress of coping up with the hurdles in showing adequate performance toward their work under the burden of fulfilling family needs and likewise going parallel. The pandemic significantly affected the women entrepreneurs who faced the closure of their business activities since the pandemic initiated, having left them with no income. Furthermore, a number of females who used to provide services like the maintenance of household and cleaning, childcare, as well as looking after older people were left with no work or earning.[74]

A significant increase has been witnessed in women's entrepreneurship over the recent years around the globe. The firms initiated and managed by women entrepreneurs have a vital role to play in economic and social growth. As COVID-19 has posed a threat to entrepreneurship worldwide, it is expected that the ventures owned by women are also vulnerable to the challenges brought about by the pandemic. It has been noted that 6% of the women-owned businesses were compelled to close their business activities, whereas 2.4% indicated to be positively impacted by the pandemic.[75] In 2008, the global economic crisis put down 47% of the women-owned businesses which is feared to be repeated by the COVID-19 crisis as the sectors that are significantly affected are those small- and medium-sized ventures owned by women, such as education, tourism, childcare, hospitality, event management, beauty salons, and other professions associated with women. Moreover, lack of labor, reduced working hours, and disruption of supply chains due to the closure of borders among countries as a result of lockdowns had adversely affected 10% of women entrepreneurs in the trading sector. According to a study, 76% of the women-owned businesses have been adversely affected by the pandemic. Among them, 33% indicated being heavily affected, and 24% reported being slightly affected. The ventures owned by women have faced different pandemic consequences, witnessing a decrease in income due to a decline or, in some cases, lack of demand and transitory stoppage of business operations in particular. The World Tourism Organization conducted a Global Report in the seven countries of the EU for the span 2012–2016 signifying 38% of the firms that are being operated in the tourism sector are owned by women.[76] The industry of tourism has been profoundly struck by the current pandemic and the steps taken to downturn its outspread. Not only the owners of touristic ventures, hotels and motels, and hospitality service providers are among the most affected in the market of tourism but also the related industries, such as food processing, handicrafts, and alike have also been affected that comprises women entrepreneurs as well. As a whole, the women entrepreneurs operating in the sector of services, hospitality, and alike have seemed to be heavily hit by the virus.[77]

2.5 POST-COVID ERA AND OPPORTUNITIES

Compared with the financial crises that occurred in the past, the COVID-19 pandemic has caused grave psychological, economic, and political consequences as mentioned above. The business milieu has undergone a profound alteration, creating redoubtable hindrances in the creation and expansion of ventures. As witnessed, the COVID-19 pandemic has induced dreadful effects on entrepreneurship in several diversified sectors, such as sports, hospitality, food, movie theatres and entertainment, hair salons education, trading, electronics travel and tourism, and many others, yet, in spite of the significant challenges inflicted by the pandemic, the world in the post-COVID era is prospective to proffer significant opportunities and prospects for startups and ventures. A number of sectors, in fact, have witnessed progress during the pandemic, including home entertainment, medical equipment suppliers, telemedicine, hospitals, technology services, robotics, Artificial intelligence, e-learning, e-commerce retailers, delivery and courier services, manufacturing of sanitary products, cybersecurity, and several others.[18] Many new ventures have drastically declined, whereas some countries acted differently. In South Korea, technology startups have been used to combat COVID-19. A number of startups began their business activities like utilizing AI (artificial intelligence) in reducing the rate of infection and managing the emergency caused by the pandemic as well as in the development of diagnostic kits. The government also put efforts to providing new opportunities by collaborating with agile startups. In South Korea, the government and particularly the measures taken by the Ministry of Startups and SMEs provided unleashed power to the startups to fight the virus.[78] The ecosystem of startups in Europe also accelerated, aspiring to make full use of the time, for example, startup and tech circle in Norway initiated a hackathon online in 2020.[79] The fintech startups in Italy also took measures to cope with the crisis.[80] Up to 25 Y, combinator-based heath-tech and biotech startups in the United States also actively participated in fighting against the virus.[81] The pandemic has compelled numerous startups to change and redesign their working strategies that were essential for their survival and may work as an opportunity for them to grow. This has led them to produce products that are greatly in demand.[82] Therefore, although the net effect of the pandemic needs some time to be utterly appreciated, entrepreneurs may successfully seize greater opportunities.

2.5.1 DIGITAL TECHNOLOGY

The acknowledgment and utilization of digital technology are among the significant changes induced by the pandemic in daily life as well as at work. Digital technology has proffered innovative resolutions to tens of thousands of individuals in lockdown not being able to carry out their work duties from their workplaces. It has facilitated medicine delivery and further healthcare requirements, education, and food while carrying out work from home. It also helped individuals to remain connected across the world. While appreciating the facilities, billions of individuals have recognized digital technology as having been comfortable with it. Moreover, the travel restrictions due to lockdowns around the world made the organizations acknowledge digital technologies to be helpful in keeping their workers productive, informed, and connected. The conventional business meetings and trips have been substituted by the Zoom meetings that are available worldwide.

For a number of new international ventures, the increasing utilization of digital technologies symbolizes better access with economical cost, greater efficiency, and improved coordination as well as lesser expenses.[83] Some entrepreneurial ventures have been also enabled by digital technologies to remain connected to business platforms that helped them to survive the obstacles brought about by the pandemic. International entrepreneurial ventures have achieved higher agility and responsiveness with the application of digital technologies and swiftly transformed to the unpredictability of their business sectors.

The pattern toward digital entrepreneurship (i.e., establishing organizations that utilize these technologies in addressing the requirements of the market) has been robust in the years before the pandemic.[84] The examples are the entrepreneurs from developing countries that have exploited the rapid espousal of smartphones in order to provide innovative services and products to clients. Likewise, a number of companies have invested in digital technology for the expansion of their businesses. Moreover, digital technology has enabled online teaching and research helping institutions and students to remain connected. As a number of individuals have experienced the potential of digital technologies and become comfortable with online ordering, this trend is expected to keep on accelerating. The businesses that survived the effects of the pandemic believe that online services will be trusted by the customer even in the post-COVID world. Online services have appeared to be reliable, economical, as well as convenient.[85]

With the success of digital entrepreneurs being more evident, the inception of new entrepreneurial ventures is likely to raise that may exploit the opportunities around the globe.[86] As several higher education institutions are offering online courses and the creation of various educational platforms, there is a possibility for new ventures to step into that market and propose programs with higher quality to various audiences at less cost. Telemedicine can also be perceived as the same. Thus, digital entrepreneurship may explicitly accelerate the inception of new ventures, enabling them to conduct their business operations successfully.

2.5.2 GLOBAL INNOVATION

The pandemic has compelled numerous startups and businesses to change and redesign their working strategies that were essential for their survival and may work as an opportunity for them to grow. This has led them to produce products that are greatly in demand such as face masks and medical equipment like ventilators. The challenges inflicted by the pandemic are expected to accelerate innovation globally as a way of discovering resolutions to the hitches encountered by entrepreneurs. As the internet has helped entrepreneurial ventures to survive through COVID, it can also act as a means to collaborate with local entrepreneurs and involve in economic innovations that may enable them to exploit the opportunities in certain niche markets. New entrepreneurial ventures may also convert the theoretical discoveries of research into goods and products to be advertised, promoted, and sold.

2.6 MANAGING THE CRISIS

Societies nowadays are growingly facing obscure mega-crises and Black Swan events,[87] signifying that unpredicted crises are occurring like the COVID-19 pandemic, which is having disastrous societal effects. As these crises are unexpected and uncertain, the prevailing strategies fail to work and thus a novel entrepreneurial strategy is required. This has called for the creation of prompt response by the government, societal leaders, and science. As it has been witnessed that the situations created by the pandemic are deeply uncertain, entrepreneurs are expected to identify the opportunities and risks that can empower them to exploit the prospects in crisis by observing the social as well as market needs of the community. As a fast-thinking approach is needed to cope with the crisis, this denotes that the provisional and extended effects of inaction can be later evaluated. Adopting a coherent and logical strategy is what it takes to deal with the crisis rationally.[88] This approach, however, cannot work in a crisis like that of the present COVID-19, in which there is a quick development of a health crisis. Instead, it is needed to utilize intuition and gut feeling to manage the effects of the virus. Thus, it is conceived that the coordination of a quick response is more reasonable, based on other societal effects. As the crisis is dynamic in nature, a quick-response approach is needed instead of a bureaucratic method. To suppress the unpredictability of the crisis, a more direct approach is needed to adopt.[89] It is plausible to take help from the available statistics and take decisions from the given analysis and information instead of adopting a wait-and-see strategy. This signifies taking a pragmatic approach to coping the crisis as well as the possible consequences of indecision.

Prevention and response to huge changes are included in managing a crisis.[90] As a crisis occurs, it is paramount to have a quick response and communication toward it. Thus, it can be implied that it is difficult to manage a crisis because the resolution of issues needs to go parallel with estimating upcoming problems. A study suggests four C's in the management of crisis: causes, consequences, caution, and copying.[91] Causes, at times, can be accredited to particular variables that can happen in an intermittent or constant way. The specific cause can refer to an occurrence or an unexpected result of a particular activity. Consequences can allude to the environmental impacts of the crisis, ranging from no impact to small or extensive societal change. Caution relates to the feeling of unpredictability and risk progressing in a particular manner. This implies that there may be some apprehension about a specific cause of action. Coping implies how people, organizations, and governments manage as an event occurs. This may incorporate specific approaches to deal with the changes that happened by utilizing an entrepreneurial approach.

2.7 ENTREPRENEURSHIP RESPONSE TO COVID-19

An unpredictable situation that occurs with a higher degree of uncertainty is referred to as a crisis. The present pandemic has instigated certain changes in the behaviors of individuals that have posed serious threats to businesses for their survival. Thus, the response of entrepreneurs toward the current COVID-19 crisis is being emphasized as well as how they cope with it through innovation and creativity.

Entrepreneurs have the potential to resolve problems with creativity as well as bring societal welfare and help society to bounce back. Nevertheless, dreadful crises can put entrepreneurs under pressure in suppressing the challenges and delivering results. Entrepreneurship comprises the assessment of opportunities and producing novel ideas. In addition, to empower different thinking patterns, it is required to have a particular degree of creativity that gives way to new ideas. Creativity implies introducing new products or ideas that are novel and hold the potential to generate profits.[92] Moreover, creativity is a vital component in solving problems. Therefore, it is contemplated that creativity or a creative leader is more significant than the conservative methods of management in fighting against such uncertain and chaotic conditions of the environment. Simultaneously, innovation is also considered a determinant of economic development, progress, and gaining competitiveness. To sustain the business in long term and to overcome the crisis, businesses must exhibit innovation by employing creativity in acquiring opportunities and solving problems.

The current crisis has severely hit entrepreneurial businesses with the cessation of business activities due to a decrease in monetary funds and increasing rent, hence resulting in the financial fragility of businesses.[93] To cope with such catastrophic circumstances, entrepreneurs are expected to come into action. For example, during the lockdown in Australia, an entrepreneur, Ann Do, turned her restaurant business to selling face masks not only to overcome her monetary loss but also to contribute toward society.[94] In more recent studies, it is indicated that the regularization of entrepreneurial ventures positively works toward mitigating the consequences of crises. Furthermore, the promotion of entrepreneurial dynamism has been viewed as a key determinant of more entrepreneurial activities that certainly affects macroeconomic variables, such as development, innovation, and employment in a positive manner.[95] Innovative startups and entrepreneurial orientation that contribute toward economic development by creating employment opportunities have become a priority for economies.[96] Though these entrepreneurial ventures are most vulnerable to the aftermaths of crises, it is also indicated that they act as a stimulus in the development and retrieval of the economy as they generate innovation and create employment opportunities.[97] Thus, how SMEs and entrepreneurs fight against these difficulties has become pertinent to be identified and understood so that it can be easier to identify the methods of managing the crises as well as reducing their consequences.

The behavior of entrepreneurs during the time of crisis is significant in handling events during economic depressions. The innovation and creativity exhibited by organizations and entrepreneurs assist in the origination of services and products that are required by the customers, for example, the establishment of incubators, technology parks, policies promoting innovation, and collaboration among innovative firms and groups.[98] Entrepreneurs who adopt innovation tend to modify their business strategies that comprise a change in business activities for value creation, development of entrepreneurial approaches, and capturing novel opportunities.[99] Thus, education needs to play its role in the development of such skills in individuals. The European Commission has stated that the development of entrepreneurial competencies is mandatory so that people can be prepared to establish abilities, for example, resilience, to facilitate businesses to employ people having essential skills that can help them in adapting new working atmosphere.[100]

2.7.1 ENTREPRENEURIAL ABILITIES AND SKILLS

The origin of novel ideas that assists society and firm in value creation is referred to as entrepreneurship.[101] An entrepreneur is considered to be an individual who tries to generate and introduce innovative processes, firms, and products, or modify ones that already exist.[102] During the time of crisis, it is required for an entrepreneur to be more dynamic and innovative.[103] Such an individual reaches this point through distinctive abilities, such as recognizing opportunities, proactivity, innovation, resilience, and risk management.[104]

An individual can establish a new venture and promote the development of society through entrepreneurial skills.[105] Such skills are indispensable in taking risks and increasing competitiveness.[106] For this reason, entrepreneurial skills are analyzed in terms of the success of a business. Training programs aiming at certain objectives are utilized in developing such competencies.

Creativity is required to approach a challenging situation with innovation .[107] In order to deal with the challenges caused by crises, entrepreneurs employ innovative ideas by utilizing risk-taking initiatives.[108] Self-efficacy refers to the point an individual depends upon one's capabilities in determining the challenges they may bear, effort in overcoming them, and to what extent they must continue to face these hindrances.[109] On the other hand, self-efficacy is considered to be a driver toward the entrepreneurial intention to establish a new venture. Entrepreneurial intention denotes the capability of an individual to establish a new venture or to improve an existing company, in the present day or in the upcoming time.[110] Furthermore, locus of internal control is also paramount as it conveys the belief that failure or success is based upon an individual's own efforts and abilities.[111]

Proactivity lets an individual to take initiatives, capture opportunities and persist on attaining objectives.[112] Being proactive enables to forecasting problems and changes the elements to solve a certain state of affairs.[113] The proactive ability of an entrepreneur is vital in identifying new business opportunities. Moreover, innovation leads toward the development of novel ideas for producing services and goods,[114] whereas resilience is considered significant in overcoming adversities.

2.7.2 RESILIENCE

In entrepreneurial crisis management, resilience is a necessary impression due to its assisting nature being utilized in apprehending the way organizations conform to or withstand a change. Resilience has become increasingly focused due to the threats caused by health emergencies. The capability to fight against hindrances brought about an unpredicted state of affairs. Resilience, in terms of business, is an entrepreneur's ability to change, survive, and progress in a time of crisis. It helps in planning the courses of action to survive amid a crisis and obtain best outcomes. It is a multidimensional construct that amalgamates individual characteristics, behavior, and qualities that are appropriate and beneficial.[115] The personal attributes that place entrepreneurial behavior within the entrepreneurship function are associated with an entrepreneur's natural predisposition to be exposed to the situation and external threats, inclination toward risk-taking, creativity, and intellectual capabilities.[116] The capability of an entrepreneur is enhanced through these characteristics in terms of identifying and discovering business opportunities as a key feature of entrepreneurship. the actions taken by entrepreneurs can help the community to bounce back. Being able to counter the crisis denotes that entrepreneurship has short as well as long-term implications for the local economy in terms of creating wealth, jobs, competitiveness, and progress.[117]

Resilience integrates innovation and creativity to change and transform business activities according to the requirements of the market and customers. Businesses are making a response toward the economic effects instigated by COVID-19 in several ways. Furthermore, in order to manage the catastrophe caused by the coronavirus, it is required to adopt an entrepreneurial orientation. The reinforcement of the connections among businesses and their ecosystem, as well as instilling a sense of resilience in them toward crisis, can support the global economy to survive any upcoming calamity.[118] The ecosystem denotes a meaningful alliance of a group of organizations who, with their communications, direct the innovative performance of national institutions.[119]

In this time of crisis, businesses and ventures have begun to think and act more strategically to uplift their digital abilities. Resilient business ventures have begun to prefer online sales and cloud-based sales as they are secure and accessible all over, all the time. The resilience of entrepreneurial ventures is also dependent upon their ecosystem which is significant in the persistence of business activities and economic progress. Thus, public policies and governmental assistance are paramount in developing resilience in entrepreneurial ventures and producing more comprehensive and long-term progress.

2.7.3 ENTREPRENEURIAL COURSES OF ACTION TO COMBAT COVID-19 CRISIS

The study of entrepreneurial courses of action in uncertain situations is central to the research on entrepreneurship.[120] Nevertheless, it has become extremely challenging to distinguish between the kind of responses that create logical human actions and spontaneous reactions.[121] The researchers who have studied spontaneous behaviors exhibited by entrepreneurs in the upshots of natural calamities have regarded the current COVID-19 crisis as similar to those past events,[122] in which entrepreneurial activities take place irrespective of the hurdles that occur in the assembling and processing of information regarding different elements favoring logical and planned response.

The question that arises is whether a planned organized response will help entrepreneurs to survive the crisis. Studies have shown that such patterns of planning, if not positively relate to the survival and performance of ventures.[123] On the whole, the response of entrepreneurs to the current pandemic crisis is yet to be completely determined. Therefore, to answer it further, researchers have put forth three perspectives that can be utilized by entrepreneurs to effectively respond to the ongoing pandemic crisis: planning of business activities, frugality, and emotional support.[124] Through this, individual characteristics of these perspectives affecting entrepreneurs' insights, preparedness, and possible responses are emphasized.

2.7.3.1 SURVIVING THE CRISIS: PLANNING OF BUSINESS ACTIVITIES IN UNPREDICTABLE SITUATIONS

For entrepreneurs, the planning of business activities has a vital role to play in the creation of their new ventures whether it is for an existing firm or a new startup.[125] The crisis caused by the current virus was completely unpredicted and was not included in the processes or results of business planning, irrespective of how formally or informally the planning was done; the investors and founders who focused on situational planning did not consider such a dreadful event or alike situations in their business planning. They considered more possible situations like hindrances in developing services/products or the processes of sales and alike in their risk management planning. Overall, the crisis caused by the current pandemic was extremely uncertain[126] that emerged promptly and posed a survival threat to a number of business ventures.

The reengaging and rapid modification of business planning processes has become necessary for business ventures, investors, and founders due to the current COVID-19 crisis. As it is evident that economic conditions are changing rapidly, entrepreneurial ventures must frequently reassess and adjust their business activities till the environment reaches stability. Nonetheless, if the planning of business activities tends to take greater resources and time, it may consume an extensive outlay of effort. Such efforts are necessarily required in the current time of crisis to add value to business actions, such as rapid production of new products, closure of contracts with clients, or direct investor interaction. Thus, entrepreneurs are required to cautiously reflect on the extent to which they must plan their business activities and the required efforts. It is advised to adopt more concise planning forms rather than formal in such a dynamic environment.

2.7.3.2 TIME TO LOOK INSIDE: THE ROLE OF FRUGALITY IN ECONOMIC TURMOIL

Frugality is associated with entrepreneurs and explained as an individual's predisposition to preserve resources as well as apply economic motives in acquiring those resources. In present days, successful entrepreneurs have regarded frugality as the reason for their success, for example, Amazon and Berkshire Hathaway founders Jeff Bezos and Warren Buffet, respectively.[127] Frugality is regarded as a dynamic mindset that can help entrepreneurs in bouncing back from the economic adversities brought about by the coronavirus. Overall, there is a fine alignment between the nature of frugality and resourcefulness,[128] hence, having frugal nature can mitigate the effects of the coronavirus pandemic on small as well as ventures that are about to emerge. Furthermore, entrepreneurs with less frugality are more vulnerable to the economic upshots of crises as well as deprived in terms of identifying and capturing opportunities.

2.7.3.3 EXTRINSIC MOTIVATION: LOOKING FOR EMOTIONAL SUPPORT

Given that the business planning process, accompanied by the exploration of frugality, can act as a beneficial behavior in such times of crisis; emotional support also needs to be studied in terms of its role in individual and professional linkages as the pandemic continue to prevail. Studies on entrepreneurship have shown that the social connections of entrepreneurs are significant in performing better[129] as they are capable of providing access to useful resources. Among these resources, social support is significant that includes informational support or emotional support (closeness, empathy, and encouragement, etc.).[130] As a matter of fact, the entrepreneurs who encountered the 2008 economic recession indicated that social relations were a significant source in buffering the effect of economic decline which consequently decreased the withdrawal intentions of entrepreneurs from entrepreneurial activities.

Overall, the concept of social support determines the performance of individuals by amalgamating four elements: stimulating positivity, enhancing positivity, buffering negativity, and exacerbating negativity.[131] In the present situation of crisis, a significant element for mitigating negativity is emotional support that has become rare and hard to gain than usual. Hence, there is an increased demand for in-person emotional support, yet it is hardly available. The circumstances bring about by crises can generate unity and a more cultural collectiveness[132] in which seeking help can be considered appropriate as well as promoted. For this purpose, online media can play its role as a source of emotional support for entrepreneurs. It is suggested by studies that online communication can significantly reduce time and location barriers, thus acting as a significant factor through which emotional support can be attained. Such online communication comprises chat rooms, e-mails, and instant messaging, etc. In general, the reciprocation of emotional support amid entrepreneurs is considered significant in the enhancement of productivity.[133]

2.8 RECOMMENDATIONS

The COVID-19 pandemic globally emerged as an unprecedented bolt from the blue, especially in referring to the economy. The virus came forward as a global calamity with its social and economic consequences throughout the world. Evidently, the current virus is going to have a significant impact on entrepreneurship. We are still fighting against COVID-19 pandemic and just begun to identify its consequences on entrepreneurship. In order to proceed further, it is not sufficient to implement a wait-and-see strategy, rather entrepreneurs must adopt resilience and become ready to capture new opportunities for entrepreneurship while encouraging emotional support. Thus, in order to fight against the dreadful economic situation caused by the COVID-19 pandemic, planning of business activities, adopting frugal behavior, as well as the availability of emotional support can act as a blessing in disguise for entrepreneurs. The type of business planning that can assist new ventures to survive must be frequent and active; encouraging to support team unity; providing a sense of direction and purpose. Moreover, frugal behavior leads toward resilience through the reassessment of startup motivations and objectives, whereas social support can help in rebuilding the entrepreneurial activities and bouncing back in the post-COVID era.

Moreover, more appropriate steps must be taken to assist the survival of entrepreneurs.[134] Government must originate fiscal policies to provide financial funding to potential startups. If such strategies are introduced, it can still be hoped for a recovery from the aftermaths of COVID-19. On the other hand, entrepreneurs must perceive the pandemic crisis as an opportunity to redirect and re-purpose their business activities through the utilization of their skills and knowledge. They must figure out the new emerging requirements of society and shape the nature of their ventures accordingly. By re-directing of business activities will help them to survive the crisis and identify market gaps. The current crisis can be converted into an opportunity by continuously encouraging entrepreneurs to establish new ventures, which, consequently, will generate employment.[136] Economic dynamism can be engendered by producing new services and products that will ameliorate the economy worldwide.[137]

KEYWORDS

- **entrepreneurship**
- **COVID-19**
- **ventures**
- **angel investors**
- **startups**

REFERENCES

1. Cortez, R. M.; Johnston, W. J. The Coronavirus Crisis in B2B Settings: Crisis Uniqueness and Managerial Implications Based on Social Exchange Theory. *Ind. Market. Manage.* **2020,** *88*, 125–135.
2. Alon, I.; Farrell, M.; Li, S. Regime Type and COVID-19 Response. *FIIB Bus. Rev.* **2020,** *9* (3), 152–160.
3. Ratten, V. Coronavirus and International Business: An Entrepreneurial Ecosystem Perspective. *Thunderbird Int. Bus. Rev.* **2020,** *62* (5), 629–634.
4. Giones, F.; Brem, A.; Pollack, J. M.; Michaelis, T. L.; Klyver, K.; Brinckmann, J. Revising Entrepreneurial Action in Response to Exogenous Shocks: Considering the COVID-19 Pandemic. *J. Bus. Ventur. Insights* **2020,** *14*, e00186.
5. WHO. WHO Director-General's Opening Remarks at the Media Briefing on COVID-19. **2020,** March 1. https://www.who.int/dg/speeches/detail/who-director-general-sopening-remarks-at-the-media-briefing-on-covid-19---11-march-2020
6. Liñán, F.; Jaén, I. The Covid-19 Pandemic and Entrepreneurship: Some Reflections. *Int. J. Emerg. Markets*. **2020,** Nov 27.
7. Sergi, B. S.; Popkova, E. G.; Bogoviz, A. V.; Ragulina, J. V. Entrepreneurship and Economic Growth: The Experience of Developed and Developing Countries. In *Entrepreneurship and Development in the 21st Century 2019 Apr 15*; Emerald Publishing Limited, 2019.
8. Kuckertz, A.; Brändle, L.; Gaudig, A.; Hinderer, S.; Reyes, C. A.; Prochotta, A.; Steinbrink, K. M.; Berger, E. S. Startups in Times of Crisis–A Rapid Response to the COVID-19 Pandemic. *J. Bus. Ventur. Insights*. 2020 *13*, e00169.
9. Goodell, J. W. COVID-19 and finance: Agendas for Future Research. *Finance Res. Lett.* **2020,** *35*, 101512.
10. Winston, R. The Takings Are Coming: How Federal Courts Can Protect Regulatory Efforts to Address California's Housing Crisis. *Ecology LQ* **2020,** *47*, ,625.
11. Baker, S. R.; Bloom, N.; Davis, S. J.; Terry, S. J. Covid-Induced Economic Uncertainty. National Bureau of Economic Research, 2020, Apr 13.
12. McKibbin, W.; Fernando, R. The Global Macroeconomic Impacts of COVID-19: Seven Scenarios. *Asian Econ. Papers*. **2021,** *20* (2), 1–30.
13. Ratten, V. Coronavirus (covid-19) and Entrepreneurship: Changing Life and Work Landscape. *J. Small Bus. Entrepreneurship* **2020,** *32* (5), 503–516.
14. GDA (Global Data Analysis). Coronavirus (COVID-19) Executive Briefing. Global Data, 2020.
15. Jackson, J. K. Global Economic Effects of COVID-19. Congressional Research Service, 2021, Nov 10.
16. Nagarjun, K. ILO: As Job Losses Escalate, Nearly Half of Global Workforce at Risk of Losing Livelihoods.
17. Vasilić, N.; Popović-Pantić, S.; Semenčenko, D. Women Entrepreneurship in the Time of COVID-19 Pandemic. *JWEE* 2020. *28* (3–4), 23–40.
18. Zahra, S. A. International Entrepreneurship in the Post COVID World. *J. World Bus.* **2021,** *56* (1), 101143.
19. Devinney, T. M.; Hartwell, C. A. Varieties of Populism. *Global Strategy J.* **2020,** *10* (1), 32–66.

20. Rodrik, D. Populism and the Economics of Globalization. *J. Int. Bus. Policy* **2018,** *1* (1), 12–33.
21. Wright, L. Annals of History: Crossroads: A Scholar of the Plague Thinks That Pandemics Wreak Havoc—and Open Minds. *The New Yorker* July 20, 2020, 18–23.
22. Wang, C. L.; Altinay, L. Social Embeddedness, Entrepreneurial Orientation and Firm Growth in Ethnic Minority Small Businesses in the UK. *Int. Small Bus. J.* **2012,** *30* (1), 3–23.
23. Ratten, V. Coronavirus (COVID-19) and Entrepreneurship: Cultural, Lifestyle and Societal Changes. *J. Entrepren. Emerg. Econ.* **2020** Sept 24.
24. Lerner, J. The Future of Public Efforts to Boost Entrepreneurship and Venture Capital. *Small Bus. Econ.* **2010,** *35* (3), 255–264.
25. McMullen, J. S.; Shepherd, D. A. Entrepreneurial Action and the Role of Uncertainty in the Theory of the Entrepreneur. *Acad. Manage. Rev.* **2006,** *31* (1), 132–152.
26. Amabile, T. M.; Conti, R.; Coon, H.; Lazenby, J.; Herron, M. Assessing the Work Environment for Creativity. *Acad. Manage. J.* **1996,** *39* (5), 1154–1184.
27. Liguori, E.; Winkler, C. From Offline to Online: Challenges and Opportunities for Entrepreneurship Education Following the COVID-19 Pandemic. *Entrepren. Educ. Pedagogy* **2020,** *3* (4), 346–351.
28. Griffith, E. Start-Ups Are Pummeled in the 'Great Unwinding'. *NY Times* 2020.
29. GEM. Adult Population Survey Dataset. Global Entrepreneurship Research Association, London Business School: London, 2019. https://www.gemconsortium.org/data
30. Tsatsenko, N. A. The Relationship Between Entrepreneurship and Economic Growth: Key Issues. *Colloquium-J.* **2020,** *61* (9), 134–136.
31. Meahjohn, I.; Persad, P. The Impact of COVID-19 on Entrepreneurship Globally. *J. Econ. Bus.* **2020,** *3* (3).
32. Vaccaro, A. R.; Getz, C. L.; Cohen, B. E.; Cole, B. J.; Donnally, III C. J. Practice Management During the COVID-19 Pandemic. *J. Am. Acad. Orthopaedic Surgeons* **2020,** Jun 1.
33. Bacq, S.; Geoghegan, W.; Josefy, M.; Stevenson, R.; Williams, T. A. The COVID-19 Virtual Idea Blitz: Marshaling Social Entrepreneurship to Rapidly Respond to Urgent Grand Challenges. *Bus. Horiz.* **2020,** *63* (6), 705–723.
34. Demirgüç-Kunt, A.; Peria, M. S.; Tressel, T. The Global Financial Crisis and the Capital Structure of Firms: Was the Impact More Severe Among SMEs and Non-Listed Firms? *J. Corp. Finance* **2020,** *60*, 101514.
35. Conti, A.; Dass, N.; Di Lorenzo, F.; Graham, S. J. Venture Capital Investment Strategies Under Financing Constraints: Evidence from the 2008 Financial Crisis. *Res. Policy* **2019,** *48* (3), 799–812.
36. Gompers, P.; Kovner, A.; Lerner, J.; Scharfstein, D. Venture Capital Investment Cycles: The Impact of Public Markets. *J. Financial Econ.* **2008,** *87* (1), 1–23.
37. Brown, R.; Rocha, A. Entrepreneurial Uncertainty During the Covid-19 Crisis: Mapping the Temporal Dynamics of Entrepreneurial Finance. *J. Bus. Ventur. Insights* **2020,** *14*, e00174.
38. De Clercq, D.; Sapienza, H. J. Effects of Relational Capital and Commitment on Venture Capitalists' Perception of Portfolio Company Performance. *J. Bus. Ventur.* **2006,** *21* (3), 326–347.
39. Clark, C. The Impact of Entrepreneurs' Oral 'Pitch' Presentation Skills on Business Angels' Initial Screening Investment Decisions. *Ventur. Cap.* **2008,** *10* (3), 257–279.

40. Howell, S. T.; Lerner, J.; Nanda, R.; Townsend, R. R. Financial Distancing: How Venture Capital Follows the Economy Down and Curtails Innovation. National Bureau of Economic Research, 2020, May 18.
41. Brown, R.; Rocha, A.; Cowling, M. Financing Entrepreneurship in Times of Crisis: Exploring the Impact of COVID-19 on the Market for Entrepreneurial Finance in the United Kingdom. *Int. Small Bus. J.* **2020,** *38* (5), 380–390.
42. Majumdar, A.; Shaw, M.; Sinha, S. K. COVID-19 Debunks the Myth of Socially Sustainable Supply Chain: A Case of the Clothing Industry in South Asian Countries. *Sustain. Product. Consumption* **2020,** *24*, 150–155.
43. Veselovská, L. Supply Chain Disruptions in the Context of Early Stages of the Global COVID-19 Outbreak. *Prob. Perspect. Manage.* **2020,** *18* (2), 490–500.
44. Barua, S. Understanding Coronanomics: The Economic Implications of the Coronavirus (COVID-19) Pandemic, 2020, Apr 1. Available at SSRN 3566477.
45. Baldwin, R.; Tomiura, E. Thinking Ahead About the Trade Impact of COVID-19. *Econ. Time COVID-19.* **2020,** *59*, 59–71.
46. Guan, D.; Wang, D.; Hallegatte, S.; Davis, S. J.; Huo, J.; Li, S.; Bai, Y.; Lei, T.; Xue, Q.; Coffman, D. M.; Cheng, D. Global Supply-Chain Effects of COVID-19 Control Measures. *Nat. Human Behav.* **2020,** *4* (6), 577–587.
47. Gupta, M.; Abdelmaksoud, A.; Jafferany, M.; Lotti, T.; Sadoughifar, R.; Goldust, M. COVID-19 and Economy. *Dermatologic Therap.* **2020,** *33* (4), e13329.
48. Shinghal, K.; Saxena, A.; Misra, R. Entrepreneurship and COVID-19. *Int. J. Sci. Res. Manage. Stud.* **2020,** *4*, 94–97.
49. Page, I. T. COVID-19 and Higher Education: Some Issues. *Univ. News*. **2020,** *58*, 23.
50. World Food Programme. Impacts of COVID-19 on Small-and Medium-Sized Enterprises in the Food System, 2020. www.gainhealth.org/sites/default/files/publications/documents/impacts-of-covid-19-on-small-and-medium-sized-enterprises-in-the-food-system-results-of-an-online-survey.pdf
51. EIT Food. Crisis vs Opportunity: How Has COVID-19 Impacted the Agrifood Sector in 2020? 2020. www.eitfood.eu/blog/post/crisis-vs-opportunity-how-has-covid-19-impacted-the-agrifood-sector-in-2020
52. Pakistan Tourism Development Corporation. Strategy to Help Mitigate the Socioeconomic Impact of COVID-19 on Pakistan's Tourism Industry, 2021. tourism.gov.pk/
53. OECD. OECD Economic Outlook, Interim Report March 2020; OECD Publishing: Paris, 2020.
54. McKinsey & Company. Reimaging The US $9 Trillion Tourism Economy-What Will It Take, 2020. www.mckinsey.com/industries/travel-logistics-and-infrastructure/our-insights/reimagining-the-9-trillion-tourism-economy-what-will-it-take
55. Sharma, A.; Nicolau, J. L. An Open Market Valuation of the Effects of COVID-19 on the Travel and Tourism Industry. *Ann. Tour. Res.* **2020,** *83*, 102990.
56. Kaushik, K. Sailing Through the Storm: Here's How COVID-19 Has Impacted the Travel Startups In India, 2020. www.outlookindia.com/outlooktraveller/explore/story/70779/impact-of-covid-19-on-indian-travel-startups
57. Invest2innovate. CVID-19 & Its Impacts on Pakistani Startups, 2020. invest2innovate.com/wp-content/uploads/2020/12/COVID-19-and-its-Impact-on-Pakistani-Startups-V2-Final-min.pdf

58. S&P Global. Tough Act to Follow: COVID-19's Implications for Media and Entertainment Industry, 2020. www.spglobal.com/en/research-insights/featured/landscape-on-media.
59. Yeo, T. J. Sport and Exercise During and Beyond the COVID-19 Pandemic. *Eur. J. Prev. Cardiol.* **2020,** *27* (12), 1239–1241.
60. Haymillian.com. Impact of the Pandemic on Media and Entertainment Industry, 2020. https://haymillian.com/impact-of-the-pandemic-on-media-and-entertainment-industry/
61. Economic Times. Coronavirus Impact: Events, Entertainment Industry Says Covid-19 Hit *60* Million Livelihoods, 2020. brandequity.economictimes.indiatimes.com/news/media/coronavirus-impact-events-entertainment-industry-says-covid-19-hit-60-million-livelihoods/74821842
62. Parnell, D.; Widdop, P.; Bond, A.; Wilson, R. COVID-19, Networks and Sport. *Maag. Sport Leisure* **2020**. DOI: 10.1080/23750472.2020.1750100
63. Adhikari, M. The Media and Entertainment Industry Post Covid-19: The Best and Worst of Times. Business Insider India, 2020. https://www.businessinsider.in/advertising/media/article/the-media-and-entertainment-industry-post-covid-19-the-best-and-worst-of-times/articleshow/80022616.cms
64. Research and Markets. The Impact of COVID-19 on the Entertainment Market, 2020. researchandmarkets.com/reports/5013572/the-impact-of-covid-19-on-the-entertainment-market
65. Dele-Ijagbulu, O.; Moos, M.; Eresia-Eke, C. The Relationship Between Environmental Hostility and Entrepreneurial Orientation of Small Businesses. *J. Entrepren. Innov. Emerg. Econ.* **2020,** *6* (2), 347–362.
66. Price, R. Impacts of COVID-19 Regulatory Measures on Small-Scale and Informal Trade in Zimbabwe.
67. Hernández-Sánchez, B. R.; Cardella, G. M.; Sánchez-García, J. C. Psychological Factors That Lessen the Impact of COVID-19 on the Self-Employment Intention of Business Administration and Economics' Students from Latin America. *Int. J. Environ. Res. Public Health* **2020,** *17* (15), 5293.
68. Mickiewicz, T.; Rebmann, A. Entrepreneurship as Trust. *Foundations Trends Entrepren.* **2020,** *16* (3), 244–309.
69. Bodas, M.; Peleg, K. Self-Isolation Compliance in the COVID-19 Era Influenced by Compensation: Findings from a Recent Survey in Israel: Public Attitudes Toward the COVID-19 Outbreak and Self-Isolation: A Cross Sectional Study of the Adult Population of Israel. *Health Aff.* **2020,** *39* (6), 936–941.
70. Swinnen, J.; McDermott, J. COVID-19 and Global Food Security. *EuroChoices* **2020,** *19* (3), 26–33.
71. Bartik, A. W.; Bertrand, M.; Cullen, Z.; Glaeser, E. L.; Luca, M.; Stanton, C. The Impact of COVID-19 on Small Business Outcomes and Expectations. *Proc. Natl. Acad. Sci.* **2020,** *117* (30), 17656–17666.
72. Youth Co:Lab. Youth Co:Lab Survey Reveals How COVID-19 Is Affecting Youth-Led Businesses in Asia-Pacific. UNDP Asia and the Pacific, 2020, Mar 31. https://www.asia-pacific.undp.org/content/rbap/en/home/presscenter/articles/2020/youth-co-lab-survey-reveals-how-covid-19-is-affecting-youth-led-.html
73. Beraha, I.; Đuričin, S. The impact of COVID-19 Crisis on Medium-Sized Enterprises in Serbia. *Econ. Analy.* **2020,** *53* (1), 14–27.

74. UNWOMEN. Survey Impact of the COVID-19 Pandemic on Specialist Services for Victims and Survivors of Violence in Serbia, 2020. https://www2.unwomen.org//media/field%20office%20eca/attachments/publications/2020/05/unw_covid-vaw_report_final.pdf?la=en&vs=5317 30.09.2020.
75. SeCons. *Consequences of COVID-19 on Women's and Men's Economic Empowerment*; UNWOMEN: Serbia, 2020
76. World Tourism Organization. Global Report on Women and Tourism, 2019.
77. SeCons. *Impact of the COVID-19 Pandemic and Measures for Its Prevention on Women Entrepreneurs in Serbia*; UNWOMEN: Serbia, 2020.
78. Salamzadeh, A.; Dana, L. P. The Coronavirus (COVID-19) Pandemic: Challenges Among Iranian Startups. *J. Small Bus. Entrepren.* **2021,** *33* (5), 489–512.
79. EU Startups. Apply by Midnight Today to Join the Online COVID-19 Hackathon run by Norway's Tech Community, 2020. https://www.eu-startups.com/ 2020/03/apply-by-midnight-tonight-to-join-the-online-covid-19-hackathon-run-by-the-norweigan-tech-community/ (accessed 2 Apr 2020).
80. EU Startups. Our Fintech Community has Come Together to Fight Against COVID19: Interview with Head of Fintech District, Alessandro, 2020. www.eu-startups.com/2020/03/our-fintech-community-has-come-together-to-support-thefight-against-covid-19-interview-with-head-of-fintech-district-alessandro
81. Y Combinator. YC Companies Responding to COVID-19, 2020. https://www.ycombinator.com/covid
82. Sedlacek, P.; Sterk, V. Startups and Employment Following the COVID-19 Pandemic: A Calculator.
83. Kim, J. D.; Cavusgil, E. Antecedents and Outcomes of Digital Platform Risk for International New Ventures' Internationalization. *J. World Bus*. **2020,** *55* (1), 101021.
84. Nambisan, S. Digital entrepreneurship: Toward a Digital Technology Perspective of entrepreneurship. *Entrepren. Theor. Practice*. **2017,** *41* (6), 1029–1055.
85. Reuber, A. R.; Fischer, E. International Entrepreneurship in Internet-Enabled Markets. *J. Bus. Ventur*. **2011,** *26* (6), 660–679.
86. Ojala, A.; Evers, N.; Rialp, A. Extending the International New Venture Phenomenon to Digital Platform Providers: A Longitudinal Case Study. *J. World Bus*. **2018,** *53* (5), 725–739.
87. Ansell, C.; Boin, A. Taming Deep Uncertainty: The Potential of Pragmatist Principles for Understanding and Improving Strategic Crisis Management. *Admin. Soc*. **2019,** *51* (7), 1079–112.
88. Liu, Y.; Shankar, V.; Yun, W. Crisis Management Strategies and the Long-Term Effects of Product Recalls on Firm Value. *J. Market*. **2017,** *81* (5), 30–48.
89. Weick, K. E.; Sutcliffe, K. M. *Managing the Unexpected: Resilient Performance in an Age of Uncertainty*; John Wiley & Sons, 2011.
90. Doern, R. Entrepreneurship and Crisis Management: The Experiences of Small Businesses During the London 2011 Riots. *Int. Small Bus. J.* **2016,** *34* (3), 276–302.
91. Shrivastava, P. Crisis Theory/Practice: Towards a Sustainable Future. *Ind. Environ. Crisis Quart*. **1993,** *7* (1), 23–42.
92. Fillis, I.; Rentschler, R. The Role of Creativity in Entrepreneurship. *J. Enterpris. Cult.* **2010,** *18* (01), 49–81.

93. Petropoulos, P. IBISWorld: Industry Insider: How Disruption from COVID-19 Is Affecting SMEs, 2020. https://www.ibisworld. com/industry-insider/coronavirus-insights/how-disruption-from-COV ID-19-is-affecting-smes/
94. Fang, J.; Renaldi, E.; Lange, E. Meet the Businesses Adapting to Thrive Amid the Coronavirus Lockdown in Australia, 2020. https://www.abc.net.au/news/2020–09–05/small-australian-business es-adapting-to-survive-coronavirus/12622654
95. Barba-Sánchez, V.; Atienza-Sahuquillo, C. Entrepreneurial Intention Among Engineering Students: The Role of Entrepreneurship Education. *Eur. Res. Manag. Bus. Econ.* **2018,** *24* (1), 53–61.
96. Kraus, S. W.; Meshberg-Cohen, S.; Martino, S.; Quinones, L. J.; Potenza, M. N. Treatment of Compulsive Pornography Use with Naltrexone: A Case Report. *Am. J. Psych.* **2015,** *172* (12), 1260–1261.
97. Vodă, A. I.; Florea, N. Impact of Personality Traits and Entrepreneurship Education on Entrepreneurial Intentions of Business and Engineering Students. *Sustainability* **2019,** *11* (4), 1192.
98. Castro, M. P.; Zermeño, M. G. Being an Entrepreneur Post-COVID-19–Resilience in Times of Crisis: A Systematic Literature Review. *J. Entrepren. Emerg. Econ.* **2020,** Nov 6.
99. Cucculelli, M.; Bettinelli, C. Business Models, Intangibles and Firm Performance: Evidence on Corporate Entrepreneurship from Italian Manufacturing SMEs. *Small Bus. Econ.* **2015,** *45* (2), 329–350.
100. European Commission. Commission Presents European Skills Agenda for Sustainable Competitiveness, Social Fairness, and Resilience, 2020. https://ec.europa.eu/commission/presscorner/detail/en/ip_20_1196
101. Fisher, G.; Stevenson, R.; Burnell, D. Permission to Hustle: Igniting Entrepreneurship in an Organization. *J. Bus. Ventur. Insights* **2020,** *14*, e00173.
102. Swedberg, R. *The Social Science View of Entrepreneurship: Introduction and Practical Applications*; Entrepreneurship and Small Business Research Institute (ESBRI), 2001.
103. Salisu, I.; Hashim, N.; Mashi, M. S.; Aliyu, H. G. Perseverance of Effort and Consistency of Interest for Entrepreneurial Career Success: Does Resilience Matter? *J. Entrepren. Emerg. Econ.* **2020,** Jan 24.
104. Castro, M. P.; Scheede, C. R.; Zermeño, M. G. Entrepreneur Profile and Entrepreneurship Skills: Expert's Analysis in the Mexican Entrepreneurial Ecosystem. In *2020 International Conference on Technology and Entrepreneurship-Virtual (ICTE-V)*, Vol. 10; San Jose, CA, USA, 2020, Apr 20.
105. Saptono, A. Entrepreneurship Education and Its Influence on Financial Literacy and Entrepreneurship Skills in College. *J. Entrepren. Educ.* **2018,** *21* (4), 1–1.
106. Chew, L. M.; Hoe, L.; Kim, T.; Wan, L. Self-Perceived Entrepreneurship Skills for Undergraduates of Private University in Malaysia. *Am. J. Appl. Sci.* **2016,** *13* (6), 715–725.
107. Kusmintarti, A.; Anshori, A.; Sulasari, A.; Ismanu, S. Student's Entrepreneur Profile: A Cluster of Student's Entrepreneurial Characteristics. *J. Entrepren. Educ.* **2018,** *21*, 1–12.
108. Abdullah, N.; Hadi, N.; Dana, L. The Nexus Between Entrepreneur Skills and Successful Business: A Decompositional Analysis. *Int. J. Entrepren. Small Bus.* 2018, *34* (2), 249–265. https://doi.org/10.1504/ijesb.2018.10013260
109. Mauer, R.; Neergaard, H.; Linstad, A. K. Self-Efficacy: Conditioning the Entrepreneurial Mindset. In *Revisiting the Entrepreneurial Mind: International Studies*

in Entrepreneurship; Brännback, M., Carsrud, A., Eds.; Springer: Cham, 2017; pp 293–317.

110. Palazzechi, L.; Bucci, O.; Di Fabio, A. High Entrepreneurship, Leadership, and Professionalism (HELP), a New Resource for Workers in the 21st Century. *Front. Psychol.* **2018,** *9*, 1–8.
111. Fernandes, J. M.; Afonso, P.; Fonte, V.; Alves, V.; Ribeiro, A. N. Promoting Entrepreneurship Among Informatics Engineering Students: Insights from a Case Study. *Eur. J. Eng. Educ.* **2017,** *42* (1), 91–108.
112. Kozubíková, L.; Čepel, M.; Zlámalová, M. Attitude Toward Innovativeness Based on Personality Traits in the SME Sector. Czech Republic Case Study. *Manage. Market. Challenges Knowl. Soc.* **2018,** *13* (2), 913–928.
113. Yan, X.; Gu, D.; Liang, C.; Zhao, S.; Lu, W. Fostering Sustainable Entrepreneurs: Evidence from China College Students': Internet Plus Innovation and Entrepreneurship Competition. *Sustainability* **2018,** *10*, 1–23.
114. Martens, C. D.; Machado, F. J.; Martens, M. L.; de Freitas, H. M. Linking Entrepreneurial Orientation to Project Success. *Int. J. Project Manage.* **2018,** *36* (2), 255–266.
115. Ayala, J. C.; Manzano, G. The Resilience of the Entrepreneur. Influence on the Success of the Business: A Longitudinal Analysis. *J. Econ. Psychol.* 2014. *42*, 126–135.
116. Rüdiger, K.; Peris-Ortiz, M.; Blanco-González, A. *Entrepreneurship, Innovation and Economic Crisis: Lessons for Research, Policy and Practice*; Springer International Publishing: Gewerbestrasse, Switzerland, 2014.
117. Williams, N.; Vorley, T. Economic Resilience and Entrepreneurship: Lessons from the Sheffield City Region. *Entrepren. Regional Dev.* **2014,** *26* (3–4), 257–281.
118. International Trade Centre. COVID-19: The Great Lockdown and Its Impact on Small Business. International Trade Centre, 2020. https://www.intracen.org/uploadedFiles/intracenorg/Content/Publica tions/ITCSMECO2020.pdf
119. Sussan, F.; Acs, Z. J. The Digital Entrepreneurial Ecosystem. *Small Bus. Econ.* **2017,** *49* (1), 55–73.
120. Bylund, P. L.; McCaffrey, M. A Theory of Entrepreneurship and Institutional Uncertainty. *J. Bus. Ventur.* **2017,** *32* (5), 461–475.
121. Brown, L.; Packard, M.; Bylund, P. Judgment, Fast and Slow: Toward a Judgment View of Entrepreneurs' Impulsivity. *J. Bus. Ventur. Insights* **2018,** *10*, e00095.
122. Villar, E. B.; Miralles, F. Purpose-Driven Improvisation During Organisational Shocks: Case Narrative of Three Critical Organisations and Typhoon Haiyan. *Disasters* **2021,** *45* (2), 477–497.
123. Chrisman, J. J.; McMullan, E.; Hall, J. The Influence of Guided Preparation on the Long-Term Performance of New Ventures. *J. Bus. Ventur.* 2005 *20* (6), 769–791.
124. Klyver, K.; Honig, B.; Steffens, P. Social Support Timing and Persistence in Nascent Entrepreneurship: Exploring When Instrumental and Emotional Support Is Most Effective. *Small Bus. Econ.* **2018,** *51* (3), 709–734.
125. Michaelis, T. L.; Carr, J. C.; Scheaf, D. J.; Pollack, J. M. The Frugal Entrepreneur: A Self-Regulatory Perspective of Resourceful Entrepreneurial Behavior. *J. Bus. Ventur.* **2020,** *35* (4), 105969.
126. Loch, C. H.; Solt, M. E.; Bailey, E. M. Diagnosing Unforeseeable Uncertainty in a New Venture. *J. Product Innov. Manage.* **2008,** *25* (1), 28–46.
127. Montag, A. Here's Why Jeff Bezos Still Drove a Honda Long After He Was a Billionaire [WWW Document]. *CNBC* **2018.** www.cnbc.com/2018/01/18/

whyamazons-jeff-bezos-drove-a-honda-after-he-was-a-billionaire.html (accessed 15 Apr 2020).
128. Bradley, S. W. Entrepreneurial Resourcefulness. *Wiley Encyclopedia Manage.* **2015,** *5*, 1–3.
129. Stam, W.; Arzlanian, S.; Elfring, T. Social Capital of Entrepreneurs and Small Firm Performance: A Meta-Analysis of Contextual and Methodological Moderators. *J. Bus. Ventur.* **2014,** *29* (1), 152–173.
130. Clough, D. R.; Fang, T. P.; Vissa, B.; Wu, A. Turning Lead Into Gold: How Do Entrepreneurs Mobilize Resources to Exploit Opportunities? *Acad. Manage. Ann.* **2019,** *13* (1), 240–271.
131. Bavik, Y. L.; Shaw, J. D.; Wang, X. H. Social Support: Multidisciplinary Review, Synthesis, and Future Agenda. *Acad. Manage. Ann.* **2020,** *14* (2), 726–758.
132. Bennett, D. L.; Nikolaev, B. Historical Disease Prevalence, Cultural Values, and Global Innovation. *Enterpren. Theor. Pract.*
133. Kuhn, K. M.; Galloway, T. L. With a Little Help from My Competitors: Peer Networking Among Artisan Entrepreneurs. *Enterpren. Theor. Pract.* **2015,** *39* (3), 571–600.
134. Giotopoulos, I.; Kontolaimou, A.; Tsakanikas, A. Drivers of High-Quality Entrepreneurship: What Changes Did the Crisis Bring About? *Small Bus. Econ.* **2017,** *48* (4), 913–930.
135. Fairlie, R. W. The Impact of COVID-19 on Small Business Owners: Continued Losses and the Partial Rebound in May 2020.
136. Ioannides, D.; Gyimóthy, S. The COVID-19 Crisis as an Opportunity for Escaping the Unsustainable Global Tourism Path. *Tour. Geogr.* **2020,** *22* (3), 624–632.
137. Padilla, J.; Petit, N. Competition Policy and the COVID-19 Opportunity (Preprint).

CHAPTER 3

Agriculture and COVID-19

MUHAMMAD TARIQ[1], MUHAMMAD AYAZ KHAN[2], ARWA ABDULKREEM AL-HUQAIL[3], and SHAKEEL AHMAD[4]

[1]*Central Cotton Research Institute, Multan, Pakistan*

[2]*Department of Agriculture Extension and Adoptive Research, Punjab, Pakistan*

[3]*Department of Biology, College of Science, Princess Nourah bint Abdulrahman University, Riyadh, Saudi Arabia*

[4]*Department of Agronomy, Bahauddin Zakariya University Multan, Pakistan*

ABSTRACT

Since COVID-19 pandemic affected all sectors of life; agriculture was equally affected during this crisis. The main impact of COVID-19 on agriculture has been in the form of changing demand and supply ratio, labor shortage, and impacts on rural economies. Agriculture is the main source of earning, particularly in low-income countries. The commodities are few and the impact of COVID-19 on such countries may be very high. The agriculture production of underdeveloped countries is very prone to COVID-19 due to their high level of dependency upon labor in farming systems. The most affected sectors in agriculture were dairy farming, fruit and vegetable farming, poultry farming, and fisheries because of their perishable nature. There had been fear of a food shortage, but it did not happen due to an undisrupted grains supply, and the calorie intake was partially affected due to the shortage of the above-mentioned perishable commodities. The limited activities in the local fruit and vegetable and grains market resulted in low

Post-Pandemic Economy, Technology, and Innovation: Global Outlook and Context.
Samina Yaqoob, Arwa Abdulkreem AL-Huqail, and Fakhra Aziz (Eds.)

income generations and ultimately reduced economic access to food items. The price fluctuations were more for vegetables and fruits than grains and other field crops. Small and medium enterprises were quite vulnerable to COVID-19 shocks due to their small cash reserves. The COVID-19 affected food availability through its impacts on production, transportation/supply disruption, and higher retail prices along with lesser purchasing capacity of consumers. Being a major food source, agricultural activities remained a major focus to ensure food supply on regular basis. Moreover, an undisrupted agro-input supply may be ensured for achieving food security goals through higher target yields. It was realized that agriculture activities should be retrieved through the provision of safety kits, incentives, and health insurance to farm workers, along with financial and marketing assistance to farm owners.

3.1 INTRODUCTION

The first outbreak of COVID-19 was reported from Wuhan in China in December 2019. Despite the massive quarantine and preventive measures, its spread extended to many parts of the world. Besides its devastating effects on health, it disrupted almost all sectors of life on this planet. Agriculture and food security were among the most severely affected sectors after health by COVID-19. Being a main source of food, many efforts and initiatives have been taken at the government level to ensure food supply on a regular basis. Exempting the opening of agro-inputs markets and fruit, vegetables, and grains markets during peak days of COVID-19 spread is an example of importance of agriculture business for food security. It was essential because it was realized in many countries that famine is more hazardous as compared to COVID-19.

Global agriculture sector has been hit by the pandemic in multiple ways, like farm labor shortage, shortage of farm inputs due to border closure and cancellation of deals, operational problems in food processing industries, reduced agriculture trade (export and import of commodities), disruption in food supply chain, price hikes of farm inputs due to shortages, health risks to farmers, and financial difficulties faced by growers. If this pandemic continues, global food security may become a core issue especially in developing countries. Food supply is a main factor of life, and thanks to food chains for uninterrupted supply. Demand and supply channels were disrupted in many countries. For instance, the demand for food items with a long shelf life emerged in Italy during the emergency period. The food items like meat, fruits and vegetables were adversely affected by imbalances in the supply-demand ratio, which resulted in remarkable changes in prices. The meat sector was at the top among food items, which worsened during this period and ultimately resulted in a reduction in the price of live animals. The prices of Grana cheese in Italy were reduced, and shortage of fresh milk and fresh cheese was also noted due to logistic restrictions.[1] The demands were contracted due to slow economic growth and purchase power of the consumers. The seasonal workers moved to their hometowns, and countries and the tasks of harvesting and planting were not completed, which further disrupted demand and supply. Agriculture is a source of earning for millions of people in developing countries and stopping of farming activities impose economic threats, leading to limited access to food. Most of industries and markets remained closed, which left no earning source for manpower of various sectors. The preferred places for shopping were neighboring markets to avoid movements. The impact of COVID-19 and future strategies for agriculture are given and summarized in Figure 3.1.

Special relief and assistance packages were announced by the governments for the sake of purchase of essential food packages. Even food packets were also distributed among poor people by locals, non-government organization and government agencies in certain regions across the world. All these efforts did not completely fulfill the target objective due to several issues, including social, economic, and administrative. Furthermore, the volume of assistance and relief packages were too small in proportionate to the affected population. This chapter elaborates on COVID-19 impact on various aspects of agriculture production, processing & marketing.

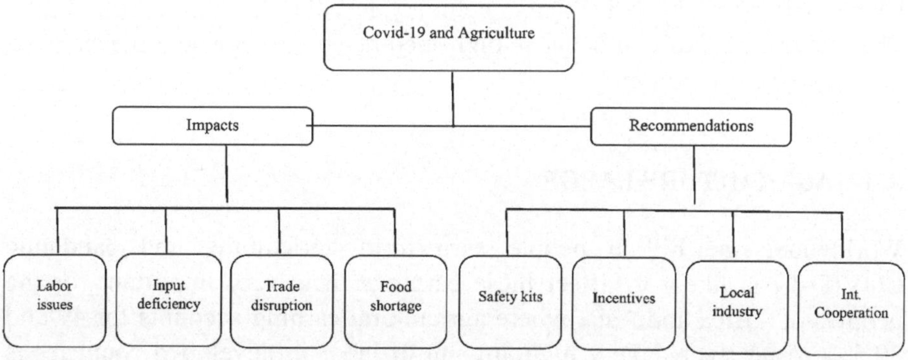

FIGURE 3.1 Impact and future strategies for agriculture during COVID-19 pandemic.

3.2 AGRICULTURAL INPUTS

Agriculture production involves intermediate inputs and fixed cost. The seeds, fertilizers, pesticides, feeds, and energy are included in the intermediate inputs. There is a strong relationship between intermediate input supply and overall production. Countries with higher incomes use high inputs and thus harvest a high yield, and vice versa for poor countries. The share of intermediate inputs is 80 and 10% in developed and less developed countries, respectively.[2] Therefore, high income countries are likely to suffer more from disrupted intermediate input supply. Disruptions in the flow of inputs, either from local or international suppliers, had key impacts on farm production. Such impacts were more visible in countries that were affected at very early stages. For instance, the pesticide production in China was reduced sharply and resumed after lockdown. The low pesticides production, accompanied with less transportation facilities and high costs resulted in a sever outbreak of locust in East Africa, which further threatened the food security. The fertilizers and other agro-chemicals are imported and exported, which were severely disrupted due COVID-19 spread. China exports highest amount of phosphorus fertilizer and also ranks second in exports of nitrogen fertilizer. On the other hand, Brazil is the largest importer of nitrogen and phosphorus fertilizer. Unfortunately, both the countries were severely affected by COVID-19 and fertilizers demand and supply remained imbalance.[3]

The machinery and structures are another input in the crop production. The lack of spare parts due to market closures and the unavailability of storage facility further hamper agriculture production. The lack of mechanization means that farmers would require labor to carry out various field operations which was otherwise to be completed with machinery. Because labor use is more expensive than machinery, it will reduce farm profitability. These are more likely to occur in high-income countries where mechanized farming is very common.

3.3 AGRICULTURE LABOR

Worldwide, one billion people earn from agriculture, and pandemic COVID-19 is likely to affect these earnings. It is very important for the peoples of Africa and Asia, where agricultural earning accounts for 49 and 30.5%, respectively.[4] Very high amount of labor in developed countries is from the underdeveloped world; the closure of borders and flight operations along with sending back laborers to their home countries resulted in a labor shortage in those countries. Consequently, upon labor shortage, some proportion of the produce may be lost in the field. The harvesting and processing processes of fruits and vegetables were adversely affected in Italy due to a shortage of labor, which returned to their home countries.[1] The other aspects of COVID-19 on the agriculture-based food system lacks processing due to labor shortages. It would adversely affect the supply, and consumers would have to pay high prices. The illness of the workers reduces their physical capacity to perform field duties. The harvesting operations were delayed due to a labor shortage, which resulted in yield losses in the field. Furthermore, the sowing of subsequent crops is also delayed as a result of late harvesting of preceding crop.[5,6] Similarly, delayed harvesting of forage crops deteriorates the quality.[7–9] There are pre-sowing training sessions for crops in different countries. The farmers gather at local places, and agriculture experts impart trainings on various aspects of crop production. Gathering was restricted in COVID-19 pandemic and farmers cannot get trained, which is expected to reduce the crops yield.

Being sector specific, the impact of labor issues was quite apparent in both low- and high-income countries. The agricultural production is expected to be reduced by 3.11% in south Asia because of COVID-19 during the first quarter of 2020, and this happened mainly because of labor shortage. In economic value, it is equal to USD 3.76 billion, and the GDP of the south Asia region was expected to decline by 1.4%.[10] The practical guidance was issued by several governments to encourage the cross-border movement of seasonal workers to carry on various agricultural activities. Certain precautions and protective measures including adjustments in working hours, reviewing the processes where workers interaction is high, maintaining social distancing, provision of protective kits, easy access to health facilities, and improving cleanliness, and residence facilities at the farms.

3.4 AGRICULTURE MARKETS

While evaluating COVID-19 impact on supply and price fluctuations of agro-based products, and being stakeholders, we must have information on changes in policies, production levels, market infrastructure, and weather.[11] The supply side was mainly affected by the probability that farmers may get sick and thus stop farming activities. The harvesting time of crops cannot be changed, and there are chances that the produce may spoil due to low market access. Furthermore, future markets were quite unpredictable, and farmers were confused about how much to produce. The other aspect related to supply was from low availability of agro-inputs, and future yields may decline. The transportation of goods has been restricted, and supply may be disrupted for import based markets around the world. Because inadequate transportation was permitted for the delivery of vital stuffs, numerous processing-based industries experienced shortage of raw materials and ultimately produced less quantity of products. From a demand point of view, there was fear that lockdown may last for a long time, which pushed people to buy more quantities to be stored for future. The same case was very true for non-perishable items.

The transport of essential agricultural food commodities has been exempted from the restrictions of the lockdown at local level in many countries. Even then, an imbalance between supply and demand was observed during pandemic COVID-19. It was due to the result of the closure of hotels and the changing behavior of consumer. The labor shortage and logistical restrictions further impacted the food supply at retail outlets. The mode of marketing in conventional markets has shifted to online purchases and delivery at the doorsteps. Many growers, traders, and buyers did not adopt this marketing system due to lack of infrastructure.

The wheat procurement in this region was done during COVID-19 peak spread, and government was actively involved in purchase to avoid food shortage in future COVID-19 spread. The wheat arrival in Indian markets has been lower in 2020 than in 2019 in the first and second lockdown phase; while it was recovered in later phase of lockdown. Similarly, onion supply had been lower during all phases of lockdown in 2020 over the corresponding period of previous years. While wheat prices remained higher only for the first phase of lockdown than previous trends of 2019. In case of onion, the prices were initially higher but declined with the commencement of first lockdown.[11] The tea prices were fall down due to halt of imports by China and Islamic Republic of Iran, along with postponement of the tea auction by the East Africa Tea Trade Association.[12] The prices of poultry in Pakistan declined to the minimum level during the initial spread of COVID-19, mainly with the closure of restaurants, marriage halls, and hotels.

It was reported that the first infection with COVID-19 was caused by its transmission from bats.[13] Therefore, more people were afraid of dealing with animals and consuming partially cooked animal meat. Indefinitely, the animal sector was also adversely affected by COVID-19. The labor shortage, border restrictions, low input supply for animal feed industries, and low working conditions in slaughterhouses had certain issues for animal sectors. The live movement of poultry in China was restricted, which severely damaged the sector. The breeding flock is imported to developing countries from the developed world. The process of importing poultry breeding flocks had not been carried out, and it was expected that there may be insufficient eggs available for hatching to provide chicks at the farms. Fish are among main sources of protein from animals, and the fishing sector is also expected to be adversely affected. The reduced supply of fruit and vegetables by 20% during March and April has been observed.[14]

Despite its economic value as a fiber crop,[15–18], many farmers had been very reluctant to sow cotton crops due to unstable international markets. Being raw material for textiles, it was being expected that textile industry may face deficiency and many workers might become unemployed. Moreover, the textile industry may face a labor shortage, and ultimately, less buying of raw cotton was also expected. China is the main consumer of cotton, and imports in China are likely to decrease due to the COVID-19 outbreak. The other textile manufacturing countries were also adversely affected, and cotton markets would be disrupted. Many orders have been cancelled and suspended by many brands in importing countries. If the situation stabilizes in countries like China and India, the demand for cotton will increase.

3.5 AGRICULTURE TRADE

The containment measures taken during pandemic COVID-19 in the whole world affected nearly all walks of financial activities globally. The global GDP growth is anticipated to fall from the previous estimate of 2.9% to 2.4% in 2020.[19] Apart from other economic sectors, the global agricultural trade chains were also disrupted by the pandemic. Agricultural trade consists of the import and export of agri-products. During the COVID-19 outbreak, global agricultural exports suddenly declined. China, the first pandemic hit country faced 11.6% shortfall in agriculture exports in the first two months of 2020.[20] The principal causes for radical reduction of world agri. exports are the disturbance in supply of agro-exports besides prohibitions executed on agricultural products by importing countries.

During the month of April in 2020, worldly food commodities exports regarding value-added-products like freshly picked items, milk and meat that were greatly purchased by hotels, colleges, universities, and tourism industry as compared to domestically.[21,22] In countries like United States and

Netherlands, the agriculture export worth is greater than US $100 billion, and export earnings will be adversely suffered due to a lack of export activities.[2] The agricultural export supply chain was disrupted by shut down of export commodity production and processing firms due to unavailability of labor. Globally, some countries have restricted export of many food commodities to ensure national food supplies. For instance, Russia, the globally top wheat-exporter, restricted for grain exports to maintain food security, but Serbia, Vietnam, and Kazakhstan, restricted their exports on other commodities.

Moreover, transportation charges and shipping fees increased heavily. Moreover, the operational competence of international shipping ports decreased, resulting in a reduction in transport of agriculture and other commodities.[20] Resultantly, agricultural exports from the world's top exporting countries reduced dramatically.[23,24] In addition to disruptions in the supply chain and logistics, the global demand for agricultural imports reduced due to the pandemic. About 10% (20,000 tons) of Chilean cherries were blocked at the airport as they were being transported from Chile to China.[25] Generally, certain commodities demand increased and decreased drastically for others, which created serious problems with food security.[26–28] Further, if this pandemic prevails over a longer period, then there may be a shifting of food purchases more to staples and less processed products due to shrinking budgets of consumers.[29]

Countries with import-based food systems are very prone to food shortages due to restrictions on borders. Countries like Somalia, South-Sudan, and Guinea-Bissau fulfill approximately 40% of their food requirements from imports and remain highly vulnerable to food insecurity during the critical period of COVID-19.[2] Being a developing country, Pakistan's economy was also badly affected by the pandemic. Due to the pandemic, overall loss to Pakistan's overall economy is projected to be about Rs. 1.3 trillion.[30] As per State Bank of Pakistan, entire agro-exports were on a declining trend in February 2020 due to COVID-19 and trade restrictions. After the ease in lock down by some countries during the first 6 months of 2020, global agro-based exports augmented sharply by 2.5% during the same period for 2019.[20]

3.6 POST COVID-19 AND AGRICULTURE PERSPECTIVES

COVID-19 is a health crisis that is disrupting fundamental global systems, including industries, food, and agriculture systems, and jeopardizing workers livelihoods. The world is already facing climatic change and food security challenges.[17,31–33] Across the globe, in excess of 820 M people are suffering from hunger in 2018.[34] In context of post COVID-19 agriculture perspective, the world has a unique opportunity to reevaluate and reconstruct the agriculture and farming sectors. In the post pandemic context, strategies must be initiated for incentivizing and facilitating the availability of machinery by government departments and private sectors. Mechanized farms would augment farm efficiency, resilience, and sustainability.[35] The workforce engaged in food processing industries is worse hit by this pandemic as their majority belongs to poor population. Governments must build the workforce database of the farm and food industries to support them financially in future pandemic and unemployment circumstances. Moreover, the provision of safety kits to farm and food industry workers must be ensured to keep them safe from the pandemic instead of forcing them to refrain from work.

The sustainable supply of agri-inputs like, quality seed, fertilizers, and agrochemicals are the key to maximum farm output. Due to the border closure and trade difficulty, the supply of these agri-inputs adversely affected during the pandemic.[36] Adopting the post COVID-19 policy measures the supply of these farm inputs. To meet global agri-inputs demand, the leading producer countries should expand their production capacities. Moreover, self-sufficiency is imperative to avoid future shortage of agri-inputs. At the global level, there must be an international cooperative approach towards the sustainable manufacturing and trade of these important farm inputs to avoid adverse effects on agricultural production in current and future pandemics.

During COVID-19, capital scarcity and financial problems were faced by the majority of farmers belonging to the underdeveloped agro-based economies like Pakistan and India. Farmers of high-value commodities like fruits, vegetables, flowers, dairy, and fish have suffered substantial financial losses due to COVID-19.[35] One of the prompt responses by the governments in a post-pandemic scenario should be financial support for small farm producers. This monetary support may be in the form of subsidies, support prices, interest-free loans, or direct aid. These post COVID-19 policies will not only help small and medium farmers restart their farm businesses but will also reinstate their trust on the governments.

During the pandemic, vegetables & fruits supply-chain has been limited in several urban regions of the world due to lockdown and the unavailability of transportation. This not only created food shortage in some worse viruses hit cities of the world but also the farmer suffered financial losses. Keeping in view the post pandemic policies in this context, diversification of agriculture and the food system must be the prime focus. Inclusion of highly nutritious crops and foods in agriculture and the food system must be done on a top priority. For example, quinoa (a super food) contains more and better proteins viz. other primary cereals and can be cultivated in adverse agro-environments. On the other hand, for sustainable and contactless farm supply to urban consumers, use of modern technologies like drones and online demand, supply systems must be introduced. Governments, international donors, along with NGOs should play their collaborative role in reshaping the research based sustainable and resilient agriculture and farming systems through post COVID-19 initiatives.

3.7 GOVERNMENT INITIATIVES

In response to COVID-19, different governments and funding agencies provided relief packages to agriculture sector. The major objective of these relief packages was to support the farmers and the food processing industries. In March 2020, the Pakistani Government proclaimed a relief fund of 5.66$ billion for poor citizens, as their lives had been severely affected due to COVID-19. The Chinese Council of Agriculture (COA) allocated an unusual budget amounting to USD 245 M for saving and revitalizing agricultural sector.

The Government of India announced similar financial support funds. Official authorities regulated the agricultural supply chains to ensure food security for people. Additional initiatives include free trade of fruits and vegetables to markets. The Bangladesh Government has also announced a scheme amounting BDT 50 billion for agri-business farmers. The Government of Iran is providing food, loans, sanitizers, sprayers, and other necessary equipment to farmers. The Ministry of Agriculture, Iran has launched a strategy for addressing transport related matters for ensuring well-timed delivery of crops and livestock inputs through the harmonization of concerned organizations. To ensure the availability and accessibility of food, Agriculture Ministry, Indonesia has harmonized with provincial governments for establishing Cooperative Farmers' Market to increase logistical efficiency and to lower costs and time associated with distribution.[37] The Government of Japan allocated a 989$ billion financial amount that was about 20% of GDP.[38] United States Department of Agriculture announced a US $14 billion aid package for farmers for facing market disruptions and related expenditures. The Cambodian Government announced US $50 M for nominal-interest loans for helping small farmers during the pandemic. The

South Korean Government has announced a relief package of USD 48.8 M that will be delivered to farmers. In addition to the governments, different NGOs and funding agencies are playing their part in assisting the farmers financially and technically in developing countries like Pakistan and India.

3.8 RECOMMENDATION AND CONCLUSIONS

The agricultural sector is facing significant problems due to the COVID-19 pandemic in the world. Forced isolation, social distancing, traveling restrictions, and border closures have created considerable concerns. Laborers' shortage, restrictions on transportation along with closure of borders has negatively impacted agriculture sector. The supply of perishable commodities was more affected than that of non-perishable commodities. During the pandemic situation, poor small and medium farmers in underdeveloped economies are mostly affected. The major problem was that the farmer had to face a shortage of inputs such as seeds, fertilizers, and insecticides.

During the COVID-19 pandemic, the agricultural activities were run in a safe manner in many countries to ensure a better food supply in the markets at accessible prices. The relevant organizations have been making efforts for a uniform flow of agriculture trade throughout the world. Certain well targeted and quick interventions would be required to move out of the crisis in the agriculture sector. In future, farmers support in the form of safety training of farm workers, access to protective accessories, and adopting labor saving technologies will be necessary for continuous food supply in the markets. The farm workers should get access to information sources to reshape the working environment and social norms. To avoid the labor shortage issue, the mechanization of small farms is very essential, either through government provision from or on a rental basis. The ration card may be issued to the poor people to purchase food items at subsidized prices. The farmers should be provided loans at very low interest rates for the purchase of agro-inputs to strengthen the food supply through higher crop yields. Being a major food source, there is a need for stimulating the agricultural production through takingappropriate measures, such as decent wages and other associated assistance. Social security is lacking for agriculture workers in many governments, it must be guaranteed to ensure the safety and health benefits. Stimulation of local market development will be needed to consume surplus agriculture-based commodities. Urban farming may be promoted for the supply of diversified food items to urban people. COVID-19 is a global crisis, and hence, it requires a global response to deal with it. Therefore, it needs global collaboration and assistance not only in health, but necessarily for trade, economics along with financial policies.

KEYWORDS

- **initiatives**
- **inputs**
- **labor**
- **marketing**
- **trade**

REFERENCES

1. Barcaccia, G.; Agostino, V. D.; Zotti, A.; Cozzi, B. Impact of the SARS-CoV-2 on the Italian Agri-Food Sector: An Analysis of the Quarter of Pandemic Lockdown and Clues for a Socio-Economic and Territorial Restart. *Sustainability* **2020,** *12*, 5651.
2. Schmidhuber, J.; Pound, J.; Qiao, B. *Covid-19: Channels of Transmission to Food and Agriculture*; FAO: Rome, 2020. https://doi.org/10.4060/ca8430en.
3. Seleiman, M. F.; Selim, S.; Alhammad, B. A.; Alharbi, B. M.; Juliatti, F. C. Will Novel Coronavirus (Covid-19) Pandemic Impact Agriculture, Food Security and Animal Sectors? *Biosci. J. Uberlândia* **2020,** *36* (4), 1315–1326.
4. International Labour Organization (I LO). Covid-19 and the Impact on Agriculture and Food Security. International labor organization (ILO) Sectoral Brief. Dated 17th April **2020**.
5. Tariq, M.; Ali, H.; Hussain, N,; Nasim, W.; Mubeen, M.; Ahmad, S.; Hasanuzzaman, M. Fundamentals of Crop Rotation in Agronomic Management. In *Agronomic Crops*; Hasanuzzaman, M., Ed.; Springer: Singapore, **2019**; pp XX–XX. https://doi.org/10.1007/978–981–32–9151–5_24.
6. Afzal, M. N.; Tariq, M.; Ahmed, M.; Abbas, G.; Mehmood, Z. Managing Planting Time for Cotton Production. In *Cotton Production and Uses*; Ahmad, S., Hasanuzzaman, M., Eds.; Springer: Singapore, **2020**; pp XXX–XXX. https://doi.org/10.1007/978–981–15–1472–2_3.
7. Tariq, M.; Ayub, M.; Elahi, M.; Ahmad, A. H.; Chaudhary, M. N.; Nadeem, M. A. Forage Yield and Some Quality Attributes of Millet (*Pennisetum americannum* L.) Hybrid Under Various Regimes of Nitrogen Fertilization and Harvesting Dates. *Afr. J. Agric. Res.* **2011,** *6* (16), 3883–3890.

8. Ayub, M.; Abbas, H.; Tariq, M.; Tahir, M.; Nadeem, M. A.; Siddiqui, M. H. Periodic Assessment of Dry Matter Production and Nutritional Value of Millet Legumes Mix Fodder. *Agric. Res.* **2013,** *2* (3), 265–269.
9. Ijaz, M. K.; Tariq, M.; Nadeem, M. A.; Tahir, M.; Shah, S. A. S.; Anwer, A. Forage Production and Pattern of Forage Quality Indices During Reproductive Development of Millet Genotypes. *J. Environ. Agric. Sci.* **2016,** *8*, 54–59.
10. Gregorio, G. B.; Ancog, R. C. Assessing the Impact of the COVID-19 Pandemic on Agricultural Production in Southeast Asia: Toward Transformative Change in Agricultural Food Systems. *Asian J. Agric. Dev.* **2020,** *17* (1), 1–13.
11. Varshney, D.; Roy, D.; Meenakshi, J. V. Impact of COVID-19 on Agricultural Markets: Assessing the Roles of Commodity Characteristics, Disease Caseload and Market Reforms. *Indian Econ. Revi.* **2020.** https://doi.org/10.1007/s41775–020–00095–1.
12. https://theexchange.africa/industry-and-trade/panic-as-coronavirus-forces-africas-largest-tea-auction-shut/
13. Zhou, P.; Yang, X.; Wang, X. G. et al. A Pneumonia Outbreak Associated with a New Coronavirus of Probable Bat Origin. *Nature* **2020,** *579*, 270–273.
14. Mahajan, K.; Tomar, S. Here Today, Gone Tomorrow: COVID-19 and Supply Chain Disruption. Working Paper No. 28, Ashoka University, Department of Economics, 2020.
15. Afzal, M. N.; Tariq, M.; Ahmad, M.; Mubeen, K.; Khan, M. A.; Afzal, M. U.; Ahmad, S. Dry Matter, Lint Mass and Fiber Properties of Cotton in Response to Nitrogen Application and Planting Densities. *Pak. J. Agric. Res.* **2019,** *32* (2), 229–240.
16. Tariq, M.; Yasmeen, A.; Ahmad, S.; Hussain, N.; Afzal, M. N.; Hasanuzzaman, M. Shedding of Fruiting Structures in Cotton: Factors, Compensation and Prevention. *Trop. Subtrop Agroecosys.* **2017,** 20, 251–262.
17. Tariq, M.; Ahmad, S.; Fahad, S.; Abbas, G.; Hussain, S.; Fatima, Z.; Nasim, W.; Mubeen, M.; Rehman, M. H.; Khan, M. A.; Adnan, M. The Impact of Climate Warming and Crop Management on Phenology of Sunflower-Based Cropping Systems in Punjab, Pakistan. *Agric. Forest Meteorol.* **2018,** *256*, 270–282.
18. Tariq, M.; Afzal, M. N.; Muhammad, D.; Ahmad, S.; Shahzad, A. N.; Kiran, A.; Wakeel, A. Relationship of Tissue Potassium Content with Yield and Fiber Quality Components of Bt Cotton as Influenced by Potassium Application Methods. *Field Crops Res.* **2018,** *229*, 37–43.
19. OECD Interim Economic Assessment. Coronavirus: The World Economy at Risk 2nd March, 2020.
20. Cao, L.; Li, T.; Wang, R.; Zhu, J. Impact of COVID-19 on China's Agricultural Trade. *China Agric. Econ. Rev.* **2020.**
21. World Trade Organization . Covid-19 and Agriculture: A Story of Resilience, 2020; pp 1–12.
22. Fisher, M. WTO Report Assesses Impact of COVID-19 on Agricultural Trade. *Newsletter* August, **2020.**
23. Zhang, Y.; Diao, X.; Chen, K. Z.; Robinson, S.; Fan, S. Impact of COVID-19 on China's Macroeconomy and Agri-Food System—An Economy-Wide Multiplier Model Analysis. *China Agric. Econ. Rev.* **2020,** *12* (3), 387–407.
24. Barichello, R. The COVID-19 Pandemic: Anticipating Its Effects on Canada's Agricultural Trade. *Can. J. Agric. Econ.* **2020,** *68* (2), 219–224.
25. http://www.fruitnet.com/asiafruit/article/181021/coronavirus-measuring-the-market-impact.

26. Glauber, J.; Laborde, D.; Martin, W.; Vos, J. Trade Restrictions Are Worst Possible Response to Safeguard Food Security, IFPRI Blog, **2020**. www.ifpri.org/blog/COVID-19-traderestrictions-are-worst-possible-response-safeguard-food-security (accessed 27 March 2020).
27. Fan, S. Ensuring Food for All, Beijing Review, **2020**. www.bjreview.com/Opinion/202004/t20200410_800200584.html?from5groupmessage&isappinstalled50NO.16 (accessed 16 April 2020).
28. Fan, S.; Si, W.; Zhang, Y.; How to prevent a global food and nutrition security crisis under COVID-19? *China Agric. Econ. Rev.* **2020,** *12* (3), 471–480.
29. Kerr, W. A. The COVID-19 Pandemic and Agriculture: Short- and Long-Run Implications for International Trade Relations. *Can. J. Agric. Econ.* **2020,** *68*, 225–229.
30. Haider, M. Coronavirus: Pakistan May Face Initial Economic Loss of Rs 1.3 tr'. *News Int.* March 20, 2020. Viewed 28 March **2020**. https://www.thenews.com.pk/print/631789-coronavirus-pakistan-may-faceinitialeconomicloss-of-rs1–3tr
31. Ahmad, S.; Abbas, G.; Fatima, Z.; Khan, R. J.; Anjum, M. A.; Ahmed, M.; Khan, M. A.; Porter, C. H.; Hoogenboom, G. Quantification of the Impacts of Climate Warming and Crop Management on Canola Phenology in Punjab, Pakistan. *J. Agron. Crop Sci.* **2017,** *203* (5), 442–452.
32. Ahmad, S.; Abbas, Q.; Abbas, G.; Fatima, Z.; Naz, S.; Younis, H.; Khan, R. J.; Nasim, W.; Rehman, M. H.; Ahmad, A.; Rasul, G. Quantification of Climate Warming and Crop Management Impacts on Cotton Phenology. *Plants* **2017**, *6* (1), 7.
33. Rahman, M. H.; Ahmad, I.; Ghaffar, A.; Haider, G.; Ahmad, A.; Ahmad, B.; Tariq, M.; Nasim, W.; Rasul, G.; Fahad, S.; Ahmad, S. Climate Resilient Cotton Production System: A Case Study in Pakistan. In *Cotton Production and Uses*; Ahmad, S., Hasanuzzaman, M., Eds.; Springer: Singapore, **2020**; pp XX–XX. https://doi.org/10.1007/978–981–15–1472–2_22.
34. Food and Agriculture Organization F A O.; IFAD, UNICEF, WFP and WHO. *The State of Food Security and Nutrition in the World 2019. Safeguarding Against Economic Slowdowns and Downturns*; FAO: Rome, 2019.
35. Kumar, A.; Padhee, A. K.; Kumar, S. How Indian Agriculture Should Change After COVID-19. *Food Security* **2020,** *12* (4), 837–840.
36. Timilsina, B.; Adhikari, N.; Kafle, S.; Paudel, S.; Poudel, S.; Gautam, D. Addressing Impact of COVID-19 Post Pandemic on Farming and Agricultural Deeds. *Asian J. Adv. Res. Rep.* **2020,** 28–35.
37. BKP. Pasar Mitra Tani di Semua Provinsi Siap Jaga Pasokan dan Stabilitas Pangan di Tengah Pandemi Covid-19. (Farmers' Markets in All Provinces Ready to Maintain Supply and Stability of Food in the Middle of Pandemic Covid-19. Ministry of Agriculture, Food Security Agency (English version), 2020. https://doi.org/10.31752/idea.2020.17.
38. Takeo, Y. Japan's Virus Stimulus Package to Come in Two Phases, 2020. https://www.bloomberg. com/news/articles/2020–04–06/japan-s-virus-stimulus-package-to-come-in-two-phases-documents-k8nuj552 (assessed on 15 Apr 2020).

CHAPTER 4

Role of Health Professionals During and Post COVID-19

FARKHANDA ASAD[1], ASMA ASHRAF[1], MUHAMMAD MEHROZ KHAN[2], ZUNAIRA SHAHEEN[1], and CATALINA GEORGETA DINU[3]

[1]*Department of Zoology, Government College University, Faisalabad, Punjab, Pakistan*

[2]*Department of Biochemistry, Government College University, Faisalabad, Punjab, Pakistan*

[3]*Faculty of Law, Transilvania University of Brasov, Brasov, Romania*

ABSTRACT

COVID-19, as a global pandemic, has caused serious complications increasing mortality rate and chaos in the medical field all around the globe. The first and foremost step in fighting this disease was preventive measures and immunity boosting. Healthcare workers and health professionals including surgeons, doctors, pharmacists, nurses, and psychiatrist had a major role to play in controlling and eradicating this infection from the world. Researchers applied their findings in preventing the spread through the US Center of disease control and prevention. Worldwide lockdowns and medical care were applied to control the spread, all through the help and guidelines of health professionals. In the way of preventing and curing this disease while vaccine is still on the run-in various countries, healthcare workers had to go through various challenges and issues regarding availability of resources and medical awareness of the society. Many health workers, who previously had no idea about dealing with a pandemic, also got experience and lesson from the ongoing pandemic.

Post-Pandemic Economy, Technology, and Innovation: Global Outlook and Context.
Samina Yaqoob, Arwa Abdulkreem AL-Huqail, and Fakhra Aziz (Eds.)

4.1 INTRODUCTION

Since the start of 2020, there have been a global pandemic of COVID-19 going on till date. As the outbreak started in Wuhan, China, it was initially thought that the virus will not spread to other countries and would soon be handled by the Chinese government and health professionals. But due to the peculiar and sudden symptoms of this virus, it was unable to be detected commonly in areas without special equipment, so it spread rapidly in different parts of the world. A public emergency was declared on January 30th by World Health Organization at a global level.[1]

COVID-19 has drastically affected lifestyles of everybody including resulting in worldwide economic crisis, international stock market collapse, medicinal shortage, and sudden increase in mortality rate. It was not only a great concern for underdeveloped countries but developed countries were also affected equally and badly. Complete lockdown over the countries seizing life gave way to increased hunger and joblessness. Hospitals piled up with patients in underdevelopied countries having very low availability of resources and medical equipment to treat new patients with no prior experience of the disease, which was a great disaster. Quick availability of ventilators and increased number of beds in intensive care units of hospitals in both public and private sector of underdeveloped countries could not be meet over night as the virus spread rapidly.

There is no age limit for the people getting affected by the virus because it affects every individual equally; however, symptoms may vary from mild-to-severe depending upon the immunity of affected person. According to guidelines published by the Center of Disease Control and Prevention, common symptoms of COVID-19 include dry cough, fever, and fatigue while rare symptoms vary from person to person include sore throat, diarrhea, loss of taste and smell, headache, and conjunctivitis. Severe symptoms include difficulty in breathing, loss of speech and movement, and chest pain or pressure.[2] In all the scenarios, the major role in controlling and dealing with this pandemic was of health professionals and public health workers. Proper awareness among people regarding the virus and precaution was the preliminary step taken by health workers in the way of preventing this disease to spread. Different health professionals, including doctors, pharmacist, researchers, nurses, and healthcare worker at the hospitals, performed valuable roles in controlling and fighting COVID-19, given the short time period and scarcity of resources due to fast outspread of the disease. Researchers had the most important role in determining the type of disease and providing preventive measures for the viral spread control and to help doctors and hospital staffs in controlling the mortality rate. Center of Disease Control and Management (CDC) played a major role in providing information regarding prevention of viral infection. All the standard operating procedure relating to health professionals and social distancing were provided by CDC. Different medications were applied on hit-and-trial basis in a short time period to find possible help in controlling the infecting of virus in body. In this chapter, we will discuss thoroughly the major and most important role of health professionals in dealing with this pandemic in the most efficient way, the challenges they had to face during the ongoing pandemic in hospitals of every kind, structural and resource flaws they had to face during the pandemic, and social values of healthcare workers.

4.1.1 QUARANTINE AND LOCKDOWNS

Over more than one million people have died worldwide due to the SARS coronavirus whose vaccine availability still remains a question despite tall claims of the global powers of clinical trials. A vaccine takes almost two years to be fully available in the market to patients after a viral disease outbreak occurs. So what was the initial step taken by CDC to prevent the outbreak from spreading and to decrease number of patients in hospitals and leash the burden? Quarantine, the process of separating people who are not ill but have the risk of getting infected in coming days by exposed infection from the area where there's widespread viral infection,[3] and lockdowns were applied worldwide immediately to prevent social interactions and crowd buildup in virus-affected areas. Transports were closed all over the world, and patient with any kind of symptoms were advised to self-quarantine themselves even from their families. Strict lockdowns in cities were applied and any kind of social gatherings were banned. This helps in preventing spread of disease and mitigates the burden on hospital. It also helps to lower the risk of hospital staff and all the people the infected person didn't meet during quarantine from getting infected. According to the US Department of Health and Human Services CDC, the criteria for quarantine includes measures like providing food, water, medical facilities, and other everyday useful items for survival so that the quarantine person or family does not have to go out in the open.[4] Quarantine for the suspected individual or family lasts for up to 14 days and it might extend depending on the laboratory test conditions and infection.

A well-managed lockdown citywide and family quarantine can mitigate the risk of infection spread but it usually depends on the resources available, the extent of quarantine, and the management of officials in dealing with quarantine issues.[3] Authorities have to closely monitor the process and cover the flaws during lockdown because unchecked quarantine will have serious consequences. Moreover, imbalance provision of resources may lead to chaos and hunger. People in quarantine feel like a prisoner without committing any crime so their psychological grooming is necessary to keep them out of depression and anxiety as well. Proper check and balance is necessary otherwise quarantine may lead to whole system collapse and increase in problems during any pandemic.

4.2 DURING AND POST COVID-19 ROLE OF SURGEONS

In the start of 2020, as the coronavirus disease came up with a huge challenge to the medical community worldwide it shook the medical infrastructure of every country to the ground. Health-care professionals might have had the ability to adopt the current emergency situation, but surgeons had no previous or ongoing experience to cope up with the ongoing pandemic. They were pushed to compete with the ongoing crisis and help other medical staff in coping up with the situation, getting out of their own personal surgery room into a public outpatient department, and treat patients out of their field of interest.

4.2.1 SURGEONS BEFORE COVID-19 PANDEMIC

Before the start of COVID-19 pandemic, surgeons' one duty role of surgery had no impact on the infrastructure of hospitals as patient surgery department is a single field lightly related to medical complications. The likelihood of getting infection during surgery is already minimized by the use of antiseptics and antibacterial drug usage. The pressure upon medical system of a hospital from surgery department is not a great concern. Unlike medical department dealing with daily outdoor patients were piling up with more and more patients because COVID-19, diagnosis was not started back then and it was treated as common flu or throat infection. In case of surgeons, they had no relation with dealing any medical issues or complications because coronavirus had no relation to surgery field, so surgeons had very little to do with increasing number of outdoor patients without knowing the actual cause.

4.2.2 *SURGEONS DURING COVID-19 PEAK*

There is no separate department in the time of an emergency; all kinds of specialists including surgeons, neurologists, urologists, and orthopedics become lifesavers in the time of need. Dr. Daniele Macchini explained the pandemic situation in Italy and emphasized the importance of surgeons to fill up the gap created in medical staff on call due to the huge number of patients coming in and low number of health professionals available to treat and deal with them.[5]

As the COVID-19 peak infection started all around the world every hospital mended their systematic strategies from separate ward system to one public ward quarantine with proper sanitizing equipment and social distance. Doctors were well equipped with masks and medical kits to protect them from getting infected during treatment. On March 13th, as number of cases in America increased beyond repair, their council American college of surgeons decided to suspend and delay all kind, of surgeries for the coming time.[6] In order to cope up with increasing coronavirus patients and low number of medical staff, surgery departments all over the world decided to reconstruct their duty schedule to provide hospital management with their surgical as well as non-surgical needs during pandemic. They constructed three teams in the form of daytime, nighttime, and backup call team to cover the overflowing burden of corona patients in outdoor departments. As the number of patients increased, hospital management kept increasing the number of surgeons into their resident staff so that the burden of patient handling could be kept at minimum.[7]

Surgeons' Reorganization during COVID-19	
Surgical clinic transforming into medical ones	Only emergency surgeries were performed
Anesthesia staff was given duties to inpatient departments of medicine	Reduced surgeries allowed more ventilator availability
Alcohol scrubs used in surgeries were used as disinfectants to avoid viral transmission	Global efforts were performed to donate N95 masks, surgical masks, and food for in-residents
Internet facilities were used between staff for communications and important meetings	Discussion with senior medical staffs helped them to cope up with difficult situations

4.2.3 THE ROLE OF SURGEONS DURING THE COVID-19 PANDEMIC: IMPACT ON TRAINING AND LESSONS LEARNED FROM A SURGICAL RESIDENT'S PERSPECTIVE

Surgeons have a vast experience of dealing with traumatic situations. Because all of the crucial and lifesaving surgeries are performed in panic and trauma so dealing with pandemic trauma was not a big deal for them. This ability greatly impacts the situations in hospitals where there is patient everywhere and you have no time to spare. Trauma-informed care theory is applied throughout the time dealing with patients under stressful environment.[8] This also includes protecting physicians, families, trainees, and patients from retraumatic waves in hospitals that piles up due to hysteria of a disease. They assume a universal precaution that all patients have been exposed to pathogens and so they have to keep a safe distance while communicating and treating patients.

4.2.4 SURGEONS AFTER COVID-19 PEAK

Prior to the ongoing pandemic, surgeons used the surgery equipment and machines as a separate unit in hospitals keeping a unique identity from other medical units. During the pandemic, surgeons learned a lot of new medical emergency dealing and techniques to fight the challenges faced from the increasing inpatient numbers. Personal protective equipment like surgical masks, N95 masks, and disinfectants used as surgical items were the most important source of protection during viral outspread and dealing with pandemic patients. Surgical unit essentials in a department like beds, ventilators, and other machines can be used in medicinal wards during ongoing disease outbreak. Even physical space available in surgery wards can be used as a proper patient bed if patients outnumber the total capacity of hospital beds.

The role of ventilator is crucial in treatment of a seriously ill patient with COVID-19 present in highly intensive units or ICU. Patient condition is measured through ventilator-controlling machine; oxygen level of the patient, their respiratory conditions and heartbeat monitoring through bedside vital machines were under constant observation by the health staff dealing with the patient. Most important thing during dealing with a viral disease patient is to prevent oneself from contracting infection. In this case, the patient should be kept in isolation and use PPE during visits and avoid patient's family to come in physical or near contact with them. In order to minimize physical contact with the patient, long piped IV lines should be constructed so that medicine and drugs could be given at length keeping the safety measures in check.[7]

4.2.5 *HEALTHCARE WORKER (HCW) WELLNESS*

During COVID-19, among the frontline warriors of health system were the healthcare worker including nurses, maids, ward boys, health machine mechanic, etc.; they have played a major role in maintaining stability and keeping the overburdening of health professionals in check. Maintaining discipline in the time of chaos keeping in view the directions of senior staff under pressure of getting the infection is a great risk. Grooming and wellness of healthcare workers during the pandemic was a tremendous task which needed attention. There are a few steps in healthcare worker wellness required for a hospital staff to work without any flaw.

(a) Mental support

Working during a pandemic is extremely stressful and laborious because not only a healthworkers' life is at risk but their family members and all the people who come in contact with them are at risk of getting infected. HCW had no choice except to make hard decisions which lead to moral stress and anxiety so they needed emotional support and psychological grooming like in any disaster times.

(b) Work beyond ethnic discrimination

Private healthcare charity organization or NGOs working in aid for hospitals should work beyond the question of ethnic hate or discrimination and also teach their HCW the same lesson because it can lead to disaster in the time of chaos and panic which demands unity and patience. A patient's health depends on the behavior and treatment of healthcare staff, and it has a great impact on ethnic violence by the upper class in hospitals.

(c) Provision and availability of PPE

Providing the HCW with all kinds of personal protection equipment is the main necessity of pandemic. The risk of getting illness reduces a great time than without protective equipment and even in some cases death is avoidable.[8] They must be protected from infection causing agent in the environment of hospital premises during duty with proper equipment like sanitizers, surgical or N95 masks, and medical kits in accordance to the recommendation of CDC. Latest research shows that COVID-19 virus can stay in air for up to 3 h after it is transferred by an infection-carrying body.[10] Guideline regarding patient handling with PPE on and proper disposal of used kits must be given to HCW in the hospitals before duty to avoid health risking threats.

According to a case study in Australia, some respondents HCW gave answers to the given PPE-related questions. Out of which only 26.7% had proper gowns available at work while 23.3% were given proper masking equipment while other half were not given proper PPE and masks as shown in following table.[11] 'n' refers to number of respondents.

Always Sometimes Never						
	N	%	n	%	N	%
Surgical masks	141	26.3	183	42.3	265	45.4
P2/N95 masks	156	26.7	194	33.2	234	40.1
Gowns	276	45.5	152	29.9	167	28.6
Goggles	240	49.7	223	39.2	132	22.1

(d) Production of medical equipment

Due to the ongoing chaotic pandemic, millions of people all around glove have been affected. As a result, healthcare machinery is on shortage as hospitals have low number of bedside vitals and ventilators to deal with seriously ill patients. Huge number of COVID-19 test kits, protective kits, masks, and antiseptic liquids are being consumed for diagnostic, handling, and safety purposes, respectively.[8] Main focus of every country must be on production of these new equipment and easy accessibility to HCW in normal range of prices so that they can buy it on personal expense as well without any burden. Providing hospitals with adequate number of ventilators and other lifesaving machines is the need of the hour during a pandemic.

4.2.6 SOCIETAL ISSUES OF EQUITY AND INCLUSION

A world already dealing with hate crimes against ethnic differences was hit by a pandemic mid between. In this scenario, social biasness of HCW is inevitable and difficult to eradicate from the society. Equal provision of medical equipments and medicine without considering ethnic differences, freedom of speech for everybody so that they can give awareness to their communities, and treating rich and poor, politician or layman equally in a hospital is the most important part of societal balance during chaos. There are a few points to be considered critical while taking care of social equity and inclusion during this pandemic.

(a) Limited resources

As in COVID-19, testing kits were limited and number of patients was out of control to be considered so in order to cope up with this situation provision should be made according to available resource not on the basis of social differences.[12] For example, if somebody from upper and lower class is sick with the disease simultaneously, in order to diagnose the disease one must apply first-come-first-get basis or readily available rule. You cannot stop the treatment on the basis of ethnic differences or social poverty and provide treatment to only upper class. This would lead to social chaos and anxiety in the society and bad influence for the HCW community.

According to one plan design, the allocation of resources should be based on the following table:

Guideline for Limited Resources During COVID-19 Pandemic

Values	**Application to COVID-19**
(a) Prioritise contributors	
Retrospective- priority to those who have contributed	Maximum priority to researcher and HCW on duty
Prospective priority to those who will contribute	Maximum priority to upcoming HCW on duty
(b) Priortize to intensive patients	
Critical patients first	To enhance treatment benefits to society
Young patients first	To enhance viral spread and mortality
(c) Maximum benefit:	
Save the most lives	Highest priority
Increase the prognosis	Highest priority
(d) Equal treatment	
First come, first serve.	Not applied
Random selection	Only to those patients having similar prognosis

(b) *Freedom of speech*

During a pandemic, every voice matters. You have to listen to all the members of a society including healthcare workers, layman patients, politicians, military, and leaders. Everybody in the community plays an important role in determining various aspects for public health awareness. You cannot overlook a nonmedical person's opinion in view of a public health worker because HCW are working in hospitals while management is providing them with the necessary equipment have to communicate with other offices as well.

Public awareness is only possible through the help of communication and media means which in turn depends on freedom of speech. If hospital healthcare worker are facing any kind of issue regarding equipment shortage or poor management they can speak it out loud. Without the fear of government or any managing companies about which they give statement of wrong doing or poor management. Military and government officials may speak about their concern regarding public health threats and concerns if they are not properly able to manage the situation. Warning and precaution speech could be the first and easiest mean of providing safety to the nations while dealing with a pandemic and it must be encouraged without the fear of being misjudged or losing one's reputation.[12]

(c) *Biasness in treatment*

One of the major problems of hospitals is the healthcare worker biasness in treating people who are closer to them and treating patients who are completely strangers. This must be checked by the hospital authorities. No doubt the HCW on duty for the pandemic must be treated first and priority should be given but workers which are not on duty mush be treated as same strange patients. There should be no family or kinship priority while treating patients with COVID-19 disease. Putting a person's life at risk just for the sake of your acquaintance is ethnic crime and must be prohibited.

4.2.7 STRUCTURAL VIOLENCE

As COVID-19 pandemic started, various management flaws and structural violence came up with time. Government all around the globe had to deal with pandemic as well as economic burden due to lockdowns, loss of medical facilities due to over burden of patients, ethnic hate crisis, and unemployment due to downsizing of private and public companies. Moreover, due to ban in international travel and transport every country faced shortage of medical supplies and other important items. Increase in poverty and mental instability became the cause of structural violence from the society

(a) *Loss of medical benefits*

As burden of patients increased in hospitals, governments globally suspended free medical facilities to cope up with the crisis. Increase patient inflow in hospitals depleted hospital resources to a drastic level. Insurance companies did not provide free leverage because of bankruptcy issues. This resulted in mental and financial pressure on people specially living in countries with poverty issues like Africa, white rural communities, and brown-black communities of underdeveloped countries.[8]

(b) *Economic downfall*

Pandemic struck on countries which were already facing economic crisis due to international debts and low tax collection. Shortage of supplies like electricity, water, and other facilities was a major concern for developing countries. Even Native Americans were under a lot of pressure due to incomplete provision of electricity, water, and security which increased regional hate among people. Moreover people living without proper homes on the streets being a burden to community had no way to get treated from the hospitals on their personal expense

(c) *Poor hygienic care*

Even after proper guidelines and public awareness campaigns, people were unable to adopt complete hygienic care for protection. People who are homeless were at greater risk of getting infection from the air. Sewerage and garbage collector community were unable to properly apprehend the guidelines issued by CDC for PPE due to various mental, physical, and financial problems. People who were unable to read and understand the importance of hygiene in underdeveloped countries were the most vulnerable community during this pandemic.

(d) *Financial crisis*

Due to economic burden in underdeveloped countries in response to coronavirus, people faced disastrous financial crisis as stock markets dropped below and companies had to shut in order to apply safety precautions. Daily wagers under lockdown and quarantine had no source of income to run the house utilities so they had to face financial upheaval in the midway. As a result, consumption surpassed the daily earned money putting pressure of financial sources. Mental health and anxiety affected greatly into the society as no source of income thought struck to everyone. People below the poverty level in underdeveloped countries were at the most vulnerable to this pandemic, having the fear of getting infection and medical bills with a financial problem to cope with hunger increased depression and anxiety among them. Hate crimes and robbery increased as a result of increased difference between upper- and lower-class communities.

(e) Unemployment

According to a case study, there will be 30% increase in unemployment across United States which is more than the unemployment rate of Great Depression in 1929.[8] As lockdown and international trade stopped to prevent the spread, public and private companies went for downsizing in their employees. Daily wagers were out of market due to trade and business halt from the pandemic, people who live through selling different items in the streets were affected the most because of lockdowns. Under-developed countries GDP went below zero because of poverty and unemployment.

Surgeons had to face different cases due to this pandemic and above structural flaws in it. Patients with mental health issues, domestic violence, poverty, homeless, and drug abusers increased during pandemic. Poor medical facilities added fuel to fire. The only solution to this problem was government aid to every class regardless of the communities they belong to to compensate the financial anxiety and loss. State and federal interference are necessary to keep proper check and balance in the society to avoid domestic and drug abuse increase during pandemics.

4.3 DURING AND POST-COVID-19 ROLE OF DOCTORS

Doctors are the frontline fighter in any pandemic situations worldwide. In coronavirus, doctors were the only hope for the public in fight against this lethal pandemic. Doctors with their professional experience and knowledge help and guided public through the peak of infection and saved millions of lives. As the virus spread into whole community, burden on doctors globally became immense and challenging. They had to go through various infrastructural flaws and shortages like lack of PPE, ICU beds, hospital beds, shortage of staff, lack of training in young doctors to fight pandemic situations like COVID-19, and most of all increase in patient to doctor ratio that put a great deal of mental stress on the over working doctors in the community. Doctors of the world played different important roles in the prevention of COVID-19 including treating patients, hospital management, and thrifty use of scarce resources to providing guidelines and information to public to prevent the spread of virus in the community. Not only senior medical officers performed their duties during COVID-19 but young doctors, doctors of other department, and final year medical students of medicine also played their part in easing hospital burden.

4.3.1 ROLE OF MEDICAL STUDENTS

Although medical students are not as skilled or experience as a general doctor but they are an important asset to world because they have all the necessary knowledge regarding minor ailments and patient-handling techniques. During COVID-19, medical students played an important role in taking patient's history, communicating with patient, and diagnosis of disease and symptoms assisting in treatment process and discharge planning before a doctor could prescribe appropriate treatment.[15] It was helpful for senior doctors because during this pandemic patient influx was too much to handle so they needed more hands to cover overflow of patients into the hospitals. During pandemic, all kinds of academic activities were paused in fear of infection increase so in the meantime final-year medical student who generally do practice in hospitals had to sit in their homes without practice. In order to cover up their academic encumbrance they were called up to help doctors with their duties and practice medicine.

Medical students have a role in examining medical test reports, taking notes of every physicians visit and prescription. They treated patients in the outpatient department with minor ailments and routine checkups. Medical students can assist doctors in checkup of patients like pregnant women and their normal deliveries. Diabetes and heart patients need routine checkup which can be covered by the help of medical students. Guiding patients with use of PPE and appropriate healthcare routine were some of the duties of medical students during COVID-19 peak days.

4.3.2 PHYSICIAN SCREENING AND PROTECTION

Being at the frontline of defense against COVID-19, doctors are the most delicate and important asset that could get infected from the virus. Thousands of doctors across the globe have died fighting against this disease even on duty. Physicians have played exceptional role in the detection and fight against coronavirus. Dr. Li Wenliang, was an ophthalmologist At Wuhan Central Hospital where the outbreak started and first case was diagnosed. He detected those new cases of pneumonia had similar symptoms with SARS, happened in 2003. He also alarmed other physicians and healthcare workers about the new virus and asked them to wear appropriate personal protective equipment. But unfortunately, his fears were neglected, and he was punished for spreading false fear among healthcare workers and physicians. But when he died by contracting the virus himself while treating a patient who was already infected, this caused panic in public and forced the management to disclose the outbreak situation.[16]

Physicians had to make use of each and every PPE available for them. Because they were in hospital completely exposed to viral environment while treating patients. researchers during SARS 2003, discovered that washing hands frequently could stop viral transmission for up to 55% and wearing masks could do the same with 68% efficiency, if all of these protective measures and equipment including gloves were used the viral transmission could be prevented up to 91%.[17] So physicians had to take extra care during COVID-19; physicians were routinely screened with -19 PCR test and antibody tests. Routine temperature checkups and monitoring of symptoms for COVID-19 was must for every physician all around the globe.

4.3.3 ALLOCATION OF SCARCE RESOURCES AND TREATMENT

As stated earlier, when the pandemic was at peak, patient number surpassed the available health capacity of the world with millions of new cases every day. Physicians were in great stress of handling the crowded hospitals and allocating scarce resources equally. Public was already frightened and panic due to lockdowns and financial crisis they had to be dealt with patience and equity.

Patient-monitoring technologies like pulse oximetry and other vital health machines helped physicians to cover critical patients of COVID-19 from a safe distance and properly handle patient's health but due to scarcity of these resources in the face of increasing number of patients, physicians were under great stress in allocation of beds, equipment, and treatment to all the patients. Patients in the hospitals outnumbered available resources all over the world. Moreover, ban in international trade and lockdowns increased the inequality of treatment in the society. Once detected with coronavirus, patients were completely isolated from their families and public in isolation ward for at least 14 days depending upon their antibody tests. Patients were given extra care in isolation wards temporarily built by the health workers in order to cope up with burden of patients. Ventilators were put on patients having respiratory issues like difficulty in breathing and low oxygen level in blood. Immunity boosting medicine was used to help the body fight against the viral infection. Medicines were used to lower the fever due to infection in patients. In order to compete with the ongoing crisis, physicians decided to work in all outpatient clinics to the minimum in order to complete COVID-19 patient treatment and resource utilization. Critical patients were given priority in bed allocation and machine usage so that possible lives could be saved. Physicians paid extra attention to the wellness of their own community and governments all over the world encouraged them because in order to fight with the infection healthcare workers and physician protection was the most important thing. Without them, the health system would have collapsed.

4.3.4 MENTAL STRESS DURING COVID-19

Doctors were under great stress during COVID-19 because they had to perform extra duties with fear of getting infection and no proper resources were available at the time of peak crisis. They had no appropriate PPE available and hospitals were filling up with critical patients. Dealing with them under scarcity and lack of knowledge caused frustration in physicians to a great extent. According to a report, when a French physician was infected with the virus he committed suicide, three physicians died from cardiac arrest, which was due to mental pressure and stress.[18] The main reason for this to happen was poor management of hospital duties, family worries, and economic downfall of the world.

Another reason for the physician stress was family protection. They were working hard despite the shortage of PPE, health workers, medical staff, medicines and electric equipment. With lack of knowledge and increasing number of patients, they were worried for their families who could have contracted the virus from them because working in the hospital with scarcity of sources would have definitely transmitted virus into them; from where it would have infected their families when they met them. Some of the physicians were asked to stay in quarantine away from their families to avoid any risk of viral transmission to their families. Working in quarantine without being able to see or meet their families leads to ethical dilemmas and mental injury.[19] According to another study conducted in China, 70% of the health workers in Hubei working on coronavirus duties and suffered from mental stress, 50% had depression, 44% anxiety, and 34% insomnia due do different psychological burdens during quarantine.

4.3.5 MORTALITY IN DOCTORS

Frontline fighters against coronavirus 2020 were the most vulnerable of all in terms of getting infected and increased death rate. Continuously being in the viral environment during COVID-19 peak time exposed physicians to increased infection and mortality. Lack of proper knowledge and awareness regarding preventive measure and spread of virus was also a major cause of deaths in physicians all over the world. Physicians from otorhinolaryngology, dentistry, and anesthesiology were the most-affected community in COVID-19 because they were directly exposed to disease carrying patients without appropriate PPE in the start. Almost 12% deaths in physicians were recorded from these fields.

Physicians succumbed to this deadly virus all over the world performing their duties at hospitals. Countries that recorded the most deaths of physicians were Italy, Iran, Philippines, Indonesia, China, Spain, USA, and UK, respectively. According to an article about physician death from coronavirus, the case study of $n = 278$ physician deaths show following deaths countrywise in April.

Country	*n* (percentage %)	Median Age
Philippines	21 (8)	62
Indonesia	17 (6)	58
China	16 (6)	51
Spain	12 (4)	61
Italy	121 (43)	69
USA	12 (4)	65
Iran	43 (15)	54
UK	11 (4)	68
France	7 (3)	66
Pakistan	3 (1)	46

Country	*n* (percentage %)	Median Age
Brazil	2 (1)	53
Egypt	2 (1)	50
Mexico	2 (1)	45
Turkey	2 (1)	67
Canada	1 (1)	62
Greece	1 (0.5)	-
Germany	1 (1)	58
Honduras	1 (0.5)	56
Serbia	1 (0.5)	59
South Korea	1 (0.5)	60
Poland	1 (0.5)	-

Physicians in underdeveloped countries like in Asia and Africa were the most affected because they were already struggling with shortage of PPE and proper medical facilities so the stress increased mortality rate not only due to coronavirus but also from mental stress and lack of proper care provision to physicians.

4.4 DURING AND POST-COVID-19 ROLE OF PHARMACISTS

Pharmacy is an important part of a health system. Without them, treatment through proper medication is impossible. During pandemics, pharmacist play important role in maintaining balance during medication supply and variety in treatment. They have various applications in the field of medicine such as screening, vaccination, testing, pharmaceutical countermeasures and ensuring medication safety and accessibility during pandemics.[22] They have proved most valuable during the coronavirus crisis. Pharmacists have a role in providing prescribed medication by the physician, dispensing services, and all kinds of pharmacy-related items. They are not generally considered as healthcare professionals since they follow different rules and regulations but the professional skills of pharmacists is important in pandemic situations to provide people with over the counter medications and other easily accessible medicine related to the disease. They have the basic and important knowledge about which drug is usable for the fight against disease and what kind of personal protective equipment (PPE) is useable in this regard.[23] They are the most easily accessible healthcare workers to the public even in severe pandemic cases. They have played a great part in handling this pandemic during quarantine and lockdowns through their professional experience and help.

4.4.1 CONSULTATION AND REFERRING

As COVID-19 started, public all over the work was in shock. Hospitals piled up with patients fear of government ban and financial crisis made people to keep their illness to themselves without even consulting doctors. Pharmacist on the other hand played a major role in providing over the counter medication and proper guideline through market consultation. Pharmacist helped public through mental pressure and PPE-usage guideline. If the medicine that physician have prescribed is not available in the market or becomes short due to overflow of prescriptions, it was the duty of pharmacist to give alternate equivalent medicine to the patient so that the psychological stress for the public can be reduced. When patients enter the pharmacy, their temperature was checked to avoid any mishap in the pharmacy and to avoid viral spread. Any sign of COVID-19 symptoms was immediately being reported to nearby clinics or hospitals so that spread could be prevented and patient could be isolated. Pharmacist have a very vast role in consultation, referring public to physicians for more information and guidelines regarding self-safety from viral infection through immunity increasing drugs.[23]

4.4.2 PSYCHOLOGICAL HELP

During the coronavirus outbreak, public went under a psychological stress due to different crises that popped up due to lockdowns and trade halt. As countries banned exporting medicinal facilities, every country faced shortage of PPE and medicines that were helpful in fight against coronavirus. Public had to face medicine shortage due to overburden and reliance of patients on a single medicine, so pharmacist helped them by giving alternative equivalent of the medicine, so they do not have to stress about the lack of treatment to a bit. Moreover pharmacists helped public through their professional experience regarding the psychological fear of virus. Many people fear in going to physicians tends to visit pharmacy more often for over-the-counter medicines to get a quick relief. During pandemic, pharmacy consultancy increased to a great extent in drugs that were used to help in fight against coronavirus; in this way, many people who were officially not diagnosed with the disease took pharmacist into confidence for their treatment.

4.4.3 PUBLIC AWARENESS AND EDUCATION

People having no means of internet access and illiteracy in public were a big hurdle in the COVID-19 guideline for them. Pharmacists on the other hands were specifically educated regarding the preventive measures and medicinal use against coronavirus. They prevented the spread of false or wrong prescriptions for the infection treatment. Pharmacist experience and knowledge were particularly helpful in stopping the spread of misleading information and lack of guidance regarding coronavirus.[25]

According to a case study, almost 90% of the community pharmacists have proper knowledge related to COVID-19 preventive measures and they apply them in daily life.[26] One of the drawbacks of lack of public awareness was spread of fake news, misleading information regarding PPE usage, and wrong prescription of over-the-counter medicines to the public. Pharmacist, on the other hand, used mobile devices to access social media and article help in this regard to have adequate information and knowledge to prevent the drawbacks happening in already stressful pandemic environment.[27] COVID-19 early information regarding symptoms, use of personal protective equipment (PPE), maintaining social distance, and avoiding crowded place were necessary for public who had no access to the internet media or electronic media. Complete awareness through flyers, flex, and brochure was given by pharmacies in the community. They guided the public regarding personal hygiene, respiratory hygiene self-protecting tactics, onset of infection symptoms, and transmission ways to help them avoid the spread of disease..[28] They trained the patients to distinguish COVID-19 from common flu and when to ask for medical assistance. Avoiding unnecessary outings was preferred to keep public in homes and isolated. Pharmacist played a major role in convincing the public regarding no vaccine availability in the market and only preventive measures are the cure against this disease to avoid false information and myths of treatment. Public was trained to have a basic knowledge about over-the-counter medicine usage and application in symptoms to avoid unnecessary clinical visit.[23]

4.4.4 PATIENT HEALTH AND DISEASE MANAGEMENT

Patient's health monitoring is the most important thing during a pandemic. Patients were given guidelines regarding prescribed medicines. Taking medication on time and checking expiry dates before buying were recommended by pharmacies. Patients were given guidelines to keep a check on their own health routinely. They were advised by pharmacists to take medication if any symptom of infection appears. As some medicines were not available in the market due to shortage or overuse, pharmacist asked patients history before giving alternative equivalent medicine and asked them to inform if any adverse reaction to medicine occurred. Patients were asked to regularly check their oxygen level through gadgets and measure their blood pressure; if the blood pressure was not normal against 180 mmHg systolic or 110 mmHg diastolic, the person should immediately seek medical assistance. Complete history was taken before prescribing medicine from the pharmacist to avoid any adverse reaction.[23]

4.4.5 MAINTAINING MEDICINE SUPPLY CHAIN

During pandemic, the biggest problem faced by the public was medical supply shortage. Various medicines, PPE, and sanitizing alcohols were in huge demands used for protective measures in hospitals and homes. Pharmacist had a great challenge to ensure the proper supply chain of these materials in a routine manner. Unnecessary pharmacy visit was also a big hurdle to the prevention of disease. Underdeveloped areas of city and rural areas were completely in short supply of medicine. In order to cope up with this challenge, pharmacists set up online pharmacy and made door to door delivery facilities functional so that people under lockdown could casily access to medicines and other PPE.[25]

On March 28, the FDA issued emergency-use authorization for the COVID-19 treatment medicines including hydroxyl-chloroquine sulfate and chloroquine phosphate. This requires a fact sheet which contain all the important information regarding use, misuse, and side effects of these drugs when applied for COVID-19 treatment to certain adults and adolescent.[29] Pharmacists were given all the necessary knowledge regarding prescription and use of these drugs for the public. They were informed about the misuse and stocking of these medicines during pandemic to ensure proper supply of medicines to the needy critical patients.

4.5 TOWARD POST-COVID-19: LESSONS AND CHALLENGES

COVID-19, though not completely eradicated from the world, has been controlled to the predictable level. While vaccine discovery is still on the run, researchers and healthcare professionals have learned a lot from this ongoing pandemic. Not only healthcare professionals but all other people suffering from this pandemic had to face different challenges in fighting this disease. Many things have learned in the process of dealing with pandemic, social instability, poverty, and scarcity of resources during lockdowns and quarantine.

4.5.1 CHALLENGES FOR HEALTHCARE PROFESSIONALS

Healthcare professional is the most essential part of a community during health crisis globally. During this pandemic, healthcare professional go through various challenges that are described thoroughly as follows:

(a) *Overflow of patients and overtime duties*

As COVID-19 struck hard globally, hospitals came up with issues of shortage of healthcare professionals. Huge influx of patients in hospitals amid coronavirus demanded more healthcare workers to be on the move. As public emergency was declared, hospitals rearranged their staff duties to cover outpatient departments in hospitals. In order to cover the shortage of medical employees, they curtailed nonemergency treatments, as in New York and Seattle, hospitals had to cancel elective surgeries to cope up with increasing number of coronavirus patients.[30] As many health professionals went under isolation due to catching of the disease, there was a decrease in doctor–patient ratio in hospitals, in order to fill the gap, retired doctors, surgeons, and other medical staff not belonging to the medical department of health were given duties to deal with increasing patients. Even final year medical students and nurses were taken into consideration to cover different hospital wards with medical dealing.[31] Medical staff had to work in double shifts to cover the amount of increasing burden.

(b) *Fair allocation of scarce resources*

Even though during pandemic emergency production of medical resources was increased to unpredictable level but shortage still persisted due to over population burden globally. Lack of health workers as well computerized beds specially designed for critical medical purpose were in small amount, the major problem that came during the pandemic was to allocate these limited resources to unlimited number of patients. In order to distribute it ethically, HCW were given the top priority. PPE were in huge demand across the globe, in supplying these equipment government organization gave HCW the top priority in order to protect them from getting infection because they are the back bone of any health system especially during pandemic. For the society, next priority was for the poor, homeless, and prisoners' community because viral spread is fast and vulnerable in the community due to poor hygiene and lack of necessary PPE awareness. In order to provide them with treatment facilities, they had to be confined in their local areas to prevent influx in already filled up hospitals. Moreover, hate crimes and ethnic differences rise from neglecting these communities because they are already struggling with social anxiety and financial crisis so they need extra care while dealing with a global pandemic.[32]

After HCW, next priority group should be of older adults, people having weak immune system and the patients with comorbid diseases which are already suffering a lot. Because they are most vulnerable community of the society so they should be given priority in treatment. The next group is of people who take part in production and management of the medical supplies to keep the hospitals going against the fight with pandemic. They include pharmaceutical producers, medical reps, public health workers, fire fighters, mechanics, and the manufacturer of goods and facilities in mills and organizations necessary for PPE production and other hospital requirements production. Next priority group was of people with disabilities like physical or mental because they are usually the ones who are always left behind during chaos and crisis management.[32]

(c) *Psychological distress*

The issue of psychological distress and anxiety among healthcare worker during pandemic is common. They are just like general population in this regard because of lockdowns, quarantine, insecurities of their own family protection from infection, lack of proper resources for treatment and treatment itself, and most importantly the risk of contracting disease during duty. Moreover, they have to face issues like improper treatment resources and shortage to PPE to protect themselves. Risk of negative hit and trail on critical patients and fear of biasness in treating patients were also one of the major causes of anxiety among HCW. Extra duties and sleep deprivation due to heavy workload of patients on their shoulder are a disaster for this community.[33]

A case study in New York regarding psychological distress and coping behavior among healthcare worker shows following data in which 657 participants responded to questionnaire during peak of pandemic April 9th to April 24th, 2020. Out of them, 74% reported the fear of transmitting disease to their loved ones from them. While other source of anxiety were lack of medical equipment, shortage of PPE, testing kits, lack of proper awareness to society and guidelines, and the overtime duties due to heavy workload in hospitals.[34]

(d) *Infection risks*

Biggest challenge for healthcare worker in this pandemic was of their own protection from the infection. HCW are the backbone of any health system in a country, any mishap to this community leads to collapse of health system across the globe. Risking one's life for human welfare is a huge responsibility and favor. Protecting healthcare staff from the ongoing pandemic should be the first and foremost priority of all the hospital managements and government officials at the global level.

In start of coronavirus pandemic, 29% of patients were healthcare worker in China.[35] As time passed with experience this percentage reduced. HCW are at higher risk of getting infection because they have to live in the environment of infection, as in start due to uncertainty of the disease symptoms and asymptomatic carrier a healthcare worker could have been infected from the disease without even knowing a particular reason could be of insufficient awareness to the guidelines and viral transmission process. One of the major transmission spot for COVID-19 among HCW was meeting area where HCW usually care less and could contract the disease asymptomatically without the use of appropriate PPE. One of the case study provided that one patient exposed 41 healthcare worker to the virus resulting in 14 days of isolation to the whole healthcare staff of that hospital. Out of them only 15% were wearing N95 masks and 85% with surgical masks on.[36] As the peak of pandemic rose with time risk of HCW getting infected increased day by day creating a big hurdle in way of treatment. Healthcare staff had to keep themselves protected with PPE in accordance to the recommendation of CDC in 1987 from viral diseases.[37]

4.5.2 *CHALLENGES FOR SOCIETY*

(a) *Mental health issues in quarantine*

Pandemics are the major source of mental health degradation in the society. Any imbalance in daily life can cause psychological distress. During coronavirus there was a great increase in the number of mental health patients in the society due to quarantine and lockdowns. Psychological distress during lockdowns could be caused by inability to adopt new situations, loneliness and unkind restrictions. Poor economic conditions, increasing expenses and debts during lockdown with no source of income became a burden on the society living under fear of virus. Lack of physical activity with no source of entertainment and mind freshness caused poor physical health which resulted in causing mental problems. Difficulty in adopting frustrating restrictions and guidelines from government and international organizations during lockdowns became a source of anxiety and depression in turn causing sleep disorders, suicidal thoughts and other psychiatric issues.[38]

(b) Poverty due to lockdowns

Lockdowns and quarantine due to coronavirus in 2020 all over the world halted trade and business. People in lockdown consumed all their savings leading to poverty and income shortage. As the virus spread quickly food and income resources depleted swiftly causing people to starve and increase in street crime and robberies. The most affected were the middle class because they will get a push from socioeconomic crisis and will have to lower their standard of living people below poverty line would starve to death. Communities living on the margin of poverty line will have to face income shortage and unemployment issues due to lockdowns which will have a drastic effect on socioeconomic conditions of society.[39] It is not imaginable how much increase in poverty there would be in the world but according to the following graph shows that there would be 0.7% increase in poverty on global scale and as population increase occur there would be 49 million people pushed to extreme poverty conditions with time.

(c) Lack of public awareness

Despite WHO issuing guidelines for public to protect from infection, there were many flaws in prevention due to lack of awareness about the virus in public.[28] People lacked knowledge and preventive measures regarding the virus leading to myth and rumors that spread panic and chaos among people all over the globe. Countries with low literacy rate were affected the most. Pakistan where over all literacy rate remained at 59% caused a non-serious attitude and ignorance toward viral preventions especially in rural areas where there were no use of PPE and social distancing was at minimum they were purely living on superstitions and myths with herbal medication having no use against the virus which had to be changed to prevent deaths due to virus.[41]

(d) *Shortage of hospitals*

Coronavirus in 2020 hit real hard to the communities globally. As number of infected individuals increased beyond the capacity of a country's health system it caused a chaos among health worker and society to get treatment priority. according to American Hospital Association there were total of 5198 community hospitals comprising of 792,417 beds with 3532 emergency departments and 96500 ICU beds out of which 23,000 were for neonatal and 5100 for pediatric departments leaving on 68,400 for the public community of adult patients.[42] But number of patients in modern pandemic increased way beyond the capacity of health system to cover up. Shortage of ventilators, health workers, and other medical equipment required to deal with critical patients caused havoc among the society. Normally according to California law, the total capacity of patient treatment daily was of 100,000 patients. But coronavirus cases surpassed this capacity to unimaginable extent.[43] In order to cope up with the situation, new rooms with less facilities were created to treat patient and other options like quarantine, self-isolation and proper awareness through international agencies and media was opted.

4.5.3 LESSON LEARNED BY HEALTHCARE PROFESSIONALS

During fight with coronavirus pandemic healthcare professionals learned a lot to tackle the drastically deteriorating situation in hospital globally. Scarcity of medical resources, chaos in wards and extra duties gave many ways to adopt in the run. People were not only ill with coronavirus but cases with domestic abuse, drug abuse and mental health issues came up rising with the pandemic due to various reasons. How healthcare professionals adopted and dealt with the ongoing situation is a wonder to be praised. In order to tackle a new patient with completely different disease and unknown symptoms healthcare worker had to make new strategy and technique to monitor the situation carefully. Taking in doctors of other professional fields into medical ward was the first step in monitoring. As in coronavirus case, critical patient number increased drastically which resulted in ICU bed shortage. Hospital management only admits patients into ICU when the condition is too critical to handle but in case of coronavirus request for ICU admission increased to unmanageable extent and increased mortality rate due to improper care and admission biasness. So, healthcare professionals had to change their patient intake criteria to palliative comfort care.[44]

Next step in patient monitoring was prioritizing strategy.[45] Though in some thoughts this is not ethically considered correct but due to excessive influx of patient and limited resources this is the only option left to deal with the patients. In this scenario, patient treatment should be in accordance to the years left to live so youngest should have the priority to get treatment.[45] Although this system has various flaws such as misjudgment of patient condition and disability criteria to overcome this difficulty guideline for patient selection criteria in pandemic have been applied.[46] Another step in covering ICU bed shortage was to create new rooms or using pre-existing rooms as ICU with some amendments this idea covered the scarcity of ICU beds to a great extent. Quick help from the HCW helped in achieving this task. Although this task greatly reduced the burden of patients in original ICUs of hospitals but it lacked various necessary equipment. First newly constructed ICUs had no modern health machineries like ventilators and bed vitals properly equipped and newly appointed healthcare worker were not adequately trained for the emergency task which required time for learning. Another important step taken in way of decreasing burden of patients was transfer of less critical patient to the hospital areas where there is low influx of patients so that the treatment process could be divided equally. It might have consequences for the family of handling patient on their own for the time being but for the long run the patient was able to get proper care without chaos of overflowing patients.

Last but not least, the process of handling critical patient was formulated. Patient's family is already going through dilemmas of treatment process. Any kind of miscommunication can cause psychological distress in ICU and semi-ICU area between healthcare worker and patient's family because they will go through serious grief. As said in New York Times "*Of all the ways the coronavirus pandemic has undermined theconventions of normal life, perhaps none is as cruel as theseparation of seriously ill patients and their loved ones, now mandated at hospitals around the world.*"[47] IT communication with the patient is the best possible solution to this problem, trying one's best at treatment but in the end life and death is all on luck so preparing the family of patient with all the possible consequences is the duty of healthcare worker. Always keep in touch with patient's family regarding health condition of the patient is a crucial process because in isolation treatment patient's family is not allowed to frequently visit them in order to protect them from the infection so these were the major steps learned during pandemic by the health workers.

4.5.4 LESSONS LEARNED BY SOCIETY

(a) Preventive measurements

During COVID-19 peak time, the major drawback against fight was unpreparedness regarding the preventive measures. People were unaware of the idea that having a clean hygiene, social distancing, and wearing proper personal protective equipment could prevent the spread of diseases to a great extent. According to the guideline from WHO for preventive measures;

1. Make a routine of maintaining proper distance from people near you and wearing mask during pandemic.
2. Avoid going to crowded areas like markets and social gatherings outside avoid close contact if meeting is necessary.
3. Keep a proper ventilation check to have a clean environment where you could breathe virus free.
4. In cleanliness hygiene, wash your hands and mouth frequently, and cover your mouth and nose while coughing or sneezing.
5. Proper awareness and information regarding the disease symptom is must for everyone keep up to date information of current affair regarding corona virus research.
6. If you feel unwell or any symptom of virus quickly isolate yourself from everyone and use over the counter medication to help.
7. If the symptoms persist or become severe, seek medical assistance right away.

(b) Global solidarity and vaccine development

Pandemics demand global solidarity. As coronavirus hit really hard around the globe, countries started banning export of medical related equipment to save themselves from the shortage of medical facilities. Economic burden hiked in underdeveloped countries. Developed countries like UK, USA, China, and Germany were severely affected amid the crisis of pandemic. In this scenario, countries having good relationship with each other exchanged all kind of possible help. As the pandemic started, US president trump offered financial aid to CureVac, a German company working on COVID-19 vaccine to secure the rights of any vaccine produced for US.[48] As the outbreak expanded in Europe, Germany, and France banned export of PPE to overcome shortage crisis of medical facilities.[49] As the peak dropped in China and situation was under control it helped other countries like Pakistan by donating medical equipment to cover up the shortage. This is the only collective response to global solidarity required at the time of pandemic to fight against it.

The day this virus was discovered, vaccine development started right away but the process takes time and has to pass through various trials and difficulties in approval from world organizations. Many countries around the globe are in desperate try of developing the vaccine as soon as possible private and public sectors a have spent billions of dollars in search of effective COVID-19 vaccine.[51] Moreover even if vaccine is developed some of the under developed countries will not have the capacity to provide vaccine to billions of people all around the globe so solidarity is required among world powers to cope up with financial and technological difficulties against vaccine distribution.

(c) Health system importance

Pandemics are rare but leave dreadful effects on society in terms of mortality and imbalance in health system globally. Even countries like US having balanced economic structure than other living on the edge were under water for unprepared health system. Drug, medical equipment, and machineries like ventilators are produced in specific countries they are not vast in production due to lack of technology and resources. During COVID-19 lack of proper health system and availability of modern technology to treat patients efficiently became evident. Many countries where health system relied on imported drugs got into trouble due to shortage of medical supplies. Lockdowns and ban on international trade added more trouble and increase in mortality rate across the globe due to rare availability of life supportive drugs and ventilators. Patients who required hospitalization due to severe symptoms needed beds and proper ICU environment. This caused chaos among hospital management across the globe because of rapid influx of patients and non-availability of beds in hospitals. Underdeveloped countries were affected the most even developed countries were unable to cope up with increasing number of patients so they had to turn non-ICU beds into semi-ICU conditions quickly. In order to cope this situation ,improvement in health system is required as mentioned. It is essential to increase bed, especially ICU bed, capacities in many countries, in order to reduce stress situations where patients cannot receive required treatment, and to prevent hospitals from being overwhelmed in times of crisis, when there is a spike in patients requiring hospitalization.

Even temporary beds should be created in time of need during pandemics as said.

Shelter hospitals should be incorporated into pandemic planning as the primary destination for pandemic patients, to allow traditional hospitals to continue functioning as normal as possible (or normally as long as possible).

4.6 DURING AND POST-COVID-19 ROLE OF PARAMEDICS

Following the World Health Organization (WHO) delegated the unroll of the coronavirus disease 2019 (COVID-19) widespread, a Public Health Emergency of International Concern on January 30, 2020, COVID-19 has remarkably undisciplined clinical care decision making in pretentious countries. In March 2020, the WHO published break clinical direction on the consideration of COVID-19 patients focused on health ministers, health system administrators, and other decision-makers. In this direction, the WHO featured the discoveries of a huge necessary investigation of COVID-19 patients, noticing that 40% of patients with COVID-19 may have low disease, where treatment is generally suggestive and doesn't need inpatient care; 40% of patients have moderate disease that may require inpatient care; 15% of patients have serious disease that requires oxygen treatment or other inpatient mediations; and 5% have basic disease that requires mechanical ventilation. Where COVID-19 network transmission is set up, the WHO has suggested that clinic specialists decide portion of lifesaving assets for healthcare workers and patients. In spite of a remarkable public lockdown being pronounced in South Africa (SA) on March 15, 2020, COVID-19 cases in SA have kept on rising and community transmission is presently settled. This situation raises the possibility that a flood in cases might be up and coming, which could overpower the country's wellbeing framework. Likewise, difficult critical care triaging choices should be made, as an issue of persistence, in the country's private and state sectors. SA intensivists have significant involvement with apportioning basic considering experiences in the country's resource scare environment. However, control with regards to a pandemic "flood" is uncommon in the country's history. Such decision-making raises significant governance and morals issues. In creating rules for admission to an ICU during humanitarian emergencies, healthcare professionals are guided by wide morals standards. As a first step, it is essential to build up whether a patient wishes to approach mechanical ventilation. A few patients may have recorded their desires in such manner ahead of time healthcare directives, for example, "living wills."

Coronavirus disease has affected the lives all around world. As medical doctors, they gladly did effort on the cutting edges of any nearby, local, or worldwide disease. They care for all patients as injured and severe sick patients in the Intensive Care Unit, paying little regard to their experience, or coronavirus rank around the world. During the existing pandemic, they stay faithful and devoted to greatness in the clinical care of our patients, advancing research and proof educated practice while improving the careful workplace environment by tending to issues of bad form and disparity. The COVID-19 pandemic has now constrained us, as surgeons, to move our moral focus from singular patient-centered care to a more public health, patient-centered care approach. Rather than expanding singular patient results we should rather try to boost results for the more noteworthy population and society where we live and work. While surgical and critical care societies have been suitably making urgently required clinical guidelines, here is little direction with respect to the morals and value population gives that surgeons face when working in this new epoch of COVID-19.

The continuous COVID-19 episode has brought about more than 5.4 million cases and more than 3,30,000 deaths around the world. Governments reacting to a serious disease pandemic may participate in freedom restricting measures including the utilization of quarantine, at times without adequate legal or moral defense. However, isolate offers a chance to build up an understanding of COVID-19 that may somehow or another is not possible, through the study of disease course and transmission. Exploration on people and gatherings in isolate raises particular moral issues that require adjusting the privileges of limited individuals against the scientific and social value such examination could deliver. As cases of COVID-19 quickly increased worldwide, quick activity was important to reduce the most noticeably terrible of the outbreak. This included utilization of quarantine, the separation and restriction of development of individuals who, despite the fact that not yet ill, have been presented to an infectious agent and might get infection. Not all like social separating measures, for example, remain at home requests and business terminations, quarantine is significantly more prohibitive in that individual or gatherings are completely bound except in instances of emergency. The US Centers for Disease Control and Prevention's direction on quarantine incorporates measures for giving essential goods and services to prevent the need to access food, water, and medical services, in addition to other things. Large geographic limitations, for example, the one used to confine travel to and from Wuhan in China in the beginning stage of the Coronavirus pandemic, some of the time called cordon sanitaire, are firmly identified with quarantine activities. Quarantine can control the spread of disease: the quarantine of relatives of patients with coronavirus was demonstrated to diminish demand for concentrated consideration beds and passing from the disease, when joined with different interventions. However, quarantine can risk singular rights through control, particularly when governments use network quarantines that bind huge quantities of uncovered yet healthy people close by the individuals who are ill.

Since everybody has understood that we have actual widespread disease that could overpower clinics with COVID-19 patients and slaughter a large number of individuals around the world, it is reasonable that society is battling and worried for a successful immunization. In these conditions, the best commitment of researchers is to give dependable logical evidence through proof-based medication. As such, it is compulsory that specialists be profoundly mindful in logical exploration. In any case, it is turning out to be evident that the coronavirus has brought about a significant number of logical related articles, and the speed at which the data has been distributed isn't well matched with the time naturally spent during the examination of friend surveys.[3]

Technologies to quickly alarm people when they have been in contact with somebody conveying the COVID SARS-CoV-2 are essential for a system to manage the far and wide. Evidently in any event 47 tracking apps are open general. They are use in Australia, South Korea, and Singapore. Tracking apps are morally legitimate and right now educated advancements in France, Italy, and United Kingdom. Some governments have undertaking to protect data and privacy. Google and apple are evolving a typical partner to support apps that do not require data storage.[54]

The COVID-19 widespread threatens both lives and livelihood. To lessen the spread of coronavirus, governments initiate the crises management interference that includes quarantines, strict social distancing and force home working. Coronavirus measures are important to spare the lives of probably the weakest people inside society, but then in equal they make a scope of pessimistic ordinary impacts for as of now minimized people. Likely unintended results of the administration of the COVID-19 emergency remember raised danger for workers for low-paid, unsure and care-based employment, over-description of minority ethnic gatherings in case numbers and fatalities, and gendered boundaries to work. First time unusual effects are directed due to coronavirus widespread. In a first action of emergency procedures, the infection was developed as a danger from an external perspective. Nations, for example, Australia, shut their boundaries to companions and presented compulsory isolates for returning inhabitants and occupants. As proof of public program arose, a second rush of emergency trial was presented. Societal isolation direction that suggested people remaining six feet away from others issued by many countries. Numerous nations gave social removing direction that suggested remaining six feet from others or potentially presented "place of shelter" orders that necessary inhabitants to just leave their homes for "fundamental going on" (City and County of San Francisco, 2020). Simultaneously, these trials changed everyday life. Coronavirus strategies started from government yet were converted into act by associations. Businesses settled on choices about whether, when and how to move to distant functioning. Even though a few of us were needed to remain at home, important employees, for example, cleaners, specialists, attendants, doormen, cash keepers, and mail carrier were approached to remain at work.

Most important factor in creating fear and public worry and disturbance of daily life functioning is loss caused by unknown pathogen. COVID-19 widespread has affected nearly every aspect of medicine and raises more difficulty for clinical. Developing transmittable disease has posted such essential moral trials as coronavirus SARS COV-2 which is source of coronavirus. It arose in the wet market in Wuhan, China, in early December, making zoonoses from bat. Commonly care givers and attendants are at work to determine cases of coronavirus to saves survivors and to instruct themselves and general society about defensive measures to stop the viral spread and as yet thinking about the individuals who are not affected with the infection.

Past wellbeing laborers, a choice about who is tried or who gets treatment must fixate on precaution of SARS-CoV-2 transmission (general wellbeing), security of people at higher danger, addressing cultural needs, and advancing social equity. Securing general wellbeing may mean organizing assets for individuals in confined settings, (e.g., needy safe houses, detention centers, and nursing homes), where the infection can spread quickly from individual to individual. Assets may should be focused to regions encountering confined out-breaks to control transmission and stop hospitalizations. Gatherings at most elevated dangers, for example, more established grown-ups, individuals with weak immune responses, and individuals with fundamental situations, (e.g., heart or lung ailment or diabetes) are another need, as they are destined to turn out to be genuinely sick.[32]

In many countries caregivers are phrasing under effective barrier from this widespread. Caregivers and attendants are tolerating depression, and social suffering from differing expert standards. They are confronted with challenges by and by, with moral differences, high levels of consciousness and patient mortality, and long working hours. Many caregivers are suffered with coronavirus and dying in the lines of duty. COVID-19 is hardback infection with acute clinical abstract including deaths and 124 countries are infected with this disease.[56] Medical doctors in Italy have given critical funds such as severe care bed and ventilators to patients but due to disease outbreak Italy become the second-most affected country.

South Korea confronted most challenges, for example, due to deficiencies of beds in hospitals patients dying at home while waiting for their turn. In April 27, 2020 the COVID-19 imply 2,916,338 cases and had declared 205,923 lives. Throughout the world health issue are increasing due to coronavirus (COVID-19). People with poor immune response are most threatened due to COVID-19. In March 2020, further 300,000 surveys over the world that listed on clinicaltrials.gov. Later, there is a need to proceed some further research surveys along with the novel ideas for precaution and treatment of coronavirus. Due to this widespread disease we should predict ethical and social suggestions.[57] As of April 8, 2020, there are in excess of 100 antibody applicants for COVID-19. Human test examines include the purposeful disease of exploration members and can give an incredible logical strategy to the testing of antibodies and therapeutics and for considering host–microorganism cooperation in little quantities of members (i.e., around 25–100 individuals). Such examinations have been finished with numerous microbes. Human test examines can possibly improve the productivity of antibody progress, and in this way advantage general wellbeing sooner than would somehow or another be conceivable (both during a pestilence and in inter-epidemic periods) and lessen the quantity of members uncovered to hazard in the assessment of immunization security and viability.

Intensive care expert are confronting moral concerns identified with confirmation and non-affirmation in ICU to hang on life and speak with their families. The dangerous widespread which has disturbed the global populace caused an exceptional inflow of excessive acute respiratory distress syndrome sufferers intensely by increasing the beds in ICU in many regions of many countries. Subsequently, four new alternatives never applied to date were considered with the basic point of sparing a most extreme number of lives: to organize ICU beds for patients with the best visualization; to increment no matter what the quantity of ICU beds, consequently making venture down ICUs; to sort out exchange too far off ICUs with more beds accessible, or to quicken withdrawal of life uphold in ICUs.

Furthermore, to ensure the patients' family members, visits for families were denied or forcefully restricted and sufficient correspondence among nurses and families was interrupted, checking over 20 years of examination pointed toward improving cooperation with families and nature of care during EOL. Besides, since most medical services offices were being utilized for COVID-19 patients, the circumstance additionally raised worries inside the ICU for patients without COVID-19 requiring ICU affirmation. In such an emergency, there are fixings at risk to stir up our moral standards, improve our moral difficulties, and lead to circumstances of tolerating for nurses.[33]

Some basic moral decisions with which ICU caregivers have been challenging during COVID-19 widespread and to underline their limits. On February 21, 2020, first coronavirus was shown in Italy. As March 8, 2020, Italy become second most influenced nation on the planet. In probably the biggest report from China, 5% of COVID-19 expected admission to ICU. In light of the coronavirus widespread, specialists are being compelled to move from quiet focused morals to general wellbeing morals. This move will unavoidably cause moral sufferings for specialists as they are compelled to adjust elective clinical plans and move to different parts of patient protection. It is basic that we understand the progressions that are happening in the flow worldwide setting of total shortcomings, so specialists are best prepared to explore these difficult moral issues. Specialists have not been resistant to this suffering. It has been showed in a few different ways in the previous weeks to months, dependent on where one lives. A focal point of the pain for specialists has been the need to change our typical concentration from attempting to benefit our individual patients to concentrating on the benefit of the public. This moved from persistent focused morals to general wellbeing morals has happened in numerous manners all through the country.

As we have seen elective clinical program destroyed, specialists have been approached to organize activities that are both therapeutically essential and time touchy to carry out another cause of ethic misery for some specialists has been the command to remain at home except if we are specifically called upon to concentrate to direct patient protection. Serve it to state that remaining at home in the middle of disaster doesn't promptly fit with the character of most specialists. The vast majority of us, used to thorough working room plans and long facilities, are not acclimated with holding up at home to be brought in to assist. Though, in a setting wherein we expect numerous doctors and other clinical attendants will be contaminated with coronavirus, remaining at home permits us to protect the clinical attendants fully expecting deficiencies later on.[58]

Paramedics are at the cutting edge of medical care conveyance, and this encompasses during the current COVID-19 widespread. This pandemic causes definite issues for paramedics, which incorporate treating and moving tainted patients, yet in addition issues around sterilization and sanitization of ambulances and medical supplies. Of specific concern is the pneumonia related with the 2019 novel COVID. Information on COVID-19 pneumonia is evolving. Progressing research shows that practically all genuine results of COVID-19 component pneumonia, particularly in matured individuals and those having multiple medical conditions. Paramedics can profoundly affect the maintenance of patients with pneumonia. Successful administration of COVID-19 pneumonia by the paramedic should base on brief acknowledgment, early organization of oxygen and injecting fluids and move to medical clinic. In certain circumstances, paramedics may should be engaged with the conveyance and upkeep of aviation route supplements in patients with coronavirus pneumonia.[59]

Emergency vehicle administrations are the essential suppliers of desperate out-of-medical clinic medical care administrations. The arrangement of organize system with combat zone paramedics giving a convenient reaction to circumstances, regularly in testing conditions. Altogether, paramedics made an important aspect of the medical care continuum or connection. Regularly the main purpose of contact for the medical services framework, paramedics give both out-of-clinic and in-emergency clinic (circumstance dependent) care with a consistently advancing and extending choice of training. With progresses in Australia of expert enrollment under a public board, paramedics keep on building up itself as a medical service calling. In Australia more than 18 000 enlisted paramedics, most of which work for emergency vehicle administration (COVID-19) and the infection that causes it, SARS-CoV-2, has put a strain on ambulances services, clinics, and other medical care offices universally.

The complete overall number of affirmed cases is 1,015,850 with more than 53,216 passing to date on April 3, 2020. Due to expanded interest that COVID-19 has had on existing worldwide medical services frameworks, understudy caregivers have lately been viewed as an advantage by various governments to be used during this pandemic, anyway understudy paramedics are yet to be officially considered for consideration to the more extensive medical care reaction.[60]

After at first depending on enlisted develop on and progressed practice suppliers to staff stations, some governmentally supported testing places have increasingly changed to using emergency medical technician and paramedics. To oblige this move in faculty, they actualized more smoothed out operative methodology for instance, rather than utilizing nasopharyngeal swabs (which require RNs and APPs to control), activities using EMTs have changed to nasal swabs. Since these are basic tests the patients complete themselves, places have received frameworks of finishing predetermined assessments and guidelines to the patients in their vehicles with six-foot limits. Also, there is no need to directly contact with patients, the requirement for more elevated level personal protective equipment (e.g., N95 covers, Tyvek suits, PAPR hoods, and so on.) is significantly diminished. Emergency Medical Technicians can hope to be provided with gloves, careful covers, and disinfectant showers in places that have accepted comparative operational strategies. Despite personal protective equipment principles, obviously, normal cleansing of the workstation, including hardware, pens, seats, and tables, is required. In adding of taking care of tests, emergency medical technicians have the additional duty of overseeing different stations like enlistment. At pass through testing places, patients may just lower windows and verbally give segment data to EMTs. Otherwise, patients may hold up archives to the window, permitting EMTs to duplicate data onto enrollment structures. Nevertheless clear operational methods, medical care suppliers should feel self-confident they will be isolated from patients through physical hindrances or six feet of separation. The cycle for coronavirus testing is as yet developing. As we try to oversee cases in the United States, it is significant that EMTs and paramedics have an appropriate feeling of the structure of portable testing destinations in the event that they are to work in these conditions. With more noteworthy understanding of coronavirus testing strategies, pre-hospital suppliers will have the option to additionally add to the public exertion of containing the infection.

As you will without a doubt know coronavirus has been named a widespread by the World Health Organization (WHO) with patients actually being affirmed at an expanding rate. The circumstance with respect to coronavirus is subsequently evolving every day. Coronavirus is proceeding to put risky burdens on the National Health Services and more extensive wellbeing and social consideration administrations. As experts taking a shot at the combat zone there is a highly danger of experience to the infection, and paramedics likewise have every day contact with conceivably in danger individuals from the public. It is basic that we do everything we can to lessen the pace of transmission of coronavirus inside society, to facilitate the problem on the medical services framework overall.

These are trials for crisis clinical administrations (emergency medical services) work force on the forefronts of the COVID-19 pandemic. To clear the moral difficulties Emergency Medical Services faculty face without having justifiable PPE and offer some direction on the most direction method to outline their choices.

Emergency clinic staffs are at the combat zone due to outburst of COVID-19. The clinic staff due to stress practices rest issues in a people as of now in danger. Lack of sleep, long moves, and sleep deprivation in emergency clinic staff have been related with individual, administrative and general wellbeing dangers. These incorporate expanded danger of mental and physical issues, changed insusceptible reactions (immune response), clinical blunders, confusion, sleepy driving, and exhaustion. In March 2020, the World Health Organization called for giving admittance to psychological wellness and advising for wellbeing experts associated with the COVID-19 outburst. To answer this call, we propose everyday guidance for the administration of rest issues (lack of sleep, sleep deprivation, and move work) that can be remembered for strong intercessions. The counsel depends on psychobiological standards of rest guideline and on rules for the treatment of sleep deprivation and was applied inside an activity offering mental help to the staff of three college medical clinics in Rome.[61]

To fill in the absence of doctors during the coronavirus outburst, a few states have taken law to permit the enlistment of conclusive year clinical assistants into the workforce. Clinical understudies are usually presented to theoretical and effort related pressure, which make worse rest issues. Regularly assistants get the certain message that rest is something that is unessential so as to accomplish instructive greatness.

Emotionally preparation is mandatory for crisis paramedic training. Emotionally work supports the function of paramedics at the combat zone of patient consideration. During the COVID-19 disease where patients are at their generally powerless, it is basic that paramedics can offer both consolations to guardians and be permitted in spite of the infection. Managing coronavirus has put tension on paramedics, for whom mental prosperity is basic to their ability to adapt in remarkably testing conditions, where demise has so often categorized the most extreme instances of the infection.[62]

4.7 DURING AND POST-COVID-19 ROLE OF MEDICAL STUDENTS

The outbreak of COVID-19 has quickly turned into a global epidemic. The introductions of social segregation, the closure of unnecessary businesses and restrictions on travel have caused a dramatic change in day-to-day operations. The epidemic sent waves into the medical house, creating uncertainty, fears, and questions about the role of a medical student in times of public health crisis and toppled medical education. Due to extensive uncertainty and disagreement about the suitable roles of medical students during the epidemic, student contribution in clinical care has varied across organizations. Some schools forbid patient reunions, while others have hired students to perform hospital-based roles or even to graduate medical students in advance so that they can work as professional doctors.[63]

The Association of American Medical Colleges, On March 17, 2020, in a cooperative statement with the LCME, suggested that medical schools agree with at least a two-week postponement from their medical students' contribution in any activities concerning patient contact to develop appropriate educational strategies and separate clinical experience to better ensure safe, meaningful clinical learning of students unless there is a critical need for local healthcare workers. Many disagree with the AAMC that the involvement of medical students should provide with opportunities for clinics that will assist in patient care and can help to prevent staff shortages. History provides two relevant examples of how the epidemic can affect medical students. In the first case from 1918 of the Spanish flu pandemics, medical students were asked to replace doctors who had lost their infection and were sent to areas in need throughout Spain. As the disease spread to the US, the Minnesota Health Board's Secretary collaborated with the University of Minnesota Medical School's dean to find senior medical students to fill the position around home. The same happened in Philadelphia where fourth-year students from the University of Pennsylvania School of Medicine worked in an emergency hospital without little supervision, after receiving one talk about the disease. These examples represent a significant increase in the burden on medical students during a crisis.[65]

Contrary to the critical role of medical students providing direct patient care, most recently in 2003 during the Great Depression (SARS) outbreak, exposure of medical students to patients was significantly reduced. That year, the Faculty of Medicine at the Chinese University of Hong Kong suspended medical student training after 17 students contracted SARS c-virus from an indicative patient while they were in the wards. Similarly, the University of Toronto banned the medical treatment of their medical students during a similar outbreak.[66]

Prior to AAMC's recommendations, the decision that medical students should continue in clinical practice remained varied and controversial. Government public health advisers in the United Kingdom and Canada have suggested that medical students participate in the work to combat COVID-19 as was seen as necessary in 1918.[67] In Italy, one of the countries most affected by the COVID-19 epidemic, medical students have already been "promoted" early. The government has canceled their eligible tests and will go ahead with their normal graduation process from 8 to 9 months and endorsing the process to obtain certificates, which will result in about 10,000 medical school graduates joining Italian doctors in clinics and homes of retired people. Medical education leaders can benefit from learning about the various methods used worldwide to inform methods in their areas. This study presents the views of a panel of local researchers and medical graduates, residents, and medical students regarding the benefits and risks associated with clinical involvement of medical students during an epidemic and offer other ways to increase student contributions and education while minimizing unnecessary risk.[68]

4.7.1 TRADITIONAL ROLE OF MEDICAL STUDENTS DURING COVID-19

AAMC incorporates its direction by emphasizing that "medical students are students, not employees ... They are not yet MDs." While true, this fence fails to acknowledge that medical students have roles not only as students, but also as clinical trainers. The primary role of medical students is to study medicine. However, students are nurses who care for patients. They talk to patients, call for advice, turn pages, communicate with families, take notes, help with procedures, and help coordinate care and planning. During the COVID-19 epidemic, medical students who only work as students bring unnecessary risks to patients and other physicians. Medical students can act as additional carriers of the virus, use personal protective equipment (PPE) there is a serious shortage—and place additional responsibilities on teaching physicians. Medical education alone does not justify these risks.[15]

However, allowing medical students to work on medical roles can benefit patients entirely. There is an example of this type of involvement. During the Spanish influenza of 1918, medical students at the University of Pennsylvania cared for patients in the nursing profession. During the 1952 polio epidemic in Denmark, groups of medical students were given the task of breathing patients by hand. In the current epidemic, medical schools in the United States, Italy, and the United Kingdom are graduating from the medical profession before becoming a registered nurse. The healthcare system should not wait until it stops to invite medical students to work. Medical students are skilled in many clinical areas. Allowing them to work can improve patient care long before the healthcare system reaches a staff crisis, and in some cases can help prevent such disasters from occurring.[65]

In addition, it is noteworthy that the shortage of staff and the demand for medical students is in line with the prevalence of the epidemic and the complexity of the country's healthcare system. As major outbreaks occurred in Italy and the UK, medical students played a key role in tackling the problem compared to Germany. However, bearing in mind the undoubted desire of medical students to take part in the fight against COVID-19, the role of medical students must be considered. Volunteer students support physicians in patient care or work on the COVID-19 telephone service. The students who took on these responsibilities released doctors in administrative duties so that they could focus more fully on the critical care of critically ill patients. Volunteer students are encouraged to think for themselves about the use of their activities. Most students consider their work to be useful and see it as important for medical staff. This emphasizes that students can do specific activities for the benefit of showing doctors and students. However, it is doubtful if these students are adequately trained to perform more responsible roles, such as assisting with ventilation of patients .[69]

4.7.2 CLINICAL ROLE OF MEDICAL STUDENTS DURING COVID-19

The AAMC guidelines range mainly from concern to patient and student infection risk, PPE deficiency, and debt-related problems. These risks undoubtedly need careful consideration, but they can be minimized. We believe that allowing students to perform clinical activities, in some cases, can provide benefits to patients beyond the risks associated with student involvement. First, medical students can help with routine clinical care. Medical students can enhance the efficiency of small staff clinics by taking histories, calling in patients with laboratory test results, providing patient education, recording visits, and asking questions about COVID-19. Even in epidemics, patients with chronic conditions need ongoing care. Pregnant women need regular admission, and discharged patients need to be monitored. Many of these activities can be done with telemedicine, so there will be no risk of transmission. Second, students can provide care in nonprofit patient services with COVID-19. Under the supervision of senior residents or trained doctors, advanced medical students ("sub interns") often treat their patients. In the absence of medical students, these patients will need to be covered by house management, which may increase AAMC-related staff shortages. While this type of engagement will require appropriate PPE, hospital services with high-quality students may increase the availability of other physicians to treat patients with COVID-19. If students are allowed to work in hospitals, they may be at increased risk of developing coronavirus-2 (SARS-CoV-2). However, students are also at greater risk of acquiring SARS-CoV-2 while screening visitors to hospitals, having PPE pulses, and providing doctors with child care, all of which they are assigned to do, and some require PPE. In addition, the risk posed by student involvement may be lower than the risk of retired volunteers who are at risk of developing COVID-19 complications due to their age. However, because human risk cannot be eliminated, we agree with the AAMC that any involvement of medical students should be voluntary.[15]

A 2019 study of medical students at the National University of Ireland, Galway, showed that 59% of participants were willing to volunteer if there was an infection problem. The majority of participants agreed that health professionals are morally responsible for the epidemic and 81% believe that students should be encouraged in the same way. Moreover, of the participants, 98% indicated self-sacrifice as a compelling reason for such a commitment. Given the complexity of the COVID-19, however, is self-sacrifice alone enough to ensure student enrollment? While these incentives are commendable, they cannot be allowed to replace the skills of adequate clinics. Since students are not able to match the knowledge, skills and experience of a qualified clinic, one could argue that their involvement in caring for a patient with COVID-19 in particular will benefit students in education, rather than a meaningful provision of health care. Although we live in extraordinary times, care must be taken in order to facilitate, take the level of preparation for medical students who limit their training during this time. During the curriculum, students are introduced to the state of health care in a controlled manner. In all clinical attachments, they work in idleness, shading groups, capturing histories and observation processes. Therefore, although this program creates a stable learning environment, it does not ensure that students acquire the confidence and skills needed to perform well during the epidemic.

Finally, medical students helped far from caring for patients with COVID-19. They monitored patients with mild-COVID-19 symptoms that are not acceptable; speed up the care of approved patients by reviewing charts, taking notes, and ensuring that tests are performed; and follow-up of patients after discharge. While all roles may need to be monitored by doctors, they reduced the overall burden on clinical teams. We believe that, in moderation, they have improved patient care.[71]

In conclusion, as medical schools have decided how they have continued during COVID-19, we are wary of attempts to shelter students from volunteer work. Medical students are doctors who are responsible for the patients and who should be allowed to carry out their duties as such. In addition to the benefits for patients and the healthcare system, allowing students to participate reinforces important values, such as self-sacrifice, service in times of crisis, and solidarity with work. Students are determined and able to fight this historic disease and should be given the opportunity to do so. It is our hope that the COVID-19 epidemic will lead to the development of various programs on how medical students can best be used in the upcoming epidemic and other different situations, so that hospitals and medical schools can better prepare for future challenges. We are confident that the epidemic, especially the current one, can provide a variety of educational opportunities for medical students and should not lead to a reduction in education and feelings of complete dissatisfaction.

4.8 MENTAL HEALTH AND PSYCHOLOGICAL CONSIDERATIONS

It is a pandemic malady brought about by another strain of COVID-19. "CO" stands for corona, "VI" for virus, and "D" for disease. Once in the past, this infection was alluded to as "2019 novel COVID" or "2019-nCoV." The 2019 novel COVID (2019-nCoV) pneumonia, accepted to have begun in a wet market in Wuhan, Hubei region, China, toward the finish of 2019, has increased extraordinary consideration cross country and universally. All things considered coronaviruses are a gathering of infections having a place with the group of *Coronaviridae*, which taint the two creatures and people. Human COVID's can cause gentle sickness like a typical cold, while others cause more extreme infection (e.g., MERS—Middle East Respiratory Syndrome and SARS—severe acute respiratory syndrome). Symptoms can incorporate fever, hack, and windedness. In more serious cases, contamination can cause pneumonia or breathing troubles. The infection is sent through direct contact with respiratory beads of a contaminated individual (created through hacking and sniffling). People can likewise be tainted from and contacting surfaces defiled with the infection and contacting their face (e.g., eyes, nose, and mouth). The COVID-19 infection may make due on surfaces for a few hours, yet basic disinfectants can kill it.[28]

Psychological well-being is a basic and fundamental segment of wellbeing. WHO (2002) states: "Emotional wellness as a condition of complete physical, mental, social and otherworldly prosperity and not only the nonattendance of infection." An individual keeping up ideal degree of psychological well-being understands their own capacities, can adapt to the ordinary worries of life, can work beneficially and can add to their locale. Emotional wellness is major to group and individual capacity as people to might suspect, act out, associate with one another, gain a living and appreciate life. On this premise, the advancement, assurance, and rebuilding of emotional well-being can be viewed as a fundamental worry of people, networks, and social orders all through the world.[72]

The flare-up of COVID-19 infection 2019 (COVID-19) as of late has influenced human life generally. Other than direct physical and monetary dangers, the pandemic additionally by implications away individuals' emotional wellness conditions, which can be overpowering however hard to quantify. As indicated by World Health Organization (WHO), one out of four individuals on the planet will be influenced by mental or neurological problems eventually in their lives.[73] Mental trouble is normal in the people in question, alongside financial misery. The mental intercessions have helped the casualties to improve after some time, however the most well-known mental issues, for example, discouragement and uneasiness are relied upon to increment because of negative effect on emotional well-being.[74]

Considering the current circumstance, emotional well-being is a rising worry among the populace, particularly medical services experts working in emergency clinics for treating individuals determined to have COVID-19. They experience dread and tension because of the likelihood of infection and spreading the infection among their loved ones. Further it is resolved that wellbeing experts working in medical clinics during COVID had likewise announced manifestations of discouragement and tension. While psychological well-being issues are considered as regular issues, yet, the patients, and medical services laborers are not accepting any preparation in giving emotional wellness care. As per WHO (2020), it is basic for the medical care experts to deal with their psychological and psychosocial prosperity.[75] Dread, vulnerability, and melancholy are normal substances experienced by people during the situations of organic calamities. These issues can make hindrances and difficulties in dealing with the current circumstance and episode of the infection.[76]

Coronavirus emergency influence emotional well-being because of various factors, for example, abrupt rise and spread of Disease, Confused, blended messages, deception and bits of gossip, delayed emergency, Unpredictability, no "promising culmination of current circumstances" yet no antibody, no noteworthy control, lockdown, essential individual/social/strict necessities, customs and methods of adapting restricted, Global emergency.[77]

4.8.1 IMPACT OF COVID LOCKDOWN ON MENTAL HEALTH

Coronavirus lockdown is a proactive measure taken by the administration to guarantee the anticipation of COVID-19 spread through social separating and segregation. This implies is a need considering the flare-up of the infection on the planet where nations, for example, US, Italy, and France are battling to control the fast spread. Lockdown implies that all people are needed to remain at home and just go out for purchasing necessities.[78] While, this circumstance of lockdown can be agreeable for a few, it very well may be overpowering and freezing for other people. As per WHO (2020), more established grown-ups who are disengaged are defenseless to confront emotional wellness issues, for example, tension, stress, misery, and dissatisfaction, particularly the ones having existing intellectual issues. Grown-ups during isolate and disconnection may feel disturbed prompting alarm that impacts affect their prosperity. The prohibitive estimations taken by a few nations for social removing can have a famous adverse effect on the psychological well-being and prosperity of individuals. Because of disengagement and physical removing, COVID-19 emergency, conclusion of schools and work environments, individuals will undoubtedly feel dread, tension, and dejection. It has gotten applicable to assess the impacts of home isolate and confinement, particularly when individuals may likewise fear for getting tainted with the infection, on psychological wellness of individuals and how to beat the issues to limit the negative effects. Considering the vulnerability with respect to the time-frame of lockdown, it is ideal to address the public psychological well-being of individuals during the times of lockdown. It is uncovered that there has been a lot of increment in the quantity of psychological well-being connected cases during the COVID-19 emergency and is assessed to expand extra time, given the seriousness of the circumstance.

The psychological wellness and psychosocial conditions can be more serious for grown-ups who have endured before with various types of uneasiness issues, misery, alarm assaults, stress, OCD, despondency, or claustrophobia. The specialist decided not many of the normal medical problems during COVID lockdown:

Severe nervousness manifestations, trouble in breathing, migraines, and chest torments.

- Worsening of beforehand happening nervousness assaults and gloom.
- Encountering redundant impulses of hand-washing, checking, questioning, and cleaning.
- Feeling desolate, defenseless, and tired.
- Having negative musings and steady stressing sentiments that can't be controlled or halted. Feeling aggravated and having considerations of approaching fate.
- Difficulty in resting, eating, and focusing on any undertaking.

Such manifestations and emotional well-being issues in grown-ups can likewise prompt substance misuse. Lockdown has likewise offered ascend to joblessness where a few people have lost their positions. These grown-ups are additionally defenseless to fall in melancholy.[79] The social segregation and lockdown can demonstrate to have critical adverse effect on emotional wellness of individuals determined before to have psychological well-being issues.[73]

4.8.2 MENTAL HEALTH PROBLEMS IN HEALTHCARE WORKERS

The writing uncovered that a critical extent of HCWs during pandemic experience the ill effects of psychological wellness issues including diagnosable emotional well-being messes. They are specified as follows.

- ***Emotional distress and burnout***

  An investigation from Canada announced that 36% of the HCWs confronting the SARS pestilence encountered a significant level of trouble with medical attendants having a higher rate than specialists. Another investigation directed during the Ebola pandemic found that around 66% of HCWs experienced the enthusiastic depletion. Also, another examination from Hubei (China) found the commonness of despondency among the forefront HCWs to be 50.4% with essentially higher rates in medical caretakers, females and those working in the tertiary consideration setting.[80]

- ***Anxiety issues***

  The examinations from China in the midst of COVID-19 have revealed the commonness of tension among HCWs going from 44.6%14 to 62% (generally 30% had a moderate or serious degree of nervousness).[20]

- ***Depression/burdensome indications***

  Studies led during the SARS have announced a predominance of the downturn among the forefront HCWs to be 38.5%. Studies that have assessed pressure and misery in HCWs after 1 year of the SARS pandemic had likewise uncovered higher sorrow, nervousness, and post-awful indications.

- ***Insomnia***

  A relative report from Taiwan revealed that 37% of the HCWs working in the SARS unit experienced sleep deprivation (Pittsburgh Sleep Quality Index). The most recent examinations have announced the predominance of sleep deprivation (by Insomnia Severity Index) among the cutting edge HCWs to be around 35%–38%.

- ***Other mental issues***

  HCWs often experience the ill effects of other mental issues, for example, wellbeing is related concerns (33% of HCWs revealed this), ineffectively seen self-wellbeing, depersonalization, low close to home accomplishment and absence of power over their lives during the time of isolate.

4.8.3 FACTORS CONTRIBUTING TO MENTAL HEALTH PROBLEMS IN HCWS

Numerous natural, mental, and social/ecological elements (risk of introduction to contamination, stigma, job pressure, and isolation/isolate, and so on) and their interaction incline a person to an expanded danger of psychological wellness issues.[80]

I. *Biological factors*

History of disposition issue and prior age has been recognized to incline the HCWs for an expanded danger of emotional wellness issues during the time of pandemic. This is likewise interceded by socio natural factors, for example, having a kid or a debilitated older in the family, whom they need to also think about while conveying obligations as HCWs during the pandemic.[20]

II. *Psychological factors*

Writing recommends that the character characteristics of the HCWs are one of the significant determinants for the advancement of emotional well-being issues during the pandemic circumstances. For example, an investigation directed during SARS pandemic on HCWs found that the people having on edge avoidant character characteristics, dread of examination, and avoidant method for dealing with stress were at higher danger of psychological well-being pressure, upheld by a few different investigations. Further, HCWs enjoyed the feeling centered adapting methodologies experience the ill effects of higher enthusiastic fatigue, stress, uneasiness, sorrow, and PTSDs.[82] Writing additionally recommends that those associated with intelligent practices experience lesser mental pain, and create issue-centered adapting. Also, issue-centered adapting procedure among the HCWs during the pandemic has been accounted for to diminish their psychological pressure and lightened their dread, in this manner diminishing the emotional wellness issues.

III. *Socio natural variables*

- ***Inadequate correspondence and absence of data***

Absence of legitimate correspondence from the higher specialists to the bleeding edge HCWs and quickly changing rules with respect to contamination control measures could prompt vulnerability, trepidation, and absence of information and a feeling of wildness over the circumstance. These go about as significant arbiters for the improvement of emotional well-being issues among the HCWs.[83]

- ***Risk of introduction to disease***

The HCWs working in the high danger region (screening outpatient division (OPD), inpatient, and ICUs) are at a higher danger of introduction to disease. An investigation from Wuhan (China) reports that as high as 87.5% of HCWs got contaminated from COVID-19. Such a high danger of introduction to contamination offers ascend to dread, trepidation, and worry among the HCWs, which frequently get exacerbated by the dread of being a virus for their relatives and friends and family, bringing about noteworthy psychological well-being issues.[20]

- ***Social separating***

  Staying away from correspondence is considered as a significant measure to handle the infective episode, incredibly rehearsed in the continuous COVID-19. Accordingly, HCWs are ordered to keep up good ways from their associates, both at the working environment and outside, which denies them of in any case genuinely necessary social help.[84]

- ***Stigma***

  Seen disgrace among the HCWs has been accounted for to be a significant middle person for mental issues during the time of the pandemic. Studies led during SARS/MERS found that the predominance of noteworthy saw disgrace among the HCWs went from 20% to half.

- ***Job stress/word-related pressure***

  The HCWs contracting diseases brings about gross understaffing at the medical services foundations. Such a circumstance represents the HCWs to work with restricted assets, long working hours and much of the time evolving obligations, and to work in a new climate that, additionally with the new colleagues, brings about colossal mental pressure. This gets aggravated by the extraordinary needs of isolate/disconnection and exacting support of relational removing.[85]

4.8.4 SUGGESTIVE ACTIVITIES

Individuals have indicated more negative feelings (uneasiness, wretchedness, and outrage) and more negative feelings (bliss) after the announcement of COVID-19 and lockdown measures. Systems, for example, suitable rest, eating well food, participating in some physical movement, and investing energy with loved ones are some ways of dealing with stress. WHO has started self-improvement intercession that helps in lessening the mental and social trouble in the current circumstance of emergency. Coming up next are not many of the activities that can be followed to guarantee positive reasoning and managing psychological well-being issues.

- It is fundamental for the populace to know with respect to the offices that can be gotten to get psychological wellness and psychosocial uphold.
- People confronting psychological well-being issues must look for reasonable and enthusiastic help through their families and close ones.
- People managing emotional well-being issues can take part in online mental discussions through video visit or talk box.
- The government additionally needs to create reserves and assign them to the clinical business to guarantee the proper conveyance of guiding and mental administrations without the ordinary limitations on separation.
- Home care programs must be started as in emergency clinics, the mental beds will be probably redirected to those experiencing COVID disease.[72]

Mental health is a positive concept related to our emotions, psychological and social wellbeings. It includes how we think, act, feel, and deal with stress situations. Having a good mental health means one should know to enjoy a life in full swing, enough ability to deal with the stress condition, having a capacity to set a goal in life and to bounce back in every situation. Major mental health issues linked with COVID-19 are anxiety, depression, trauma, fear, insomnia, and anger. COVID-19 is new for the world and it affects the mental and psychological status due to its sudden emergence, misconceptions, and rumors. People don't know to react in this situation because there are a lot of things that are not properly guide as far there is no previous experience on this disease. There are lot of things that cause people restless like disruption in the daily life, life come to stand still like stagnant water, loss of old life as peoples are far away from their friends and loved ones. Loneliness and isolation such as lockdown and social distancing by the public health actions, sense of fear and anxiety about the future, about their own health. Social isolation have major role in psychiatric disorder, suicidal behavior, irregularity in sleeping pattern, and eating habits. Social stability and emotional health are linked with the connectedness with other peoples. During SARS epidemic in 2003, social detachment played a key role in increases in suicidal cases. One-third of the SARS suicidal victims experiences social isolation during the disease outbreak.

Peoples are much more worried about their financial conditions because their supporting services on which their rely are gone like daily workers who have to go out daily and earn for their family are helplessly sitting in their houses due to which they come across many psychological conditions they are ready to end their lives. Economic uncertainty leads toward the depression and stress, uncertainty make people think that something bad will happen as there is no hope or predications about the end of this disease. There is no light at the end of a tunnel no vaccine till date which makes people more worried and stressful that affects their mental health. Suicidal cases increased during COVID-19. Suicide cases are the major cause of non-corona virus death. Multiple suicidal cases has been reported from many countries for example in England a 19-year-old boy died in a hospital after a suicidal attempt due to the fear of isolation, in New York city a 65-year-old man hang himself in the hospital after being tested positive for corona virus, a Bangladeshi man shot himself because he and other villagers thought that he is infected with the corona after some fever and cold symptoms postmortem reported showed that he was not corona positive.

Alcohol consumption has increased due the COVID-19 crisis. According to some reports, alcohol spending has increase up to 55% in a week in USA. Online purchase of alcohol beverages reaches about 243%.

The groups of people which are more vulnerable to psychological impact are the older peoples with poor health conditions frontline soldiers like doctors, nurses, healthcare providers, and first responders. Doctors have daily basis contact with the COVID-19 patients and they witness the patient's suffering and their painful death which cause many psychological issues for them. A 49-year-old head of emergency department in New York committed suicide after witness the tremendous suffering of a COVID-19 patient. A survey was done in China in which mental state of many healthcare professional were examined which reveal that the 50.4% are suffering from depression, 34.0% from insomnia, 44.6% from anxiety, and 71.2% are distress. People who have existing mental health history are very much vulnerable to the psychological impact during COVID-19 because they are mentally weak and emotionally unstable than others. Communities who are jobless or have difficulties in their earning resources also face major psychological issues. Economic crisis is linked with the mental health issues. Unemployment and job insecurity represents major risk of increased depressive disorder. In USA and many other countries, suicide rate has increased during the COVID situation. As we know that COVID-19 is a viral disease it spread from one human to other that's why people who live in crowded places are in the fear of being corona positive and make them restless. Limited and confused information about the disease also cause many psychological issues.

Another important community is the COVID-19 survivors who are also at the elevated risk of psychological problems. Painful experience during the corona journey like learning about the disease, fear of infecting others, admitted to the intensive care unit, and loss of income may lead to the depression, anxiety, and posttraumatic stress disorder. Some current studies showed that 96.2% of covered COVID-19 patient are in posttraumatic stress symptoms. COVID-19 is also linked with the neurological problems like headache, dizziness, seizures, and acute ischemic stroke and about 25% of COVID patients have these neurological problems. These neurological issues are linked with the suicidal behavior.

Psycho-social support is an important approach to improve the psychological status of a community. This can be done by the mental health professionals, teachers, community worker, and the one who have training on psycho social support (PSS) which includes different type of activities which help to gain good mental health and reduce stress (MH&PSS module). Suicide prevention can be done in three approaches—universal, selective, or indicated. Universal approach is for everyone in the community regardless they have the risk of suicide. To minimize the crisis of suicide during COVID-19, it is necessary to reduce the stress, anxiety, depression, loneliness, and fear. Anxiety can be managed by adopting strategies like attach yourself with the activities that occupied your mind like watching tv, playing with kids, etc., that also consume your energy. Plan your daily routine, identify an activity and hobby that gives you joy and pleasure work in a short bursts with clear breaks that's gives you clarity in your thoughts. Loneliness can be overcome by keeping in touch with your loved ones, family friends through social media, or on the phone and be active in your family groups. Try something new every day so that your mind is occupied in a healthy activity. Write down your thoughts and experiences every day. Physical activities are very good for your health and mind like yoga or a simple exercise spent at least 1 h on your physical fitness. Seek some good meditation that will improve your contraction, do not expect too much from other because they are also sailing in the same boat.

Keep yourself away from the negative emotional like do not search about the disease on Google keep faith on the doctor, do not check the statistics on COVID-19 that will create fear in you. Maintain a distance from groups who are in habiting of spreading rumors. Share your feelings and thoughts with the person you trusted the most, be confident, and do not hesitate to ask for a help. Community organizer included first responders, pharmacist, and school employer have the opportunity to identify the individual that are at the risk of suicide and direct them to the proper treatment. Suicide prevention helpline should be available that gives helpful advices to the peoples who are mentally ill. There should be a social media campaign to encourage the mental health patients to seek help, keep going and reduce stress.

Selective approach includes the group of peoples that are at the risk of suicide like patient with the previous psychological problems history, COVID-19 survivors and front line workers like doctors, pre-medics, and elderly peoples. Patients with psychological issues should continue their treatment and keep in touch with their doctors and psychiatrics. Telemedicine is one of the effective approaches to keep contact with your doctor. COVID-19 survivors should give a proper guideline for their daily routine after COVID-19 recovery. Vulnerable individual should keep themselves away from listening, reading to the traditional, and social media stories.

An indicated approach is for those peoples who have a risk factor that make them more vulnerable to the suicide for example a group of people who have recently attempt suicide. Such persons require more than attention than others may be they keep hesitated in face to face conservation with the mental health professionals. This may be put them in contact with the COVID-19. There should be a follow up plan for these individuals' clinics should set up well design guidelines to deal with such patients.

Every citizen needs to contribute in this war against virus by doing all the necessary measures like social distancing but there are certain things that's need to do on a national level because public alone cannot fought on all sides. Government should know their responsibilities by taking measures to preserve the mental health and morals of the citizens. Government should launch an official website on COVID-19 to reduce the panic and ambiguity. Government-controlled website provides all the necessary information related to the pandemic, exhibit videos, and all the readable material on the pandemic, display the number of infected patients from the virus, number of recovered patients, and number of deaths. This would provide the actual status of pandemic and one will be not panic on the false information. There should be a helpline number for corona on the website.

The Ministry of Health should conduct a webinar to handle the mental health issues and also provide with the health workers, videos and poster that provides the necessary guideline to healthy ill people. Government should try to go hand-in-hand with the general public and try to comfort the local public by providing some kind of finical support. Banks should launch easy loan policies and try to comfort their customers. Government should give relief on utility bills and there should be monthly packages for the daily workers. NGOs should take a step forward to help the needy peoples. During such a stressful and pandemic situation, the concerned government, hospitals, and educational institute even solo individuals should try to cope up with the situation and look into the psychological intervention and seek necessary measures. In addition to focus on the social distancing, public should also well aware of mental health issues and take preventing measure.

4.9 CONCLUSIONS

Coronavirus being the center of attention worldwide in 2020 have taken thousands of lives and millions of people were infected all around the world. The world organizations were totally unaware of the pandemic and its consequences on human life. Lockdowns, trade halt, scarcity of resources, economic crisis, and increase in mortality were some of the major issues brought up by ongoing pandemic. World already on the brink of World War III faced bio war unexpectedly, shortage of resources and lack of research on virus caused a havoc in the health system globally. Country hospitals all around the globe were not adequately equipped with required machineries and personal protective equipment (PPE). Patients outnumbered the available resources to treat in every country which caused a panic in world. Mental stress also contributed to a great extent in creating issues while fighting against this pandemic. Health care professionals played a significant role in fight and prevention of coronavirus all around the globe. They performed multiple roles to cope up with the rising challenges. From treating patients, creating temporary hospitals, setting up telemedicine, and switching roles to providing awareness and psychological support to public were some of the exceptional duties healthcare professionals performed in this pandemic. Public also learned various lessons while fighting and surviving this pandemic. Proper hygiene, use of appropriate PPE, maintaining social distance, and avoiding crowded places in the tie pandemic were some of the most important lessons learned by public and healthcare professional. Proper awareness regarding disease transmission and causes must be taught to everyone so any misfortune could be avoided or at least prevented from spread. World needs more medical facilities than other machineries to cope up the rising challenges of infections. Vaccine development is under process but more research on disease causing agent is required so vaccine could be developed timely to avoid any misfortunate circumstance. As Dr. Tedros

Adhanom Ghebreyesus, Director General of WHO, said, *"This is the time for facts, not fear. This is the time for science, not rumors. This is the time for solidarity, not stigma."* We need strong worldwide relationship so world powers could help each other during times of pandemics and crisis.

KEYWORDS

- **health professionals**
- **nursing**
- **paramedics**
- **doctors**
- **physicians**
- **medical technicians**

REFERENCES

1. World Health Organization. Statement on the Second Meeting of the International Health Regulations (2005) Emergency Committee Regarding the Outbreak of Novel Coronavirus (2019-nCoV), 2020.
2. Centers for Disease Control and Prevention. Symptoms of Coronavirus, 2020.
3. Evans, N. G. Covid-19: The Ethics of Clinical Research in Quarantine. *BMJ* **2020,** *369*.
4. Prevention, CfDCa. Order for Quarantine Under Section 361 of the Public Health Service Act 42 Code of Federal Regulations Part 70 (Interstate) and Part 71 (Foreign). US Department of Health and Human Services, 2020.
5. Wady, H.; Restle, D.; Park, J.; Pryor, A.; Talamini, M.; Abdel-Misih, S. The Role of Surgeons During the COVID-19 Pandemic: Impact on Training and Lessons Learned from a Surgical Resident's Perspective. *Surg. Endosc.* **2021,** *35* (7), 3430–3436.
6. Rusch, V. W.; Wexner, S. D.; Atala, A.; Atkinson, J. L.; Denneny III, J. C.; Eberlein, T. J. et al. The American College of Surgeons Responds to COVID-19. *J. Am. College Surgeons* **2020,** *231* (4), 490–496.
7. Wady, H.; Restle, D.; Park, J.; Pryor, A.; Talamini, M.; Abdel-Misih, S. The Role of Surgeons During the COVID-19 Pandemic: Impact on Training and Lessons Learned from a Surgical Resident's Perspective. *Surg. Endosc* **2021,** *35* (7), 3430–3436.
8. Zakrison, T. L.; Martin, M.; Seamon, M.; Matthews, J.; Joseph, B.; Rattan, R. et al. COVID-19, Ethics and Equity—What Is Our Role as Surgeons? *Ann. Surg* **2020.**
9. Maunder, R. G.; Leszcz, M.; Savage, D.; Adam, M. A.; Peladeau, N.; Romano, D. et al. Applying the Lessons of SARS to Pandemic Influenza. *Can. J. Public Health* **2008,** *99* (6), 486–488.
10. Van Doremalen, N.; Bushmaker, T.; Morris, D. H.; Holbrook, M. G.; Gamble, A.; Williamson, B. N. et al. Aerosol and Surface Stability of SARS-CoV-2 as Compared with SARS-CoV-1. *New Engl. J. Med.* **2020,** *382* (16), 1564–1567..

11. Halcomb, E.; Williams, A.; Ashley, C.; McInnes, S.; Stephen, C.; Calma, K.; James, S. The Support Needs of Australian Primary Health Care Nurses During the COVID-19 Pandemic. *J. Nurs. Manage.* **2020,** *28* (7), 1553–1560.
12. Prakash, N. Doctors Are Concerned That Black Communities Might Not Be Getting Access to Coronavirus Tests. *BuzzFeed News*, March, 22, 2020.
13. Miller, D. G.; Pierson, L.; Doernberg, S. The Role of Medical Students During the COVID-19 Pandemic, 2020.
14. Udwadia, Z. F.; Raju, R. S. How to Protect the Protectors: 10 Lessons to Learn for Doctors Fighting the COVID-19 Coronavirus. *Med. J., Armed Forces India* **2020,** *76* (2), 128.
15. Liu, X.; Zhang, S. COVID-19: Face Masks and Human-to-Human Transmission. *Influenza Other Respiratory Viruses* **2020,** *14* (4), 472.
16. Labad, J.; González-Rodríguez, A.; Cobo, J.; Puntí, J.; Farré, J. M. A Systematic Review and Realist Synthesis on Toilet Paper Hoarding: COVID or Not COVID, That Is the Question. *PeerJ.* **2021,** *9*, e10771.
17. Galbraith, N.; Boyda, D.; McFeeters, D.; Hassan, T. The Mental Health of Doctors During the Covid-19 Pandemic. *B. J. Psych. Bull.* **2020,** 1–7.
18. Lai, J.; Ma, S.; Wang, Y.; Cai, Z.; Hu, J.; Wei, N. et al. Factors Associated with Mental Health Outcomes Among Health Care Workers Exposed to Coronavirus Disease 2019. *JAMA Netw. Open* **2020,** *3* (3), e203976.
19. Ing, E. B.; Xu, Q.; Salimi, A.; Torun, N. Physician deaths from corona virus (COVID-19) disease. *Occupational Medicine, 70* (5), 370–374.
20. Aruru, M.; Truong, H. A.; Clark, S. Pharmacy Emergency Preparedness and Response (PEPR): A Proposed Framework for Expanding Pharmacy Professionals' Roles and Contributions to Emergency Preparedness and Response During the COVID-19 Pandemic and Beyond. *Res. Soc. Admin. Pharm.* **2021,** *17* (1), 1967–1977.
21. Zheng, S. Q.; Yang, L.; Zhou, P. X.; Li, H. B.; Liu, F.; Zhao, R. S. Recommendations and Guidance for Providing Pharmaceutical Care Services During COVID-19 Pandemic: A China Perspective. *Res. Soc. Admin. Pharm* **2021,** *17* (1), 1819–1824.
22. Agomo, C. O. The Role of Community Pharmacists in Public Health: A Scoping Review of the Literature. *J. Pharma. Health Serv. Res.* **2012,** *3* (1), 25–33.
23. Bragazzi, N. L.; Mansour, M.; Bonsignore, A.; Ciliberti, R. The Role of Hospital and Community Pharmacists in the Management of COVID-19: Towards an Expanded Definition of the Roles, Responsibilities, and Duties of the Pharmacist. *Pharmacy* **2002,** *8* (3), 140.
24. Hoti, K.; Jakupi, A.; Hetemi, D.; Raka, D.; Hughes, J.; Desselle, S. Provision of Community Pharmacy Services During COVID-19 Pandemic: A Cross Sectional Study of Community Pharmacists' Experiences with Preventative Measures and Sources of Information. *Int. J. Clin. Pharm.* **2020,** *42* (4), 1197–1206.
25. Hamza, M. S.; Badary, O. A.; Elmazar, M. M. Cross-Sectional Study on Awareness and Knowledge of COVID-19 Among Senior Pharmacy Students. *J. Commun. Health* **2021,** *46* (1), 139–146.
26. Mannan, D. K. A.; Mannan, K. A. Knowledge and Perception Towards Novel Coronavirus (COVID 19) in Bangladesh. *Int. Res. J. Busi. Soc. Sci.* **2020,** *6* (2).
27. Guharoy, R.; Krenzelok, E. P. US Food and Drug Administration (FDA) Emergency Use Authorization: Glass Half Full or Glass Half Empty? *Clin. Infect. Dis.* **2021,** *73* (3), 549–552.

28. Weise, K.; Baker, M.; Bogel-Burroughs, N. The Coronavirus Is Forcing Hospitals to Cancel Surgeries. *NY Times* **2020**.
29. Fowler, A. J.; Dobbs, T. D.; Wan, Y. I.; Laloo, R.; Hui, S.; Nepogodiev, D. et al. Resource Requirements for Reintroducing Elective Surgery During the COVID-19 Pandemic: Modelling Study. *Br. J. Surg.* **2021,** *108* (1), 97–103.
30. Gostin, L. O.; Friedman, E. A.; Wetter, S. A. Responding to COVID-19: How to Navigate a Public Health Emergency Legally and Ethically. *Hastings Center Rep.* **2020,** *50* (2), 8–12.
31. Robert, R.; Kentish-Barnes, N.; Boyer, A.; Laurent, A.; Azoulay, E.; Reignier, J. Ethical Dilemmas Due to the Covid-19 Pandemic. *Ann. Intensive Care* **2020,** *10* (1), 1–9.
32. Shechter, A.; Diaz, F.; Moise, N.; Anstey, D. E.; Ye, S.; Agarwal, S. et al. Psychological Distress, Coping Behaviors, and Preferences for Support Among New York Healthcare Workers During the COVID-19 Pandemic. *Gen. Hosp. Psych.* **2020,** *66*, 1–8.
33. Wang, D.; Hu, B.; Hu, C.; Zhu, F.; Liu, X.; Zhang, J. et al. Clinical Characteristics of 138 Hospitalized Patients with 2019 Novel Coronavirus–Infected Pneumonia in Wuhan, China. *JAMA* **2020,** *323* (11), 1061–1069.
34. Ng, K.; Poon, B. H.; Kiat Puar, T. H.; Shan Quah, J. L.; Loh, W. J.; Wong, Y. J. et al. COVID-19 and the Risk to Health Care Workers: A Case Report. *Ann. Intern. Med.* **2020,** *172* (11), 766–767.
35. Centers for Disease Control (US). *Recommendations for Prevention of HIV Transmission in Health-Care Settings*, Vol. 37; US Department of Health and Human Services, Public Health Service, Centers for Disease Control, 1987.
36. Mukku, S. S. R.; Sivakumar, P. T. T. Mental Health Care of Older Adults During Coronavirus Disease (COVID-19) Pandemic: Challenges and Way Ahead in India. *Indian J. Psychol. Med.* **2020,** *42* (5), 495–496.
37. Buheji, M.; da Costa Cunha, K.; Beka, G.; Mavric, B.; De Souza, Y. L.; da Costa Silva, S. S. et al. The Extent of Covid-19 Pandemic Socio-Economic Impact on Global Poverty: A Global Integrative Multidisciplinary Review. *Am. J. Econ.* **2020,** *10* (4), 213–224.
38. Noreen, N.; Dil, S.; Niazi, S.; Naveed, I.; Khan, N.; Khan, F. et al. COVID 19 Pandemic & Pakistan; Limitations and Gaps. *Global Biosecur.* **2020,** *1* (4).
39. AHA, *AHA Hospital Statistics*, 2018 Edition. 2018.
40. Emanuel, E. J.; Persad, G.; Upshur, R.; Thome, B.; Parker, M.; Glickman, A. et al. Fair Allocation of Scarce Medical Resources in the Time of Covid-19, 2020.
41. Stelfox, H. T.; Hemmelgarn, B. R.; Bagshaw, S. M.; Gao, S.; Doig, C. J.; Nijssen-Jordan, C.; Manns, B. Intensive Care Unit Bed Availability and Outcomes for Hospitalized Patients with Sudden Clinical Deterioration. *Arch. Intern. Med.* **2012,** *172* (6), 467–474.
42. Biddison, E. L. D.; Faden, R.; Gwon, H. S.; Mareiniss, D. P.; Regenberg, A. C.; Schoch-Spana, M. et al. Too Many Patients… A Framework to Guide Statewide Allocation of Scarce Mechanical Ventilation During Disasters. *Chest* **2019,** *155* (4), 848–854.
43. Vergano, M.; Bertolini, G.; Giannini, A.; Gristina, G. R.; Livigni, S.; Mistraletti, G. et al. Clinical Ethics Recommendations for the Allocation of Intensive Care Treatments in Exceptional, Resource-Limited Circumstances: The Italian Perspective During the COVID-19 Epidemic, 2020.
44. Hafner, K. A Heart-Wrenching Thing': Hospital Bans on Visits Devastate Families. *NY Times* **2020,** *3*, 29.
45. Forman, R.; Atun, R.; McKee, M.; Mossialos, E. 12 Lessons Learned from the Management of the Coronavirus Pandemic. *Health Policy* **2020,** *124* (6), 577–580.

46. Anderson, M.; Mckee, M.; Mossialos, E. Covid-19 Exposes Weaknesses in European Response to Outbreaks, 2020.
47. News, M. *COVID-19 Test Kits, PPE from China Have Arrived, msn news*. **2020**.
48. CEPI, *CEPI Gets €140 Million Funding Boost from Germany While Expanding Coronavirus Vaccine Search, CEPI*. **2020**.
49. Timmis, K.; Brüssow, H. The COVID-19 Pandemic: Some Lessons Learned About Crisis Preparedness and Management, and the Need for International Benchmarking to Reduce Deficits. *Environ. Microbiol.* **2020**.
50. Singh, J. A.; Moodley, K. Critical Care Triaging in the Shadow of COVID-19: Ethics Considerations. *South Afr. Med. J.* **2020,** *110* (5), 355–359.
51. Morley, J.; Cowls, J.; Taddeo, M.; Floridi, L. Ethical Guidelines for COVID-19 Tracing Apps, 2020.
52. Branicki, L. J. COVID-19, Ethics of Care and Feminist Crisis Management. *Gender, Work Organization* **2020,** *27* (5), 872–883.
53. Turale, S.; Meechamnan, C.; Kunaviktikul, W. Challenging Times: Ethics, Nursing and the COVID-19 Pandemic. *Int. Nurs. Rev.* **2020,** *67* (2), 164–167.
54. Meagher, K. M.; Cummins, N. W.; Bharucha, A. E.; Badley, A. D.; Chlan, L. L.; Wright, R. S. COVID-19 Ethics and Research. *Mayo Clin. Proc.* **2020,** *95* (6) 1119–1123.
55. Angelos, P. Surgeons, Ethics, and COVID-19: Early Lessons Learned. *J. Am. College Surg.* **2020,** *230* (6), 1119.
56. Higginson, R.; Parry, A.; Williams, M.; Jones, B. Paramedics and Pneumonia Associated with COVID-19. *J. Paramedic Pract.* **2020,** *12* (5), 179–185.
57. Whitfield, S.; MacQuarrie, A.; Boyle, M. Trained, Ready But Under-Utilised: Using Student Paramedics During a Pandemic. *Aust. J. Paramed.* **2020,** *17*.
58. Ballesio, A.; Lombardo, C.; Lucidi, F.; Violani, C. Caring for the Carers: Advice for Dealing with Sleep Problems of Hospital Staff During the COVID-19 Outbreak. *J. Sleep Res.* **2021,** *30* (1), e13096.
59. Hayes, C.; Corrie, I.; Graham, Y. Paramedic emotional labour during COVID-19. *J. Paramedic Pract.* **2020,** *12* (8), 319–323.
60. Ferrel, M. N.; Ryan, J. J. The Impact of COVID-19 on Medical Education. *Cureus* **2020,** *12* (3).
61. Krieger, P.; Goodnough, A. Medical Students, Sidelined for Now, Find New Ways to Fight Coronavirus. *NY Times* **2020,** *23*.
62. Starr, I. Influenza in 1918: Recollections of the Epidemic in Philadelphia. *Ann. Intern. Med.* **1976,** *85* (4), 516–518.
63. Clark, J. Fear of SARS Thwarts Medical Education in Toronto. *BMJ: Br. Med. J.* **2003,** *326* (7393), 784.
64. Legraien, L. Government Is Considering Using Medical Students to Help in Coronavirus Outbreak, 2020.
65. Amante, A.; Balmer, C. Italy Rushes New Doctors Into Service as Coronavirus Deaths Rise Above 2500. *Reuters*, 2020.
66. Drexler, R.; Hambrecht, J. M.; Oldhafer, K. J. Involvement of Medical Students During the Coronavirus Disease 2019 Pandemic: A Cross-Sectional Survey Study. *Cureus* **2020,** *12* (8).
67. Gouda, P.; Kirk, A.; Sweeney, A. M.; O'Donovan, D. Attitudes of Medical Students Toward Volunteering in Emergency Situations. *Disaster Med. Public Health Preparedness* **2020,** *14* (3), 308–311.

68. Murthy, S.; Gomersall, C. D.; Fowler, R. A. Care for Critically Ill Patients with COVID-19. *JAMA* **2020,** *323* (15), 1499–1500.
69. Mamun, M. A.; Sakib, N.; Gozal, D.; Bhuiyan, A. I.; Hossain, S.; Bodrud-Doza, M. et al. The COVID-19 Pandemic and Serious Psychological Consequences in Bangladesh: A Population-Based Nationwide Study. *J. Affect. Disorders* **2021,** *279*, 462–472.
70. Li, S.; Wang, Y.; Xue, J.; Zhao, N.; Zhu, T. The impact of COVID-19 Epidemic Declaration on Psychological Consequences: A Study on Active Weibo Users. *Int. J. Environ. Res. Public Health* **2020,** *17* (6), 2032.
71. Makwana, N. Disaster and Its Impact on Mental Health: A Narrative Review. *J. Family Med. Primary Care* **2019,** *8* (10), 3090.
72. Xiang, Y. T.; Yang, Y.; Li, W.; Zhang, L.; Zhang, Q.; Cheung, T.; Ng, C. H. Timely Mental Health Care for the 2019 Novel Coronavirus Outbreak Is Urgently Needed. *Lancet Psych.* **2020,** *7* (3), 228–229.
73. Druss, B. G. Addressing the COVID-19 Pandemic in Populations with Serious Mental Illness. *JAMA Psych.* **2020,** *77* (9), 891–892.
74. Kimhi, S.; Marciano, H.; Eshel, Y.; Adini, B. Resilience and Demographic Characteristics Predicting Distress During the COVID-19 Crisis. *Soc. Sci. Med.* **2020,** *265*, 113389.
75. Nguyen, H. C.; Nguyen, M. H.; Do, B. N.; Tran, C. Q.; Nguyen, T. T.; Pham, K. M. et al. People with Suspected COVID-19 Symptoms Were More Likely Depressed and Had Lower Health-Related Quality of Life: The Potential Benefit of Health Literacy. *J. Clin. Med.* **2020,** *9* (4), 965.
76. Zhou, X.; Snoswell, C. L.; Harding, L. E.; Bambling, M.; Edirippulige, S.; Bai, X.; Smith, A. C. The Role of Telehealth in Reducing the Mental Health Burden from COVID-19. *Telemed. e-Health* **2020,** *26* (4), 377–379.
77. Gupta, S.; Sahoo, S. Pandemic and Mental Health of the Front-Line Healthcare Workers: A Review and Implications in the Indian Context Amidst COVID-19. *Gen. Psych.* **2002,** *33* (5).
78. Park, J. S.; Lee, E. H.; Park, N. R.; Choi, Y. H. Mental Health of Nurses Working at a Government-Designated Hospital During a MERS-CoV Outbreak: A Cross-Sectional Study. *Arch. Psych. Nurs.* **2018,** *32* (1), 2–6.
79. Wu, P.; Fang, Y.; Guan, Z.; Fan, B.; Kong, J.; Yao, Z. et al. The Psychological Impact of the SARS Epidemic on Hospital Employees in China: Exposure, Risk Perception, and Altruistic Acceptance of Risk. *Can. J. Psych.* **2009,** *54* (5), 302–311.
80. Chen, P.; Mao, L.; Nassis, G. P.; Harmer, P.; Ainsworth, B. E.; Li, F. Coronavirus Disease (COVID-19): The Need to Maintain Regular Physical Activity While Taking Precautions. *J. Sport Health Sci.* **2020,** *9* (2), 103–104.
81. Khee, K. S.; Lee, L. B.; Chai, O. T.; Loong, C. K.; Ming, C. W.; Kheng, T. H. The Psychological Impact of SARS on Health Care Providers. *Crit. Care Shock* **2004,** 100–106.
82. Li, D. K. T. Challenges and Responsibilities of Family Doctors in the New Global Coronavirus Outbreak. *Family Med. Commun. Health* **2020,** *8* (1).

CHAPTER 5

Impact of COVID-19 on Education

NIMRA KANWAL[1], SANA ARSHAD[1], BIRRA DAR[1], SHAHZAD SHARIF[1], FAKHRA AZIZ[2], ARWA ABDULKREEM AL-HUQAIL[3], and MARIUS IRIMIE[4]

[1]*Materials Chemistry Laboratory, Department of Chemistry, GC University Lahore, Pakistan*

[2]*STEM Education Department, Lahore College for Women University, Jail Road Lahore, Pakistan*

[3]*Department of Biology, College of Science, Princess Nourah bint Abdulrahman University, Riyadh, Saudi Arabia*

[4]*Faculty of Medicine, Transilvania University of Brasov, Brasov, Romania*

ABSTRACT

Among various sectors of the world being hit by COVID-19, the global education sector is the worst hit. As a measure to control viral infections, lockdowns were imposed in different parts of the world, which led to the closure of schools and educational institutions. To maintain education during the COVID-19 pandemic, e-learning and other digital technologies were promoted. Various online and social media platforms such as YouTube, Google Classroom, Teams, and Zoom have played vital roles in such a dreadful situation. The global education sector was not ready for this abrupt transition from traditional education to remote learning. This unprecedented workload affected the mental health of mentors and learners. e-Learning is a new dimension for teachers, and they have to struggle a lot to cope up with such a crisis. The nationwide lockdowns and curfews have compounded the lives of international students by introducing financial and health-related issues. The severe acute respiratory syndrome coronavirus

Post-Pandemic Economy, Technology, and Innovation: Global Outlook and Context.
Samina Yaqoob, Arwa Abdulkreem AL-Huqail, and Fakhra Aziz (Eds.)

2 (SARS-CoV-2) crisis has horrific effects on the mental health condition of mentors and students as they suffered from anxiety, social isolation, and depression. Different countries responded to the pandemic in their specific way. However, developed countries were aware of some e-learning modes before the pandemic; thus, they were ready for this shift in education, while developing countries were adversely affected due to poor digital infrastructure and facilities. The pandemic has changed the whole scenario of different aspects of education, and the education sector is exploring alternative ways to tackle this crisis.

5.1 INTRODUCTION

5.1.1 EDUCATION: A SOURCE OF AWARENESS

Education molds a person and makes him better than he was before. Education is based on learning which is essential to develop skills and acquire knowledge by studying, experimenting, and being taught.[1]

Among various mentors from history, Aristotle is adjudged the best mentor ever lived who defined education as:

"The creation of a sound mind in a sound body"

OR

"Education is the process of training man to fulfill his aims by exercising all the faculties to the fullest extent as a member of society"[2]

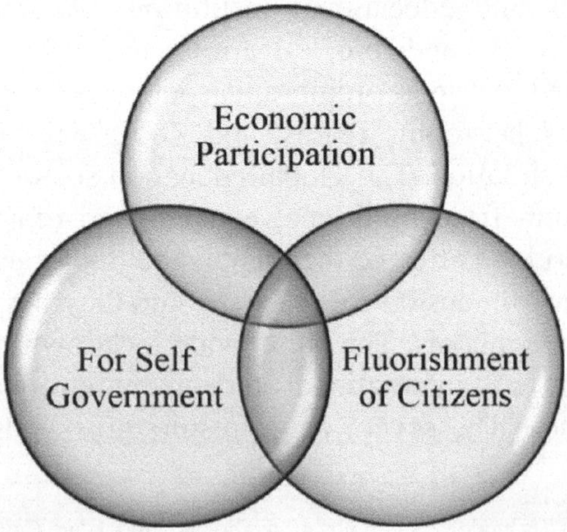

FIGURES 5.1 Aims of education.[3]

True education is not limited to pursuing a defined study course. It is meant to improve the entire life and abilities, that is, physical, spiritual, and mental powers of an individual. Education actually prepares a human being to perform services in his community.[4]

5.1.2 *WAVES OF COVID-19 IMPACTING TRADITIONAL EDUCATION*

COVID-19 is a global outbreak that started at the end of the year 2019 in the seafood market of Wuhan, China. The novel coronavirus (n-CoV) is a member of the severe acute respiratory syndrome (SARS) virus family.[5] SARS outbreak occurred in the year 2002 in China for the first time since then, the coronavirus family has received much attention. SARS and COVID-19 viruses possess quite similar sequences of genes, that is, about 79%. After 17 years of the SARS–CoV outbreak, SARS-CoV-2 first hit China. Since then, the n-CoV has spread worldwide and transmitted to many countries, including the continents of Asia, Europe, America, and Africa, and even a few cases reported in Antarctica. In March 2020, WHO proclaimed COVID-19 as a pandemic, a status which has not been declared for SARS-CoV due to the lack of severity of infection as compared to COVID-19.[6]

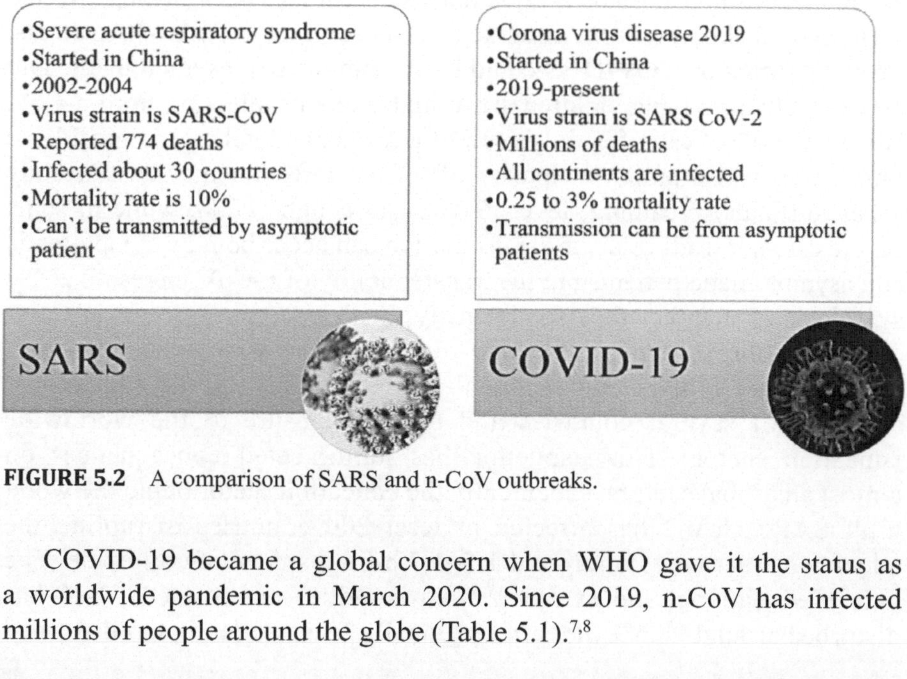

FIGURE 5.2 A comparison of SARS and n-CoV outbreaks.

COVID-19 became a global concern when WHO gave it the status as a worldwide pandemic in March 2020. Since 2019, n-CoV has infected millions of people around the globe (Table 5.1).[7,8]

TABLE 5.1 COVID-19 in Different Countries During June 2020.

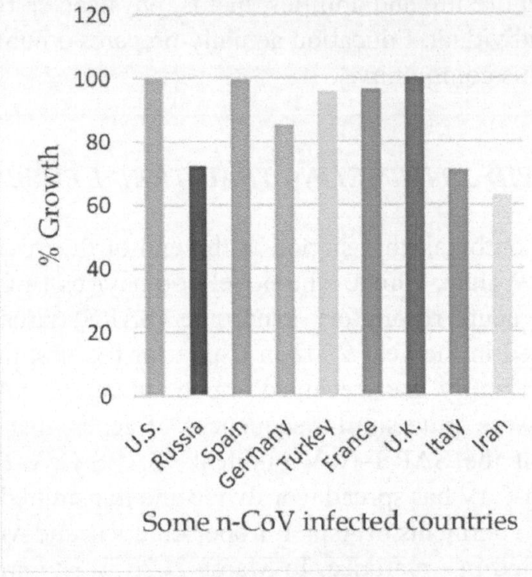

5.1.2.1 COMMON SYMPTOMS OF INFECTION

Zoonotic virus transmission is rapid that can occur through touching affected surfaces and droplets from coughing or sneezing of COVID-19 patients. People affected by COVID-19 could be symptomatic or asymptomatic. Old people and very young children are at high stake of infection from n-CoV. However, n-CoV can affect a person of any age, and nobody is considered immune to it. Common symptoms of n-CoV infection include flu, body aches, difficulty breathing, fever (97%), and cough (77%), while in some severe cases, it leads to death. Transmission can occur both by symptomatic and asymptomatic patients but the transfer ability of n-CoV increases as the symptoms of an infected person intensify.[8]

During the start of the second quarter of the year 2020, this viral epidemic had evolved into a global pandemic affecting the educational activities of several countries and brought closure to the worldwide education sector.[9] This pandemic has multifaceted consequences on almost all global sectors, specifically the education sector being the worst hit.[10] SARS-CoV-2 has affected at least 200 countries disrupting the educational activities of around 1.5–1.7 billion students worldwide. The halt in educational and extracurricular activities due to COVID-19 has disturbed around 98.6% of learners globally. The pandemic has disturbed every aspect of educational and cocurricular activities. Novel learning tools and techniques are being shared to overcome and compensate for the loss of educational activities due to the pandemic. The academic year session 2020–2021 is almost lost to the SARS-CoV-2 pandemic and there is fear of losing some more years in the future due to different waves of pandemic. However, COVID-19 has paved the way for improving e-learning modes and digital technologies.[11]

5.1.2.2 COVID-19 VARIANTS

The SARS-CoV-2 virus is producing its variants which have given rise to waves of COVID-19. One of the main reasons behind these variants and waves is that more people are infected with the virus. As a result, the virus replicates greatly, undergoes mutation, and produces variants that have given rise to different waves of COVID-19 globally. As a result of fast mutation, new COVID-19 variants become resistant to previously designed vaccines. The variants are deadlier than the original coronavirus due to mutation in spike protein. As vaccines are based on spike proteins of SARS-CoV-2 virus, thus their efficacy in building immunity is concerning.[12]

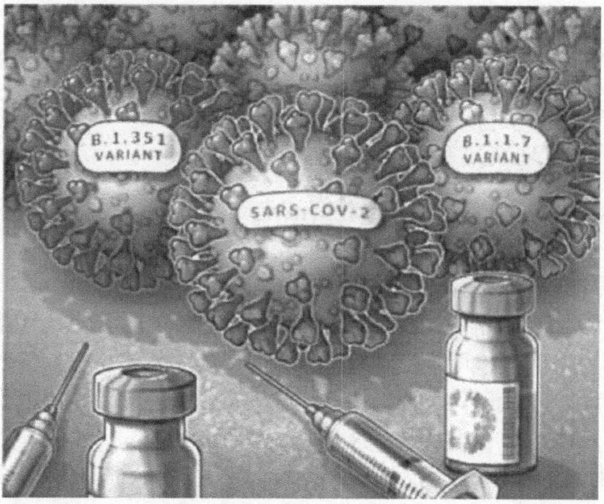

FIGURE 5.3 Variants of SARS-CoV-2.

5.1.2.3 IMPACT OF COVID-19 CRISIS ON TRADITIONAL EDUCATION

The SARS-CoV-2 pandemic has the worst footprint on global education. To control virus transmission, educational sectors have undergone different phases of lockdowns. These lockdowns have paved the way for incorporating digital technology and e-learning to compensate for the loss of education. In such a scenario, education and learning have stepped into a digital web-based world, connecting mentors and learners virtually. As an alternative to traditional education, e-learning has proven to be best for maintaining education during pandemic-induced lockdowns.[1]

The COVID-19 crisis has resulted in the closure of the global education sector as a measure to avoid viral infection. To compensate for the education loss, the world has opted for online or remote learning strategies. Educational institutions around the globe have restarted academic activities by using alternate modes of distant learning to maintain education.[9]

COVID-19 has infected around one hundred and three million people, as reported in January 2021. The USA is at the top of the list of infected countries, with more than 25 million infections and 450,000 deaths. The USA is followed by India, Brazil, and the UK in the highest number of viral infections during the first half of the year 2021. The survivors of viral infection face mental health issues and anxiety. A grim picture of reality is presented upon reviewing literature about the impact of COVID-19 on hundreds of millions of global students.[13]

5.2 PANDEMIC LED INNOVATION OF TECHNOLOGICAL INFRASTRUCTURE

The lockdowns during the SARS-CoV-2 pandemic have disturbed the conventional system of physical learning at campuses. The idea of remote learning has brought several challenges. Students have to continue their learning process by using laptops, computers, mobile phones, and television. This strategy is bringing a dramatic impact on the entire education sector as new modes of education and training of staff are required. Moreover, in developing parts of the world, an extra burden of internet connection and expenditure is evident on students and families.[14]

Building the technological infrastructure is very crucial to overcome the education loss due to the COVID-19 pandemic. As the technologies and devices used in online learning are not available in traditional physical classrooms, lack of participant's perception could be an issue. To build the required educational infrastructure, a learning management system (LMS), a system of education without a classroom but involving regular attendance, assignments, class timing, and testing is mandatory.[15]

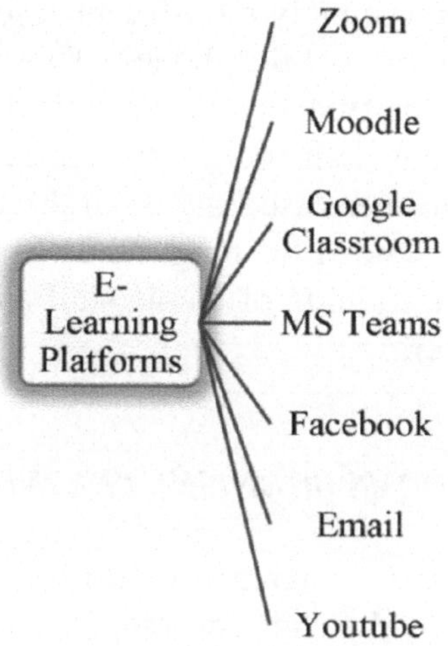

FIGURE 5.4 Variety of e-learning platforms revolutionizing the concept of education.

5.2.1 PLATFORMS FOR E-LEARNING

To combat and compensate for educational loss, the e-learning platforms, that is, Microsoft Teams and Google Classroom, are built to create educational courses and to develop professional skills for the online education system. Building and regulating such online platforms is a time taking process. These platforms share a variety of contents, that is, pre-recorded lectures, audio files, Word files, PDFs, and YouTube links. With the availability of a sea of online platforms learners are facing hiccups in using and referring to these platforms. One of the main challenges for e-learners is the affordability and accessibility of these online courses. Several students across the world have no access to digital devices and unreliable internet connections. In developing parts of the world, students cannot afford expensive electronic devices. Online learning platforms can also be adopted after lockdowns, where they would function to enhance learning and coaching. However, the selection and adoption of a specific system for all teachers and learners have not yet been achieved that can fulfill all requirements.[11]

5.2.2 CONTINUATION OF EDUCATION DURING COVID-19

Among numerous disturbances imposed by the SARS-CoV-2 pandemic, one is the closure of educational institutions across the globe. The closure of institutions has resulted in a transition from face-to-face, or physical, mode of learning to the online system of education. In online education, lectures and lessons are delivered remotely by using internet services and electronic devices, that is, laptops or mobile phones. This unwanted transition has raised many challenges for students, mentors, and educational institutions. The key difference of this transition between developed and developing countries is that in the former case, that is, in the UK, students are already aware of some form of blended learning, while in the latter case, that is, in countries like Cambodia, training of whole staff and students is required to meet the demand of the era.

5.2.2.1 DIFFERENT FORMS OF ONLINE LEARNING

Online education system is recognized by different names, that is, remote/distance learning, blended/hybrid learning, and e-learning. Each type of learning involves the integration of learning with technology.

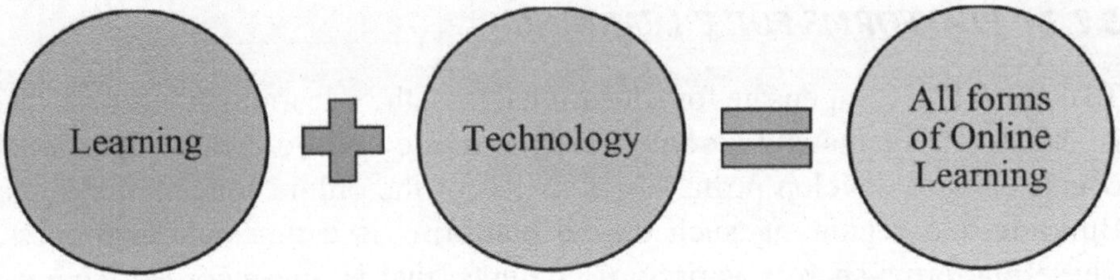

FIGURE 5.5 Transforming the process of learning by utilizing technological advancements.

However, the actual definitions of these terminologies are listed in Table 5.2.

TABLE 5.2 Differentiation Between Different Modes of Digital Learning

e-Learning	Online learning is in the form of regular lessons, discussions, or presentations, entire education is delivered through the internet, the teacher facilitates understanding, and the main responsibility is on the student.
Distance learning	It can be synchronous or asynchronous; helpful for those who are geographically far from the source of education; and used prior to COVID-19.
Hybrid learning	A more fruitful way for connecting students with mentors via integrating traditional and online learning, is not entirely dependent on the student and is comparatively better.

Educational institutions, especially in developing countries such as Pakistan, Indonesia, and Cambodia are not ready for this transition in the education system. There is a need to empower digital competence, technology infrastructure, educational equality, and assessment. Online learning is entirely dependent on the internet and technology devices; a new burden on students. Students in various parts of the world bear problems in online learning due to slow connections, outdated devices, and a lack of knowledge to run various applications. A main hurdle is the socioeconomic border that the students have to cross to benefit from e-learning.[16]

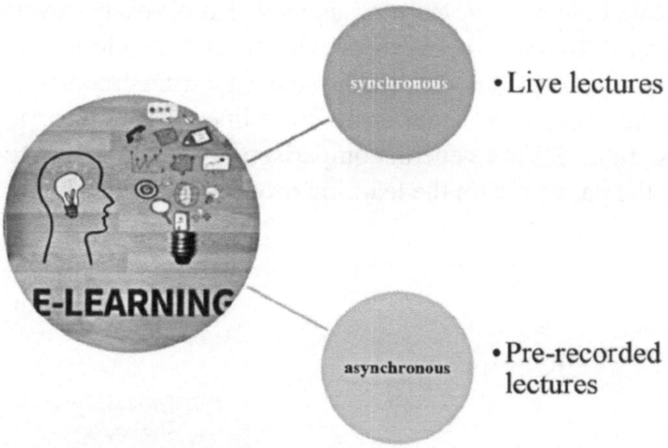

FIGURE 5.6 Types of lectures in e-learning.

Online system of learning has come up with its pros and cons. Some studies claim that online learning has the benefits of being cost effective, less complicated, technology oriented, and availability of hybrid programs. Other studies claim that e-system has fewer social interactions, unreliable assessment, and unequal cost of technology.[17] A popular phrase used in an educational circle is Maslow before Bloom, the purpose of saying this phrase is that our learners are safe, and their basic level needs to be met before the pandemic and online education. The closure of institutions has raised the risk of child abuse and domestic violence in some regions of the world. Reliable assessment and regular feedback are mandatory in educational learning. As a positive part, these requirements are met in online remote learning. Disabled students with a disability such as walking disability, visual impairment, and deafness require additional effort and guidance from their mentors and family. Many disabled students are unable to meet their educational needs. This is a need of the hour to develop and invest in alternative and better ways for the special educational needs (SEN) of this group of students.[11]

5.2.2.2 A COMPARISON OF POSITIVE AND NEGATIVE IMPACTS OF E-LEARNING

Despite all the difficulties that emerged in the transition from traditional methods of learning to digital learning, the pandemic has paved the way for some positive outcomes in learning as well. However, the overall impacts are observed differences between developed and developing countries as some developing countries lack the basic digital infrastructure while developed countries have used some forms of online tools before the pandemic lockdowns. Table 5.3 is a general comparison of some positive and negative impacts of the pandemic on the learning process and education.[18]

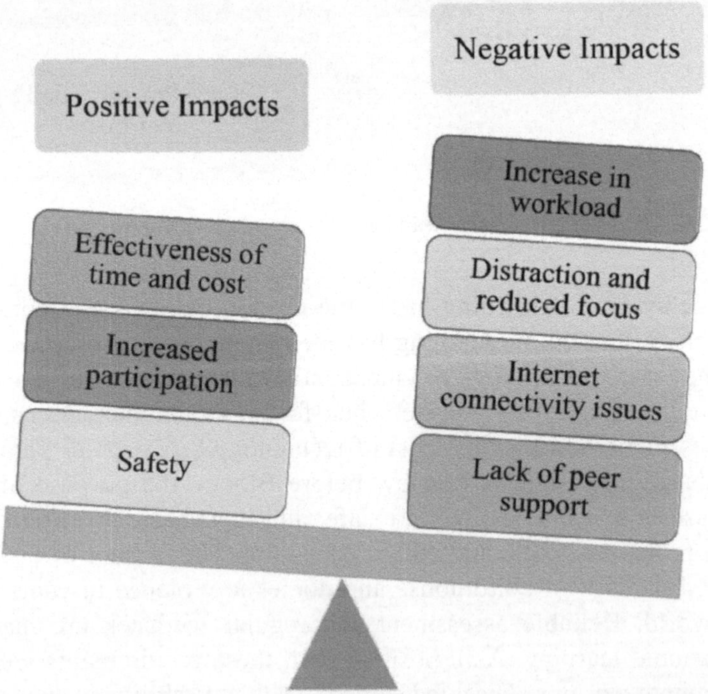

FIGURE 5.7 Maintaining a strict balance between pros and cons to acquire maximum advantage from e-learning.

TABLE 5.3 General Impacts of e-Learning on Students.

Negative Impacts	Categories	Positive Impacts	Categories
Increase in workload	➢ More online assignments, presentations, and quizzes ➢ Classwork became homework	**Effectiveness of time and cost**	➢ Less transportation cost ➢ Less time is consumed in getting ready to go outside to study
Distraction and reduced focus	➢ Due to the physical absence of a mentor, students feel less committed ➢ Incorporating non-educational tasks during online lectures	**Increased participation**	➢ Ease of access to class materials ➢ Ease of expressing ideas
Internet connectivity and technology issues	➢ Due to large number of simultaneous users, slow connectivity ➢ No access to expensive devices ➢ No technology literacy	**Safety**	➢ Reduced danger of getting COVID-19 infection ➢ Decline in number of daily accidents
Inadequate support	➢ No direct access to admins, instructors, and peers ➢ Difficulty in using online platforms		

5.2.2.3 ASSESSMENT IN E-LEARNING

The assessment process is essential for the evaluation of students during pandemic-led lockdowns and digital learning periods. Numerous methods are incorporated by the administration to build an understanding of students' learning abilities during the e-learning phase. Mock tests are considered a systematic way of assessment among many methods available to assess student's learning ability.[1] Most common ways for assessing students in digital learning include

- Open-book exam
- Online quizzes
- PowerPoint presentation
- Case studies
- Online oral
- Report writing
- Essay writings
- Reviews

- Abstracts
- Problem-based assessment methods

5.2.3 COMPARISON BETWEEN TRADITIONAL AND E-LEARNING

This comparison was carried out by taking into account three major aspects of education:

I. In terms of satisfaction and usefulness.
II. In terms of practical applications.
III. In terms of technological issues.

5.2.3.1 IN TERMS OF SATISFACTION AND USEFULNESS

e-Learning has the advantage of maximum coverage to convey instructions to the target audience. By using this type of strategy, similar training is ensured for all learners. However, a large number of students do not find online modes of education feasible despite their benefits and traditional education is still the choice of the majority of students. Traditional education allows the students to participate in classroom debates and discussions with fellows and mentors. A global survey conducted for 175 participants showed 42% of total participants were satisfied with e-learning as they find this type of education to be technology oriented and essential for the present job market. Around 29% of students preferred classroom learning over e-learning. This survey proves that most students find e-learning useful, productive, and satisfactory (Table 5.4).

TABLE 5.4 Response of Participants Toward Traditional and e-Learning in Terms of Satisfaction.

Participants	Percentage	Response
175	**100**	
51	29.1	No
74	42.2	Yes
50	28.5	May be

5.2.3.2 IN TERMS OF PRACTICAL APPLICATIONS

e-Learning has nothing to do with a practical demonstration of learned concepts which becomes highly challenging for medical and research students around the globe. The results of this survey are listed in Table 5.5.

TABLE 5.5 Response Toward Traditional and e-Learning in Terms of Practical Applications.

Participants	Percentage	Response
175	**100**	
13	7.4	No
140	80	Yes
22	12.5	May be

5.2.3.3 *IN TERMS OF TECHNOLOGICAL ISSUES*

Online learning is totally based on powerful internet connections and electronic devices. If there is poor internet connectivity or a power shortage, then online data cannot be accessed. Due to the lack of digital infrastructure in rural areas, students fail to attend virtual classes. The results of the survey on technical issues for learners are listed in Table 5.6.

TABLE 5.6 Response of Learners Toward Traditional and e-Learning in Terms of Technological Issues.

Participants	% age	Response
175	**100**	
94	53.7	No
47	26.8	Yes
34	19.4	May be

5.3 TRAINING MENTORS FOR DIGITAL LEARNING

The SARS-CoV-2 pandemic has brought a transition from face-to-face learning to e-learning. As educational institutes shift to an alternate and innovative online education system, more stress is given to online teaching programs, that is, emergency remote teaching ERT, to prepare mentors around the globe for online education and assessment. COVID-19 has forced teachers and learners to adapt to this digital environment. However, mentors are not ready for the abrupt shifting of traditional education to online education. To compensate the educational loss due to the pandemic, institutes around the world have shifted to digital learning. As a result, teachers are being trained via webinars to facilitate them digital learning. Educators have adopted the "Education in Emergency" strategy to survive in an alternate education system. Adaptation to these new challenges requires supporting and gauging the staff accordingly. While governments and health officials are trying to slow down the spread of COVID-19 infections, educators are trying to impart quality education during this challenging period. However, mentors are confused about which tools should be used for teaching, that is, either pre-recorded lectures or online face-to-face classes. Some teachers recommend online classes, while those with poor internet connection recommend prerecorded video lectures.[11]

Before training students, it is mandatory for institutes to train mentors for this big shift. Online training webinars are an efficient tool during a pandemic to remotely train teachers and enhance their virtual teaching techniques. Online webinars are being a modern method for professional training and pedagogical skill development of tutors to combat difficulties in the online systems. After the completion of online training via webinars, online certificates are awarded to teachers.[20]

5.3.1 ICT FOR TRAINING MENTORS

The COVID-19 crisis has forced the education sector to rethink and reconsider the role of information and communication technology (ICT).[21] The use of pedagogy for the online education system is dependent on the exposure and expertise of educators and mentors to ICT. Online teaching platforms, that is, Microsoft Teams, Zoom Meetings, and Google Classroom have been introduced to build online educational courses and skill development. Teachers are being trained to adopt creative ideas to overcome the limitations imparted by the online education system. To improve online teaching methods, mentors are collaborating among themselves at the local level. Many organizations of education are offering free tools for supporting the learning of mentors in a more creative and engaging environment. Unlike mentoring in traditional classrooms, e-learning has innovated the ideas and ways of learning. A range of techniques has been devised for the digital training and development of technologically backward mentors.[11] ICT (Information and Communication Technology) has helped a lot in training teachers for a big shift in education. The use of ICT is revolutionizing the interaction between mentors and students. ICT trains the teachers

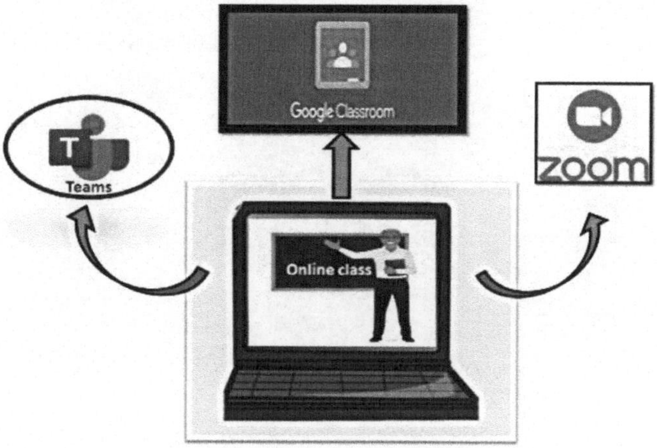

FIGURE 5.8 Training mentors to cope with revolutionization during pandemic.

- To improve their professional skills
- To develop critical thinking
- To engage the students in an online system for efficient learning[22]

Regarding changes in the traditional modes of learning, instructors have to face many problems. So, it was a massive challenge for the mentors to fulfill their duty efficiently and get used to this type of teaching.[23] Instructors play a key role in e-learning but due to the unforeseen shift of learning from off-line to the online system, mentors have to face many difficulties. Mentors were trained to use different applications for virtual learning, for example, Teams, Zoom, and Google Classroom.[24]

The establishment of the desired type of learning and mentoring is also included in ICT training during the designing and planning of online courses. Hence, mentors are trained professionally to fulfill all their obligations during drastic circumstances.[25]

5.3.2 E-MENTORING

Mentorships play a vital role in the education system. e-Mentoring helps oneself with videos, texts, and audio-type communications. e-Mentoring includes asynchronous modes, such as emails, and synchronous such as phone calls, video calls, etc., to develop a connection between mentor and mentee.[26]

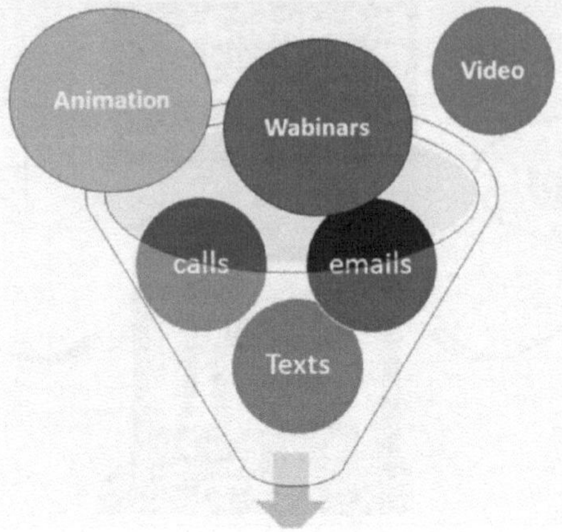

FIGURE 5.9 Different modes in e-mentoring.

New technologies are being used to search for new teaching techniques and strategies for mentors. Utilization information and communication technologies (ICTs) proved to be very helpful as a source of education and efficient interaction between teachers and students.[27]

Major difficulties are faced by mentors during transition of educational system. As teachers were not used to digital teaching method thus their mentoring was more important than students so that they could deliver quality education to students.[28] Placement period of teacher–student is the main part of teaching programs.[29] Special instructors and classes have been arranged for the training of teaching staff. It was time consuming process but proved to be much fruitful. Learning sessions were offered on daily basis at first and they were joined by large number of lecturers.[30] Recordings of those sessions were distributed later to those lecturers who missed them. Essential on-campus facilities were made accessible in soft form for teachers and students.[23] Informal support such as Microsoft Team and Zoom meetings strengthened the online teaching system, which enabled mentors to share their knowledge efficiently with their students and peers.[31]

e-Mentoring exposed mentors to new ways of evaluation to explore students' skills and enhance their creativity. Hence, distinctive modes of evaluation and assessment were organized rather than simple paper–pen tests. These assessment tools included Microsoft assignments, PowerPoint presentations, oral quizzes, reports, and essay writing, which proved to be helpful for mentors to determine the online skills of students in the innovative educational atmosphere.[32]

Teachers are being educated on the following:

- How to communicate with students during online meetings.
- How to maintain the decorum of classroom during an online session.
- How to organize online discussions in classrooms.
- How to keep check and balance during the online examination.
- How to keep students engage in the discussion so that they could not lose their focus during online classes.
- How to have class recordings and feedback after class sessions.[33]

5.3.2.1 PROBLEMS FACED BY MENTORS IN E-MENTORING

During the COVID-19 crisis, the main objective of every educational institute is to sustain the education system during lockdowns and curfews. As teachers and students were unable to attend any physical class during this time so the system could collapse badly. For such an alarming situation, teachers were introduced to this new mode of teaching system that could help them in their interaction with students.[34] Most of the teachers were unaware of such type of online learning, so special classes and webinars were arranged at that time for their training.[35] Surely, it was a challenge to transfer what is taught face to face in online classes. The main challenge was the disconnection between the way that teachers were taught to teach because teachers were not used to such type of teaching method and how the course will be delivered effectively in online classes.[36] Without clear guidelines for mentors to follow, the effectiveness of these online classes could be void. The key issues raised during e-mentoring are as follows:

- Reduced confidence of teachers as there is no face-to-face interaction with learners.
- Less connection with students.
- More pressure on mentors to attain students' attention.
- No efficient assessment system to evaluate students.
- Many teachers struggled with the delivery of content due to a lack of visual contact with their students[37]
- Long hours of sitting in front of cameras caused adverse effects on physical and mental health of mentors.
- Lack of students' attention despite enormous effort.[38]

Mentors struggled a lot in polishing their techno–pedagogical proficiency. Teachers have to step out of their comfort zones to flourish their skills, and to engage students in collaborative activities. Instructors were exposed to new methodologies and jargon like dragon dreaming methodology, flipped classrooms, and self-paced learning. Poor internet connections also caused great hindrance to mentors in delivering their lectures and developing communication with their students.[39]

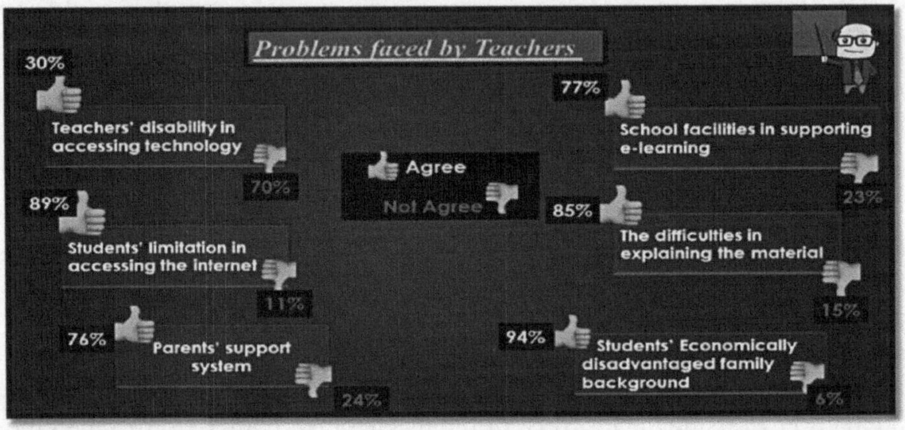

FIGURE 5.10 Results of a survey conducted on problems mentors faced during e-mentoring.

5.3.2.2 STRATEGIES OF E-TEACHING

A survey was conducted to analyze which strategy of e-mentoring was most suitable for the students. The results of which are summarized in Table 5.7.

TABLE 5.7 Strategies for E-Mentoring.

No	Teaching strategies	Percentage %	%	%	%
		Strongly agree	**Agree**	**Disagree**	**Strongly disagree**
1.	Applying video conference	3.6	23.2	64.3	8.9
2.	Using only online chat (WA Group, Google Classroom, zoom)	17.9	58.9	19.6	3.6
3.	Combining both online chat and video conference	4.5	2.5	69.6	5.4
	Average	8.6	34.2	51.2	6

The absence of video communication affects the proper connection between mentors and learners. Different online learning apps such as Zoom meetings, Google Classroom, and Teams were used to maintain an efficient connection between mentors and their students. Students and mentors suffered equally; however, despite all hurdles, they managed to sustain the learning system efficiently. e-Mentoring helped all mentors to flourish their skills for the upcoming technological era. One thing that was agreed upon by all is that mentors worked harder than ever before, and struggled enough to deliver their efforts just to have a pinch of fruitful results during the pandemic.[40]

5.4 WORKLOAD OF EDUCATIONAL INSTITUTIONS

An unprecedented workload has been produced by shifting face-to-face learning to e-learning for students and mentors. For education institutions, leaving the traditional mode of classroom education and integrating external software into their system needs great effort.[16]

5.4.1 WORKLOAD ON TEACHERS

According to a survey conducted in May 2020 in Australia, some teachers describe that this pandemic has engulfed their holiday time, and now there is no time for respite, whereas other mentors complain this paradigm shift as exhausting, draining, and time consuming. The key challenges faced by teachers during this abrupt transition and increase in workload are as follows:

- Insufficient time to fulfill the demands of teaching and learning.
- Working more than contract.
- Not paid for overburden due to work-from-home strategy.
- Self-preparation for teaching online without proper initial training.

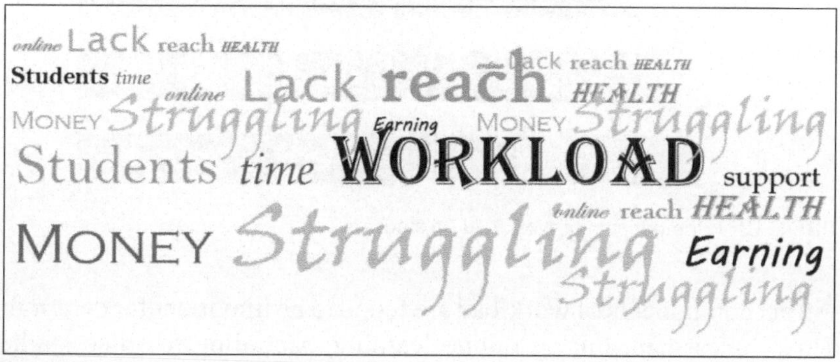

FIGURE 5.11 Most frequent words in response to a survey on the workload of teachers.

Online learning and education system can be innovative for education in the long run but for the academic years 2020–2021, the teachers and students are only surviving to make it through, exhausted beyond measure.[41]

In response to maintaining education, online methods of assessment such as online assignments and quizzes were adopted for which the entire education sector was not ready. Some educational institutions around the globe offered online courses prior to lockdowns. However, for the educational institutions which were not familiar with digital learning and its practical application before the pandemic, the unprecedented shift and navigation were challenging.[18]

5.4.2 WORKLOAD ON STUDENTS

COVID-19 has forced most educational institutions around the world to switch to online learning in an emergency mode as a measure to ensure safety.[42] As a result, during online learning, student workload must be measured and reduced. The workload of e-learning on students is assessed with the following components:

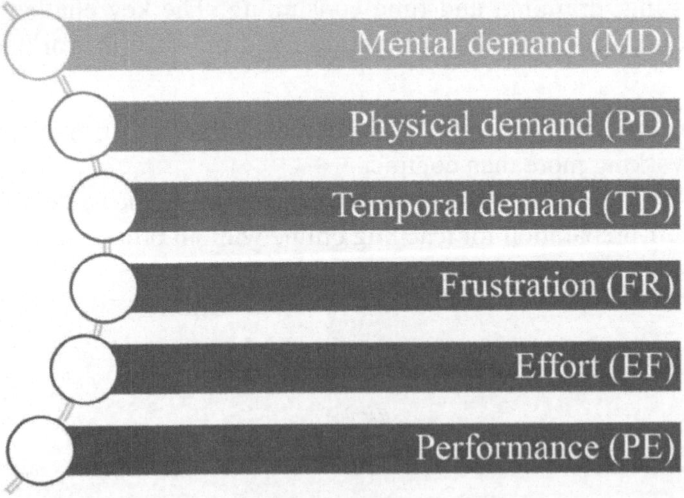

FIGURE 5.12 Components of workload on students.

All six components of workload are found to be important for determining students` assessment during online learning, according to some studies.[43] Many students may struggle to cope with the avalanche of chores they are required to complete and may fall into "survival mode," when their primary emphasis is on completing the absolute minimum of work to meet the next deadline.[44] This fact could have a negative influence on learning quality since students in this mode are more likely to use the surface learning strategy as a coping mechanism to manage their workload.[45]

Some learners may get disheartened and disillusioned, which can lead to a significant drop in situation-specific motivation to learn. With the new normal of remote and hybrid learning, institutes must examine the amount of academic workload students endure, as well as its impact on their learning behavior and motivation.[46,47]

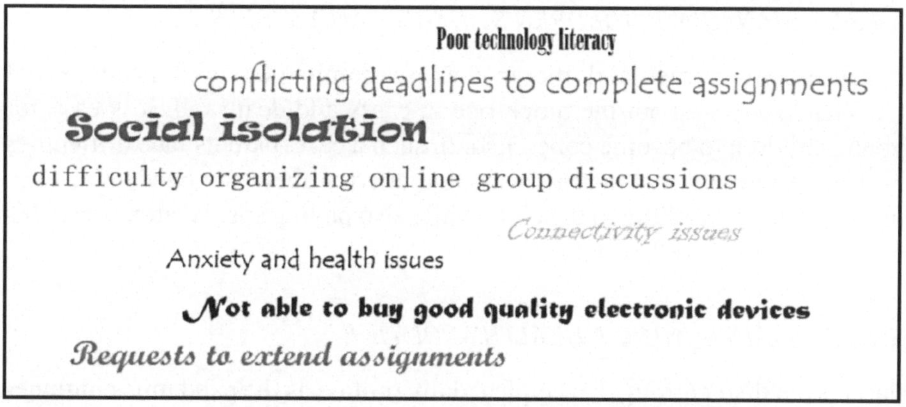

FIGURE 5.13 Feedback from students on key issues during online education.

The number of students who report such issues is quite greater in developing countries in contrast to the number of students in developed and industrialized countries. For instructors, it is mandatory to create learning assignments and module structures based on a set of principles.[48]

5.4.3 WORKLOAD ON FAMILY

Families all over the world have been affected by the COVID-19 pandemic. Parents are in a bind as their homes serve as a school, an office, and a living space all at the same time.[49] Even if parents have more time with their children, the stress of juggling several roles makes it difficult for them to devote time to parenting. Parents are finding it challenging to focus on different parts of their children's overall development since youngsters and parents remain confined to their houses.[50]

5.4.3.1 PROVIDING ASSISTANCE TO CHILDREN DURING ONLINE CLASSES

Parents have become actually home–school instructors and tuition teachers as a result of the COVID-19 pandemic. Parents are struggling to keep their children on track and assist them with homework. If the children are in different grades, the challenge is multiplied. Many parents are concerned about ensuring that their children attend online lessons on time, finish their homework and give it to the teacher, and are prepared for the next day's class.[51]

5.4.3.2 MANAGING CHILDREN'S ANXIETY AND STRESS

Because the internet and the media are bombarded with headlines of COVID-19 news about the quick rise in cases and death toll, it is easy for young children to become concerned. In such a case, parents face difficulties in dealing with their children's fears and queries about the pandemic. They must explain everything to the child while also paying special attention to his or her emotional well-being.[52]

5.4.3.3 MAINTAINING A HEALTHY ROUTINE

Parents are disregarding their typical daily routine as the pandemic continues and the weight of domestic and professional duties grows. As a result, children's habits and routines tend to be erratic.[53] It has become increasingly difficult for parents to keep their children on a strict schedule, with set times for meals, studying, and sleeping.[54]

Routine provides comforting predictability for young children, and they remain enthusiastic throughout the day. Parents, on the other hand, are unable to restore a framework, and as a result, youngsters lose interest in almost everything.[55] Routine provides comforting predictability for young children, and they remain enthusiastic throughout the day. Parents, on the other hand, are unable to restore a framework, and as a result, youngsters lose interest in almost everything.[56]

5.4.3.4 MANAGING BEHAVIORAL ISSUES

During the pandemic, children are unable to see their friends, play outside, or spend an evening in the park because they are restricted to their houses.

As a result, they get stressed and tend to misbehave to vent their frustration.[57] Young children may exhibit their dissatisfaction in a variety of ways, including temper tantrums, violence, and increased clinginess. Parents are having a difficult time reassuring and assisting their children in dealing with this stressful scenario.[58]

5.4.3.5 MAINTAINING CHILDREN'S INTEREST

COVID-19 isn't just a viral disease; it is also a mentally and psychologically exhausting crisis. People are unable to interact with one another or meet their loved ones. Not just adults, but also youngsters, are having difficulty adjusting to this environment.[59] Parents of small children are finding it difficult to keep them involved in meaningful activities since schools have closed. In this situation, the role of parents is critical. Many parents lack the necessary teaching resources and hence are unable to successfully teach their children. As a result, youngsters miss out on a critical stage in their educational and developmental journey.[60]

5.5 INTERNATIONAL STUDENT MOBILITY

The international student mobility (ISM) is a basic component of sets of multinational movements and migrations.[61] To achieve personal and professional skills, geographical movement of youth arises.[19]

5.5.1 BENEFITS OF ISM

- Cross-cultural communication.
- Cultural awareness and tolerance.
- Development of knowledge and skills.
- Global citizenship.
- Professional development.
- Self-confidence due to mixed cultures.
- Comfortability in a multicultural setting.
- Improved ability to expression.
- Enhanced critical thinking ability.
- Economic contribution.[62,63]

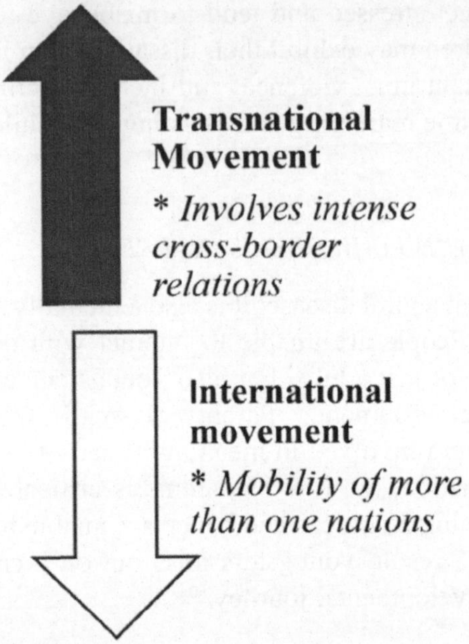

FIGURE 5.14 Types of movements.

In response to SARS-CoV-2 pandemic, the movement of students across the world is disrupted due to flight curtailment, travel restrictions, and closure of borders. Due to the abrupt closure, international students were stuck at deserted education campuses and hostels.[19] In some countries, foreign students faced social exclusion.[64] Many students have delayed their plan of going abroad to study as a measure to avoid infection. Thus, the higher education institutes (HEIs) of host countries, such as the US, Canada, Australia, and the UK, have predicted a decline in the numbers of global students for the academic year 2020–2022.[19,21,65,66]

5.5.2 COVID CRISIS AND ISM

Unlike regional disasters, such as earthquakes, the pandemic spreads with mobility; thus, special restrictive measures are taken to control its expansion. International students, particularly, the southern learners, require more support from the host northern countries during movement halt in response to the pandemic. Global northern countries are those countries that lead the global education system. Learners from the south, being less developed, are attracted to northern global countries. The pandemic has socially and economically affected the mobility and lives of international students.[67]

A halt in the social and physical activities of youth has resulted in the adoption of sedentary behavior, that is, the behavior performed in a sitting position that requires $\leq$1.5 metabolic equivalent of task (METs) of energy. Inactivity has adverse effects on cardiovascular, muscular, and metabolic functions. The World Health Organization (WHO) recommends about 75 min of excessive physical activity per 1 week. A study conducted in three Italian universities at the end of the first lockdown showed increased use of electronic devices, that is, laptops and mobile phones, that is, +52.4 min/day.[68] The delayed academic activities, lack of social interaction, and halt in physical activities have declined students' mental health and functioning.[65]

International students have faced social, economic, education, equalization, and health issues during COVID-crisis. The host countries have also faced economic and employment issues due to the frozen mobility of global students.[19]

5.5.2.1 TRENDS OF ISM IN TWO DECADES

Trends in ISM have been changing continuously with the passage of time.[69,70] Evidently, the trend alteration is affected by a plethora of factors ranging from the political decisions of superpowers to the financial and economic conditions prevailing all around the globe. A keen analysis of the trends to affect ISM determines three major waves in these two decades.[71]

5.5.2.1.1 Trend #1

This trend was observed for a sexennial starting from 1999 to 2006.[72] During this period of 6 years, the mobility of international students was determined by the unfortunate incident of 9/11 and the desire of students and institutes for research excellence. The factor that stimulated the students was the financial funding while institutes were looking for young, creative minds.[73]

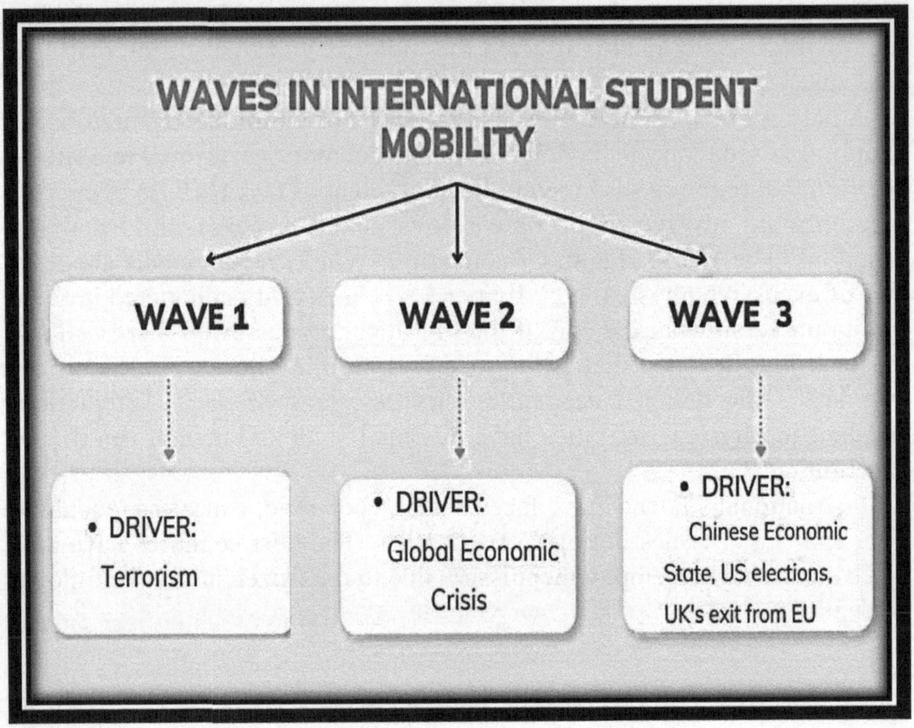

FIGURE 5.15 Waves in international student mobility.

5.5.2.1.2 Trend #2

The determinant behind this trend was an economic decline and downturn on a global scale.[74] Nations were struggling, so the higher education departments of countries were compelled to admit international students as they were a source of capital. This transformed the platform into a market where institutes were advertised to get a hold of the buyers, that is, in this case, the international students.[75] This wave lasted longer than the first one, that is, from 2006 to 2013.

5.5.2.1.3 Trend #3

The latest wave was shaped by the declining economy of China, the mandate of the UK to leave from the European Union (EU), and the presidential election in the United States.[76] This trend lasted till 2020.

5.5.3 PREVAILING TREND

The trend prevailing, although not defined yet, is most probably shaped by the pandemic. The institutes in the current situation are pressurized to ensure maximum international admittance and also retain the balance between the well-being of institute and the facilities and services provided to the international students.[62]

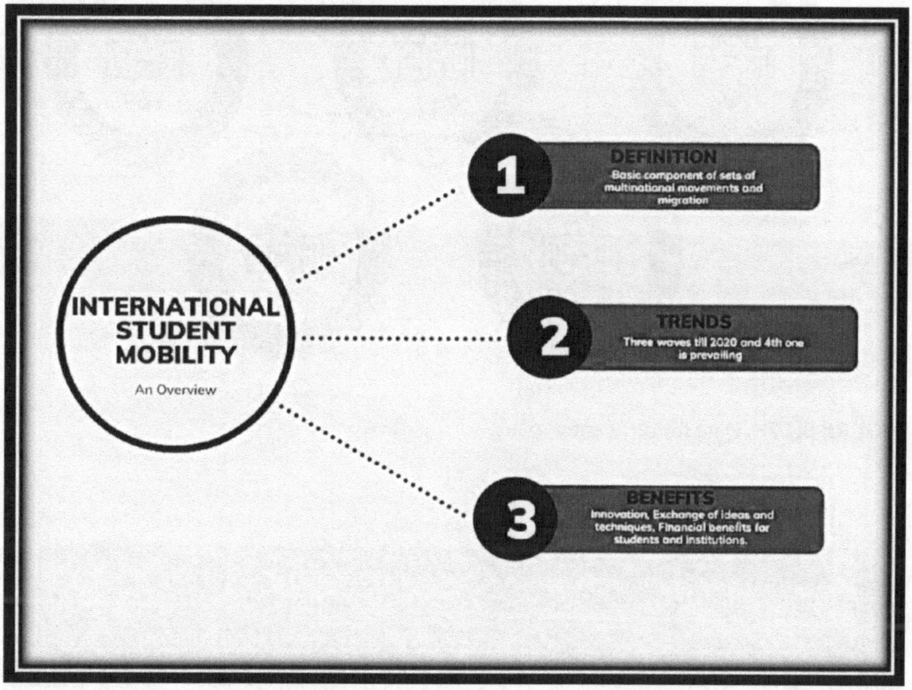

FIGURE 5.16 A general description of ISM.

The mobility of students, nationally or internationally, is related to education, training, and internship processes.[77] According to a survey of the year 2020–2021, the number of students declined to 15% as compared to recent years. Due to the pandemic, the enrollment of international students declined to 64%, which is much more striking.[78] Main purpose of developed countries accepting students from other countries is to encourage students to return to play a vital role in the development of their homeland.[79] Nearly 33 universities worldwide supported the mobility of students during the pandemic, while 60% of worldwide universities increased virtual mobility during the pandemic. Developed countries such as Australia, Canada, the UK, China, and the USA host most of the students every year and assist them to fulfill their dreams.[80] This public health crisis has many negative impacts on the mobility of students, as described in Figure 5.8.[81]

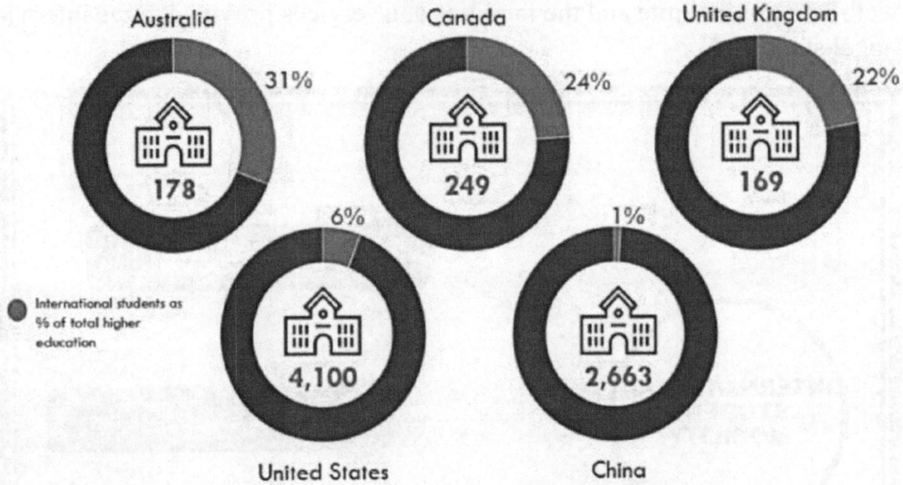

FIGURE 5.17 Data for different regions.

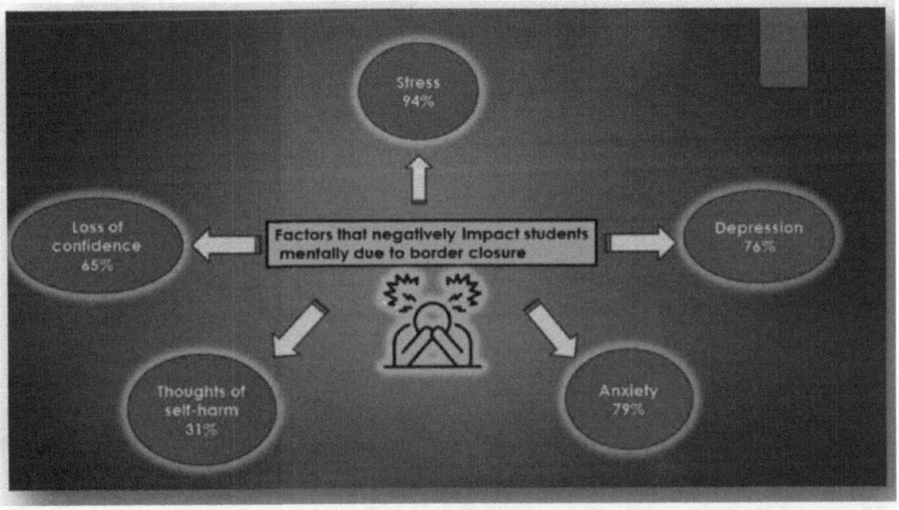

FIGURE 5.18 Impact of SARS-CoV-2 crisis in disrupting ISM and related factors.

5.5.4 CHALLENGES FACED BY INTERNATIONAL STUDENTS DURING PANDEMIC

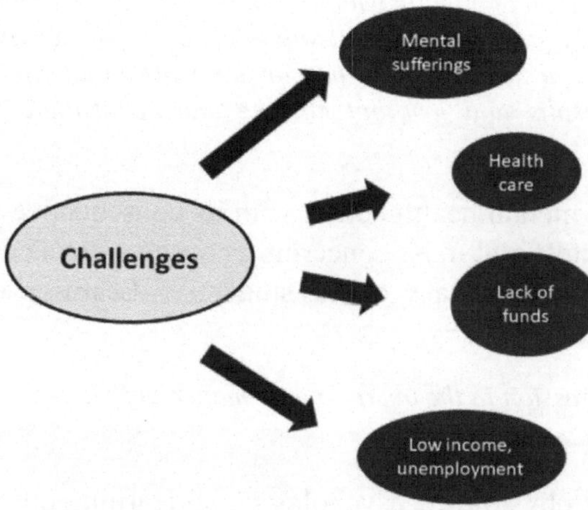

FIGURE 5.19 Challenges faced by international students during pandemic.

Due to the pandemic, the students settled abroad had to face many challenges and hindrances listed as follows:

- Lack of adequate funding.
- Unemployment.
- Difficulty in the adoption of e-learning.[82]
- Protection and safety measures against lethal COVID-19.[83]
- Social isolation in host countries.

These challenges have pushed many students toward anxiety, depression, frustration, and boredom and also affected their academic patterns badly.[67]

5.6 MENTAL HEALTH AND LEARNING EFFICIENCY DURING PANDEMIC

Pandemics have a history of impacting the mental well-being of students in an adverse manner.[84] This pattern was repeated once again by the latest pandemic of SARS-CoV-2 in 2019.[85,86] The COVID-19 crisis not only affected mental health but also created such physiological alterations that, in turn, resulted in the deterioration of the mental health of individuals, especially the student body all-round the globe.[87,88] The precisely described definition of mental health was coined by the organization WHO:

> *A state or condition of mind in which an individual or a person is precisely able to deal with common stressful situations of his or her life, recognize the traits and abilities present in him or her, work in an efficient manner to produce results and last but not the least contribute towards the community.*[89]

This effect on mental health comes with its consequences. Talking about students, the greatest and most concerning consequence is the effect on the learning capacity and efficacy of the students.[90] Learning efficacy can be defined as follows:

> *Extent of progression in the overall performance definiteness and the ratio of speed to the learning time.*[91]

Evidently, the physiology, psychology, and learning efficacy of an individual are closely interlinked. Changing one will alter the other two. Let us first discuss the physical, social, and physiological effects that can influence the mental status and condition of the students amid the prevailing pandemic.

5.6.1 ASPECTS AFFECTING THE MENTAL STATUS OF STUDENTS

Although there are many factors during the pandemic that can lead to deteriorated mental health, some are more important than others. Some of these factors are as follows:

5.6.1.1 FINANCIAL SETBACK

Most of the students in their high school and college years earn for themselves. They strike a healthy balance between study, recreation, and their part-time jobs. However, owing to the lockdowns, over time, a greater percentage of students lost their part-time jobs due to the closure of the commercial sector. Apart from this, most of the students relied on the school to provide them with at least one free meal a day. The closure of educational institutions and the shift toward remote learning systems deprived them of this facility. Now, students, especially those who were located away from their homes, have to worry about their necessities, more than they had to do prior to the pandemic. In this time of crisis, when most adults were struggling to cope with the financial setback, it became stressful for the young minds to maintain the previously stroked balance, which then resulted in compromised mental health.

5.6.1.2 LOSS OF FOCUS OWING TO DISTRACTIONS

Students were not able to focus on their studies, considering the plethora of distractions around them. For instance, most of the students had lost someone in their immediate family at the hands of COVID-19. This not only created fear but also distracted them from their educational goals. Moreover, screen time had increased exponentially. Students try to distract themselves from the problems and stresses of daily life, but unknowingly they distracted them from their studies. Besides, they become more anxious due to the great amount of unfiltered information that they receive about the prevailing situation. Evidently, we can say that the students become distressed to distracted.[92]

5.6.1.3 STRESSORS, EXACERBATING ANXIETY IN STUDENTS

In most third world countries where the internet is not a necessity but a facility, a stable internet connection is not a facility that everyone can access. This creates a gap between those who have and those who lack and, in the long run, serves as a stressor for students who are already dealing with a lot of problems.[93] Apart from this, grades, and assignments, as well as the monetary issues, also burden the young sapling minds to the extent that their mental well-being is compromised.[94]

5.6.1.4 PHYSIOLOGICAL ALTERATIONS

The mental status of any individual is best revealed by his or her physiological practices such as sleeping and eating. Staying inside the residences has disturbed the sleep–wake cycle. Some sleep a lot, while others do not get the necessary amount of sleep. Another form of sleep regularity is the difficulty in sleeping or waking up.[95] Similarly, eating habits have been altered in the wrong way. Besides, people also indulge in emotional eating. These changes in the physiological habits, directly affect the psychological and mental health of the students.[96]

Some students also face mental illnesses when they are not able to work efficiently due to altered physiological working of their body, after their post-recovery from infection.

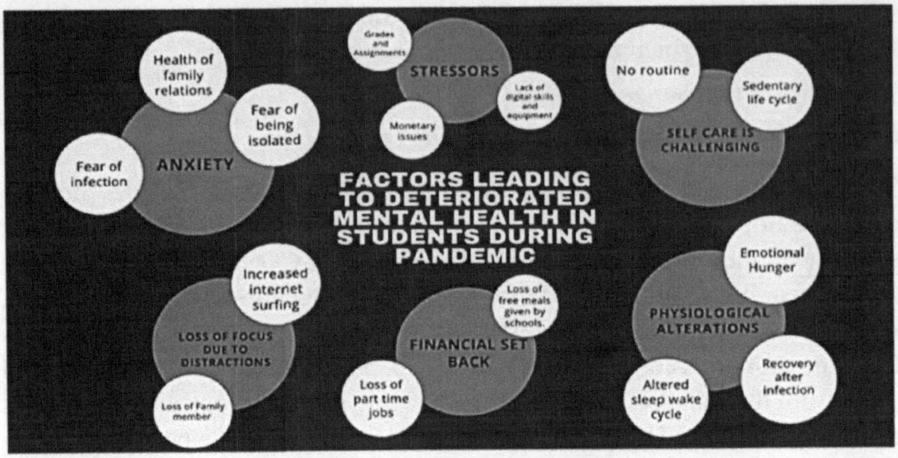

FIGURE 5.20 Factors impacting the mental health of learners during the SARS-CoV-2 crisis.

5.6.1.5 FEAR OF INFECTION AND SOCIAL ISOLATION

Studies have revealed that students are known to show some abnormalities in their behavior owing to the pandemic. A keen analysis of students in Turkey revealed that they want to use gloves for even their everyday tasks, and they also show an abnormal handwashing routine.[97] Moreover, the biggest concern that creates enormous fear is the fear of getting isolated. Students cope with the stressors through recreational activities and going out and meeting with people. However, the pandemic has left the students in isolation.[98] Besides, students living in distant locations from their families are also concerned about the health of their families.[99]

5.6.1.6 CHALLENGES FACED DURING SELF-CARE

Maintaining discipline during isolation and quarantine is a very difficult task. This has made self-care an extremely difficult feat. Moreover, the sedentary lifestyle not only alters the body physiologically but also psychologically.[100]

5.6.2 RELATIONSHIP BETWEEN THE PROSPECTS AND LEARNING EFFICACY OF THE STUDENT

These prospects are closely related to the learning ability and the efficacy of students all around the globe. This relation can be best explained by the fact that learning efficacy can be enhanced greatly by engaging students in real-life situations and by ensuring proper engagement and communication with other students around them. However, as a result of the quarantine and isolation, students are not allowed to leave their residences, due to which they cannot apply their studies to their real life. Moreover, they are not able to engage with their class fellows as effectively as they did before. This has largely affected their learning capability and impacted their efficacy in an adverse manner.[101]

5.6.3 METHODS TO COPE WITH MENTAL STRESS AND ANXIETY

The need of the hour is to find ways to cope with the above-mentioned factors that are maliciously affecting the mental well-being of the scholars. For this purpose, following steps can be taken:

FIGURE 5.21 Ways to cope with mental illness during pandemic.

5.6.3.1 PROMOTING THE IDEA OF PHYSICAL DISTANCING RATHER THAN SOCIAL DISTANCING

First, we need to make corrections in the term distancing. The term commonly used is social distancing when the need of the hour is physical distancing and not social distancing.[102] If we want to alleviate the anxiety and stress, then we need to stay connected. Promoting this feeling of connectedness will decrease the fear of isolation and solitude during the long periods of quarantine and lockdown. In this way, students will never feel lonely and will be able to study properly and maintain their mental health along with it.

5.6.3.2 *DIFFUSING APPROPRIATE AWARENESS*

As we have heard that half knowledge is more dangerous than ignorance. The same is the case with the present condition. People are not completely educated and aware of the limitation, symptoms, and manifestations of the virus. Therefore, our priority is to make the students aware of the proper knowledge about the virus and its manifestations.[103]

5.6.3.3 *DECREASE IN SCREEN TIME*

Internet surfing is the most serious cause of depression in youngsters, specifically students, even on normal days. Greater the on-screen time, the greater the intake of information and the lesser the time to process it. In this way, the person accepts the information as it is without thinking about anything. So, decreasing screen time will allow the students to give more time to their studies and keep them away from information from unauthorized sites.

5.6.3.4 *DEVELOPING A SENSE OF SELF-CONTROL*

Having a sense of control is the greatest achievement for an individual. Self-control creates self-discipline. If a student works to achieve his goal, then he will be able to cope with the distractions and focus on his studies as a result of which he or she can learn efficiently even in this era of remote and online studies.[104]

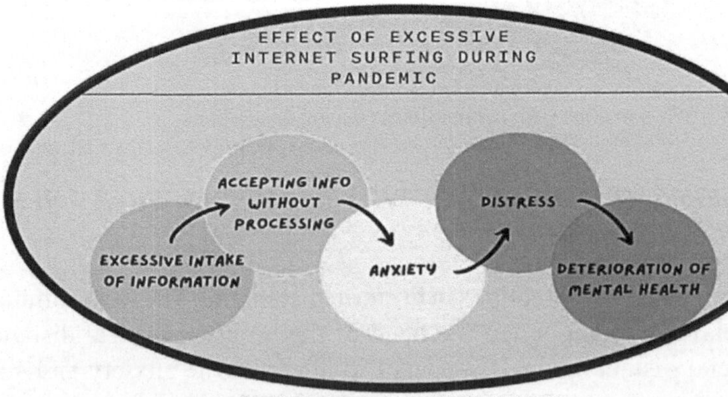

FIGURE 5.22 Negative impacts of internet surfing.

5.7 RESPONSE OF GLOBAL EDUCATION SECTOR TOWARD PANDEMIC/COVID CRISIS

The COVID-19 pandemic has disrupted the quality of learning and teaching, career goals, and academic activities of students and mentors. According to a survey carried out by UNESCO, the educational activities of more than half of the world's students have been disturbed by nationwide lockdowns and educational institutions' closures in more than 100 countries. Boris Johnson, the Prime Minister of Britain, acknowledged the lockdown of educational institutions to lower the rising curve of COVID-19 infections. The COVID-19 pandemic has created gaps in the global education system. Apart from destroying the global health sector, it has also disrupted the worldwide traditional education system. This outbreak has caused the closure of educational institutions, the transition from physical classes to online lectures, the loss of tutor's jobs, and much more, as presented in Fig. 5.27:

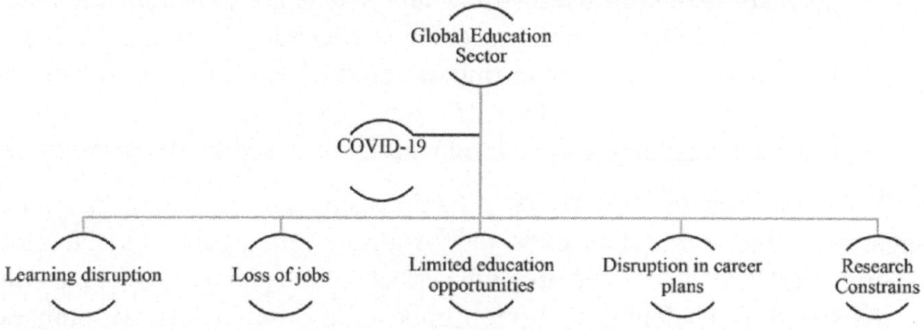

FIGURE 5.23 Presentation of global education sector responses toward the pandemic.

From America to Asia, no nation is immune to the SARS-CoV-2 pandemic. Educational sectors of many nations, including the giant powers, were not prepared for the pandemic. In response to WHO guidelines to reduce the lockdowns due to coronavirus infections and standard operating procedures (SOPs) were imposed worldwide. Here is an overview of responses from the education sectors of developed and developing nations:

- ➢ In the USA, schools were closed during the waves of the pandemic, which resulted in affecting around 60 million students.
- ➢ In Spain, school closure disrupted the job contracts of people working in special education and cafeterias, apart from affecting some 11 million learners.
- ➢ Ministry of Education in Saudi Arabia ordered the closure of schools and universities and opted for virtual schooling.

- In Australia, some schools were closed and few remained open with strict SOPs. The government of Australia believed that children are at low risk of this viral infection.
- In Italy, the military was deployed to ensure school closure.
- In India, a curfew was imposed, and all educational institutions were closed.
- The Government of Zambia ordered curtailment of all educational activities and closure of academic institutions as of March 2020. In a district of Zambia, three mentors were interviewed. The data collected from these interviews predicted a decline in performance as a consequence of lost student–mentor interaction.[10]
- Similarly, in France, Iran, Pakistan, China, South Africa, Nigeria, North and South Korea, Lebanon, Ghana, Ethiopia, Vietnam, Germany, and Russia, school closures and lockdowns were ensured.
- While on the other hand, in some countries such as Brazil and Singapore, some regions of Australia, and Sweden schools remained open with strict SOPs. The unprecedented education institutions' closure has proved to be supporting in curtailment of viral infections. However, millions of students around the globe have been exposed to severe challenges in their education, imposed by the pandemic.

Disruption due to COVID-19 infections and curfews may last much longer than the world has expected. Andrey Azoulayals, the Director–General of UNESCO, warned about the effects of the pandemic on education as "the speed of academic disruption imposed by the COVID-19 outbreak could threaten the educational rights of students if prolonged." During this critical period of the pandemic, if the students are not productively engaged in curricular activities, it could give rise to the following incidents:

- Involvement of students in crime.
- Poor academic performance.
- Mental health concerns.

The education of disabled students is worst hit by the pandemic as the needs for guidance and extra physical attention are not met.

5.7.1 MODES OF EDUCATIONAL INSTITUTIONS CLOSURE

Apart from special students, laboratory researchers are also facing disruption in their usual work. They are allowed to work in laboratories under strict SOPs devised by the administration of the institution.

Governments of COVID-19-affected countries have imposed lockdowns, initiated home–schooling systems, and academic campuses closure as a measure to avoid the contagion. A paradigm shift from traditional education to online learning has been imposed. COVID-19 imposed closure of campuses has impeded cognition, learning and caused anxiety among students and staff.

5.7.2 RESPONSE OF MEDICAL AND DENTAL UNIVERSITIES

As far education of medical students is concerned, they are more likely to exhibit impaired competency and performance due to the suspension of internships in hospitals. In the UK, medical students have exhibited poor performance in examinations due to the suspension of attendance at clinical practices. During the pandemic, the assessment of final-year medical students in the UK is comparatively poor than the pre-COVID assessment. The measures taken to tackle the pandemic's adverse impact on education include online problem-based learning strategies. In China, medical colleges were sealed, and all examinations were delayed as a response to combat the pandemic. During the first wave of COVID-19, Canadian Government paused clinical clerkships for at least 6 weeks. The Association of American Medical Colleges in March of 2020 halted clinical rotations of medical students, and colleges were allowed to take decisions according to their particular circumstances. Training of neurosurgery residents was impacted as they were ordered to cancel all educational gatherings. The rotations were postponed for the preservation of personal protective equipment PPE. Medical organizations suggest suspension of contact between patients and non-essential surgery residents to protect residents without compromising practice and knowledge. During the pandemic, at the University of Washington, the general surgery residency program was rebuilt and restructured as an emergency requirement.

In the USA, a report on alternative ways of learning and assessment, along with the schedule of curricular changes, was submitted to Commission on Dental Accreditation (CODA) by all dental schools to ensure safety without disrupting education. Owing to the pandemic emergency, many dental schools suspended clinical practices. The European dental academies resorted to synchronous non-clinical learning, virtual tools, online meetings, and pedagogical software.[10]

5.8 CONCLUSIONS

The SARS-CoV-2 crisis was initiated in the last month of 2019 and since then, it has created havoc and disrupted a plethora of different sectors of the world. Unfortunately, one of the most highly influenced sectors is the educational sector. To compensate for the educational loss to some extent and to ensure safety, e-learning, and e-mentoring were introduced as alternative modes. Teachers and students were not prepared for such a drastic deviation from the conventional trends and thus their minds were clouded by anxiety, depression, and fear, which in turn gave rise to learning disabilities. Data reveal that the most commonly employed modes used for lecturing are prerecorded audios and videos; powerful software that includes Microsoft Teams, Zoom, Doodle, and Google Classroom. As known earlier, any institute harbors two types of students, one local student, and the other international students. During this critical time, international students faced issues of being stuck at deserted campuses; thus, their academic year 2020–2021 was lost. Owing to these problems faced by the students, each nation adopted a different form of combat strategy that primarily depended on its available sources, that is, both economic as well as digital). However, challenges are aggravated in countries that lack digital infrastructure, and thus they are not able to provide a stable internet connection to their learners.

KEYWORDS

- **COVID-19**
- **universities**
- **blended learning**
- **virtual learning**
- **distance learning**
- **science education**

REFERENCES

1. Radha, R. et al. E-Learning During Lockdown of Covid-19 Pandemic: A Global Perspective. *Int. J. Control Autom.* **2020,** *13* (4), 1088–1099.
2. Robb, F. C. Aristotle and Education. *Peabody J. Educ.* **1943,** *20* (4), 202–213.
3. Brighouse, H. *On Education*; Routledge, 2006.
4. White, E. G. H. *Education*; AB Publishing, 1903.
5. Toquero, C. M. Challenges and Opportunities for Higher Education Amid the COVID-19 Pandemic: The Philippine Context. *Pedagogical Res.* **2020,** *5* (4).
6. Liu, Q. et al. From SARS to COVID-19: What Lessons Have We Learned? *J. Infect. Public Health* **2020.**
7. Bozkurt, A. et al. A Global Outlook to the Interruption of Education Due to COVID-19 Pandemic: Navigating in a Time of Uncertainty and Crisis. *Asian J. Dist. Educ.* **2020,** *15* (1), 1–126.
8. Abebe, E. C. et al. The Newly Emerged COVID-19 Disease: A Systemic Review. *Virol. J.* **2020,** *17* (1), 1–8.
9. Zhuo, H. Learning from Global Education Arrangement During COVID-19 Pandemic Period. *Int. J. Manage. Educ. Human Dev.* **2021,** *1* (02), 80–85.
10. De, S. *Impacts of the Covid-19 Pandemic on Global Education*, 2020.
11. Pokhrel, S.; Chhetri, R. A Literature Review on Impact of COVID-19 Pandemic on Teaching and Learning. *High. Educ. Fut.* **2021,** *8* (1), 133–141.
12. Rubin, R. COVID-19 Vaccines vs Variants—Determining How Much Immunity Is Enough. *JAMA* **2021,** *325* (13), 1241–1243.
13. Bajaba, S., Mandurah, K.; Yamin, M. A Framework for Pandemic Compliant Higher Education National System. *Int. J. Info. Technol.* **2021**, 1–8.
14. Schleicher, A. The Impact of COVID-19 on Education Insights from Education at a Glance, 2020. oecd.org website: https://www. oecd. org/education/the-impact-of-covid-19-on-education-insights-education-at-a-glance-2020,pdf
15. Sari, T.; Nayır, F. Challenges in Distance Education During the (Covid-19) Pandemic Period. *Qual. Res. Educ.* **2020,** *9* (3), 328–360.
16. Piseth, N.; Charungkaittikul, S. Proposed Strategies to Strengthen Community Participation in Community Learning Centers in The Kingdom of Cambodia. Humanities, Arts and Social Sciences Studies (Former Name Silpakorn University Journal of Social Sciences, Humanities, and Arts), 2021, 436–446.
17. Ramij, M.; Sultana, A. Preparedness of Online Classes in Developing Countries Amid COVID-19 Outbreak: A Perspective from Bangladesh. Afrin, Preparedness of Online Classes in Developing Countries amid COVID-19 Outbreak: A Perspective from Bangladesh, June 29, 2020.
18. Maqableh, M.; Alia, M. Evaluation Online Learning of Undergraduate Students Under Lockdown Amidst COVID-19 Pandemic: The Online Learning Experience and Students' Satisfaction. *Child. Youth Serv. Rev.* **2021,** *128*, 106160.
19. Yıldırım, S. et al. Rethinking Mobility of International University Students During COVID-19 Pandemic. *High. Educ. Eval. Dev.* **2021.**
20. Toquero, C. M.; Talidong, K. J. Webinar Technology: Developing Teacher Training Programs for Emergency Remote Teaching Amid COVID-19. *Interdisc. J. Virtual Learn. Med. Sci.* **2020,** *11* (3), 200–203.

21. Mok, K. H. et al. Impact of COVID-19 Pandemic on International Higher Education and Student Mobility: Student Perspectives from Mainland China and Hong Kong. *Int. J. Educ. Res.* **2021,** *105*, 101718.
22. Paudel, P. Online Education: Benefits, Challenges and Strategies During and After COVID-19 in Higher Education. *Int. J. Stud. Educ.* **2021,** *3* (2), 70–85.
23. Howard, C. Mentoring Teacher Trainees in Times of COVID-19: Reflection on Practice. *Practice* **2021,** *3* (2), 128–134.
24. Wiyono, B. B.; Indreswari, H.; Putra, A. P. The Utilization of "Google Meet" and "Zoom Meetings" to Support the Lecturing Process During the Pandemic of COVID-19. In *2021 International Conference on Computing, Electronics & Communications Engineering (iCCECE)*, 2021, IEEE.
25. Donitsa-Schmidt, S.; Ramot, R. Opportunities and Challenges: Teacher Education in Israel in the Covid-19 Pandemic. *J. Educ. Teach.* **2020,** *46* (4), 586–595.
26. Lasater, K. et al. Redefining Mentorship in an Era of Crisis: Responding to COVID-19 Through Compassionate Relationships. *Int J. Mentor.Coach Educ.* **2021**. DOI: 10.1108/IJMCE-11-2020-0078
27. Sepulveda-Escobar, P.; Morrison, A. Online Teaching Placement During the COVID-19 Pandemic in Chile: Challenges and Opportunities. *Eur. J. Teacher Educ.* **2020,** *43* (4), 587–607.
28. Mutton, T. Teacher Education and Covid-19: Responses and Opportunities for New Pedagogical Initiatives. *J. Educ Teach. Int. Res. Pedal.* **2020,** *46*, 439–441.
29. Iqbal, H. E-Mentoring: An Effective Platform for Distance Learning. *e-mentor* **2020,** *84* (2), 54–61.
30. Moorhouse, B. L. Adaptations to a Face-to-Face Initial Teacher Education Course 'Forced'online Due to the COVID-19 Pandemic. *J. Educ. Teach. Int. Res. Pedal.* **2020,** *46* (4), 609–611.
31. Assunção Flores, M.; Gago, M. Teacher Education in Times of COVID-19 Pandemic in Portugal: National, Institutional and Pedagogical Responses. *J. Educ. Teach. Int. Res. Pedal.* **2020,** *46* (4), 507–516.
32. Deepika, V. et al. 'Learning from Home': Role of E-Learning Methodologies and Tools During Novel Coronavirus Pandemic Outbreak. *Postgraduate Med. J.* **2021,** *97* (1151), 590–597.
33. OECD. *Teachers' Training and Use of Information and Communications Technology in the Face of the COVID-19 Crisis*; OECD Publishing, 2020.
34. Alqahtani, A. Y.; Rajkhan, A. A. E-Learning Critical Success Factors During the COVID-19 Pandemic: A Comprehensive Analysis of E-Learning Managerial Perspectives. *Educ. Sci.* **2020,** *10* (9), 216.
35. Maatuk, A. M. et al. The COVID-19 Pandemic and e-learning: Challenges and Opportunities from the Perspective of Students and Instructors. *J. Comput. High. Educ.* **2021**, 1–18.
36. Adedoyin, O. B.; Soykan, E. Covid-19 Pandemic and Online Learning: the Challenges and Opportunities. *Interact. Learn. Environ.* **2020,** 1–13.
37. Almaiah, M. A. et al. Exploring the Critical Challenges and Factors Influencing the E-Learning System Usage During COVID-19 Pandemic. *Educ. Info. Technol.* **2020,** *25*, 5261–5280.

38. Polhun, K., et al. Shift from Blended Learning to Distance One During the Lockdown Period Using Moodle: Test Control of Students' Academic Achievement and Analysis of Its Results. In *Journal of Physics: Conference Series*; IOP Publishing, 2021.
39. Sari, T.; Nayır, F. Challenges in Distance Education During the (Covid-19) Pandemic Period. *Qual. Res. Educ.* **2020,** *9* (3), 328–360.
40. Lestiyanawati, R. J. C. The Strategies and Problems Faced by Indonesian Teachers in Conducting E-Learning During COVID-19 Outbreak. *Cllient J.* **2020,** *2* (1), 71–82.
41. Phillips, L.; Cain, M. Exhausted Beyond Measure': What Teachers Are Saying About COVID-19 and the Disruption to Education. *Conversation* **2020,** *4*.
42. Yang, C., Chen, A.; Chen, Y. College Students' Stress and Health in the COVID-19 Pandemic: The Role of Academic Workload, Separation from School, and Fears of Contagion. *PloS One* **2021,** *16* (2), e0246676.
43. Therisa Beena, K. K. Sony, M. Student Workload Assessment for Online Learning: An Empirical Analysis During Covid-19. *Cogent Eng.* **2022,** *9* (1), 2010509.
44. Kuei, C. T. Student Academic Workload During the COVID-19 Pandemic.
45. Biggs, J.; Tang, C. *Teaching for Quality Learning at University*; McGraw-Hill Education, 2011.
46. Brophy, J. *Motivating Students to Learn*; Routledge, 2004.
47. Häfner, A., Stock, A.; Oberst, V. Decreasing Students' Stress Through Time Management Training: An Intervention Study. *Eur. J. Psychol. Educ.* **2015,** *30* (1), 81–94.
48. Scully, G. Kerr, R. Student Workload and Assessment: Strategies to Manage Expectations and Inform Curriculum Development. *Acc. Educ.* **2014,** *23* (5), 443–466.
49. Morelli, M. et al. Parents and Children During the COVID-19 Lockdown: The Influence of Parenting Distress and Parenting Self-Efficacy on Children's Emotional Well-Being. *Front. Psychol.* **2020,** *11*, 2584.
50. Spinelli, M. et al. Parents' Stress and Children's Psychological Problems in Families Facing the COVID-19 Outbreak in Italy. *Front. Psychol.* **2020,** *11*, 1713.
51. Chen, C. Y.-C.; Byrne, E.; Vélez, T. Impact of the 2020 Pandemic of COVID-19 on Families with School-aged Children in the United States: Roles of Income Level and Race. *J. Family Iss.* **2021,** 0192513X21994153.
52. Vanderhout, S. M. et al. Family Perspectives of COVID-19 Research. *Res. Involve. Engage.* **2020,** *6* (1), 1–3.
53. Gadermann, A. C. et al. Examining the Impacts of the COVID-19 Pandemic on Family Mental Health in Canada: Findings from a National Cross-Sectional Study. *BMJ Open* **2021,** *11* (1), e042871.
54. Lantsoght, E. O. et al. Challenges and Opportunities for Academic Parents During COVID-19. *Front. Psychol.* **2021,** 3353.
55. Christner, N. et al. Children's Psychological Well-Being and Problem Behavior During the COVID-19 Pandemic: An Online Study During the Lockdown Period in Germany. *Plos One* **2021,** *16* (6), e0253473.
56. Aker, N. et al. Challenges Faced During the COVID-19 Pandemic by Family Carers of People Living with Dementia Towards the End of Life. *BMC Health Serv. Res.* **2021,** *21* (1), 1–10.
57. Maheshwari, S.; Mehndiratta, S. Parental Outlook and Problems Faced during Lockdown in COVID-19 Pandemic: Experience from a Paediatric Haematology-Oncology Unit in a Developing Country—A Questionnaire-Based Survey. *J. Clin. Diagn. Res.* **2021,** *15* (4).

58. Feinberg, M. E. et al. Impact of the COVID-19 Pandemic on Parent, Child, and Family Functioning. *Fam. Process* **2021**.
59. Ragavan, M. I. et al. Supporting Adolescents and Young Adults Exposed to or Experiencing Violence During the COVID-19 Pandemic. *J. Adolesc. Health* **2020,** *67* (1), 18.
60. Chung, G., Lanier, P.; Wong, P. Y. J. Mediating Effects of Parental Stress on Harsh Parenting and Parent-Child Relationship During Coronavirus (COVID-19) Pandemic in Singapore. *J. Fam. Violence* **2020,** 1–12.
61. Hari, A.; Nardon, L.; Zhang, H. *A Transnational Lens Into International Student Experiences of the COVID-19 Pandemic*; Global Networks, 2021.
62. Ghosh, R.; Jing, X. Fostering Global Citizenship Through Student Mobility: Covid-19 and the 4th Wave in Internationalization of Education. *Beijing Int. Rev. Educ.* **2020,** *2* (4), 553–570.
63. Wu, S.-J.; Chang, D.-F.; Sun, F.-R. Exploring College Student's Perspectives on Global Mobility During the COVID-19 Pandemic Recovery. *Educ. Sci.* **2020,** *10* (9), 218.
64. Bilecen, B. Commentary: COVID19 Pandemic and Higher Education: International Mobility and Students' Social Protection. *Int. Migration* **2020,** *58* (4), 263–266.
65. Savage, M. J. et al. Mental Health and Movement Behaviour During the COVID-19 Pandemic in UK University Students: Prospective Cohort Study. *Ment. Health Phys. Act.* **2020,** *19*, 100357.
66. Hu, Y.; Xu, C. L.; Tu, M. Family-Mediated Migration Infrastructure: Chinese International Students and Parents Navigating (Im) Mobilities During the COVID-19 Pandemic. *Chin. Sociol. Rev.* **2020,** 1–26.
67. Malet Calvo, D. et al. 'There Was No Freedom to Leave': Global South International Students in Portugal During the COVID-19 Pandemic. *Policy Fut. Educ.* **2021,** 14782103211025428.
68. Gallè, F. et al. Sedentary Behaviors and Physical Activity of Italian Undergraduate Students During Lockdown at the Time of CoViD-19 Pandemic. *Int. J. Environ. Res. Public Health* **2020,** *17* (17), 6171.
69. Choudaha, R.; Chang, L. Trends in International Student Mobility. *World Educ. News Rev.* **2012,** *25* (2).
70. Verbik, L.; Lasanowski, V. International Student Mobility: Patterns and Trends. *World Educ. News Rev.* **2007,** *20* (10), 1–16.
71. Choudaha, R. Three Waves of International Student Mobility (1999–2020). *Stud. High Educ.* **2017,** *42* (5), 825–832.
72. Choudaha, R.; Chang, L.; Kono, Y. International Student Mobility Trends 2013: Towards Responsive Recruitment Strategies. *World Educ. News Rev.* **2013,** *26* (2).
73. De Wit, H. Changing Dynamics in International Student Circulation: Meanings, Push and Pull Factors, Trends, and Data. In *The Dynamics of International Student Circulation in a Global Context*; Brill Sense, 2008; pp 15–45.
74. Petersa, M. A. et al. The Changing Map of International Student Mobility. *ACCESS: Contemp. Iss. Educ.* **2021,** *41* (1), 7–28.
75. Lörz, M.; Netz, N.; Quast, H. *Why Do Students from Underprivileged Families Less Often Intend to Study Abroad? High. Educ.* **2016,** *72* (2), 153–174.
76. Choudaha, R. A Third Wave of International Student Mobility: Global Competitiveness and American Higher Education. Research & Occasional Paper Series, The Center for Studies in Higher Education, UC Berkeley, CSHE, 2018; p 8.

77. Novoselec, L. J. C. *International Student Mobility During Pandemic*, 2021.
78. Yıldırım, S. et al. *Rethinking Mobility of International University Students During COVID-19 Pandemic*, 2021.
79. Bista, K.; Allen, R. M.; Chan, R. Y. *Impacts of COVID-19 on International Students and the Future of Student Mobility: International Perspectives and Experiences*; Routledge, 2021.
80. Profatilova, A. *Student Mobility in the Wake of COVID-19: The Mainland Chinese Parent Perspective*, 2021.
81. Dahdouh-Guebas, F.; Vandebroek, I. Impacts of the COVID-19 Pandemic on International Academic Study Exchange and Research Mobility Programs. *Ethnol. Conserv.* **2021,** *10*, 17.
82. Gomes, C.; Forbes-Mewett, H. International Students in the Time of COVID-19: International Education at the Crossroads. *J. Int. Stud.* **2021,** *11* (S2).
83. Hari, A.; Nardon, L.; Zhang, H. A transnational lens into international student experiences of the COVID-19 pandemic. *Glob Netw.* **2021**.
84. Lukács, A. Mental Well-Being of University Students in Social Isolation. *Eur. J. Health Psychol.* **2021**.
85. Wieczorek, T. et al. Class of 2020 in Poland: Students' Mental Health during the COVID-19 Outbreak in an Academic Setting. *Int. J. Environ. Res. Public Health* **2021,** *18* (6), 2884.
86. Zhai, Y.; Du, X. Addressing Collegiate Mental Health Amid COVID-19 Pandemic. *Psych. Res.* **2020,** *288*, 113003.
87. Rathod, S. R. et al. Change in Sleep-Wake Cycle, Use of Digital Media and Emotional Wellbeing Amidst COVID-19 Lockdown Amongst Dental Students in India. *SRM J. Res. Dent. Sci.* **2021,** *12* (3), 128.
88. Srinivasan, V. et al. Impact of COVID-19 Online Classes on Morningness-Eveningness Personality Among Adult College Students: A Survey Study. *Work* **2021,** (Preprint), 1–6.
89. Galderisi, S. et al. Toward a New Definition of Mental Health. *World Psych.* **2015,** *14* (2), 231.
90. Gurung, R. A.; Stone, A. M. You Can't Always Get What You Want and It Hurts: Learning During the Pandemic. *Scholarship Teach. Learn. Psychol.* **2020**.
91. Bruce, G. S. Learning Efficiency Goes to College. In *Evidence-Based Educational Methods*; Elsevier, 2004; pp 267–275.
92. Mesghina, A. et al. Distressed to Distracted: Examining Undergraduate Learning and Stress Regulation During the COVID-19 Pandemic. *Aera Open*, **2021,** *7*, 23328584211065721.
93. Azzahra, N. F. Addressing Distance Learning Barriers in Indonesia Amid the Covid-19 Pandemic, 2020.
94. Hasan, N.; Bao, Y. Impact of "E-Learning Crack-Up" Perception on Psychological Distress Among College Students During COVID-19 Pandemic: A Mediating Role of "Fear of Academic Year Loss". *Child. Youth Serv. Rev.* **2020,** *118*, 105355.
95. Li, Y. et al. Impact of the COVID-19 Pandemic on the Mental Health of College Students: A Systematic Review and Meta-Analysis. *Front. Psychol.* **2021,** *12*.
96. Bemanian, M. et al. Emotional Eating in Relation to Worries and Psychological Distress Amid the COVID-19 Pandemic: A Population-Based Survey on Adults in Norway. *Int. J. Environ. Res. Public Health* **2021,** *18* (1), 130.

97. Akdeniz, G. et al. A Survey of Attitudes, Anxiety Status, and Protective Behaviors of the University Students During the COVID-19 Outbreak in Turkey. *Front. Psych.* **2020,** *11*.
98. Suhail, A.; Iqbal, N.; Smith, J. *Lived Experiences of Indian Youth Amid COVID-19 Crisis: An Interpretative Phenomenological Analysis. Int. J. Soc. Psych.* **2021,** *67* (5), 559.
99. Taubman–Ben-Ari, O. et al. Distress and Anxiety Associated with COVID-19 Among Jewish and Arab Pregnant Women in Israel. *J. Reprod. Infant Psychol.* **2020,** *38* (3), 340–348.
100. Caroppo, E. et al. Will Nothing Be the Same Again? Changes in Lifestyle During COVID-19 Pandemic and Consequences on Mental Health. *Int. J. Environ. Res. Public Health* **2021,** *18* (16), 8433.
101. Kim, S.-H.; Park, S. Influence of Learning Flow and Distance E-Learning Satisfaction on Learning Outcomes and the Moderated Mediation Effect of Social-Evaluative Anxiety in Nursing College Students During the COVID-19 Pandemic: A Cross-Sectional Study. *Nurse Educ. Pract.* **2021,** *56*, 103197.
102. Talidong, K. J. B.; Toquero, C. M. D. Philippine Teachers' Practices to Deal with Anxiety Amid COVID-19. *J. Loss Trauma* **2020,** *25* (6–7), 573–579.
103. Baloran, E. T. Knowledge, Attitudes, Anxiety, and Coping Strategies of Students During COVID-19 Pandemic. *J. Loss Trauma* **2020,** *25* (8), 635–642.
104. Xiao, S.; Yan, Z.; Zhao, L. Physical Activity, Screen Time, and Mood Disturbance Among Chinese Adolescents During COVID-19. *J. Psychosoc. Nurs. Ment. Health Serv.* **2021,** *59* (4), 14–20.
105. Onyema, E. M. et al. Impact of Coronavirus Pandemic on Education. J. Educ. Pract. **2020,** *11* (13), 108–121.

CHAPTER 6

Impact of COVID-19 on Innovations and Intellectual Property Laws

MAHAM SAEED[1], SHAHZAD SHARIF[1], IZAZ AHMAD[1], GHULAM MUJTABA[2], and M. ZIA-UL-HAQ[3]

[1]*Materials Chemistry Laboratory, Department of Chemistry, GC University, Lahore, Pakistan*

[2]*Intellectual Property Organization of Pakistan, Islamabad, Pakistan*

[3]*Office of Research, Innovation and Commercialization (ORIC), Lahore College for Women University, Lahore, Pakistan*

ABSTRACT

The arrival of the coronavirus pandemic provoked the governments and World Health Organization to have a globally coordinated response to meet all the challenges in every field. The developing and least-developed countries are considerably at a more risk to be affected by health crises. After going through lockdowns, reduced innovative, scientific, and business activities in the early pandemic days, the scientific community eradicated all the conventional barriers so that COVID-19-related innovations, publications, and research could be made swiftly. COVID-19 innovation system, through pull and push efforts, incentivized the public response to support late-stage research, product development, and agreements of advanced purchasing to kick off innovation. Crises happening intensively demand a reduction of patent protection cost to link patents with R & D. Before pandemic, patent landscape based on biomedical research shaped the motives for the successive innovative development. A big share of patent applications also shifted toward remote technologies to carry on innovative incentives. These prevailing conditions have also altered the mindset of community about the impacts of IPR on

Post-Pandemic Economy, Technology, and Innovation: Global Outlook and Context.
Samina Yaqoob, Arwa Abdulkreem AL-Huqail, and Fakhra Aziz (Eds.)

the fields of research, development, and technology. Mostly, it is seen that it has negative impacts, but later evidences revel positive impacts to a greater extent. IPR not only provides monetary benefits for funding but also ensures the correct use of the researcher's data. WHO developed a site for pooling data during the pandemic so that the data liked by the general community is not hindered and can be utilized for the manufacture of pharmaceutical therapeutic drugs, making the information more accessible.

6.1 INTRODUCTION

It was the end of 2019 when Wuhan (China) was detected with a novel disease, coronavirus. This infectious disease crossed the borders quickly and got spread worldwide. World Health Organization declared public health emergency of international concern due to COVID-19 for an internationally collaborated public health response. COVID-19 was declared as a "pandemic" by WHO on March 11, 2020 to drive instant development of resources and actions, as a huge population was getting affected globally.1 Although the lockdown was announced in many countries, the director general of WHO still noted inefficacy at an alarming level. During that period, more than 12 million people were affected, among which 258,495 approximately got recovered and more than 60,000 died. The emerging cases of coronavirus showed that the health agencies, on national and international levels, were not ready to handle this novel outbreak. Reaching of COVID-19 in countries having weak health systems made the mandatory requirement of coordination and solidarity at the international level. The government gave instructions for early detection, isolation, and treatment of coronavirus cases. The best way for all the steps taken to be effective is the prevention of viral transmission; otherwise, infectious number of people will increase rapidly.

There is utmost need of assistance for the enhancement of workforce, testing capacity, and healthcare infrastructure in the underdeveloped and other developing countries of Asia, Africa, and Latin America. No prediction has been found for the unfolding of public health emergency scale in such poor countries.[2,3] At present, there is a severe shortage of personal protective equipment such as shortfall of beds, testing kits, and ventilators even in the economically developed countries like France. Moreover, insufficiency of necessary medical products is due to ban on exports by the government. For the fast, cost-effective, and accessible testing coordination is needed globally. COVID-19 detection began with the effective collaboration of China in SARS-CoV genome sequencing and releasing, which enabled the

FIGURE 6.1 A depiction of COVID-19 precautionary measures.

development of test kits. Though large-scale testing is lacking, advanced diagnostic techniques and testing are being prompted.[4]

Development of different strategies and diagnostic techniques is under struggle by different countries. Mostly, diagnosis methods are being developed with the aid of proprietary and commercial technology. It means that a license allocation with terms of agreement is required for their manufacturing, sale, and export. These conditions may lead to high prices. It may lift up the profit and enhance the strategies of commercial vendors, but the health of public remains ignorant. As the demand is increasing globally, exports are not being increased in the same way to meet them. All the laboratories and research institutes under the government can facilitate the sharing or transfer of these technologies. It is mandatory to enhance the production capacity in the developing countries. Funding is required to bring cost-effective diagnostics to the least developing and developing countries. Development of these diagnostics requires a collaborative effort by the government to cope with patent, contractual barriers, and trade secrets, which play a barrier role in this regard.[4]

6.2 IMPACT OF COVID-19 ON INNOVATION

Innovation is related to the creation and implementation of new thoughts and ideas. It is important in the field of process, product development, business, and organizations. The outbreak of the novel disease COVID-19 led to the suffering of economics due to lockdowns, which resulted in the budget continence, uncertainty in the innovation perspectives, and uncertainty in the future developments. In general, global pandemic has affected every sector, firm, or a country.[5,6]

6.2.1 CRISES OF INNOVATION MANAGEMENT

Prior to research investigation, the enhancement of uncertainty, inconsistency, complexity, and ambiguity has made the innovation management a crisis. A collaborative decision making is a high need to make the ways for overcoming this crisis, with the consideration of future aspects.[7,8] In spite of available information, these decisions are mainly improvised on gut feelings. For example, investment in the innovation management is cutoff regardless of consequences with long-term negative effects like reduction of patent filings and future firms being forfeited. On the other side, economical constraints can encourage innovation with the ongoing research.[9–13] Although, the crises led to increase in innovative activities, which explored the new strategies and innovative firms to bear the shortcomings because of crises. This also emerged some firms strongly like AirBNB and Uber, which arose like ashes in the fire and fulfilled the marketing requirements.[14–16] It has become a challenge to merely rely on these firms without having a proper data for taking backup steps. Moreover, it is also surprising that only slight information is available on how to investigate the possibilities based on knowledge available that publicly offers for making the organizational decisions during the coronavirus pandemic and other crises like this.[17,18]

Patent analytics play an important role in shaping the innovation management during crises. Four distinct cases have been studied by observing patent data in a longitudinal and cross-sectional way.[19–21] Two cases are related to negative effects, that is, how the efforts in innovation can be continued with free budget, how lockdown can cause reduction in expenses, and how decisions based on driven data can yield excess incomings, like by identification of license for technology and reducing the number of candidates. Other cases are related to identification of success by using the data related to innovation and technology like detection of most promising system for treatment/ vaccination of coronavirus.[19,22]

6.2.2 RECOVERING AND PERSISTENCE OF INNOVATIONS

Existence of some unpredictable situations like crises acts as a barrier for innovation, as in the start of 20th century, the economy crises led to changed behavior of firms to innovate. In such situation, some innovation activities

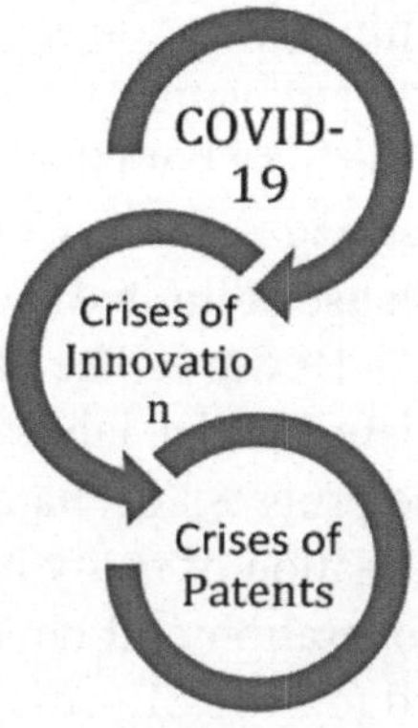

FIGURE 6.2 Triadic relation among COVID-19, crises of innovation management, and patents.

are maintained by firms to support the public, which actually caused decrease in proprietary innovative activities. Reduction of firms also slows down the R & D and therefore, innovations.[23,24]

On the other hand, crises have perks too, for example, by thriving innovative activities to meet the necessary requirements of market and manage the changes induced by crises. Some authors also define innovation as "It is a way induced through crises to evaluate the uncertainties which yield greater firm value with more certainty."[25–27]

It has also been observed that the cooperative management gets more advantage from thoroughly ongoing innovation rather than reducing costs. Firms basically provide a shield to innovative activities during crises than other actions like slightly cutting off the production prices.[28] Likewise, no matter how the financial condition is, innovative firms have greater chance to survive during crises in comparison to noninnovative firms.[29]

6.2.3 *BUSINESS INNOVATION AND COVID-19*

6.2.3.1 *EFFECT OF LOCKDOWN ON INNOVATIVE COMPANIES*

When the lockdown was employed in cities, many business-related innovative activities got reduced. A survey which was done in 2020 by the federal minister for economic affairs and energy (Germany) revealed that research activities related to many innovation projects were temporarily stopped in more than 50% of companies, while 24% of companies made their projects brought to an end.[30] Interviews of more than 200 executives were taken and it was found that during the pandemic period, only innovation activities in the field of biologics and pharmaceutics arose, while innovation for industrial growth to pursue as business got decreased. It was because both the government and public sectors prioritized overcoming the challenges due to COVID-19.[31]

Innovation got affected because of limited access to the research and development during the first COVID-19 wave. The happening of lockdowns led to the shutting down of many science parks, laboratories, and hence, innovation in them. This also affected the progress of many firms to carry out research, development, and commercialization of many business-related products. The organization of economic cooperation and development (OECD) suggested that innovation activity related to 30% of firms would be terminated without the involvement of the government. Another survey in Israel found that 54% of firms were not able to continue their research progress after 6 months, leading to running out of business agreements and plans.[32,33]

6.2.3.2 INITIALIZATION OF BUSINESS INNOVATIONS OWING TO COVID-19

Apart from public health domains, industrial organizations also took steps for innovative research activities to cope with COVID-19 challenges. A survey was performed which declared that about a quarter, that is, 23% of companies initialized innovation in healthcare, sanitization, and communication services, though it was their secondary industry.[34] Increased research activities thrived the patent companies, as was seen in USPTO at the start of 2020, which supported a huge number of patent applications supporting science, technology, and working from home.[35]

At the beginning of COVID-19 pandemic, to deal with shortage of supply in emergency and healthcare products, many steps were taken to increase the development of prudent innovations.[36] At the mid of March 2020, an Italian research team developed a 3-D printed type of respiratory valve and quickly supplied hundreds of them to Chiari medical centers. After this, a snorkeling mask was also modified into emergency ventilating mask by an engineering team.[37] Other firms in sporting, consumer, automotive, and aeronautic goods were redeployed for the quick production of hand sanitizers, face masks, and other respiratory and face protection equipment.

On the other side, recently initialized academic companies also stepped forward to deal with the outcomes coming in response to pandemic. A biotechnology company which is associated to University of Liege named "Zantac" developed an antibody rapid testing kit, "Qiagen" specially designed for healthcare professionals.[38] Following the way of research and development, many biotechnology companies coordinated with universities' research sectors to develop a suitable vaccine for coronavirus.[39] Another start-up was taken by Indian technology section, "Asimov Robotics" for the development of robots to provide services for coronavirus patients like serving food, medicines, cleaning, disinfection, and contact with a doctor.

Likewise earlier sessions of crises, the COVID-19 pandemic also faced the issues of fall in business activities and rise of bankruptcy, especially during the first wave of 2020. The countries with high entrepreneurship in 2019, like Sweden, Norway, Netherlands, and Japan, observed high registrations of business as compared to those with less enterprise, like Belgium, Germany, and France. Evidence taken from experts in the USA states that first shocking wave of COVID-19 led to a rush and strengthening of business creations.[40] The national statistics office in the UK reported that business activities have seen a fall period in early 2020, after which slightly arose from July to September 2020 as compared to the same period in 2019.[41] This phenomenon is considered positive with provisional uncertainties of future. Also, many business innovative activities stemmed from the private business creations by some unemployed individuals' personal efforts.

6.2.3.3 VENTURE CAPITAL FUNDING FOR INNOVATION IN BUSINESS

Venture capital funding is a key step for the beginning of innovations, but with the arrival of shocking COVID-19 wave, it got affected.[42] An analysis revealed that from January to August 2020, venture capital funding got declined to the minimum level, as was seen in 2013. Moreover, during the first 6 months of 2020, US-based venture capitalists also found out that investment speed was reduced to 71% of normal. This decline in investment speed devastated the companies at the early stage in the countries like the UK, the US, China, and Ireland.

However, the reduction of venture capital was not potent as the economic crises of 2008 to 2009. By July 2020, it got recovered and came back to a high level speedily. Gompers and his fellows demonstrated through studies that the declining of investment was not as bad as the internet bust of 2001 to 2002 leading to more than 50% reduction, and the financial crises of 2008 to 2009 at global level leading to more than 30% reduction.[43–45] This can be attributed to greater funding for the establishment of companies at the pandemic time so that large number of firms can innovate. But, it is to be considered that the change in venture capital funding may be challenging for the innovations taking place in different sectors affecting more to the companies at the early stages.

6.2.4 SCIENCE, TECHNOLOGY, AND INNOVATION (STI) POLICY IN RESPONSE TO COVID-19

The policymakers for science, technology, and innovation briskly took steps to both prepare and protect the STI system due to the coronavirus pandemic. The main focus was on the research and development in the field of medicine to manufacture vaccines. To deal with the crises of the socioeconomic field, the government granted STI so that innovation like production of digital devices may happen. Moreover, the education and industrial domain capacity was also enhanced to spread awareness and prohibit misinformation. For the proper implementation of measures and to ensure the response of science, technology, and innovation system, counseling organizations were developed by the government such as national command council of South Africa and national action plan on COVID-19 in Ireland.[46]

The economy got affected due to the coronavirus pandemic, but unequally. Those areas which were characterized by less innovation suffered more than those with comparatively more innovation level. Lockdowns and social distancing not only affected businesses, industries, and retailing, but also tourism. These firms and sectors also got affected due to incarceration when the second wave of COVID-19 arrived. Results and discussions in the business sector have less impact, but those with greater investments and global supply, like electronics and automotive, get affected intensely when their demand drops. As the lockdown was lifted off, the demand gradually increased excluding the manufacturing sectors and tourism. But as the world has become global village, the digital business sectors like online shopping, online teaching, webinars, cloud services, and telemedicines thrived in the era with more urge to innovate to fulfil the increased demand of products.[46]

6.2.4.1 SPEEDING UP INNOVATION TO RESPOND PANDEMIC

To respond COVID-19, many innovative steps have been taken by the countries including the preventive measures to avoid virus spread, production of emergency essentials, resist misinformation, and manipulating the effects caused by lockdowns. The approaches in the situation included:

6.2.4.1.1 Open Competitions to Produce Advanced Results

The point refers to the stimulations of research efforts, greater firms, and inventions at an individual level. To address the COVID-19 issues, many countries took steps to evaluate the relevance of inventions by the applicants, such as rapid response calls in Ireland and the initialization of businesses leading to innovation for worldwide disruption due to COVID-19.

6.2.4.1.2 Support and Organization of Virtual Datathon

Datathon is related to a 2-day event in which participants have to innovate a product as per data provided. After which, winners are encouraged with funds to widen their ideas. At the end of April 2020, the EU v/s virus datathon happened to address the problems caused by the COVID-19. More than 30,000 individuals participated in this event hosted by European innovation council and commission for the 20 pandemic issues. The outcomes were more than 2000 from which over 800 solutions were based on health and life. Other solutions contributed toward education, business, work, digital finance services, union of society, and politics. More than 100 solutions were related to the innovations to monitor the coronavirus patients so that physical contact with the doctor can be minimized.[47] All the winners from the event were invited to collaborate with accelerators and investors, in order to develop a product from the innovation. It led to the rise of over 200 partnerships.[48]

6.2.4.1.3 Promotion of Collaborative Research

Many initiatives are taken by the government to support and stimulate the innovative research. For example, Canada has launched a program named as "national research council pandemic response challenge" which allows Canadian and outsider researchers from the educational institutions or government to do a collaborative work on the specified issues of COVID-19.[33,49]

6.2.4.1.4 Sharing of Knowledge and Data

Some initiatives have been specially launched to share the data related to clinics, genome, and epidemiology. The standards and protocols involved in getting the data are also shared. The government of the US, several foundations, publishers, and Allen institute for artificial language collaboratively created machine learning techniques to address the COVID-19 issues. It included more than 2 lakhs scholarly articles related to coronavirus based on machine reading.[50] These articles also included the knowledge on antiviral compounds for coronavirus, structural–chemical data, genomic data, study on clinical trials, and modeling of research data on COVID-19.[51]

6.2.4.1.5 *Introduction of Flexibilities to Regulate*

To ensure rapid responding system, regulatory flexibilities were introduced as per feasibility. A branch of health department in Australia named as "therapeutic goods administration" is prioritized to assess the therapeutic goods for the COVID-19. Regulatory measures are also introduced in the medicine/healthcare products agency of the UK to ensure expedited reviews owing to clinical trial applications, swift scientific advice, and investigation system for therapeutic devices.[52]

6.2.4.1.6 *Ease the Access to Research Frameworks*

For the acceleration of research initiatives, many tools, laboratories, and databases have been developed. For example, the research infrastructures in Europe and the US have given access to researchers around the world for an excellent research capacity for in vivo/in vitro studies being done on coronavirus and high-performance computing.[53]

6.2.4.1.7 *Encouragement of Intellectual Property Rights*

To address the challenges related to COVID-19, the US patent and trademark office launched a program to swiftly examine the patent applications dropped by small entities without taking any additional fee.[54] A debate is ongoing regarding intellectual property right incentives to provide the solutions in such a way that are easily accessible.

6.2.5 *COVID-19 INNOVATION POLICY*

The pandemic period is well known for innovations in research which led to development and evaluation of novel therapies and vaccines. According to a data report, about 200 vaccines and nearly 362 therapeutics were developed to undergo preliminary allowance and clinical trials for COVID-19 treatment. In this regard, new policies have been featured in comparison to challenges coming this way.[55,56]

Before coronavirus pandemic, the innovation policy in biomedicine was dependent on two main approaches, that is, "Push mechanism" which deals with direct funding to be put in the category of R & D (research and development) and "Pull mechanism" which deals with rewarding when products are developed successfully.[57] The huge role as push sector in the world is played by NIH (national institutes of health), which had a budget of 40 billion dollars in 2019. This institute funding is greatly oriented toward medical schools and universities, basically for the purpose of research. Some basic discoveries were highly supported through push actions, but with a little attention that how conclusive research will help in development of products and their diffusion in the medical system. Grants for the clinical trials and late-stage product development are handled by private industry.

The most dominant way to pull the private sector is the patent system. It causes nullified competition between the innovators for a selected period. This duration leads to charging of high prices by the innovators, and innovations get promoted by getting large profits through patents. In the field of drug industry, patents are very important as a stimulant of innovation. After expiration of a patent, prices decrease with the enhancement of competition.[58] Policymakers get motivated to limit the effects created by patents in terms of restricted access and high prices. In the least developed countries, patents are not much effective to promote research and discussion for a particular disease. These limitations were overcome by economists in 1990 through commitments in the advanced marketing and proposed prizes. At the arrival of COVID-19, policy related to innovation concerns with patent, other policies, and funding for the public before coronavirus era.[59,60]

Owing to COVID-19, organization whether linked to government or not and other philanthropies around the world have financially supported the R & D for the vaccines and therapeutics. As no complete record is available, funding sources may be proprietary or nontransparent. Further, there is complete discussion based on support by the public sector for R & D and products.[61]

Push mechanism: In the US, the huge funding was provided by the government, which roughly ranged from 14 to 15 billion dollars out of 4 trillion dollars, designated for the research and development of vaccines and therapeutics. This funding enhanced the research in the US by 1/3rd in comparison to NIH funding; however, it is potentially small for avoiding a disease to come in normalcy pattern.[62,63]

6.2.5.1 ROLE OF NIH

As the coronavirus broke out, NIH activities and perspectives changed in the innovation system. On the allocation of 3.5 billion dollars by the congress, research caught the speed for the development of treatment and vaccines for COVID-19. NIH played an important role in the coordination of all the researchers around the world in order to concentrate on promising one with the avoidance of repeating research. It has also supported in the clinical trials for the development of therapeutic interventions.[64,65] In May 2020, the US first program for the development of therapeutics, diagnostics, and vaccines known as "operation warp speed" substituted the efforts of NIH. In January 2021, it had the goal to secure about 300 million doses for the American public.[66] To deal with COVID-19, an association between human/health services and defense department has financed more than 15 billion dollars by pull or push funding and combining these two.[62]

BARDA (biomedical advanced research and development authority), which was established in 2006, has been among the major sources of funding for operation warp speed. More than 4000 requests have been received by BARDA with the expectations of greater than 500 recipients.[55] The organization was questioned many times for their processes of taking decisions. Operation warp speed had a definite goal, but it also coordinated with others globally, especially China, for epidemic preparedness innovations. During this time, burden was more on military rather than health ministry with the lack of coordination with NIH, and deficient transparent contracts in accordance with rights of taxpayers.[66,67]

Both NIH and BARDA have spent a huge portion, like 2 and 15 billion dollars, respectively on research related to vaccine. Earlier, NIH accounted for 5% grants and 8% funding, but with COVID-19, funding was raised to 47% with 30% grants. BARDA has granted 77 and 13% for vaccines and therapeutics with extra funding for other diagnosis and technologies.[68] For the reservation of manufacturing in funded projects by BARDA, investment is done for clinical trials and enhanced scaled-up productivity, rather than for result and discussion only. Before the approval of all the results and discussions, investments done in manufacturing process is regarded as a risk.

To support the therapeutics, BARDA followed the similar ways. Justice department of the US also permitted the therapeutic manufacturers to provide production information so that they can be widened rapidly.[55,69]

6.2.5.2 PUSH EFFORTS

The funding for the production of vaccines and therapeutics has been contributed globally. To respond the pandemic, over 25 billion dollars loan has been provided by the European investment bank. To facilitate research for late-stage development, several members of European states like Germany and France also granted funding, while the UK supported to enhance capacity for vaccine production. The data provided by a scientific analytical company "Airfinity" show that the public funding in the US is higher than in Europe, but its approach is similar, that is, it is focused on development of vaccines. To strengthen the production capability, just like the US, Europe also collaborated with other organizations so that supply won't face scarcity. These efforts specifically included the reoccurring of clinical trials to evaluate the potential of coronavirus medications. In this scenario, the government of the UK financed the "recovery" based trials which assessed multiple antibiotics, steroids, antivirals, and antibodies. On the international level, WHO contributed toward the examination of four medications, which also included remdesivir and hydroxychloroquine.[55,70]

The funding information for the countries like Russia and China is not available, though they played a significant role in the research and development, and managed to produce seven out of 14 vaccines in the phase III clinical trial. As per the data available on "Airfinity," out of 81 vaccines that have gone through clinical trials, 15 were produced in China and four were from Russia. Another vaccine producing organization "coalition for epidemic preparedness"(CEPI), which was founded by Bill and Melinda Gates, has contributed about 1.2 billion dollars toward COVID-19.[71,72] But its contribution is much lesser than the US contribution toward recipients, thus limiting the guidance for vaccine allocation. CEPI has also played a collaborative role to discover the global vaccine producers in order to match the demand worldwide. Other philanthropies have not only been active for vaccine development but also contributed for the treatment methods.[73]

In order to speed up and widen the COVID-19 vaccine development, Bill's foundation collaborated with "Wellcome trust" and "Mastercard" for the establishment of therapeutics accelerator. It made 11 contributions so that approved medications could be evaluated, and novel therapeutics could be studied. CEPI coordinates with the ACT (COVID-19 tools accelerator), which is WHO's vaccine pillar, while Wellcome trust majorly contributes toward treatments.[74]

Generally, global push efforts are very different in the pandemic, which have strong concentration on vaccines/therapeutics development. Earlier, public support toward vaccine development was also there, but it was reflected during COVID-19 with shift for increased production capacity, trials at late stage, and risk manufacturing. Also, these push efforts supported the private philanthropies for variety of firms.[75]

6.3 IMPACT OF COVID-19 ON PATENTS

After filing, it takes about 1.5 years for the patent applications to be published, and then many years for the grant. It is also not clear that patent protection will initiate a pull mechanism to innovate. After the start of pandemic in 2020, many patent applications were filed, but arrival of their significant protection may be late after qualifying from the US patent and trademark office. One of the uncertainties for those, who always participates in pharmaceutical research and development is the competitor, who may file for multiple claims. It is also least expected from the firms the acknowledgment of patents and how to use them to direct high prices during COVID-19. Patent applications, filed before the pandemic may incentivize more than those filed during the pandemic.[55] In this scenario, mRNA technology domain is being patented highly as firms, which may provide a platform for innovation. At the same time, therapeutics having a patent term like remdesivir, which was under examination, may be more attractive for coronavirus than those patent applications not involving the term. Principally, push efforts can also offer investments in the older studied drugs too, like the recovery trial of dexamethasone; however, sponsor's interest in the type of drugs to be patented is not clear.[55,76]

6.3.1 CRISES OF PATENT ANALYTICS

Patents acquire intense cost during their whole lifetime, ranging from their filing to maintenance expenditure in every administration for their protection. When it comes to crises happening in the country, filing or maintaining of new patents become a challenge due to fluctuating budget.[76] In such a situation, reduction of expenditure is mandatory, especially linking the patents with the innovations and technologies. It ensures that patents are the valuable assets for exploiting the capabilities so that promising business opportunities can be deployed. However, scholars believe that to overcome the knowledge gap, useful information found in patent applications can be applied in the results and discussions, business strategies, and technological platforms.[78,79]

As suggested by the patent data, COVID-19 first wave did not put long-term impacts. Since the start of COVID-19 outbreak, a comparison of patent filings in PCT (patent cooperation treaty) showed downfall of patent applications from December 2019 to June 2020. However, overall patent applications were not reduced strikingly during the pandemic. In China, number of patent applications filed in March 2020 was almost equal to those filed in March 2019. Further, in coming months, a reduction can be seen in innovation activities due to COVID-19. As we are living in a global village, so the digital innovations are in high demand and this may reflect various trends for inventions.[34] Several evidences showed that beginning of pandemic led to onset of different innovation activities, followed by about 247 patent filings and hence a rise in patenting.[35]

In the current pandemic situation, this approach is related to reaching the biology, characteristic causes, and the effect of the virus. Otherwise to handle the coronavirus becomes impromptu and unpredictable. The reaction of human body in response to coronavirus has been revealed by the studies, which states that proteins named as cytokines are released to respond infections, autoimmune diseases, and genetic disorders. It leads to inflammation in the attacked area. However in rare cases, there is limitless release of cytokines causing proinflammation and leading to the failure of many organs, as one's own immune system starts working against it. This uncontrolled expression of cytokines and other immune cells is referred to as "cytokine storm." The pandemic situations like H5N1 influenza virus and COVID-19 reported the cytokine storms in the patients. This has also been seen in the diseases such as pancreatitis, juvenile arthritis, multiple sclerosis, and Still's disease, which are noninfectious.[80,81]

The coronavirus provokes the similar response when enters the lungs of a victim. The COVID-19 patient has to deal with failure of immune system due to unrestricted production of cytokines causing cell death and rupturing the wall of the lungs, resulting in difficulty in breathing and pneumonia. This failure of lungs further causes acute respiratory distress syndrome leading to failure of other organs as well. Studies have been performed to produce the drugs (immunosuppressants) that block the cytokines.[82,83]

No antidote is available against the coronavirus. The research that is undergoing to evaluate treatment methods is based on the prior knowledge collected from MERS and SARS epidemics, the diseases which are related to respiration.[84] Two treatment methods have been considered against SARS-CoV-2. The first is related to the production of antibodies that can attack spike protein of virus, and the second is related to the triggering of body immune system to work against virus by development of mRNA vaccine.[83]

6.3.2 PULL EFFORTS TO INCENTIVIZE PATENTS

Since the start of pandemic, economists announced the prizes and commitment of advanced marketing to motivate research and drug manufacturing. On the other side, philanthropists and the governments purchased huge amount of volumes for their easy and cost-effective availability to public. Countries other than the US, like the UK, Japan, Israel, and Canada have also invested in advanced purchasing. On the multilateral level, the most significant innovative step is the "COVAX" agreement, which is accompanied by WHO, GAVI, and CEPI. It is a pooled purchasing initiative, which includes advanced marketing in order to thrive funding for the development of sufficient doses of vaccine that would be available to 20% of population in the developing and underdeveloped countries.[55]

This agreement also facilitates the countries with good economy, which have also purchased several vaccine doses directly from the donors. The global push funding is basically focused on vaccines instead of therapeutics. CEPI also approached a pharmaceutical company, Eli Lilly for the supply of antibodies against coronavirus to the developing and least developing countries. This simultaneous global collaboration of countries has incentivized the innovative mechanisms regarding vaccines and also their easy access. Other motives for many firms beside these agreements/contracts are the competitors and expectations to meet the demand.[85]

6.3.3 PATENTS AND ACCESS TO MEDICINE

Before the pandemic, it was expected that the high cost of medicines could make their access difficult to the public. To reduce these concerns, some tools are being explored in COVID-19 to overcome patents. For advanced purchasing, these tools, however, may not be so applicable but are very fine to reduce the price of products to be forwarded.[60]

It was suggested in the US, to enhance the global competition for the development of vaccines and drugs by public funding, the government should be allowed the legal use of patents. The government rights the public to participate in the late-stage development, but it is also the fact in some of the government agreements that the taxpayer rights are limited.[67] Activists have made use of certain measures to enhance drug development competition in the developing countries, such as patent pools and mandatory licensing.

At the time of AIDS and HIV crises, India went through the off-patent drug manufacturing which considerably enhanced the public access to treatments. This era showed that the limitation of patent applications is useful for the products, that is, small molecule pharmaceutics, which can be synthesized abundantly as for AIDS and HIV. On the other side, formulation of complex molecules like vaccines and other therapeutics with limited intellectual property rights cannot generate sufficient potent global competition.[86,87]

Some aspects like commendatory technologies, knowledge applied for manufacturing, and other capabilities may restrict nonpatent entry. Besides taking steps for innovations, the foremost challenge is the widening of vaccine doses to fulfill the global demand. An association of a suitable technology between pharmaceutics developing companies can be helpful in scaling up the required doses. The COVID-19 technology access tool is a way for transferring the technology, licensing of many firms related to biologics and other information, but still a less potent participation has been seen through this way.[88] Many activists have also not provided sufficient financial encouragement to the firms so that an association may occur through technology share. This sharing may also be difficult to achieve thorough decree/contracts due to discouragement of participation in research and development, firms' quality, and dealing of issues present to attain the goals.[89]

6.3.3.1 CONTRACTS FOR ACCESS, PRICES, AND PURCHASE

The drifts in purchasing commitments are helpful in shaping the prices of vaccines and getting the access. Although, the health professionals can charge for doses, but in the BARDA agreement, already purchased vaccines are there to be distributed by the US government without any charges. Also, the COVAX has given access to its doses with less prices. Some pharmaceutical companies have sold their doses costly, but worldwide how much the vaccine doses were charged is not clear. Access to these vaccine doses can finally be shaped by infrequent administration.[90,91] The doses developed in 2021 are not limited to the countries' government only which provided push funding, but also to those with rich economy. Some companies have provided the sufficient supply and some philanthropists have also given an ethical scheme for allocation.[92] It has also been observed that solving the problems related to access and transfer of technology between the pharmaceutical companies can help in diffusing the allocation disputes.[69]

6.3.4 SHIFTING OF PATENTS TOWARD TECHNOLOGIES SUPPORTING WORK FROM HOME

As it got compulsory to stay at home due to COVID-19, immense amount of work was also performed from home. Several American servants performed half of the work from home; moreover in March 2020, it was decided to do 23% work by staying at home till the end of COVID-19 as compared to only 5% work done from home in 2017–2018. The top and bottom growing return differential was 19.4% at first half of 2020, shifting of stock prices also reflected the work from home. Employees performed jobs at home on resilient firms keeping in view the scenario of COVID-19 so that physical proximity may not happen.[93,94]

The acceleration of pandemic innovations supported working from home through shifting technologies like telecommunication, video conference, remote interaction, etc. Sharing of all the big work remotely takes toward the implement of advanced technology for working from home. To bring a technical change, a large number of skilled workers has been implied in the market to complement the technologies. This change has brought a sudden, immense, and surprising response in arrangements of performing work. In this situation, those patent applications were preferably read, which shared the technologies supporting working from home. About more than 3 million applications were filed from 2010 to 2020, out of which over 20,000 patents are about the technologies supporting work from home.[34]

Patent applications that were based on working from home contained the titles as:

- Optimizing a video conference by using contextual information.
- Method, apparatus, and system for video conferencing.
- Sales management through mobile and remote web system.
- Proper defining of contents for a video conferencing.
- How to summarize and recognize the speech.

As the COVID-19 cases increased in number by March 2020, with the induction of lockdowns and social distancing, half of the work was performed by staying at home. Later in September, the number of patent applications reached 1.16% exceeding the percentage experienced before the pandemic. This clearly provides the evidence that COVID-19 brought acceleration in innovation, but by working from home.[95,96] A directional drift in innovations can bring an improvement in the technologies that support remote work. Enhancing the productivity and quality of working by staying at home shifted a rush toward the patent filings. The involvement of all these mechanisms made a better experience than expectations with diminishing of stigma associated with working from home.[34]

6.4 IMPACT OF COVID-19 ON INTELLECTUAL PROPERTY LAWS

Intellectual property is the output of the innovation, technology, and new products for their protections so that they can thrive in marketplaces. It is a vast spectrum that is further categorized for the sake of immaterial, protected by the company or a person legally. Intellectual property aims to boost different types of goods, encourage people, respect their businesses, and permit people to get maximum benefits from the goods they create. It prevents copyrights of the presented ideas.[97,98]

FIGURE 6.3 Significance of IPR.

6.4.1 A CORE ISSUE DURING PANDEMIC

The outbreak of COVID-19 started from the capital city of Hubei "Wuhan" in December 2019. A health emergency was announced by the WHO on January 30, 2020 and it became a pandemic on March 11, 2020.[99] COVID-19 not only affects the educational sectors worldwide but also has an impact on the trademark. In reality, we see that during the period of the pandemic, especially from March to May, which was the beginning period of COVID-19, huge number of trademarks rose, but the number of trademarks has also fallen.[100]

6.4.1.1 IMPACT OF COVID-19 ON TRADEMARKS

During the period of the pandemic, trademark lines in Turkey and other countries declined due to the economically unstable situation.[100] Some trademarks converted to online through which their worth increased drastically. The official statistics about the trademark application in 2019 during the first period of COVID-19 decreased from 29.2% in January to 20.5% in February. Turkish patents decreased by 4% when the first case of COVID-19 was detected in Turkey; a drastic decrease happened in April when COVID-19 rose to its peak in Turkey. The decrease was noticed about 22.6%. The following graph shows the Turkish patent trademark during the pandemic.

Similarly, trademark application in Europe during the pandemic neither decreased nor increased during March to May, in comparison to the patents of Turkey. The trademark application decreased from January to April 2020 in Turkey; later on, a gradual increase was seen. The graph of European Union intellectual property is shown below.

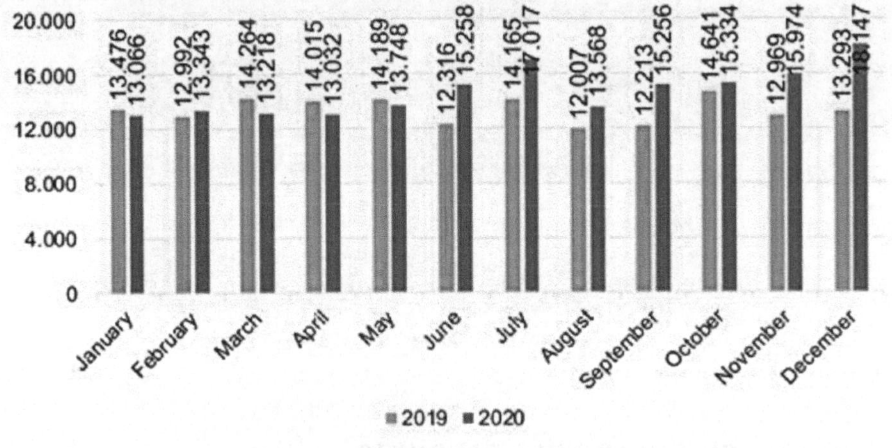

FIGURE 6.4 European trademark statistics in 2019–2020.

6.4.1.2 IMPACT OF COVID-19 ON INTERNATIONAL TRADE

COVID-19 affected the global trades badly in 2020, especially in first quarter, the decrease noticed was about 3% due to the restriction on international flights all over the world. The international supplies and demands ceased due to the sudden fall of about 30% of international flights. Exports noticed a very low figure, especially in April and May. Due to restrictions of international flights, a drastic decline was noticed in trade values. The effect of the pandemic impacted both countries that were affected mostly or not yet affected with COVID-19. The United Nations conference on trade and development figured the value of trade in the first quarter of 2020 that was 3% decrease with respect to the previous quarter, and the price index of UNCTAD loss was 1.2% in first month of 2020, 8.5% in second month, and 20.4% in March. Such a decline never happened before, even in 2008 and 2009, when the global financial crisis happened. During that time, the loss was figured about 18.6%.

6.4.1.3 IMPACT OF COVID-19 ON TRADEMARK APPLICATIONS

With the emergence of COVID-19, certain phrases like social distancing, "Korona," and "Evde Kal" (stay at home) have not only influenced our life but also exerted an influence on trademark applications. Because of that, phrases comparable to pandemic like COVID-19, "Sosyal Mesafe," "COVID," and "Korona" can be observed as a part of trademark applications.

According to research that was conducted on trademark records, it has been observed that after first examination, certain trademark applications have been refused. Trademark applications having the name "Korona" (COVID-19) when applied for Classes 05, 03, 09, and 10, which basically refer to cleaning, health, medical, and other protective materials have been rejected, except for those having some descriptive phrases as a trademark application. It was decided that registration process will continue for trademark application numbered 2020/32607 which will be used for classes 03 and 05, and for the trademark application numbered 2020/79814, the registration process for classes 03 and 35 will also continue. Similarly, the trademark application for "Hyper Corona" numbered 2020/35062 published in official Trademark Bulletin has not been refused for class 05.

Class 13 includes firearms, mortars, rockets, air guns, and defense gases. For this class, trademark application Corona numbered 2020/14479 has been approved and registered after examination, and also published in official Trademark Bulletin. For classes 38 and 41, the rejected trademark application is COVID-19 "Korona Salgin" numbered 2020/60308. The trademark applications relevant to COVID-19 having phrases "Sosyal Mesafe" (social distancing) and "Evde Kal" (stay at home), which are not descriptive and distinctive, are rejected by the office.

For class 35, trademark application numbered 63883 has been recognized for publication in official Trademark Bulletin.

6.4.1.4 *PERSPECTIVE OF EXISTING TRADEMARK IN PANDEMIC*

During the pandemic, the existing trademarks also tried to raise awareness about corona virus by changing their logo designs. Trademark applications which can be utilized for the demonstration of social distancing have been adopted by various existing trademarks as shown below.

In Turkey, certain trademarks became the part of this awareness and changed their logo designs in this manner.

It can be seen that the COVID-19 not only affected the health of the people but also affected the trademarks law and all areas of law. Indirectly, it affected all aspects of life. When the pandemic had begun, it adversely decreased the trademark applications, but then the trademark applications with distinctive phrases related to corona like "Korona," "Corona," "Sosyal Mesafe," and "Evde Kal" started emerging. After a comparison with 2019, it was observed that the trademark applications increased significantly.

Trademarks that already existed have also made alteration in their slogans and trademark applications according to the COVID-19.

6.4.2 ACCESS ISSUES TO INTELLECTUAL PROPERTY LAWS

Before understanding the impact of COVID-19 on intellectual property laws, there is a need to understand the concept of laws. These laws are made for the protection and implementation of the rights of the creator who is the owner of any invention, writing, music, design, etc. which is also termed as intellectual property. Different areas of intellectual property are:

- Copyright
- Trademark
- Patent
- Trade secret.

6.4.2.1 COPYRIGHT LAW

This law is designed to protect the rights of owners in their works in fine arts, designing any software, and entertainment. If any person tries to copy the work of the creator without getting his permission, this law protects the name of the owner.

6.4.2.2 TRADEMARK LAW

If any company or a person creates a design phrase for the identification of their products, this law protects the design, symbols, and phrases. For example, the apple company has the logo of "Apple." No one can make a similar logo that would confuse people about the source according to this law.

6.4.2.3 PATENT LAW

This law protects the invention of new products, processes, and designs by providing a complete mechanism. The patent owner can protect the third party from producing or designing the protected product.

6.4.2.4 TRADE SECRETS

It includes all the business ideas, practices, and formulas that can be used for the success of a business. These secrets are not shared with any outsider. For example, the formula used for Coca-Cola manufacturing is a trade secret that is protected without registration.

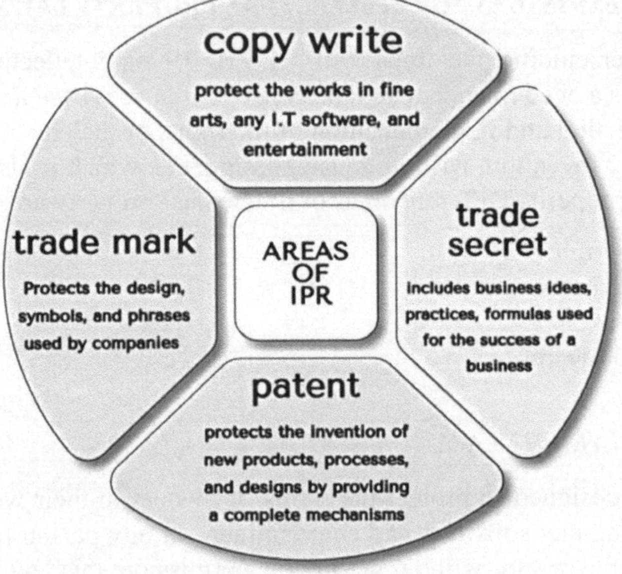

FIGURE 6.5 Areas related to IPR.

COVID-19 affected all the business sectors badly. It not only affected business health but also the protection given to intellectual property rights and also exert an effect on intellectual property right in getting protection.

Under a normal situation, third party is not allowed to use the intellectual property of the intellectual property holder due to the protection given to the right holder by the IP laws. But, COVID-19 puts pressure on the right holder to allow the third party to use their protected product for the public interest.

According to patent law, all the medical equipment is protected by patent law, which provides the company the legal rights to stop the third party from using their patented product or information. Due to COVID-19 crises, the demand of medicine and medical equipment increased manyfolds. There is a need to produce and design important product like masks, ventilators etc. which is not possible due to IP laws.

So, several governments allow the suspension of IP laws just for the sake of human health. In Malta, the government has the right to suspend IP rights, which is mentioned in the patent and design Act of the laws of Malta where national security so require. According to this law, permission is allowed to all the companies to manufacture the invention without authorization of the patent. This suspension of IP rules not only affects the IP laws but also the quality of the products. Production of vaccine and medical devices is not an easy task. By using shared information of the owner, no one can make the actual product effectively. The quantity of the products increased by this step, but the quality of the products got affected badly.

If we talk about the education sector, coronavirus puts restriction on the open movement of public. Classes were shifted to online mood. Certain research sites do not provide open access to public due to copyright issues. But due to COVID-19, these sites are also forced to give open access so that students can get quality education effectively, and the outside movement of people can be restricted, which indirectly helped in the control of the pandemic. This measure helped in restricting the spread of virus, but affected the IP laws and rights holders significantly.

6.4.3 INTELLECTUAL PROPERTY LAWS AS A DRIVER OF RESEARCH AND DEVELOPMENT DURING COVID-19

COVID-19 has opened a Pandora's box since its very emergence at the end of the year 2019. It has created problems and complications in every field of life. At a cursory glance, it might appear that only the health and education are most extremely affected, but it's not the truth. It has created havoc in every field, from health to education, finance to economy, and research to commercialization of the products. Not only this, but it has altered the general point of view of the public toward various matters in their ambience. The thoughts of people and general community have been clouded by the anxiety, fear, and suspicions that are closely interlinked with the rapid spread of COVID-19, and the corresponding causalities all-round the globe. One such matter, which was initially free of doubt but is transformed into a controversial matter since the inception of COVID-19, is the intellectual property law, a bon or a bane during the crises. We will observe the point of views of both the parties, those against the proposition and those in the favor of the proposition. But our foremost priority is to understand the link between the intellectual property laws or rights and the field of research and development. And for this purpose, there must be a sound understanding of the term under consideration, that is, research and development.

The best and most authentic description of this domain has been coined by the OECD.[101] According to OECD, R & D can be described as:

An innovative and inventive endeavor that is launched on an efficient, methodical ground so as to upgrade the bulk of knowledge and learning (this can incorporate the know-how about the human himself, about the civilization, and last but not least about the community) and the utilization of this upgraded learning for the sake of formulating applications.

There are three basic actions that come under the field of research and development. These activities are basic, applied, and experimental advancement and development.[102,103]

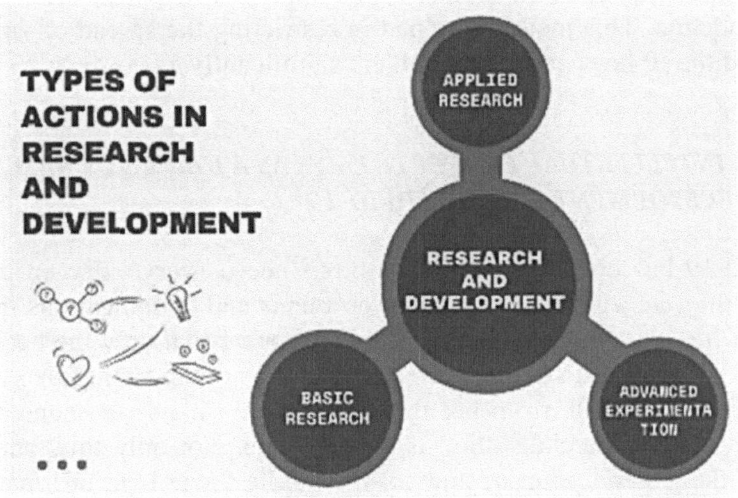

FIGURE 6.6 Types of actions in research and development.

6.4.3.1 CORRELATION BETWEEN RESEARCH AND DEVELOPMENT AND THE LAWS OF INTELLECTUAL PROPERTY

After getting a sound understanding of the proper description of the field of research and development, our next step is to highlight the connection between this field of R & D and the rights or laws of intellectual property.[104]

According to the previously available information and the perception of the community before COVID-19, laws on the intellectual property were considered as an essential step to defend and safeguard one's inventions from any kind of unwarranted and unapproved approach. Elaborating the point, we can say that if for instance any of the researcher was able to stumble upon something novel, then their foremost concern would be to be certain that he/she is the only one to get monetary benefits from that novel idea, since he/she strenuously worked and spent his/her time, energy, and resources on that purpose.[105]

But once the idea is released in the general public (in the form of a commodity, service, or a scheme), there are a lot of chances that any competitor gets hold of it and utilize it for his/her purpose. The sole purpose of IPR is to assure the researcher that his or her innovation whenever commercialized, he or she will be the first to be benefited from it and will get pecuniary benefits for the hard work. In a nutshell, we can say that IPR gives the contractual authority to the researcher for his/her fair share of work.[106,107]

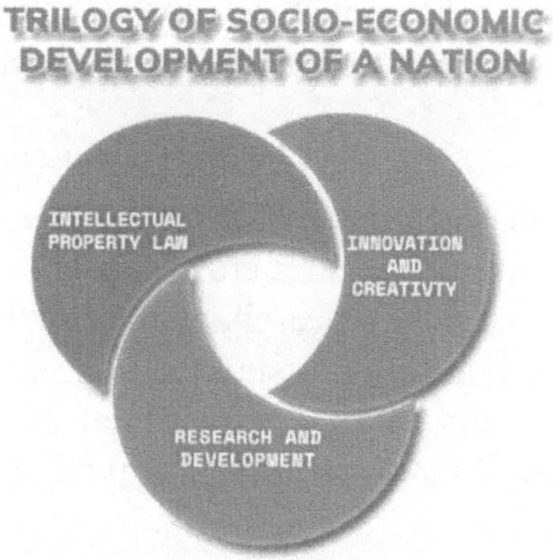

FIGURE 16.7 Socioeconomic indicators of development.

6.4.3.2 A COMPLETE TRILOGY: IPR, RESEARCH AND DEVELOPMENT, AND INNOVATION

Recapping the aforementioned statements, we can say that these three concepts of IPR, innovation, and R & D constitute a trilogy, in which each concept although has its own importance and existence but altering any one of them can automatically alter the other two. So, it is inevitable to discuss any one of them without discussing the effect of that alteration on the other two. Moreover, this trilogy is responsible for shaping the social as well as economic working and development of a nation.[108] Evidently, this is the reason why the countries aim to legislate stronger and comprehensive laws on intellectual property, as in the longer run these laws will shape the R & D, which will later affect the innovative ideas produced by the researchers and the commercialization of these ideas to upgrade the previously present ideas. These were the concepts before the pandemic. Since the initial introduction of this pandemic in our lives has changed the mindsets of many; some are strictly against these laws, while some deem them more significant during this prevailing condition of COVID-19. For the sake of analyzing the contradictory idea much more keenly, both ideas will be discussed one by one and then a conclusion will be derived in the end.[109]

6.4.3.2.1 Allegations of the Adversary Against IPR During the Pandemic

Although IPR was well accepted prior to COVID-19, but since the pandemic created a feeling of urgency in the general public, they started to deem IPR as a hurdle and requested continuously to remove it in the last 2 years.[110] The following allegations were imposed by the critics on this system of laws and regulations:

It can obstruct the access toward useful knowledge and the work previously done on the concerned topic. Moreover, they also claimed that it would most likely refrain the researchers and scientists from revealing the results and conclusions of their research, as they will wait for the desirable patent. These reasons will in turn forestall the treatment and may also hinder the processing and preparation of crisis critical pharmaceutical products. Besides, they also claimed that it will transform this field into a market.

6.4.3.2.2 Evidential Response of the Supporters of IPR w.r.t Pandemic

These allegations imposed by the critics were proved wrong with the passage of time. The supporters were of the view that IPR did not obstruct the spread of knowledge rather it allows those to access the knowledge, who are extremely serious about its utilization to produce upgraded results. Besides, there are many major obstructions in comparison to IPR. For instance, working on the vaccine and drugs for COVID-19 requires proper lab facilities, infrastructure, and resources.[111]

Moreover, it did not hinder the process of producing pharmaceutical product as during a single year from January 2020 to 2021, almost three effectual and secure vaccines have been produced. Apart from this, it allows the researchers to collaborate with platforms, and both of them share their sensitive information without being afraid of any misuse or disclosure.[112,113]

Secondly, the biggest concern of critic was that IPR will affect markets, and it is nothing but a monopoly to control the markets. Supporters answered this by highlighting the fact that for any illness, a single drug is available under numerous brand names. This point proves that none of the patent holder controls the market trend, as the patents are always presented with alternatives.[114] Moreover, these alternatives also change from nation to nation as there are local as well as international brands, while the generic name remains the same. It is visible from the treatment of hepatitis C.[115] Thirdly, it allows the researchers to select the most highly skilled and equipped of all for the collaboration, which results in more efficient working. Fourthly, it promotes collective effort from the nations all-round the globe. For instance, China, South Korea, India, and the inventors of AstraZeneca collaborated to produce almost 2 billion doses. Evidently, all of them used their resources and in this way, they acquired a complete set of resources, skills, knowledge, and proper lab infrastructure.

In short, development, mass production, distribution of COVID-19 vaccines, and development of various treatment procedures over the past 1 year has been nothing less than a successful conquest of innovations. Researchers along with life sciences companies have worked day and night to meet the requirements and demands, and this could not have been possible without the IPRs. IPs have played a crucial role in drug development in recent times, and are the most important platform in providing resources to developers and encouraging their trust in manufacturers and traders.[116,117]

6.4.4 IP POOLING INSTRUMENTS TO COPE WITH COVID-19 PANDEMIC

IP pooling is chronological assortment of a range of single or multiple pool configurations. IP refers to creations of mind in every field and aspect of life. Patent, trademark, copyrights, and trade secrets are the four major IP pooling instruments.

6.4.4.1 COVID-19 TECHNOLOGY ACCESS POOL (C-TAP)

The C-Tap, a COVID-19 IP pooling instruments is launched in partnership with Costa Rica's government by WHO to provide a platform to developers, to share knowledge, data and research to manufacturers, and for the development of COVID-19-related health products (therapeutics, diagnostics, vaccines, etc.). This tool gives the manufacturers and developers the untapped resources to mass produce and sell COVID-19-related healthcare products legally.

The President of Costa Rica in 2020 came forward to Director General of WHO with the idea to develop IP instruments for the detection, prevention, control, and treatment of the COVID-19 pandemic; as a result, C-TAP came to existence. As a result, after careful consultations with the stakeholders, letters were written and given to anyone who was eligible to contribute to the pool.

The purpose of developing C-TAP was to accelerate the development of diagnostic and therapeutic products for COVID-19, and upscale the production by providing resources and removing any possible obstacle; thus making them available globally. As estimated by the international monetary fund (IMF), by the end of 2021, COVID could cost the economy about 12 trillion dollars. This alarming figure indicates the urgency to develop IP instruments for COVID-19.

6.4.4.1.1 C-TAP Bodies

The implementing partners for C-TAP program by WHO that play a role in providing rightful health technologies timely and affordably to the world include:

- The Medicines Patent Pool
- Open COVID Pledge
- UN Technology Bank and Unit-aid
- The Tech Access Partnership (TAP)
- Global Initiative on Sharing All Influenza Data (GISAID)
- The WHO Global Observatory on Health R & D
- The WHO C-TAP database.

FIGURE 6.13 Some C-TAP bodies.

6.4.5 *FEARS CONCERNING COVID-19 IP*

IP as a tool to promote and accelerate any process has faced its own share of critics since the pandemic started in 2019. Where some consider it a blessing in disguise, others consider it an evil tool of destruction and believe that IP rights are a roadblock toward development. Since the process of development of IP, its haters have called for its cancellation and have been working day and night against it. It is feared by people.

- IP rights make the availability and manufacture of products difficult due to patentship
- IP rights make the product way more costly
- IP rights give full power to manufacturer

However, there is a need to understand that IP is a tool for promotion and acceleration rather than an obstacle.[118]

- **IP and R & D:** IP is a smooth road toward R & D collaborations. Earlier, it was believed that IP pools play a role in minimizing collaborations of R & D and intellect; however, it is the total opposite since the enforcement of IP partnership and collaborations between R & D, intellect, and companies have become easier.
- **Patent Healthcare Products:** The demand of lower-priced products like vaccines for developing countries has, however, led to the suspension of certain patent rights in IP, including the price of the products. But looking at the scale with which mass production is being done and also the number of companies producing the vaccine, it is impossible for companies to meet the competition with higher-priced products. It is predicted that soon there might be 20 manufactured types of vaccines leading to low prices to meet the competition.

6.4.6 *IP A SOLUTION NOT A THREAT*

Every now and then, IP rights have proved to be a blessing in disguise while dealing with the pandemic. For example, the manufacturing license allows various manufacturers to produce the same product under one company label. It is seen by the end of 2021, 2 billion doses of AstraZeneca were mass manufactured by issuing the manufacturing license to multiple agencies. Some factors that support the IP laws and COVID-19 vaccine development are as under:_

- IP encourages investments and discoveries, suspending it would detrack the innovation process.
- IP encourages partnership with researchers and life science companies, upscaling the mass production.
- IP laws will protect us from further coronavirus destruction and prepare for future pandemics.
- There is a need to put aside all the differences, as IP waiver discussions have slowed down the vaccine production.[119]

6.5 CONCLUSIONS

After suffering with uncertainties in innovation and research and development due to lockdowns, COVID-19 crises also changed the behavior of firms to initialize innovative activities. Patent applications incentivized innovation through technologies that supported working by staying at home. Innovation system of COVID-19 developed and influenced the technologies through private and public sectors to fight with the pandemic challenges. Knowledge in prepandemic patent applications also motivated the researchers and provided a platform for innovations. However during these times, the impact of patents on prices and medicine access is ambiguous. When it comes to IP laws, they may seem unfavorable for research and development, especially in the time of pandemic when urgency in actions is requisite, but actually it has proved to be a blessing. It not only helped the researchers and scientists to get proper funding but also segregated the platforms, which were strenuously working for manufacturing of crisis critical pharmaceutical products. IPR proved to be a bane and not a bon when it comes to the field of research, development, and innovation.

KEYWORDS

- **IPRs**
- **patents**
- **pharmaceutical patents**
- **compulsory licensing**
- **research and development**
- **pandemic**

REFERENCES

1. Guderian, C. C.; Bican, P. M.; Riar, F. J.; Chattopadhyay, S. Innovation Management in Crisis: Patent Analytics as a Response to the COVID-19 Pandemic. *R&D Manag.* **2021,** *51* (2), 223–239.
2. Liu, Y. et al. The Reproductive Number of COVID-19 Is Higher Compared to SARS coronavirus. *J. Travel Med.* **2020.**
3. Bendavid, E. et al. *COVID-19 Antibody Seroprevalence in Santa Clara Country*; MedRxiv: California, 2020.
4. Tellez, V. M. The COVID-19 Pandemic: R&D and Intellectual Property Management for Access to Diagnostics, Medicines and Vaccines. *Policy Brief* **2020,** *73*, 1–8.
5. Paunov, C. The Global Crisis and Firms' Investments in Innovation. *Res. Policy* **2021,** *41* (1), 24–35.
6. Tietze, F.; Vimalnath, P.; Aristodemou, L.; Molloy, J. Crisis-Critical Intellectual Property: Findings from the COVID-19 Pandemic. IEEE Trans. Eng. Manag. **2020,** 1–18.
7. Davis, J.P.; Eisenhardt, K.M.; Bingham, C.B. Optimal Structure, Market Dynamism, and the Strategy of Simple Rules. Admin. Sci. Quart. **2009,** *54* (3) 413–452.
8. Martin-Rios, C.; Pasamar, S. Service Innovation in Times of Economic Crisis: The Strategic Adaptation Activities of the Top EU Service Firms. R&D Manag. **2018,** *48* **(2),** 195–209.
9. Teece, D.; Peteraf, M.; Leih, S. Dynamic Capabilities and Organizational Agility: Risk, Uncertainty, and Strategy in the Innovation Economy. Calif. Manag. Rev. **2016,** *58 (*4), 13–35.
10. Müller, R. Corporate Crisis Management. Long Range Plan. **1985,** *18* (5) 38–48.
11. Cooper, R. G.; Edgett, S. J. Developing a Product Innovation and Technology Strategy for Your Business. *Res.-Technol. Manag.* **2010,** *53* (3), 33–40.
12. Archibugi, D.; Filippetti, A.; Frenz, M. The Impact of the Economic Crisis on Innovation: Evidence from Europe. *Technol. Forecast. Soc. Change* **2013,** *80* (7), 1247–1260.
13. Hingley, P.; Park, W. G. Do Business Cycles Affect Patenting? Evidence from European Patent Office Filings. *Technol. Forecast. Soc. Change* **2017,** *116*, 76–86.
14. Hoegl, M.; Gibbert, M.; Mazursky, D. Financial Constraints in Innovation Projects: When Is Less More? *Res. Policy* **2008,** *37* (8), 1382–1391.
15. Oskam, J.; Boswijk, A. Airbnb: The Future of Networked Hospitality Businesses. *J. Tour. Fut.* **2016.**
16. Zervas, G.; Proserpio, D.; Byers, J. W. The Rise of the Sharing Economy: Estimating the Impact of Airbnb on the Hotel Industry. *J. Market. Res.* **2017,** *54* (5), 687–705.
17. Christensen, M.; Knudsen, T. Design of Decision-Making Organizations. *Manage. Sci.* **2010,** *56* (1), 71–89.
18. Denrell, J.; Fang, C. Predicting the Next Big Thing: Success as a Signal of Poor Judgment. *Manag. Sci.* **2010,** *56* (10), 1653–1667.
19. Campbell, R. S. Patent Trends as a Technological Forecasting Tool. *World Patent Info.* **1983,** *5* (3), 137–143.
20. Ashton, W. B.; Sen, R. K. Using Patent Information in Technology Business Planning—I. *Res.-Technol. Manage.* **1988,** *31* (6), 42–46.
21. Ernst, H. Patent Information for Strategic Technology Management. *World Patent Info.* **2003,** *25* (3), 233–242.

22. Archibugi, D.; Filippetti, A.; Frenz, M. Economic Crisis and Innovation: Is Destruction Prevailing Over Accumulation? *Res. Policy* **2013,** *42* (2), 303–314.
23. Teplykh, G. V. Innovations and Productivity: The Shift During the 2008 Crisis. *Ind. Innov.* **2018,** *25* (1), 53–83.
24. Ferreira, A.; Teixeira, A. L. Intra-and Extra-Organisational Foundations of Innovation Processes—The Information and Communication Technology Sector Under the Crisis in Portugal. *Int. J. Innov. Manag.* **2016,** *20* (06), 1650056.
25. Ulmer, R. R.; Sellnow, T. L.; Seeger, M. W. *Effective Crisis Communication: Moving from Crisis to Opportunity*; Sage Publications, 2017.
26. Cefis, E.; Marsili, O. Good Times, Bad Times: Innovation and Survival Over the Business Cycle. *Ind. Corp. Change* **2019,** *28* (3), 565–587.
27. Heyden, M. L.; Wilden, R.; Wise, C. Navigating Crisis from the Backseat? How Top Managers Can Support Radical Change Initiatives by Middle Managers. *Ind. Market. Manage.* **2020,** *88*, 305–313.
28. Gupta, A. R&D and Firm Resilience During Bad Times, 2020. Available at SSRN 3703103.
29. Cefis, E.; Bartoloni, E.; Bonati, M. Show Me How to Live: Firms' Financial Conditions and Innovation During the Crisis. *Struct. Change Econ. Dyn.* **2020,** *52*, 63–81.
30. Paunov, C.; Planes-Satorra, S. Science, Technology and Innovation in the Time of COVID-19, 2021.
31. Am, J. B.; Furstenthal, L.; Jorge, F.; Roth, E. *Innovation in a Crisis: Why It Is More Critical Than Ever*; McKinsey & Company, 2020.
32. Organisation for Economic Co-operation and Development. *Corporate Sector Vulnerabilities During the Covid-19 Outbreak: Assessment and Policy Responses*; OECD Publishing, 2020.
33. Paunov, C.; Planes-Satorra, S. Science, Technology and Innovation in Times of Covid-19 and Policy Responses. Preliminary Overview in June 2020. *Sci. Technol. Innov. Times Covid-19 Policy Responses* **2020.**
34. Kanesarajah, V.; White, E. Chasing Change: Innovation and Patent Activity During COVID-19: A Report on the Pandemic's Impact on the Global R&D Community and Innovation Lifecycle, 2020; p 18.
35. Bloom, N.; Davis, S. J.; Zhestkova, Y. Covid-19 Shifted Patent Applications Toward Technologies That Support Working from Home. *AEA Papers Proc.* **2021,** *111*, 263–266).
36. Wakeman, S. E.; Green, T. C.; Rich, J. An Overdose Surge Will Compound the COVID-19 Pandemic If Urgent Action Is Not Taken. *Nat. Med.* **2020,** *26* (6), 819–820.
37. Frazer, J. S.; Shard, A.; Herdman, J. Involvement of the Open-Source Community in Combating the Worldwide COVID-19 Pandemic: A Review. *J. Med. Eng. Technol.* **2020,** *44* (4), 169–176.
38. Kartoglu, U. H.; Moore, K. L.; Lloyd, J. S. Logistical Challenges for Potential SARS-CoV-2 Vaccine and a Call to Research Institutions, Developers and Manufacturers. *Vaccine* **2020,** *38* (34), 5393.
39. Persson, M. COVID-19 Vaccines: A Literature Analysis of the Three First Approved COVID-19 Vaccines in the EU, 2021.
40. Dinlersoz, E.; Dunne, T.; Haltiwanger, J.; Penciakova, V. Business Formation: A Tale of Two Recessions. *AEA Papers Proc.* **2021,** *111*, 253–257.
41. Office for National Statistics. Coronavirus (COVID-19) Roundup, 2020.

42. Gavrila, S. G.; de Lucas Ancillo, A. COVID-19 as an Entrepreneurship, Innovation, Digitization and Digitalization Accelerator: Spanish Internet Domains Registration Analysis. *Br. Food J.* 2021.
43. Holmes, E. A.; O'Connor, R. C.; Perry, V. H.; Tracey, I.; Wessely, S.; Arseneault, L. et al. Multidisciplinary Research Priorities for the COVID-19 Pandemic: A Call for Action for Mental Health Science. *Lancet Psych.* **2020,** *7* (6), 547–560.
44. Gompers, P.; Gornall, W.; Kaplan, S. N.; Strebulaev, I. A. Venture Capitalists and COVID-19. *J. Fin. Quant. Anal.* **2021,** *56* (7), 2474–2499.
45. Howell, S. T.; Lerner, J.; Nanda, R.; Townsend, R. R. *Financial Distancing: How Venture Capital Follows the Economy Down and Curtails Innovation* (No. w27150); National Bureau of Economic Research, 2020.
46. Ambrasat, J.; Fabian, G. One Year After the Outbreak–Involvement of Scientists in the Covid-19 Pandemic Findings from a Germany-Wide Study, 2021.
47. Molitorisová, A.; Purnhagen, K. P.; Šístek, P. Techno-Regulation: Technological Collaboration Between EU Administrations, 2021.
48. Blanchard, A.; Schwalm, H. Guidelines on Designing, Implementing and Evaluating Open Innovation Activities, 2020.
49. Baker, N. These Cancer Scientists Turned Their Lab into a Coronavirus-Testing Facility. *Nature* **2020,** *580* (7804), 441–442.
50. Minello, A. The Pandemic and the Female Academic. *Nature* **2020,** *17*, 2020.
51. Organisation for Economic Co-operation and Development. *Women at the Core of the Fight Against COVID-19 Crisis*; OECD Publishing, 2020.
52. Castelvecchi, D. 'Loving the Minimal FOMO': First Major Physics Conference to Go Virtual Sees Record Attendance. *Nature* **2020,** *580* (7805), 574–575.
53. Amano-Patiño, N.; Faraglia, E.; Giannitsarou, C.; Hasna, Z. Who Is Doing New Research in the Time of COVID-19? Not the Female Economists. *Vox EU* **2020,** *2*.
54. Yanisky-Ravid, S.; Jin, R. Summoning a New Artificial Intelligence Patent Model: In the Age of Pandemic. *Soc. Sci. Res. Netw.* **2020.**
55. Sampat, B. N.; Shadlen, K. C. The COVID-19 Innovation System: Article Describes Innovations that Emerged During the COVID-19 pandemic. *Health Affairs* **2021,** *40* (3), 400–409.
56. Freeman, C. The 'National System of Innovation' in Historical Perspective. *Camb. J. Econ.* **1995,** *19* (1), 5–24.
57. Kremer, M.; Williams, H. Incentivizing Innovation: Adding to the Tool Kit. *Innov. Policy Econ.* **2010,** *10* (1), 1–17.
58. Levin, R. C.; Klevorick, A. K.; Nelson, R. R.; Winter, S. G.; Gilbert, R.; Griliches, Z. Appropriating the Returns from Industrial Research and Development. *Brook. Papers Econ. Act.* **1987,** *1987* (3), 783–831.
59. Frank, R. G.; Salkever, D. S. *Pricing, Patent Loss and the Market for Pharmaceuticals* (No. w3803); National Bureau of Economic Research, 1991.
60. Reichman, J. H. Comment: Compulsory Licensing of Patented Pharmaceutical Inventions: Evaluating the Options. *J. Law Med. Ethics* **2009,** *37* (2), 247–263.
61. Whoriskey, P.; MacMillan, D.; O'Connell, J. 'Doomed to Fail': Why a US $4 Trillion Bailout Couldn't Revive the American Economy. *The Washington Post* **2020.**
62. Tozzi, J.; Griffin, R.; Stein, S. Trump Administration Dips Into Protective Gear, CDC Funds to Fund Vaccine Push. *Bloomberg [Serial on the Internet]*, 2020.

63. Athey, S.; Kremer, M.; Snyder, C.; Tabarrok, A. In the Race for a Coronavirus Vaccine, We Must Go Big: Really, Really Big. *New York Times* **2020,** *4*.
64. Nguyen, L. H.; Drew, D. A.; Graham, M. S.; Joshi, A. D.; Guo, C. G.; Ma, W. et al. Risk of COVID-19 Among Front-Line Health-Care Workers and the General Community: A Prospective Cohort Study. *Lancet Public Health* **2020,** *5* (9), e475–e483.
65. Pololi, L. H.; Vasiliou, V.; Bloom-Feshbach, K. Midcareer Medical School Research Faculty Perspectives on Vitality and Professionalism During the COVID-19 Pandemic. *JAMA Netw. Open* **2021,** *4* (8), e2120642.
66. Slaoui, M.; Hepburn, M. Developing Safe and Effective Covid Vaccines—Operation Warp Speed's Strategy and Approach. *New Engl. J. Med.* **2020,** *383* (18), 1701–1703.
67. Ardizzone, K.; Love, J.; OTAs, P. Other Transaction Agreements: Government Contracts That Eliminate Protections for the Public on Pricing, Access and Competition, Including in Connection with COVID-19 Vaccines and Treatments, 2020.
68. Tracker, R. Z. B. F. Tracker Details Billions in Taxpayer Funds Supporting COVID-19 R&D Efforts. *Public Citizen* **2020,** *2*.
69. Price, W. N.; Rai, A. K.; Minssen, T. Knowledge Transfer for Large-Scale Vaccine Manufacturing. *Science* **2020,** *369* (6506), 912–914.
70. Van Dorn, A. COVID-19 and Readjusting Clinical Trials. *Lancet* **2020,** *396* (10250), 523–524.
71. Lurie, N.; Saville, M.; Hatchett, R.; Halton, J. Developing Covid-19 Vaccines at Pandemic Speed. *New Engl. J. Med.* **2020,** *382* (21), 1969–1973.
72. Kumar, A.; Bernasconi, V.; Manak, M.; de Almeida Aranha, A. P.; Kristiansen, P. A. The CEPI Centralised Laboratory Network: Supporting COVID-19 Vaccine Development. *Lancet* **2021,** *397* (10290), 2148–2149.
73. Cross, S.; Rho, Y.; Reddy, H.; Pepperrell, T.; Rodgers, F.; Osborne, R. et al. Who Funded the Research Behind the Oxford–AstraZeneca COVID-19 Vaccine? *BMJ Global Health* **2021,** *6* (12), e007321.
74. Peacocke, E. F.; Heupink, L. F.; Frønsdal, K.; Dahl, E. H.; Chola, L. Global Access to COVID-19 Vaccines: A Scoping Review of Factors That May Influence Equitable Access for Low and Middle-Income Countries. *BMJ Open* **2021,** *11* (9), e049505.
75. Hoyt, K. *Long Shot*. Harvard University Press, 2012.
76. Contarino, L.; Purnell, E. The Patent Landscape Behind COVID-19 Vaccines. *Int. Pharma. Ind. [Serial on the Internet]* 2020.
77. Duhigg, C.; Lohr, S. The Patent, Used as a Sword. *New York Times* **2012,** *7* (10), 2012.
78. Helfgott, S. Patent Filing Costs Around the World. *J. Pat. Trademark Off. Soc'y* **1993,** *75*, 567.
79. Machuca-Martinez, F.; Amado, R. C.; Gutierrez, O. Coronaviruses: A Patent Dataset Report for Research and Development (R&D) Analysis. *Data Brief* **2020,** *30*.
80. Testar, J. Cytokines: Introduction, 2020.
81. Yuen, K. Y.; Wong, S. S. Y. Human Infection by Avian Influenza A H5N1. *Hong Kong Med. J.* **2005**.
82. Goodman, B. Cytokine Storms May Be Fueling Some COVID Deaths. *WebMD Health News*. April 17, 2020.
83. Liu, C.; Zhou, Q.; Li, Y.; Garner, L. V.; Watkins, S. P.; Carter, L. J. et al. Research and Development on Therapeutic Agents and Vaccines for COVID-19 and Related Human Coronavirus Diseases, 2020.

84. Park, M.; Thwaites, R. S.; Openshaw, P. J. COVID-19: Lessons from SARS and MERS. *Eur. J. Immunol.* **2020,** *50* (3), 308.
85. Price, N.; Sachs, R.; Sherkow, J. S.; Ouellette, L. L. Are COVID-19 Vaccine Advance Purchases a form of Vaccine Nationalism, an Effective Spur to Innovation, or Something in Between? *Written Description [blog on the Internet]*, 2020.
86. Usher, A. D. South Africa and India Push for COVID-19 Patents Ban. *Lancet 396* (10265), 1790–1791.
87. Waning, B.; Diedrichsen, E.; Moon, S. A Lifeline to Treatment: The Role of Indian Generic Manufacturers in Supplying Antiretroviral Medicines to Developing Countries. *J. Int. AIDS Soc.* **2010,** *13* (1), 1–9.
88. Cox, K. L. The Medicines Patent Pool: Promoting Access and Innovation for Life-Saving Medicines Through Voluntary Licenses. *Hast. Sci. Tech. L. J.* **2012,** *4*, 291.
89. Arora, A. Contracting for Tacit Knowledge: The Provision of Technical Services in Technology Licensing Contracts. *J. Dev. Econ.* **1996,** *50* (2), 233–256.
90. So, A. D.; Woo, J. Reserving Coronavirus Disease 2019 Vaccines for Global Access: Cross Sectional Analysis. *BMJ* **2020,** *371*.
91. McAdams, D.; McDade, K. K.; Ogbuoji, O.; Johnson, M.; Dixit, S.; Yamey, G. Incentivising Wealthy Nations to Participate in the COVID-19 Vaccine Global Access Facility (COVAX): A Game Theory Perspective. *BMJ Global Health* **2020,** *5* (11), e003627.
92. Chen, Z.; Zhang, L. Meet the Challenges of Mass Vaccination Against COVID-19. *Exploratory Res. Hypoth. Med.* **2021,** *6* (2), 77–79.
93. Barrero, J. M.; Bloom, N.; Davis, S. J.; Meyer, B. H. COVID-19 Is a Persistent Reallocation Shock. In *AEA Papers Proc.* **2021,** *111*, 287–91.
94. Pagano, M.; Wagner, C.; Zechner, J. Disaster Resilience and Asset Prices. COVID Economics: Vetted and Real-Time Papers, May 22, 2020.
95. Papanikolaou, D.; Schmidt, L. D. *Working Remotely and the Supply-Side Impact of Covid-19* (No. w27330); National Bureau of Economic Research, 2020.
96. Bick, A.; Blandin, A.; Mertens, K. Work from Home After the COVID-19 Outbreak, 2020.
97. Guloglu, B.; Tekin, R. B. A Panel Causality Analysis of the Relationship Among Research and Development, Innovation, and Economic Growth in High-Income OECD Countries. *Eurasian Econ. Rev.* **2012,** *2* (1), 32–47.
98. Henard, D. H.; McFadyen, M. A. The Complementary Roles of Applied and basic research: a knowledge-based perspective. *J. Product Innov. Manag.* **2005,** *22* (6), 503–514.
99. Gulbrandsen, M.; Kyvik, S. Are the Concepts Basic Research, Applied Research and Experimental Development Still Useful? An Empirical Investigation Among Norwegian Academics. *Sci. Public Policy* **2010,** *37* (5), 343–353.
100. Falvey, R.; Foster, N.; Greenaway, D. Intellectual Property Rights and Economic Growth. *Rev. Dev. Econ.* **2006,** *10* (4), 700–719.
101. Willinsky, J. *The Intellectual Properties of Learning*; University of Chicago Press, 2018.
102. WHO, G. Statement on the second meeting of the International Health Regulations (2005) Emergency Committee Regarding the Outbreak of Novel Coronavirus (2019-nCoV). *World Health Organization*, 2020.
103. Şahin, M. Impact of Weather on COVID-19 Pandemic in Turkey. *Sci. Total Environ.* **2020,** *728*, 138810.

104. Guloglu, B.; Tekin, R. B. A Panel Causality Analysis of the Relationship Among Research and Development, Innovation, and Economic Growth in High-Income OECD Countries. *Eurasian Econ. Rev.* **2012,** *2* (1), 32–47.
105. Henard, D. H.; McFadyen, M. A. The Complementary Roles of Applied and Basic Research: A Knowledge-Based Perspective. *J. Product Innov. Manage.* **2005,** *22* (6), 503–514.
106. Gulbrandsen, M.; Kyvik, S. Are the Concepts Basic Research, Applied Research and Experimental Development Still Useful? An Empirical Investigation Among Norwegian Academics. *Sci. Public Policy* **2010,** *37* (5), 343–353.
107. Bosch, M.; Lederman, D.; Maloney, W. F. Patenting and Research and Development: A Global View, 2005.
108. Zhao, M. Conducting R&D in Countries with Weak Intellectual Property Rights Protection. *Manag. Sci.* **2006,** *52* (8), 1185–1199.
109. Falk, M. What Drives Business Research and Development (R&D) Intensity Across Organisation for Economic Co-operation and Development (OECD) Countries? *Appl. Econ.* **2006,** *38* (5), 533–547.
110. Habib, M.; Abbas, J.; Noman, R. Are Human Capital, Intellectual Property Rights, and Research and Development Expenditures Really Important for Total Factor Productivity? An Empirical Analysis. *Int. J. Soc. Econ. 2019.*
111. Chen, Y.; Puttitanun, T. Intellectual Property Rights and Innovation in Developing Countries. *J. Dev. Econ.* **2005,** *78* (2), 474–493.
112. Park, W. G.; Ginarte, J. C. Intellectual Property Rights and Economic Growth. *Contemp. Econ. Policy* **1997,** *15* (3), 51–61.
113. Gulbrandsen, M.; Kyvik, S. Are the Concepts Basic Research, Applied Research and Experimental Development Still Useful? An Empirical Investigation Among Norwegian Academics. *Sci. Public Policy* **2010,** *37* (5), 343–353.
114. Boldrin, M.; Levine, D. The Case Against Intellectual Property. *Am. Econ. Rev.* **2002,** *92* (2), 209–212.
115. Murthy, N. The Impact of the 1991 Economic Reforms on Indian Businesses. *India Transformed: Twenty-Five Years of Economic Reforms*; 2018; p 582.
116. Andrews, L. B. Genes and Patent Policy: Rethinking Intellectual Property Rights. *Nat. Rev. Genet.* **2002,** *3* (10), 803–808.
117. Forero-Pineda, C. The Impact of Stronger Intellectual Property Rights on Science and Technology in Developing Countries. *Res. Policy* **2006,** *35* (6), 808–824.
118. Anuar, H. S.; Zulhumadi, F.; Udin, Z. M. Intellectual Property Rights: Issues and Challenges in Research and Development Activities.
119. Carroll, M. W. Sharing Research Data and Intellectual Property Law: A Primer. *PLoS Biol.* **2015,** *13* (8), e1002235.

CHAPTER 7

Impact of COVID-19 on the Marketing Sector

MUHAMMAD SHAHBAZ[1], SHAHZAD SHARIF[1], ABIA MAHBOOB[1], AYOUB RASID CHAUDHARY[2], and SAMINA YAQOOB[3]

[1]*Materials Chemistry Laboratory, Department of Chemistry, GC University, Lahore, Pakistan*

[2]*Department of Chemistry, GC University, Lahore, Pakistan*

[3]*Dr Hasan Murad School of Management (HSM), University of Management and Technology, Lahore, Pakistan*

ABSTRACT

After the World War II, the Coronavirus disease (COVID-19) is considered one of the greatest global challenges experienced by human beings. Undoubtedly, it has dented badly living style of human beings covering every aspect of life. Precautionary measures such as lockdown, social distancing, and standard operating procedure have resulted in closure of physical businesses. Economic activities of business sectors around the world have been jolted completely. Individual behavior has shifted toward online systems via different devices supported by Internet. People visit different websites launched by different business sectors to fulfill the basis amenities of life. Online purchasing has become a "new norm" as consumers have shifted toward online platforms. The unprecedented scenario calls for radical adaptations to new marketing techniques and working environment to address the problems posed by COVID-19. Consequently, marketing policies and strategies have been modified significantly. As consumer behavior has modified, the business sectors have reshaped their strategies. Study of consumer

Post-Pandemic Economy, Technology, and Innovation: Global Outlook and Context.
Samina Yaqoob, Arwa Abdulkreem AL-Huqail, and Fakhra Aziz (Eds.)

segment, business competitors, development of strong relationship with the consumer, and meeting the expectation of consumer is the need of the hour. Growth demands agility in marketing without compromising with the brand value. Creative approach and customer's satisfaction nourishes the business. Different brands have handled the situation very tactfully by critical evaluation of consumers' plight. Customer relationship management (CRM) is responsible for the initiatives like personalization, email marketing, and coupons. Various brands have prioritized e-commerce to stay connected with consumers and are utilizing different tactics such as promotional devices for the survival of business.

7.1 INTRODUCTION

Life of human beings has been affected severely by the pandemic of coronavirus disease (COVID-19).[1] It has caused massive financial loss and created global economic and health crises.[2] Different strategies have been adopted internationally to prevent the spread of COVID-19. Lockdown, social distancing, and various strict standard operating procedures have limited the movement of the people and they are confined to their home. It has modified buying habits of customers and they have resorted to buy at home through online shopping using Internet connected to various devices like smartphones, laptops, etc. E-commerce marketing has shown a great improvement.[3] Coronavirus affects the respiratory system of human being and it is spread from one person to another so its transmission accelerates by cash handling and physical visitation of business sectors.[4] With the awareness of the outbreak, people have opted to take precautionary measures. The consumer's behavior has affected greatly as the worldwide recession has substantial consequences for working, living, and shopping.[5] All the businesses have been affected and, to maintain employment levels, the business sectors must react positively to curtail the demage.[6] The most effective tool to boost up the sale is effective marketing.[7] Marketing policies and strategies have been changed drastically with the modification in the behavior of consumers.

7.2 CONCEPT OF MARKETING

Marketing is the business or actions taken for selling and promoting products or services. It also includes advertising and market research. To develop marketing strategies, there exist some fundamental elements that are known as the marketing mix. The term of marketing mix was coined by Borden[8] and became more familiar when McCarthy introduced the concept of some essential elements such as product, place, price, and promotion, commonly known as 4 Ps.[9] Later, Booms and Bitner[10] put forward a specific marketing mix consisting of seven elements regarding services, adding physical evidence, people, and processes in the 4 Ps which makes it 7 Ps. All the 7Ps focus on satisfying the needs of the consumer profitably.

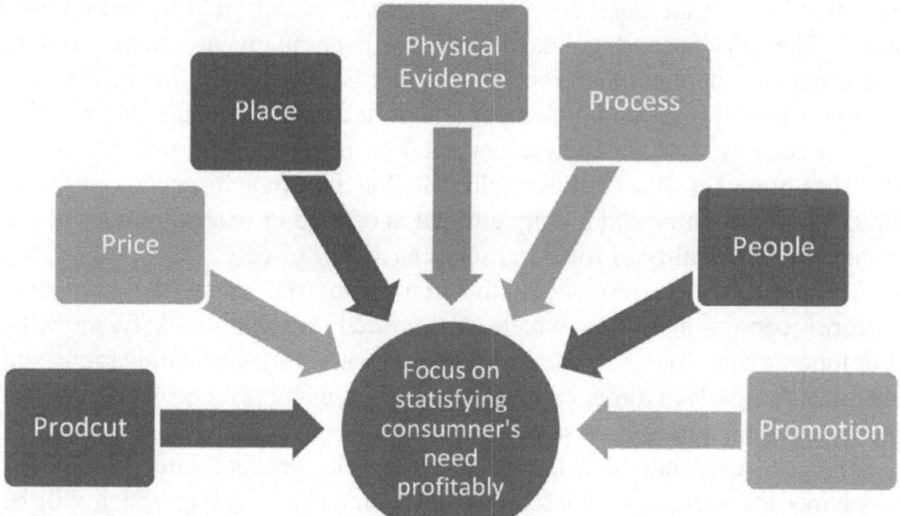

FIGURE 7.1 7Ps of marketing.

The marketing starts from product which generates revenue for the company.[11] Company offers product in the market whether it is an intangible (service) or tangible goods. The product involves a number of development stages and depends on various factors. Product life cycle, need, and its positioning play a vital role in product synthesis. Decision regarding price via online sale is very important and it is very crucial and critical for companies to standardize price.[12]

Price plays a vital role in success of product in the market. Having high price will put a question on its quality and it may affect the sale in the market. The price should be fixed in such a manner that there should be win–win situation for consumers as well as for the company. The consumer may show negative feedback if the price is very high and the quality of the product is below par. Several pricing models are presented by different researchers. Competitive Pricing Strategy is one of them which targets at the penetration into the market to get maximum market share while maintaining product positioning and customer base. A company has to charge what other companies are charging. Different strategies such as offering discounts and coupons are adopted by various companies to increase the sale.[13] Through promotions, companies communicate with customers to persuade them to buy their products.[11]

The place element is very important and mobile applications provide an easy platform. It includes distribution channels which help in maximizing sale.[14] The service and goods offered by a company are transferred to consumers by the manufacturer. The product is presented in the market and the place is a very essential element which determines whether the product is being seen by the right audience or not. For instance, the brand of McDonald's has branches all over the world. McDonald's franchises are opened in almost every country and a unique menu is offered in each country without compromising quality of food and services at low prices.

To showcase the product in the market in true sense, the marketers perform certain activities which are termed "Promotion." Technically, promotional activities rest upon multi-level marketing communications and channels. It involves direct calling, advertising, using print, as well as social media channels to promote sale.

Physical evidence constitutes the tangible product and it includes brochures, packaging, business card, and company branding which will be noticed by the consumer at first sight. However, certain intangible products also include tangible cues. When somebody sees a FedEx delivery vehicle, he will recognize it immediately due to its orange and purple color scheme.

Every person in the company is important as he is involved in preparing, distributing, and selling the product. While dealing with the intangible offerings (services), the marketing mix focuses on individuals who present the product in the market. Employees working in a factory and a field will leave a long-lasting impression on the consumer. The dealing of the employees will help in developing a strong relationship with the brand. Employees represent companies and they should be adequately trained to communicate with customers[15] as miscommunication can affect marketing efforts.[16] This element is considered one of the most essential elements of the marketing mix because service represents performance and performance cannot be separated from the performer.[17]

The product is made by the company which has to reach to the consumer ultimately. The whole process of manufacturing and delivering the product to the consumer is very important. It will drive the product in the market. It is not a mere process of delivering a product to the consumer but a road map for the company to operate.

7.3 IMPACTS OF THE COVID-19 PANDEMIC ON MARKETING

The outspread of COVID-19 has affected life of every person. Movement of people has been restrained by the government agencies to prevent its spread. They are confined to their home, but they have to meet their basic needs of living, that is, food, clothing, education, etc. An alternate has been developed in the form of e-commerce; a platform to satiate basic amenities of life. It has put a great pressure on the company to handle the shift of the consumer toward online system and they have redesigned their approach of marketing. Industrial sectors are the one which has got a deep dent on the economic growth. No doubt, during the pandemic of COVID-19, advertising and marketing departments were striving hard to navigate the business through innovative and creative marketing strategies. Marketing policies have been altered to face the increasing competition for survival of business, while considering sustainability, operational options with strategic planning in uncertain environment, analysis of issues regarding brand reputation, identification of new products as well as services required to meet the needs and expectations of consumers. Development of operative strategies, creative marketing campaigns, and effective use of social media is inevitable.

All the companies have revised their budget for marketing. There is a significant decrease in the marketing budget due to COVID-19. The budget for marketing was 10.5% in the year of 2019. With the outbreak of disease, the companies increased the budget to 11% in 2020 more in advertisement hoping to sustain their business, but the same did not borne fruit. Consequently, the strategy was changed and a significant cut was made on the advertisement budget in the year 2021 which reached to 6.4%. The firms have started to focus on e-commerce.[18]

According to the annual Gartner CMO Spend Survey-2021, company or industry of every size has cut down their marketing budgets. Companies involving manufacturing, hospitality, and technology suffered a lot during the year 2021. Budget for consumer product was 10.8% in 2020 which has been reduced to 8.3% in 2021. For financial services, it has dropped from 10.7 to 7.4%. Healthcare got cut from 9.9 to 7.2%. Budget for travel and hospitality has gone down from 10.2 to 5.4%. Manufacturing sector reduced their marketing budget from 12.7 to 5.8%. The area of IT and business services curtail their marketing budget from 9.6 to 5.9% within 1 year. Overall, budget of marketing has shrunk from 11 to 6.4% within 1 year, that is, 2020 to 2021

Undoubtedly, it was expected to decrease spending on advertisement due to COVID-19. For instance, online home rental bookings were suspended to save millions of dollars.[19] Many businesses refocused on purpose-driven, cause-related, and admission-based marketing strategies to meet the demands of the customer working from home. It was observed that the use of social media and online video streaming increased by 26% and there is a dramatic rise in the number of people availing online purchasing of essential goods.[20] Consequently, various brands revitalized their policies for marketing to enhance online communication and transactions.

During quarantine, consumers avoided in-store shopping which curtailed investment on in-store promotional materials. The consumers are using social media to satiate basis amenities of life. The behavior of the consumer is affected by external entities as the society persuades him to imitate behavior of other people. A consumer takes purchasing decision if trusted source recommends him to do so from a definite platform.[21]

The consumption of health and wellness items has increased dramatically. People prefer to buy medical and nutritional goods like vitamin supplements, fever reducers, pain killers, and antibiotics recommended by medical physicians. As the coronavirus spread by social gathering, people have restrained themselves from visiting public places including restaurants, cinemas, parks, and shopping malls. The situation has posed a big challenge for marketers to get attention of the customers. Health organizations as well as governmental agencies have an ideal opportunity to promote consumption of items relating to health.[22]

During COVID-19, supply chains disruption has resulted in shortage of consumer goods. Demand of Chinese products has increased significantly as most of the international firms depend on their manufacturing skills.[23] As a result of government restrictions, the business of imports and exports has suffered a lot due to the delay caused by of transportation of goods for firms. This factor has not only increased the prices of product but also created shortage of goods in the market.

Moreover, movement of the consumer has been restricted by government to maintain social distancing which has prevented the firms from reaching their customers.[24] Online or digital marketing involving email marketing, search engine optimization, social media marketing, content marketing, display marketing, and social pay per click is the sole medium for the companies to stay connected with the consumer. E-commerce and live streaming have become common for online business.[25] To maintain stable stream of revenue, the firms are reconsidering their philosophies regarding marketing campaigns and advertising programs spending more on promotions and media.[19]

No doubt, all the firms are looking to adopt fruitful tactics to manage the negative effects of worldwide health emergency, but they have to take radical steps to tackle tough competition, market alteration, and demand for creative and innovative marketing practices. Behavioral and psychological change of the consumer staying at home most of the time has resulted in low demand of products. Many firms are facing critical challenges so they are using e-commerce to get in touch with the customer.[26]

7.3.1 CONSUMER BEHAVIOR

To understand the marketing process, it is necessary to grasp the concept of consumer behavior as it will define the product and services rendered by the companies or firms.[27] The era of COVID-19 has provided an opportunity to observe the insights of the consumer behavior in an environment of uncertainty. With the outbreak of pandemic, the consumer has moved toward social media.[28] Stimulus, Organism, Response (S-O-R) Theory[29] and the Consumer Decision-Making Model[30] help to understand the impacts of COVID-19 on consumer behavior. The S-O-R theory explains environmental and psychological aspects on behavior.[31] An external stimulus influences the organism which causes a change in the behavioral response. It affects the cognitive process of the consumer which modifies the behavior.

Mehrabian and Russell proposed the Stimulus–Organism–Response Theory.[32] It has a powerful and explanatory nature in various fields and attracted considerable attention in the recent past. It has been implied to investigate behavior of human.[33] According to this theory, the behavioral responses (R) like approach or avoidance is influenced by emotions (O) that change with change in the environmental stimuli (S).[32] As it is widely applicable in a number of fields, it can be modified according to different research contexts and applied in different factors like effective and cognitive elements into the framework. Lennon and Kim evaluated the comprehensive model to find out the purchase intention based on the S-O-R approach. Stimulus was taken as reputation of sources and website quality whereas emotion and cognition as organisms.[34] S-O-R approach is a very comprehensive model to examine the behavior of a person. The atmosphere, as a stimulus, affects those emotional qualities and guides the activities of a person. In some cases emotion can be incorporated in emotion in stimulus or organism.[35] It can be linked in the situation of coronavirus pandemic where stimulus (S) is the prevailing circumstance, precautionary measures are emotional attitude (O) and shifting toward e-commerce is intention (R). For tourism, a positive link was observed between cognition (S), emotional attitude (O), and intention (R) of tourism.[36]

Nicosia's Consumer Decision-Making Model is also very helpful in the determination of behavioral changes due to the COVID-19 pandemic. The model contains five stages, that is, identification of product needs, product information searches, evaluation of product alternatives, purchase decisions, and post-purchase behaviors.[37]

The first step includes identifying the product needs. In this recession, healthcare and electronics supporting e-commerce are the products which are needed to the consumer. The products are supplied to the consumer and stock is maintained to prevent shortage. In case of nonavailability of a product, different alternatives can be considered and, after complete assessment of quality and price, decision is made to purchase such a product. The consumer uses the product after buying from the market and expresses his satisfaction or dissatisfaction. Post purchase behavior is very necessary because it will determine the success of the product.

Consumers have reevaluated their life priorities reshaping new criteria for life spending. They search for stability and values so there is a strong emotional connection with reliable suppliers. Digitalization is very important and reflects functioning of consumer, employees, and employers in the future. Different services such as "Google Meet," "Microsoft Team," and "Zoom" are used more often than ever.

Consumers have adopted product and service-oriented tendency and prefer to attach with notable and reliable brands. They search for trusted information regarding COVID-19 pandemic and rely on different noncommercial website as well as TV broadcasting.

People have developed holistic approach for a safer and healthier lifestyle outside and inside home. COVID-19 has left an unprecedented impact on economy of many firms and consumers belonging to lower and middle classes. The pandemic has made it difficult for them to maintain their lifestyle. Unemployment has increased dramatically and situation has worsened life of people living in developing countries.[38]

Consumers prefer to shop online to maintain social distancing which has increased turnover of online stores. Consumers who were not familiar with online shopping have excelled the field. There is a change in consumer spending on different items. Luxury goods have shown a greater decrease in buying. There is also negative impact on personal accessories, apparel and footwear, eye-ware, tobacco, and beauty and personal care. Fresh food purchase has positive trend. People have preferred to buy home and garden equipment, home care, packaged food, etc.[39]

The data illustrate that COVID-19 has a negative impact on marketing relating to packaged food, home care etc. Use of puzzles, games, and indoor activities is becoming more popular. Sale of hygiene products and wellness, gardening material, digital products, do-it-yourself product, furniture, streaming services, and consumer electronics show positive effect. Nonfood online sale in many countries has been increased. For instance, sale of nonfood items in the Netherlands has increased from 16–18 to 60–70% in the month of April 2020. Sale of cars, shoes, clothes etc. has been decreased substantially around 40–60% and many international companies have been closed to bankruptcy. With the closure of restaurants, the business of beverage and food items has downturned.

7.3.2 STRATEGIC DECISION-MAKING

Leading marketers have responded to the recession due to COVID-19. They have revised their strategies dividing marketing plan into long-term and short-term plans. However, they are facing difficulties in ensuring the actions of the short-term planning in line with long-term plans. Many companies have redefined and calibrated their purposes, channels, target customers, and products during the invading slump in marketing.

"Cause-related marketing" or "purpose marketing" are the activities which are redesigned to tackle negative effects of COVID-19. Call centers are working to support and encourage emotionally depressed people. Although cause-related activities may show negative influence[39] but research has found that positive attitude of the consumer has developed that increased purchase intention.[40] Many companies have altered their strategies of marketing and have engaged in COVID-19-related activities to strengthen the customer-brand relationship.[41] The companies are not only doing good deed but have also made good reputation.[42]

Different companies have redefined their product portfolio. Nutritional and plastic companies have started to produce mattresses and face masks. Cloths, dry cleaners, disinfectants production firms have developed partnership for the manufacturing of disinfection cabinet which are being used in hospitals. Different brands of alcohol distillation and synthesis of lemonade syrups are now focusing on the production of hand sanitizers. Artificial snow cannons are converted into aerosol machine. Take-away and home delivery services have been introduced by many restaurants.

It is a big challenge for the marketers to reach the buyers during COVID-19 crises. Distribution and retail chains have been forced to closure. Companies running online channels have taken the advantage over offline stores. Local transportation means are frequently used for delivery of products. Different mobile applications such as FaceTime, Facebook, or WhatsApp have raised the digital sale. Different concerts and events are being broadcasted live. About 10% expenditures on advertisement have been reduced globally. Many companies are focusing on investment in advertisement.

Classical and social media used in combination have proved to be more advantageous.[43] Use of proactive email provides an effective means to communicate with existing clients.[44] Many companies have taken benefit from the COVID-19 pandemic and have attracted new customers who are using online channels. They have collected data regarding needs of the new customers to identify buying behavior. Suitable or customized offers are given to the new customers and sale has been enhanced.

7.3.3 MARKETING POLICIES

To tackle the era of COVID-19, marketing policies in the fields of private label, price promotion, assortment, and communication can be modified. Companies have re-evaluated critically their range of production to increase profit. It is not always beneficial to increase number of products. Short-term loss can be seen on reducing number of products, but it does not show a significant negative effect in the long run.[45] The customers have reconsidered their needs during COVID-19, and this trend is being observed and followed by the companies in assessing the supply of the products.

The downturns of COVID-19 have increased the share held by private labels which goes down during flourished business. It is also noted that the share occupied by branded products does not increase significantly and it needs investment.[46] During a contraction, the consumers become more sensitive.[47] The need and value of the branded products affect the consumers. If the consumers feel that the products offer "value for money," they will be very pleased in buying. Paying more than the value of the products or services dissatisfies the consumers.[48]

Price sensitivity can be increased by giving temporary discount offers. Different types of promotion offers such as gift and additional services may decrease the risk of the consumers' thinking about the quality of the products. During crises, companies try to cut down the advertisement/communication expenses[49] which are more important than business fluctuations. The private label sales grow in countries having cyclic advertisement spending which results in substantial loss to brand manufacturers. Advertising sensitivity is observed to be more affected in the time of contraction than expansion.[50]

Current situation is being kept in mind while formulating contents of communication. Radio, television, and online advertisements are need of the hour. Emails prove to be more effective as compared to messages on social media and many managers use targeted techniques to capture the customers.[44]

7.3.4 MARKETERS STRATEGIC PLAN

The consumers remain unaware of the efforts made by the finance of a company during the pandemic. Marketing is depicted by every message, channel, or advertisement campaign.[51] The ever-emerging business scenario can create difficulty in communication with customers.[52] It is very important for the brands to maintain trust and integrity. Company having well-suited product and services in difficult times should be very careful; otherwise, it will develop negative impression on the customer that the companies are grinding their own axes.[53]

A marketer should have knowledge about the consumer, service, and product to re-evaluate the marketing plans. Distinctive strategies must be devised which draw a sharp difference between companies. Evaluation of the crisis and reformulation plans with clear viewpoint will find a way to analyze alternate possibilities. Unbiased data utilization helps in modification of goals to tackle the pandemic by launching initiative designs.[39] Moving toward e-commerce influences the companies, supply chains, and resources.[54] To take the potential reward or to avoid downside of the business, future marking actions should be planned intelligently in the dynamic environment.[55] No doubt, it is very important to limit the resources but capitalization on possibility cannot be ignored as well.[56] It is good for the organization to pay attention to the changing circumstances and make adjustments accordingly.[21] The following adjustments in investment and marketing are frequently adopted.

- While maintaining brand-building initiative, investment in marketing strategies is made to increase internet sale which promotes short-term business.
- Funds are shifted to promote delivery bases choices such as grocery delivery or at-home fitness solutions/apps/equipment.
- Different prices are observed on the basis of demand of products so allocation of the media to a fine tuning level is made part of the strategy.
- Cost is affected by changes in demand and media supply. A marketer ensures control over the specific expenditure areas.
- Marketing activities can be reorganized by analyzing local geographies data having different levels of effect. It helps to assess trend and highlights social sentiment.
- Being aware of the changing in marketing costs and devising effective plans, tackling the negative effects on the business will be beneficial for the company.

7.4 ADAPTATIONS DURING COVID-19

Online purchasing has become a "new norm" as consumers have shifted toward online platforms. E-commerce businesses are expanding swiftly worldwide. Customers have become more conscious about their health, freedom to travel, and purchasing basic amenities of life. They have modified their habits for fulfilment of their needs. Restriction on movement imposed during pandemic has influenced purchasing. No doubt, Movement Control Order (MCO) not only affects buying behavior but also changes mode and time of shopping.[57]

Due to COVID-19, physical contact with the customer has been reduced to 39% and there is 25% increase in online marketing platforms. Cost operation has been declined to 16%. Bargaining power of suppliers has reached to 9%. Reduction in total sales, number of customers, and other factors showed a figure of 11%.[58]

To improve communication with customers, investment has been navigated toward back-end infrastructure opportunities which have improved automation technology to 42.8%. Customer-facing digital interface has increased to 73.6% whereas trend for going market has reduced from 56.2 to 54.4% in February 2021.[59]

According to the CMO Survey conducted in February 2021, the biggest decrease at -3.9% has been observed in marketing spend. On the other hand, digital marketing spending showed 11.5% increase. It is expected that the marketing spend will increase around 10.1% in next twelve months.

It is a big challenge for the marketers to deliver their products during lockdown as retail chains and distributions are temporarily closed. Companies having online as well as offline channels have an edge over the companies having only one mode of business.[60] Many stores have launched different digital sales coaching related to Live streaming, WhatsApp, Facebook, and FaceTime.[21] During COVID-19, the demand of the consumers has decreased as they have modified their purchasing behavior. To boost up the business, retail clients should lower prices. Advertisement strengthens brand loyalty and social media synergizes the sales subject to consumers' standpoint in decision loop. Acquisition of data about new clients is possible from the web usage and it paves the way in establishing comparison of consumers on the basis of purchasing habits. New target groups can be identified as well.[60]

The year of 2020 was very challenging for marketing and it is not guaranteed that 2021 will reverse the things to normal. The marketers are devising new plans to neutralize the effects of pandemic. They have aimed the followings for fast growth of companies.

7.4.1 CONSUMER SEGMENT

During the COVID-19 crisis, brands have to communicate with the specific consumers in special circumstance. True understanding of the situation is very vital which may be different from city by city, state by state, and country by country. Businesses like restaurants, retailer, or banks may modify store by store communications. The marketing messages are personally relevant and in line with the situation and values of the individuals. Consumer segment is required to be defined to create connection between human and commercial message. A research was conducted by the EY Future Consumer Index involving 14500 individuals which shows five different groups of consumers.

1. About 32% of the individuals preferred to live within the budget and means, choosing product over brands.

2. 25% of the people involved in research were very sensitive in protecting their health including family members while selecting trusted product avoiding risk of shopping from a new platform.
3. 16% people preferred to minimize environmental pollution and chose the brands reflecting their beliefs.
4. Nearly 15% opted to buy goods from the brands that are honest with the consumer.
5. Around 12% people under research selected to have new experience by trying new products.

To have deeper insights into creative marketing and media strategies, it is very important to utilize customer segmentation.

7.4.2 COMPETING WITH COMPETITOR

The consumer always expects more from the brand and the marketers take radical steps for survival and growth of the business. Before COVID-19, there was a rise in the consumer expectations but post-recession demanded more from the brands to meet the challenges. No doubt, there is sharp increase in the digital transformation overnight and the expectation of the consumer has skyrocketed and the companies have to do more than what they are capable of providing digital experience. To deliver good experience to the customers, three strategies should be followed by companies.

1. Real-time analysis should be used for brand scores for the full customer-facing organization.
2. Real data analysis and building technology foundation by proper consumer journey.
3. The customer journey should be aligned with the collective and individual goals so that disconnection between functional silos such as customer services, sales, and marketing remain invisible to end consumers.

7.4.3 EXPECTATIONS OF THE CUSTOMER

The customer always expects that the company has every product he wants and renders good services. With the passage of time, the bar always rises and new values are set by the customer. Frictionless, relevant, anticipatory, and connected experience is required by the consumers. They only focus on what they want and when they want.

Experiences demanded by the consumers are placed by the companies in the core data of the organization. Artificial intelligence or machine learning is involved in this task which incorporates the date into market mix. No doubt, this activity is very helpful for creating relevant experiences across all the dimensions of 4Cs of marketing which are as under:

1. Content are gathered from the experiences such as mobile apps or mail.
2. Commerce involving e-commerce, a hybrid experience, or physical retail.
3. Community
4. Convenience which includes coupons or benefits for the consumers

"One-size-fits-all" approaches are used to deliver four Cs. Most of the companies are delivering but demand of the consumer is increasing with passage of time. Companies need more data as well as intelligence for effective decision-making and focus to have greater relevance in interacting with the customers for building strong connection.

7.4.4 DEALING WITH CUSTOMER

Courting a customer is similar to dating. It is an old concept that marketing relates to large buying mass with best rates in media to earn more profit. More and more parties are visited hoping that special someone will meet. It has been observed that brand marketing has been shifted to performance marketing. The pandemic has accelerated the digital channels. No doubt, performance marketing has developed an important and strong position in the marketing mix, but best results are obtained by balancing it with the brand marketing. Customer relationship management (CRM) is responsible for the initiatives like personalization, email marketing, and coupons, and it is empowered by customer data acquired by the companies with the consent of consumer.

7.4.5 CUSTOMER JOURNEY

The customer sits in the heart of marketing strategy. Customer-centricity concept is not new, but politics, technologies, or geography may disconnect the functional silos interacting with customers. Marketing is the start of relationship with the consumer. A journey is made by the companies in engaging the customer, getting sale from them directly or indirectly, and retaining them with the hope that they will advocate the brand.

7.4.6 RELATIONSHIP WITH CONSUMER

It is very vital for the companies to build a strong relationship with customers. A feeling of trust should be developed in the consumer who will prefer the product offered by the company without hesitation and also persuade others to try it. While advertising, a promise is made with the consumer and it will be reflected by the service, experience, and products. COVID-19 has emphasized on the relationship between the companies and customers as virtual sale environment has maintained revenue momentum due to the strong bond with the consumers. New customers are hard to find for the brands and it required a lot of skills.

Integrity and trust is the fundamental need for both cases. To have better sale, it is inevitable to select talented people suited for the development of relationship with the client in the emerging era of online interactions. Today, the world is primarily focusing on the insights and solutions rather than charm. To build trust, needs of the consumer must be met followed by crafting solutions to meet such needs. Trust plays a vital role in marketing sector as it rests upon the foundation of a company aimed to exchange value between the customer and company. Company acquires personal data from the consumer with his free consent but the data should not be misused. Rules and regulations should be followed by the companies. Moreover, the trust can be strengthened by developing more transparent interfaces for securing personal information. Choice to share data with company must rest with the consumer and he should be clarified regarding use of such data which will definitely foster deeper trust in the consumer.

7.4.7 AGILITY IN MARKETING

Agile cycle in technological development will be fruitful instead of linear approach. Due to COVID-19, irreversible trend has been developed in the field of marketing. In this crisis, a company should have to act quickly to find out any fault in supply chain or improper messaging to the consumer through advertisement. A permanent mindset of marketing agility should be developed in this recession. Demand sensing and consumer listening is very beneficial not only for marketing but also for companies to capture the consumers' sentiment. It is also meant for the rapid decision cycles and provides flexibility in the area of media, budgeting, and creativeness.

7.4.8 BRAND VALUE

A company should stand behind its brand. During the pandemic, brand loyalty has been challenged. According to the EY Future Consumer Index, 61% of the consumers preferred to choose brands. In the social unrest of 2020, the consumers have developed more awareness and the brands must be focused on the values. No doubt, convenience, quality, and price still matter for the consumers' choice, but the social responsibility, ethical sourcing, and trust play a key role for consumers' selection for products and services.

7.4.9 MARKETING AND GROWTH

At a time, it was thought that the marketing was cost center and a company focused primarily on the maximum benefit on investment. However, during the pandemic when topline results are compromised, the preferences have changed. The companies are reconsidering and modifying their objectives. Digital transformation is a key leader to conduct customer journey. Without accessing the scenario of marketplace in good or bad time, adaptations in marketing strategies can be brought about to create fruitful opportunities. There is an urgent need for resilience in this time of lurch which has developed a leadership culture based on collaboration.

The marketers are charged and utilizing art and science. A perfect balance of human and automation will unlock a better future. Data must be used as a fuel for driving effective human connections. Performance marketing and brand marketing should hang in the balance while keeping in view current situation. Understanding the priority areas which are to be centralized and identifying actions that are to be taken or avoided will definitely help. Blend of all the discussed truths highlights the operations, technologies, and strategies needed for the growth in business after COVID-19. It is the path for recovery of pandemic which will ensure long-term success. Companies and marketers are accustomed to traditional ways, but adjustment is inevitable for survival. The perspective of the consumers should be prioritized.[61]

7.5 TIPS FOR MARKETING AND ADVERTISEMENT DURING COVID-19

It is the key of success for the brands to respond tactfully during the time of lurch. Critical evaluation of consumers' plight and employment of clever, mindful, and proactive marketing strategies guarantee survival of business. To attract the consumers during the crisis, companies should exhibit positive values. Marketing campaigns can be adjusted with the evaluation of imagery and language used in advertisement accompanied by awareness of consumer behavior which will establish strong relation between consumers with brands. The following tips will have positive effects on marketing sector.

7.5.1 CREATIVE APPROACH

Old market strategies will definitely not work during COVID-19 and new norms are to be set to get through this tough time. Although there is risk in modifying the traditional methods but we have left with no choice to go for second plan. Creative marketing is the only way to keep the business on the right footings. Marketing of products and services in a unique way will stand you out from competition. Different promotions and offerings may help to attract the customers. Virtual options such as meetings, showcases, and online classes are also useful.

7.5.2 USE OF SOCIAL MEDIA: INFLUENCERS AND ENDORSERS

Undoubtedly, social media was king before the outbreak of global pandemic but, as compared to 79% social media profile of Americans before COVID-19, the figure has increased as more and more people are going virtually. Social media is relatively inexpensive and creates buzz about your business. It is being used to grow business in the middle of coronavirus by online offerings. To make the online business active, the following practices can be made.

- Joining or starting conversations.
- Utilizing paid advertisement and sponsored posts.
- Online contest, for example, has chance to win by sharing add.
- Remaining in contact with the customers by providing store updates.
- Limited-time or special offers.

The brands should ensure direct and clear disclosure of language. The company should abide by the prescribed rules and regulations while using bloggers and influencers for social media advertisement. Accurate and clear content should be spread from endorsers and influencers. Brands are represented by employees, endorsers, and influencers, and it is imperative to disclose the relation of speakers with the brands. Consumers will give a considerable weight to the contents of communication when the conspicuous, clear, and unavoidable connection material is disclosed.

Brands must show vigilance by ensuring compliance efforts of the speakers as they are accountable for communication. Buying behavior of the consumers is affected by social media. They respond by sharing products usage tips, service experiences, and product reviews. Social media has proved to be a very important tool in marketing during COVID-19 pandemic. It helps the consumers in the decision-making process. Hence, the social media should be made an integral part of every business.

7.5.3 USE OF PROMOTIONAL DEVICES

During COVID-19, the brands want to be connected with the consumers. The brands may adopt different strategies to increase business. Promotional devices such as giveaways, contests, and sweepstakes strategies may help the brands to engage the consumers during the pandemic. Awarding gift card to retailers and restaurants by brands may enhance the loyalty and goodwill. The brands should abide by all the rules and regulations formulated for the use of promotional devices.

7.5.4 CAUSE-RELATED MARKETING

During COVID-19 pandemic, the brands have come forward to help millions of people affected by the unprecedented disease. For-cause marketing campaigns have become a very popular way for the brands to connect their services and products with the consumers facing the COVID-19. Different states have regulated commercial coventure regulations. There should be a complete disclosure of contract provisions, advertisement relating to charity name along with amount of gift and percentage of unit price of the products.

7.5.5 *CUSTOMERS' SATISFACTION*

Every customer is very important. He purchases products and gives benefits to the company. Without customers, business cannot be successful. In the time of uncertainty, there must be assurance of the services to the customers anytime and anywhere. It is a great tactics to capture the new customers as well as establishing a strong bond with the existing ones. The sense of presence of a brand can be relighted by sending email updates, regular posts on social media, as well as information of adds to the customers' accounts. This is a calm situation of staying in contact with the consumers who will approach you in time of need.

In the midst of coronavirus, building online relationships with the consumers is more effective than in-person. The communication must be clear, thoughtful, and genuine. Strong online presence of the business will help the brand to build credibility to attract customers. Access to the information regarding needs of the customers will have positive impacts. The use of Internet has been increased 50 to 70% due to the outbreak of COVID-19. People are spending more time on Internet so the marketers should grab the opportunities with both hands and propagate their businesses online. A business may be at the top-notch, but there is always some room for improvement so the online business must be boosted up.

Marketing is always important for running a business and it requires continuous improvement. During COVID-19, the marketing can be improved by moving ahead of your competitors, having knowledge about consumers' requirements, building strong business relationship, and planning to be successful after global pandemic.[62]

7.6 CONCLUSIONS

Billions of people around the world have been affected by the COVID-19. It has resulted in shattering the industries, organizations, and global economy. Small business enterprises and corporates have been affected significantly. The supply of the goods from different countries has been cut down which has increased the price and shortage of the products in the market. Traditional marketing strategies have become ineffective during lockdown. The people have been limited to their home which changed their behavior. They have moved toward online shopping. Marketers have responded well and have modified their strategies. Social media has been used effectively in furtherance of advertisement. Online purchasing has become a "new norm" so e-commerce businesses are expanding rapidly worldwide. Marketers have reacted practically to deliver their products during lockdown and have adopted online as well as offline channels. The brands have handled the situation very tactfully by critical evaluation of consumers' plight. Promotional devices such as giveaways, contests, and sweepstakes strategies have helped the brands to engage the consumers during the pandemic. Awarding gift cards to retailers and restaurants by brands may enhance the loyalty and goodwill of the customers. The brands should abide by all the rules and regulations formulated for the use of promotional devices. For-cause marketing campaigns have become a very popular way for the brands to connect their services and products with the consumers facing the COVID-19.

KEYWORDS

- **epidemic**
- **performance**
- **marketing sector**
- **digital marketing**
- **online**

REFERENCES

1. Soliman, M.; Ivanov, S.; Webster, C. JThe Psychological Impacts of COVID-19 Outbreak on Research Productivity: A Comparative Study of Tourism and Non-Tourism Scholars **2021,** *35*, 23–52.
2. Anderson, R. M.; Heesterbeek, H.; Klinkenberg, D.; Hollingsworth, T. DHow Will Country-Based Mitigation Measures Influence the Course of the COVID-19 Epidemic? **2020,** *395* (10228), 931–934.
3. El-Ebiary, Y. A. B.; Aseh, K.; Bamansoor, S.; Pande, B.; Abu-Ulbeh, W.; Yusoff, M. H.; Pathmanathan, P. R.; Jusoh, J. A.; Al Moaiad, Y. In *Mobile Commerce and its Apps-Opportunities and Threats in Malaysia*, 2021 2nd International Conference on Smart Computing and Electronic Enterprise (ICSCEE), IEEE, 2021; pp 180–185.
4. Natali, D.; Terlizzi, A. The Impact of COVID-19 on the Future of Pensions in the EU, 2021; pp 44–57.
5. Hassan, S. B.; Soliman, M. COVID-19 and Repeat Visitation: Assessing the Role of Destination Social Responsibility, Destination Reputation, Holidaymakers' Trust and Fear Arousal. *J. Destin. Market. Manage.* **2021,** *19*, 100495.
6. Widjaja, Y. I.; Khalifa, G. S.; Abuelhassan, A. E. The Effect of Destination Reputation on the Revisit Intention to Halal Tourism Destination of Jakarta. *Int. J. Bus. Econ. L.* **2019,** *20* (5), 104–111.

7. Ahmad, M.; Lasi, M. A. The Attitudes on Consumer Perception Towards Viral Marketing: A Study on Foodpanda Food Delivery in Malaysia. *Int. J. Res. Sci. Innov.* **2020,** *7* (9), 251–255.
8. Borden, N. H. The Concept of the Marketing Mix. *J. Advert. Res.* **1964,** *4* (2), 2–7.
9. Gutierrez-Leefmans, C.; Nava-Rogel, R. M.; Trujillo-Leon, M. A. Marketing Digital Num País Emergente: Estudo Exploratório Do Marketing Mix De Pme Com Selo De Confiança. *Revista Brasileira de Market.* **2016,** *15* (2), 207.
10. Booms, B. H.; Bitner, M. J. Marketing Strategies and Organizational Structures for Service Firms. In *Marketing of Services*, American Marketing Association: Chicago, 1981; pp 47-51.
11. Kotler, P.; Turner, R. E., *Marketing Management: Analysis, Planning, Implementation, and Control*, Vool. 9; Prentice Hall: Upper Saddle River, NJ, 1997.
12. Allen, E.; Fjermestad, J. E-commerce Marketing Strategies: An Integrated Framework and Case Analysis. **2001**.
13. Glanz, K.; Bader, M. D.; Iyer, S. Retail Grocery Store Marketing Strategies and Obesity: An Integrative Review. **2012,** *42* (5), 503–512.
14. Pogorelova, E.; Yakhneeva, I.; Agafonova, A.; Prokubovskaya, A. Marketing Mix for E-commerce. **2016,** *11* (14), 6744–6759.
15. Judd, V. C. Differentiate with the 5th P: People. *Ind. Market Manag.* **1987,** *16* (4), 241–247.
16. Kushwaha, G. S.; Agrawal, S. R. An Indian Customer Surrounding 7's of Service Marketing. *J. Retail. Consumer Serv.* **2015,** *22*, 85–95.
17. Ramus, K.; Nielsen, N. A. Online Grocery Retailing: What Do Consumers Think? *Internet Res.* **2005,** *15*, 335.
18. https://www.gartner.com/en/newsroom/press-releases/-gartner-says-marketing-budgets-have-plummeted-to-6–4--of-overal
19. DiResta, A. E.; Williford, K. T.; Cohen, D. A.; Genn, B. A. The Impact of COVID-19 on Your Advertising and Marketing Campaigns, 2020. https://www.hklaw.com/en/insights/publications/2020/04/the-impact-of-COVID19-on-your-advertising-and-marketing-campaigns
20. Mander, J. Coronavirus: Insights from Our Multinational Study. **2020.**
21. Mason, A. N.; Narcum, J.; Mason, K. Social Media Marketing Gains Importance After COVID-19. *Cogent Bus. Manag.* **2021,** *8* (1), 1870797.
22. He, H.; Harris, L. The Impact of COVID-19 Pandemic on Corporate Social Responsibility and Marketing Philosophy. *J Bus. Res.* **2020,** *116*, 176–182.
23. Ansari, B.; Ganjoo, M. Impact of COVID-19 on Advertising: A Perception Study on the Effects on Print and Broadcast Media and Consumer Behavior. **2020,** *31* (28), 52–62.
24. Omar, A. R. C.; Ishak, S.; Jusoh, M. A. The Impact of COVID-19 Movement Control Order on SMEs' Businesses and Survival Strategies. *Geografia. Malasian J. Soc Space* **2020,** *16* (2).
25. Köse, U.; Deperlioglu, O. An Augmented Reality Based Intelligent Diagnosis Platform for Medical Training. In *Augmented Reality in Educational Settings*; Brill Sense, 2019; pp 217–235.
26. Wang, Y.; Hong, A.; Li, X.; Gao, J. Marketing Innovations During a Global Crisis: A Study of China Firms' Response to COVID-19. *J. Bus. Res.* **2020,** *116*, 214–220.
27. Gul, S.; Ali, A.; Saeed, I. JRevisiting Organizational Justice and Employees Job Satisfaction: A Stakeholders Perspectiveof NGOs in Khyber Pakhtunkhwa. **2021,** *15*.

28. Laato, S.; Islam, A. N.; Farooq, A.; Dhir, A. Unusual Purchasing Behavior During the Early Stages of the COVID-19 Pandemic: The Stimulus-Organism-Response Approach. *J. Retail. Consumer Serv.* **2020,** *57*, 102224.
29. Russell, J. A.; Mehrabian, A. Distinguishing Anger and Anxiety in Terms of Emotional Response Factors. *J. Consult. Clin. Psychol.* **1974,** *42* (1), 79.
30. Nicosia, R. F.; Tchao, R.; Leighton, J. Histotypic Angiogenesis In Vitro: Light Microscopic, Ultrastructural, and Radioautographic Studies. *In Vitro* **1982,** *18* (6), 538–549.
31. Liu, J.; Li, S.; Wei, G.; Xu, N.; Cheng, Y.; Wang, B.; Wu, J. A New Species of the Asian Toad Genus Megophrys Sensu Lato (Anura: Megophryidae) from Guizhou Province, China. *Asian Herpetol. Res.* **2020,** *11* (1), 1–18I.
32. Mehrabian, A.; Russell, J. A. *An Approach to Environmental Psychology*; MIT Press, 1974.
33. Kim, M. J.; Lee, C.-K.; Jung, T. J. Exploring Consumer Behavior in Virtual Reality Tourism Using an Extended Stimulus-Organism-Response Model. *J. Travel Res.* **2020,** *59* (1), 69–89.
34. Kim, J.; Lennon, S. J. JEffects of Reputation and Website Quality on Online Consumers' Emotion, Perceived Risk and Purchase Intention: Based on the Stimulus-Organism-Response Model, 2013.
35. Chang, C.-H.; Shu, S.; King, B. J. Novelty in Theme Park Physical Surroundings: An Application of the Stimulus–Organism–Response Paradigm. *Asian Pac. J. Tour. Res.* **2014,** *19* (6), 680–699.
36. Qiu, Q.; Zheng, T.; Xiang, Z.; Zhang, M. J. Visiting Intangible Cultural Heritage Tourism Sites: From Value Cognition to Attitude and Intention. *Sustainability* **2020,** *12* (1), 132.
37. Nicosia, F. M. Consumer Decision Processes: A Futuristic View, 1982.
38. Eckhardt, G. M.; Houston, M. B.; Jiang, B.; Lamberton, C.; Rindfleisch, A.; Zervas, G. Marketing in the Sharing Economy. *J Market.* **2019,** *83* (5), 5–27.
39. Hoekstra, J. C.; Leeflang, P. S. Marketing in the Era of COVID-19. *Italian J. Market.* **2020,** *2020* (4), 249–260.
40. Trimble, C. S.; Rifon, N. J. Consumer Perceptions of Compatibility in Cause-Related Marketing Messages. *J Philanthropy Market.* **2006,** *11* (1), 29–47.
41. Fan, X.; Deng, N.; Qian, Y.; Dong, X. J. Factors Affecting the Effectiveness of Cause-Related Marketing: A Meta-Analysis. *J. Bus. Ethics.* **2020**, 1–22.
42. Morhart, F.; Malär, L.; Guèvremont, A.; Girardin, F.; Grohmann, B. J. Brand Authenticity: An Integrative Framework and Measurement Scale. *J. Consumer Psychol.* **2015,** *25* (2), 200–218.
43. De Vries, L.; Gensler, S.; Leeflang, P. S. Effects of Traditional Advertising and Social Messages on Brand-Building Metrics and Customer Acquisition. *J. Market.* **2017,** *81* (5), 1–15.
44. Steimer, S. How Marketers Are Working During The Pandemic, 2020.
45. Sloot, L. M.; Fok, D.; Verhoef, P. C. The Short-and Long-Term Impact of an Assortment Reduction on Category Sales. *J. Market. Res.* **2006,** *43* (4), 536–548.
46. Lamey, L.; Deleersnyder, B.; Dekimpe, M. G.; Steenkamp, J.-B. E. How Business Cycles Contribute to Private-Label Success: Evidence from the United States and Europe. *J. Market.* **2007,** *71* (1), 1–15.
47. Van Heerde, H. J.; Gijsenberg, M. J.; Dekimpe, M. G.; Steenkamp, J.-B. E.Price and Advertising Effectiveness Over the Business Cycle. *J. Market. Res.* **2013,** *50* (2), 177–193.

48. Hunneman, A. The Do's and Don'ts for Marketing in a Recession, 2020.
49. Deleersnyder, B.; Dekimpe, M. G.; Steenkamp, J.-B. E.; Leeflang, P. S. The Role of National Culture in Advertising's Sensitivity to Business Cycles: An Investigation Across Continents. *J. Market. Res.* **2009,** *46* (5), 623–636.
50. Steenkamp, J.-B. E.; Fang, E. The Impact of Economic Contractions on the Effectiveness of R&D and Advertising: Evidence from US Companies Spanning Three Decades. *Market Sci.* **2011,** *30* (4), 628–645.
51. Widjaja, Y. I.; Khalifa, G. S.; Abuelhassan, A. E. Tourism, the Effect of Islamic Attributes and Destination Affective Image on the Reputation of the Halal Tourism Destination of Jakarta. *J. Environ. Manag. Tour.* **2020,** *11* (2), 299–313.
52. Suleyman, G.; Fadel, R. A.; Malette, K. M.; Hammond, C.; Abdulla, H.; Entz, A.; Demertzis, Z.; Hanna, Z.; Failla, A.; Dagher, C. Clinical Characteristics and Morbidity Associated with Coronavirus Disease 2019 in a Series of Patients in Metropolitan Detroit. *JAMA Netw. Open* **2020,** *3* (6), e2012270.
53. Loey, M.; Smarandache, F.; Khalifa, N. E. Within the Lack of Chest COVID-19 X-ray Dataset: A Novel Detection Model Based on GAN and Deep Transfer Learning. *Symmetry* **2020,** *12* (4), 651.
54. El-Ebiary, Y. A. B.; Pathmanathan, P. R.; Tarshany, Y. M. A.; Jusoh, J. A.; Aseh, K.; Al Moaiad, Y.; Al-Kofahi, M.; Pande, B.; Bamansoor, S. In *Determinants of Customer Purchase Intention Using Zalora Mobile Commerce Application*, 2021 2nd International Conference on Smart Computing and Electronic Enterprise (ICSCEE), IEEE, 2021; pp 159–163.
55. Alharthi, M.; Khalifa, G. S. Business Continuity Management and Crisis Leadership: An Approach to Re-Engineer Crisis Performance within Abu Dhabi Governmental Entities. *Int. J. Emerg. Technol.* **2019,** *10* (2), 32–40.
56. Taylor, C. R. *The Urgent Need for More Research on Influencer Marketing*; Taylor & Francis, 2020.
57. Ramli, M. W.; Jamri, M. H. The Impact of COVID-19 Pandemic: A Closer Look at the Night Market Traders' Experience in Penang, Malaysia. *Int. J. Acad. Res. Bus. Soc. Sci.* **2021,** *11* (1), 741–760.
58. Khudhair, H. Y.; Alsaud, A. B.; Alsharm, A.; Alkaabi, A.; AlAdeedi, A. The Impact of COVID-19 on Supply Chain and Human Resource Management Practices and Future Marketing. *Int. J. Supply Chain Manag.* **2020,** *9* (5), 1681.
59. https://cmosurvey.org/results/26th-edition-february-2021
60. Altay, B. C.; Okumuş, A.; Mercangöz, B. A. An Intelligent Approach for Analyzing the Impacts of the COVID-19 Pandemic on Marketing Mix Elements (7Ps) of the on-Demand Grocery Delivery Service. 2021, 1–12.
61. https://hbr.org/2021/03/10-truths-about-marketing-after-the-pandemic
62. https://www.forbes.com/sites/mikekappel/2020/07/22/marketing-your-business-during-COVID-19/?sh=282c801e5c92

CHAPTER 8

Impact of COVID-19 on the Banking Sector

JAVED HUSSAIN SHAH[1], SHAHZAD SHARIF[1], SIDRA FARID[1], RAHAT AJMAL[2], and SAMINA YAQOOB[3]

[1]*Materials Chemistry Laboratory, Department of Chemistry, GC University Lahore, Pakistan*

[2]*Department of Arabic, Lahore College for Women University, Lahore, Pakistan*

[3]*Dr Hasan Murad School of Management (HSM), University of Management and Technology, Lahore, Pakistan*

ABSTRACT

COVID-19 pandemic put severe impacts on the banking sector of the world. The pandemic has warned the investors, policy makers, and public that such pandemics can cause large economic damages to the world economies. The impacts of pandemic on financial institutions like foreign remittance, foreign trades (imports and exports), local trades, foods and agriculture, government revenue, and employment create a big pressure on the world reforms agenda. The pandemic disturbed the working style of the banking system. It caused a decrease in the capacity and performance of debtors. Ratio of credit risk has been increased due to the pandemic. To stabilize financial integrity and to minimize the impacts of the pandemic, financial institutions have to take some legal and performance-based steps. The government and regulatory authorities have made it possible to counter the pandemic by applying restrictive policies. It is the need of the hour to bring banking sector restructuring to minimize the impacts of natural calamities and pandemics. Global banking sector challenges like digitization of banks, low interest rates, depression of bank valuation, and strength of banks must be reevaluated to face future

Post-Pandemic Economy, Technology, and Innovation: Global Outlook and Context.
Samina Yaqoob, Arwa Abdulkreem AL-Huqail, and Fakhra Aziz (Eds.)

pandemics. The role of government to sustain banking system is imperatives and such government financial packages are helpful for smooth running of the homes of financially crunched families. Government responses in three main indexes like economic support index, health index, and stringency index are playing its pivotal role to face the pandemic.

8.1 INTRODUCTION

By examining the history, it is known that the world has faced many fatal viruses. The most recent virus is COVID-19 virus. It has affected almost every sector of life, that is, health, education, banking system, transport, aviation, tourism, retail and trades, production industries, sports, entertainment, etc. Banking sector has been affected severely by COVID-19 after the global financial crisis (GFC) 2008–2009. Various researches are suggesting that the pandemic has started to ruin the major economies of the world by creating problems in macro-economic indicators of economy that may include supply, trade flows, demand, production, savings, investments, and employment that are ultimately resulting poverty and instability in society.[1]

During the COVID-19 and after COVID-19 era, these financial losses may destroy sustainability and survival of such financial institutions (F.Is), economic certainty, solidity, and adjustment parameters around the world, whether these are developing or not.[2] Banks have to face a large number of risks and this pandemic has increased the risks of loss. COVID-19 has increased the severity of risks by credit compression, liquidity crunch, increasing in resources and decreasing rates of interests of market, diminishing returns through investments with loans with demolishing bank strategies.[3] COVID-19 pandemic affected much under-developing countries as compared to developed countries or economies. For example, a big default in loans, recoveries of loans become more hard and complex, customer's savings become exhausted to enhance quality of life, minimizing funds availability for loan purposes with compressing novel business demands.[4] Banks are considered to be the most important triggers for economic growth in under-developing countries and emerging economies. Banks are marked as a biggest source for both short- and long-term financing. In under-developing countries, banks have a major role in sustaining economic matters. Here banks play a pivotal role in continuing financial matters, developing economical infrastructure, for fulfilling necessary and innovative financial instruments while technology and innovation plays an important role in upgrading economy.[5]

COVID-19 pandemic has stressed down the economy of world, whereas banking system of most developing countries collapsed. In developing countries, growth, survival, and performance of banks were affected due to long term and fatal impacts of this pandemic. By observing crunch effects of virus on the banking system, resulting huge loss of economies and suffering financial matters cause a big damage to economy.[6]

COVID-19 has affected the banking system at an extreme level as banks were not prepared to face such long-term restrictions after global financial crisis (GFC) 2008–2009. The presence of this pandemic over a long period has threatened the economy because of imposing complete or partial lockdowns and restricting the financial matters to be dealt with ease and accuracy. By imposing varieties of restrictions and keeping social distances in reference to this pandemic, production has been decreased, demands of goods and services have been diminished, logistics and transports have been restricted, offices and industries have been shut down partially or completely, and overall public participation and movement has been restricted due to this curse.[7]

8.2 IMPACTS OF PANDEMICS ON FINANCIAL INSTITUTIONS

COVID-19 has put deep impacts on almost all sectors of life. But the economy of the world has been destroyed much as the health sector has been affected. This virus has been proved to be as dangerous economically as it is for medically. This pandemic has crunched the economy of developed countries specially and under-developing countries specifically. Daily commodities consumption and per capita income has been contracted due to international monitory policies. This virus has become the major factor for other economic policies and monetary fallout.[8]

Financial institutions play a vital role in running the economy of the world. But COVID-19 affected the economy very badly. Financial institutions all over the world are countering the impacts of pandemic, which work to counter main confrontations to societies with financial matters putting major impacts on interconnected banking processes. These are trying best to facilitate buyers for maintaining better economies.[9]

The worst economic crisis has created panic, massive unemployment, homelessness, and poverty. The United States has already claimed that this pandemic has created 4.6 million unemployment in COVID-19 restrictions. This unemployment and lockdown has brought the ratio of deaths more than the pandemic itself. This pandemic has affected health system and economy very badly.[10]

The under-developing countries face double loss as compared to developed countries. They bear not only the health sector loss but also poverty loss due to unemployment created through lockdown and emergencies. These countries face costly medications and unsuccessful health markets, extra expenditures, overloaded with nontransmittable diseases, less financial possibilities with decline in socioeconomic activities.[11]

The impacts of pandemics on financial institutions may be categorized as follows.

i. Foreign Remittances
ii. Foreign Trade (Export and Import)
iii. Local Trade
iv. Foods and Agriculture
v. Government Revenue
vi. Employment

Similar to other markets pandemic has badly affected the money market and stock market. Both of these markets have deteriorated the financial status of common people as well as national and international economies. Due to consecutive lockdowns, supply chain closure, as well as factory closure, small- and medium-scale industries have been badly affected.

COVID-19 crises warn the humanity to predict the financial cost of expected upcoming epidemics. This pandemic has shuttered down the economics of the world due to bad and unexpected banks policy. This economic failure has put forward the health failure. Social distancing, lockdowns, and restrictions in movement and restricted tourism have created impacts on foreign direct investment.[12]

8.3 RESPONSE OF BANKS TO COVID-19

COVID-19 affected the working of banks through multifaceted targets like large losses of profits, widespread bankruptcies, liquidity shortages, as well as unemployment in almost every sector and department of government and private organizations. Banks themselves have faced big losses and lesser demand and supply for both borrowers and lenders.[13]

During this pandemic, government put additional restrictions on banking working as well as on expansion of different businesses. Major central banks extended its purchasing capacities by enhancing its power through online services. It resulted in safety measures to counter liquidity as well as monetary dysfunction to make it functional in a smooth way. After covering the primary markets, banks started working to cover secondary markets by purchasing private and public sector securities.[14]

COVID-19 crisis put financial sector under strain. Major markets changed their location. Banks faced massive capital outburst, challenges of liquidity and repayment due to sustained interest rates on banking system.[15]

To counter the impacts of COVID-19 on the banking system, World Bank (WB), Asian Development Bank (ADB), and other main banking authorities modified their strategies and policies to escape this pandemic. The policy of financial sphere responses to the pandemic comprised of three actions. First, policy makers and researchers support public welfare policy before, during, and post pandemic era. Second, COVID-19 Financial Policy Response Activity Index, which is a regional-type signal, refers to track the amount of initiatives taken. Third, in reference to policy response, banks tried to engage all profitable resources of economy to counter this pandemic. Many surveillance efforts were made by banks to track the monetary aspects on their routes.[16]

To counter the pandemic, banks and financial institutes of some countries lowered specific risks, relaxed the classification patterns of economy, treatment of nonperforming loans, and followed the guidelines settled by the World Bank and IMF. These countries may have to adopt such measures to be successful at the peak of this pandemic.[17]

8.4 REGULATORY REACTION TO PANDEMIC

After the transmission of pandemic in December 2019, definitely first response must be of governments and regulators of the world. When emergency was declared at national and international levels, the world leaders found themselves responsible for its not early prediction and prompt response. Soon after its spread, its fatal ratio not only was predicted but also was detected in upcoming days with big ramification, big danger for whole of world, as described by World Health Organization (WHO). By observing the unpreparedness to counter the COVID-19 virus, the world was not ready to offer regulatory response to this pandemic. Although, having some hesitation and with controversial statements, the regulatory response of most countries was remarkable.[18,19]

Although regulatory response to COVID-19 was not satisfactory, but still it was used as a strongest tool to make a strategy to face this pandemic. COVID-19 precautionary measures including "social distancing" working through regulatory responses put a good response to this curse. The most important regulatory measures were as follows:

i. Stay at home policies
ii. Isolation of infected persons
iii. Quarantine of healthy individuals
iv. Educational institutions closure
v. Markets/Workplaces Closure
vi. Steps taken for special population[20]

8.5 NEED OF BANK'S RESTRUCTURING

COVID-19 disturbed the working style of the banking system. It resulted in decreasing the performance and capacity of debtors. The debtor's reduced capacity and performance may directly increase the ratio of credit risk. Keeping in view these facts, governments and financial institutions have taken some legal steps to provide stability and good performance to banks. These steps were taken to minimize the impacts of COVID-19 and to stabilize financial integrity.[21]

The policies relevant to mechanism and restructuring of finance or credit which is named as restructured financing or credit may be easily checked. When loan is up to Rs. 10 billion, credit quality assessment of other funds may be utilized. Credit or finance restructuring is carried out by

a) Lowest interest rates
b) Period extension
c) Reduction of principal arrears
d) Lessening of interest arrears
e) Adding of credit or finance facilities
f) Transformation of credit or financing to temporary equity participation.[22]

8.6 GLOBAL BANKING SECTOR CHALLENGES

COVID-19 has created many global challenges that made the world to focus on global development on practical grounds in true sense. Global development paradigm has been recognized by the devastation of this pandemic which affected almost every sector of human interest.[23] COVID-19 challenged the paradigm of global development that relies on three main factors. First, the lack of interconnectivity among the countries. Second, the world has to face climate change and sustain development. Third, a concept of global inequality that generated many challenges for all countries.[24]

The pandemic has created many global challenges. Although health challenge is one of the biggest challenges but the challenge of economy has surpassed the rest. After the medical sector, COVID-19 caused "the one of the biggest harmful and monetary crunch of lifetimes." Billions of people of the world have lost their jobs and livelihood.[25]

a) Digitalization of Banks

The pandemic has created one of the main challenges for banks, which is lack of complete global digitalization in banking sector. Digitalization not only in banks but in all sectors is the need of the hour. The pandemic has disrupted almost all physical movements and restricted the world on digitalization. Online working and digitally managed style of working played a vital role in decreasing these impacts and will sustain up to the restoration of normal conditions. Digital technology managed the economy platform or economy firms to continue to grow minimizing the impacts. Economic firms or companies such as Alibaba, Amazon, and Google are playing its pivotal role to sustain infrastructure.[26] To respond to the pandemic, gig economic system has been utilized but they also face physical work challenges.[27]

b) Low Interest Rates

The pandemic has diverse impacts on interest rates of banks. Policy of central banks regarding money depended minimum on interest rate cut than its time-bound lender. Low interest rates of banks have to be implemented as the lender has to face the present global crisis. This adaptation of interest rates is simply repetition of behavior that has already been demonstrated during the Global Financial Crisis (2008–2009) due to fast expansion of market-place interest comparative to financial interest. Central banks performed as suppliers or purchasers of tourist center. Hence, banks tried to stabilize markets by purchasing securities on a large scale. Emerging market economies (EMEs) involving central banks repeated this practice and foreign investors showed a great interest.[28]

c) Depression of Bank Valuation

The pandemic has made high volatility in stock market and depressed the banks valuation. Instability and major volatility was created in international market due to the pandemic. The most affected sector is financial sector where banks valuation quickly dropped around the globe. Specifically, P/NAV faced an acute downfall from 1.00x on 31-12-2019 to 0.69x on 30-04-2020. North American banks were trading at P/NAV at 1.15x, whereas Asian and European banks were trading at P/NAV at 0.56x and 0.52x respectively. The pandemic affected banking sectors a lot. From 31-12-2019 to 30-04-2020 many banks faced price decline. European banks were affected much as the EURO STOXX banks index faced a big downfall of 40.18%, stock North America 600 banks index 31.23%, and stock Asia/Pacific 600 banks index was 26.09% for the designated period.[29]

d) Strength of Banks must be Compromised

The pandemic affected not only the working of banks but also its strength. Strength of banks means the effective working to be performed under such stress and in emergency situations. Like the health experts, banking system experts are also observing the emergency situations and are making sure the working of banks must not be affected. Banking supervisors with a complete list of suggestions deal with natural calamities, functional threat circumstances, and financial pressure chapters. Some big financial institutes suggest some key points for working in such a pandemic.

i. Don't change the rules
ii. Usage of buffers
iii. Encourage loan modification
iv. Don't hide the losses
v. Clarify regulatory treatment of support measures
vi. Strengthen communication
vii. Coordinate across borders[30]

8.7 SECTORS AFFECTED BY BANKING SECTOR DURING COVID-19

The pandemic influenced almost every sector of human interest but the banking sector was affected much. The pandemic disrupted the banking sector very severely in that it affected many other sectors.

a) Tourism Industry

Tourism industry is badly affected by the pandemic. Local, regional, national, and international level restrictions of movement, traveling affected the whole tourism industry. Domestic tourism, international traveling, visitation as manifold as public transportation, air transport, sea voyages, lodgings, coffee-shops and eating houses, sports events, meetings, celebrations and conventions. A lot of states imposed traveling restrictions, closed boundaries, and managing quarantine intervals; ultimately domestic, national, and international tourism got severely affected and stopped within a couple of days after the start of the pandemic. After worldwide lockdowns, travelers of almost all the countries return to their homes as hundred to thousand residents across the globe.[31]

It is very crucial to mention here that world touristy has been vulnerable to a large-scale spectrum of crises in previous times.

b) Transport and Aviation

The pandemic COVID-19 originating from Wuhan China and spreading all over the world warned the authorities that if serious steps could not be taken, the whole world may be at high risk. Later on by observing infection ratio, World Health Organization (WHO) announced COVID-19 a public health calamity of worldwide level and issued directions to authorities and governments to take serious and prompt actions for safety. One of the major actions after the WHO instructions is to contain the masses at their places and to restrict the movement. Transport and aviation system was stopped to decrease the infection ratio.[32]

There are three major types of transport.

i. Air Transport
ii. Freight Transport
iii. Urban Transport

One of the main steps taken by most governments after the declaration of emergency was travel ban at national and international levels and border control. This is because one of the major causes of spread of the pandemic is social mobility and gathering.[33] Our enormous traffic systems specially aviation and across the ocean transportation are the major cause of human-to-human transference and are the biggest contributor for the unstoppable spread of virus worldwide.[34] Ultimately, individuals play a pivotal role in the spread of pandemic when they move from one place to another although they have no symptoms of virus.[35,36] After restrictions on transport and aviation, other major steps were taken as quarantine, isolation, social distancing, and public containment.

c) Energy Sector

COVID-19 affected all other sectors, energy sector is also affected much. The virus put a dramatic decline in foreign trade, tourism, and air transport in different states. It affected the energy sector by increasing consumption of electricity at highest level due to restrictions of people at homes.[37] Energy sector or electricity is directly or indirectly related to oil and the prices of oil fluctuated after the spread of the pandemic. During the pandemic period demand shocks and negative supply were observed in oil market. Due to travel restrictions, stoppage of busses and other vehicles, limited business activities, labor unavailability direct or indirect caused by supply shocks through negative. These demand shocks in negative were because of economic instability, interruption of value chains globally, and reduction of oil demand. These negative demand shocks of oil were taken to minimize world utilization and investment.[38] There are various studies that reflected the impacts of virus on oil prices. Efficiency of energy sector was severely affected due to decline of oil prices caused by the pandemic.[39–43]

The pandemic affected oil prices, uncertainty in energy market volatility and also determined a negative relation between stock return and oil. The pandemic affected both oil importer countries and oil exporter countries.[44]

It happened first time in the history of the world that oil prices faced severe irregularity and reached to a negative value, that is, 36.98 $ on April 20th, 2020. Production process involves crude oil as a main ingredient. Low oil costs can decrease production cost and expand profits in financial expansion, ultimately affecting monetary policy.[45]

There is a duplet role of crude oil for net oil exporting and net oil importing countries. Low oil prices could be beneficial for states that import oil. On the contrary, the states that export oil have to face a great decline in income of oil, stock market got down and financial market became volatile. Oil exporting countries faced rapid depression during pandemic era, such as Russia (-6.6%), Saudi Arabia (-6.8%), and Nigeria (-5.4%).[46]

d) Retail and Trade

The Pandemic also affected retail and trade all over the world. The behavior of retail investors financially affected very badly. Financial attitude has six dimensions, that is, economic stability, benefits in financial matters, deliberative thinking, optimism, economic uncertainty, and requirement of safety measures, on dealing activities of retail investors during the virus era. Financial attitude has drawn vital importance during the fatal pandemic. The rapid and unexpected expansion of pandemic-COVID-19 outbreak made financial markets so uncertain that retail investors had to bear big losses in a very short time.[47] It is very unbearable to estimate the financial loss during the pandemic, as during Severe Acute Respiratory Syndrome (SARS) outbreak in 2003 an economic state, that is, China got financial loss globally around 30 to 100 billion US dollar.[48] If we compare COVID-19 that is "1st in history" and affected countries higher than 200, with SARS of 2003, much loss may be expected.[49] Although there is much uncertainty in market due to global health crisis, but investors could not escape from the situations. It is believed that an open and easy approach to stock market may get attention of retail investors to take interest in various economic fields. Specifically, they are limited and quarantined at their homes due to pandemic lockdown restrictions having a lot of spare time. With such circumstances they would prefer to take interest in online trading. However, on the other hand, investing in such online and volatile markets may be risky and may leave the retail investors at big losses.[50] It is therefore concluded that when there is uncertainty in market due to prevailing situation of COVID-19, retail investors could not be convinced to invest in market. There is an acute need to suggest such key insights at the time when health crisis affected the investor's financial behavior. To protect retail investors from unexpected loss and risks, there is acute need to formulate such policies during such pandemics.

To understand the COVID-19 impacts on the banking sector involves impacts on trading activities of retail investors and impacts on financial dimensions or instruments. These dimensions like financial security, interest in financial issues, deliberative thinking, optimism, financial anxiety, and requirements for safety measures decide the trading activities of retail investors. Two main points arise here to check the affectivity of these financial dimensions on trading. First, either these financial dimensions affect the trading activities of investors or not? Second, at what level the influence of financial dimensions on trading working of retail investors during the pandemic. To check the influence of financial dimensions on investing decisions to buy insurance policies may be checked and justified.[51]

Psychological factors are very important to convince the investors to invest in the market during health crisis and uncertainty in the market. Investors should avoid investment-related decisions that are not capable of effective mode of decision and opinion formation. Researchers may identify psychological processes of investment attitude by utilizing the outline "ostrich effect" for further investor's intention to gain knowledge related to relevant investments in stock market that is continuously falling.[52]

e) Multidimensional Poverty

Among many other factors, the biggest responsible result of COVID-19 is that it created multidimensional poverty. The pandemic created world economic depression as a result of limited trade and stock exchange working. The pandemic created directly or indirectly unemployment due to lockdown policies for decreasing the impacts of virus. The United Nations study shows that poverty of world may increase for the first time since 1990 due to the pandemic. It means the pandemic put significant threats on the economic status and caused poverty and there is a big danger on sustainable development goals (SDGs) to minimize poverty by 2030.[53]

One survey depicts that people of numbers almost 1.4 billion are living in severe poverty. According to one estimate, 1.4 billion of people residing in developing countries are trapped in extreme poverty. It has caused many states of Africa with big population suffering from severe poverty. A few countries are having some serious impacts of the pandemic at the same ratio as was recorded some 30 years ago. By observing the most critical situations of income contraction of 20%, people living in poverty may increase by 420–580 millions.[53]

The pandemic put severe threats on income as well as on financial institutions. Poverty is a phenomenon which describes deficiency of basic necessities to take part actively in social activities. There is no abundant food with clothing of family having access to school and health clinic, scarcity of land where food can grow, scarcity to have support or credit. It can be concluded that poverty is insecurity, powerlessness, absence of households, and communities. Poor means one is vulnerable to disease and lack of basic necessities.

8.8 ROLE OF GOVERNMENTS TO SUSTAIN BANKING SYSTEM DURING PANDEMIC

With the commencement of COVID-19, the governments all over the world scrabbled with crisis and prompt actions. Government actions include transportations ban, lockdowns, quarantine, and diagnosis with financial aids. The major objective of such restrictions is to stop or minimize the spread of virus on one side and to decline the adverse impacts of virus on economy on the other side. However, these actions of lockdown policy have created some sort of uncertainty and fear. For example, the main action of lockdown may be good in controlling infection spread, but it could be dangerous for economic purposes where millions of people have lost jobs and livelihood. Impacts of government actions on stock market may also be elaborated in detail.[54]

To minimize the impacts of the pandemic, government actions must be utilized and followed in true sense. Best managing restrictions like safe distance, that is, social distance, quarantine policy, diagnosis, vaccinating process, and government financial support programs could be useful in reducing infection ratio. Financial markets like Stock Exchange all over the world have faced severe negative reports but with government support and guidance financial and other crises could be addressed during the pandemic.[55]

Government response to COVID-19 can be quantified by using Oxford Covid-19 Government Response Tracker (OxCGRT) database. This database measured government actions in three main categories.

i. Health Index
ii. Stringency Index
iii. Economic Support Index

Health index is assisted with four indicators showing public awareness movement and struggle, contact tracing, diagnosis policy, and vaccination. Health index represents government emergency actions for providing health facilities to public.

Stringency index is assisted by social distancing with major government actions as school closure, closing of workplace, restrictions on gathering or events, closure of public transport, restrictions on travel and tourism internally and externally.

Economic support index describes the government actions to support income and relief packages for debt/ contract for domestic financial programs.[56] The major government actions regarding finance are imperative to sustain the working policies of banks. Government made such actions for the banking sector to be best utilized for economic activities. Government economic support programs are positive to stock market. To counter the negative effects of lockdown and restrictions on travel and tour as well as unemployment and low income, government economic support programs are very useful. Direct cash programs to the accounts of affected persons to meet the basic and essential needs are very helpful to minimize the effects of COVID-19. Compliance to restrictions at home is not fully obeyed by low-income groups and they are more likely to get infected by the virus. So, government income support programs are more helpful to low-income group, which can further be enhanced to convince them for staying at home.[57] Ultimately, government support programs for the banking sector are very important initiatives for the banking sector all over the world.

8.9 FUTURE PROSPECTS OF PANDEMIC COVID-19

There are numerous future prospects of pandemic COVID-19 which can be utilized in the future for its best treatment. Post COVID-19 period is the period, where a civil society may be stronger in civil and social agendas. The primary focus may be on business and economy. Ecological burdens may also be utilized. Basically, there are two main points to address in the post COVID-19 scenario. A global and renewed new deal called "green new deal" focused on such development and circular financial matters. The future prospects are comparable with theories of green growth and coupling of ecological burdens.[58]

There are also many unanswered questions linked to the pandemic, especially the immunity system. Different types of vaccines for different ages, that is, infants and children, young and mature ages, pregnant women, individuals with immune compromised status, as most of vaccines being under development, have targets on healthy masses. So, it is also a future prospect of the pandemic that there should be a regulatory route for safe usage of vaccines for different groups of human development. The modifications that may happen may take many years as compliance with immunization or epidemics may change original assumption of vaccine.[59]

The pandemic may also be countered as China responded to it. Although there was some initial delay from Chinese Authorities to respond to it, but later on with strong governance, strong vigilance of Chinese people, strict regulation, and quick and wise use of data and digital technologies have been considered among the major causes for successes of China against war of COVID-19 pandemic.

Still, there is a need of further research for early diagnosis, treatment with advanced technologies, post treatment precautionary measures, and using sophisticated technologies to preserve human rights and privacy with high standards.

8.10 CONCLUSIONS

It can be concluded from the above discussion that the COVID-19 pandemic put severe impacts on the banking sector of the world. The pandemic has warned the investors, policy makers, and public that such pandemics can put large economic damages to the world economies. Unlike the other dangers and fear like nuclear war that could not be survived and could not escape at related cost, with global warming and climate change that is slow operating as well as localized disasters that respond to market actions, the pandemic COVID-19 put a destructive impact on global economy and banking sector. The impacts of pandemic on financial institutions like foreign remittance, foreign trades (imports and exports), local trades, foods and agriculture, government revenue, and employment put a big pressure on the world reforms agenda. The pandemic disturbed the working style of the banking system. It caused decreasing the capacity and performance of debtors. Ratio of credit risk has been increased due to the pandemic. To stabilize financial integrity and to minimize the impacts of the pandemic, financial institutions have to take some legal and performance-based steps.

The government and regulatory authorities have made it possible to counter the pandemic by applying restrictive policies. Although regulatory response was not satisfactory, still it is used as a strongest tool to minimize the impacts of the pandemic. Applying social distancing policy put a better response to this curse.

It is the need of the hour to bring banking sector restructuring to minimize the impacts of natural calamities and pandemics. Global banking sector challenges like digitization of banks, low interest rates, depression of bank valuation, and strength of banks must be reevaluated to face the in-future pandemics. Also many other sectors that are affected by the banking sector are retail and trade, energy sector, transport and aviation, and tourism sector and multifaceted poverty spread over the world. The role of government to sustain banking system is imperative and such government financial packages are helpful for the smooth running of the homes of financially crunched families. Government responses in three main indexes like economic support index, health index, and stringency index are playing its pivotal role in facing the pandemic. There are also many future prospects of the pandemic to counter the pandemic using sophisticated technologies to preserve human rights and privacy with high standards.

KEYWORDS

- **epidemic**
- **performance**
- **banking sector**
- **digital banking**
- **online banking**

REFERENCES

1. Chen, H.; Qian, W.; Wen, Q. The Impact of the COVID-19 Pandemic on Consumption: Learning from High Frequency Transaction Data, 2020. SSRN 3568574.
2. Stiller, M.; Zink, T. Impact of COVID-19 on the European Banking Industry. IDC Perspective. International Data Corporation. https://www.idc.com/getdoc.jsp?ContainerId=EUR246178520 (accessed 27 June 2020).
3. Cecchetti, S. G.; Schoenholtz, K. L. Contagion: Bank Runs and COVID-19. In: *Economics in the time of COVID-19*; Baldwin and di Mauro, Eds.; CEPR Press, 2020; pp 77–80.
4. Lagoarde-Segot, T.; Leoni, P. Pandemics of the Poor and Banking Stability. *J. Bank Fin.* **2013,** *37* (11), 4574–4583. https://doi.org/10.1016/j.jbank fin.2013.04.004.
5. Barua, S. Financing Sustainable Development Goals: A Review of Challenges and Mitigation Strategies. *Bus. Strategy Dev.* **2019,** *3* (3):277–293. https://doi.org/10.1002/bsd2.94.
6. Damak, M.; Freue, C.; Chugh, G.; Yalovskaya, N.; Tan, M.; Tan, I. et al. Banks in Emerging Markets 15 Countries, Three COVID-19 Shocks; S&P Global. https://www.spglo bal.com/_asset s/documents/ratin gs/resea rch/2020-05-26-banks -in-emerg ing-marke ts-15-count ries-three -covid -19-shocks.pdf.
7. Barua, S. Understanding Coronanomics: The Economic Implications of the Coronavirus (COVID-19) Pandemic. *SSRN Electron J.* **2020**. https://doi.org/10.2139/ssrn.35664 77.

8. Guerrieri, V.; Lorenzoni, G.; Straub, L.; Werning, H. I. Macroeconomic Implications of COVID-19: Can Negative Supply Shocks Cause Demand Shortages? https://www.nber.org/papers/w26918.
9. Sumner, A.; Hoy, C.; Ortiz-Juarez, E. WIDER Working Paper 2020/43-Estimates of the Impact of COVID-19 on Global Poverty, 2020. indiaenvironmentportal.org.in. https://doi.org/10.35188/UNU-WIDER/2020/800-9.
10. Reger, M. A.; Stanley, I. H.; Joiner, T. E. Suicide Mortality and Coronavirus Disease 2019—A Perfect Storm? In *JAMA Psychiatry*; American Medical Association, 2020. https://doi.org/10.1001/jamapsychiatry.2020.1060.
11. Rodela, T.; Tasnim, S.; Mazumder, H.; Faizah, F. Economic Impacts of Coronavirus Disease (COVID-19) in Developing Countries, 2020. https://osf.io/preprints/socarxiv/wygpk/.
12. Bloom, D. E.; Canning, D. Epidemics and Economics: Interactions Between Global Change and Human Health. *Scripta Varia* **2004,** *106*, 304–331.
13. Lee, S. W.; Mullineaux, D. J. Monitoring, Financial Distress, and the Structure of commercial lending syndicates. *Fin. Manag.* **2004,** 107–130.
14. Bhojraj, S.; Sengupta, P. Effect of Corporate Governance on Bond Ratings and Yields: The Role of Institutional Investors and Outside Directors. *J. Bus.* **2003,** *76* (3),455–475.
15. Beck, T.; Mazzaferro, F.; Portes, R.; Quin, J.; Schett, C. Preserving Capital in the Financial Sector to Weather the Storm. VOX CEPR Column, 2020. https://voxeu.org/article/preserving-capital-financial-sector-weather-storm.
16. Benmelech, E.; Tzur-Ilan, N. The Determinants of Fiscal and Monetary Policies During the Covid-19 Crisis, NBER Working Paper (No. 27461). National Bureau of Economic Research, Cambridge, MA, USA, 2020.
17. World Bank & IMF Report, 2020.
18. See also, eg, theWHO published its first Disease Outbreak News on the new virus on 5 January 2020. It contained a risk assessment and advice and reported on what China had told the WHO about the status of patients and the public health response on the cluster of pneumonia cases in Wuhan: https://www.who.int/csr/don/05-january-2020-pneumonia-of-unkown-cause-china/en. The ECDC reported the following on 25 January: "In light of the currently available information, ECDC considers that the potential impact of 2019-nCoV outbreaks is high and further global spread is likely".
19. On the Swedish approach and its major sanitary and legal implications, see E Herlin-Karnell, "Corona and the Absence of a Real Constitutional Debate in Sweden", VerfBlog, 10 April 2020 https://verfassungsblog.de/coronaand-the-absence-of-a-real-constitutional-debate-in-sweden; "Why Swedes Are Not Yet Locked Down", *The Economist*, April 4, 2020.
20. Although to slightly different degrees, the only EUMember States that have adopted such a draconian measure areItaly, Spain and France. See European Commission, "Governmental Measure Data Base" https://webcritech.jrc.ec. europa.eu/covidSt
21. March 31, 2021 through the implementation of POJK No. 11/POJK.03/2020 concerning National Economic Stimulus as a Countercyclical Policy on the Impact of Coronavirus Disease 2019 (POJK No. 11/POJK.03/2020).
22. Wanura, G. I. Prinsip Kehati-Hatian Bank Untuk Mencegah Indikasi Tindak Pidana Korupsi Dalam Pemberian Kredit Usaha Rakyat Pembibitan Hewan Ternak. *Jurist Diction* **2020,** *3* (1), 111–130. DOI: http://dx.doi.org/10.20473/jd.v3i1.17626.

23. Horner, R. Towards a New Paradigm of Global Development? Beyond the Limits of International Development. *Progress Human Geogr.* **2020,** *44* (3), 415–436. https://doi.org/10.1177/0309132519836158.
24. Fukuda-Parr, S.; Muchhala, B. The Southern Origins of Sustainable Development Goals: Ideas, Actors, Aspirations. *World Dev.* **2020,** *126*, 104706. https://doi.org/10.1016/j.worlddev.2019.104706.
25. The Economist The Covid and Climate Crises Are Connected. *The Economist* May 21, 2020. https://www.economist.com/leaders/2020/05/21/the-covid-and-climatecrises-are connected.
26. Klein, N. Screen New Deal: Under Cover of Mass Death, Andrew Cuomo Calls in the BillionairestoBuildaHigh-TechDystopia. *TheIntercept*.May08,2020.https://theintercept.com/2020/05/08/andrew-cuomo-eric-schmidt-coronavirus-techshock-doctrine/
27. Fairwork The Gig Economy and Covid-19: Fairwork Report on Platform Policies. *Fairwork*, 2020. https://fair.work/wpcontent/uploads/sites/97/2020/04/COVID19-Report-Final.pdf
28. Arslan, Y.; Drehmann, M.; Hofmann, B. Central Bank Bond Purchases in Emerging Market Economies. *BIS Bulletin* no. 20, June 2, 2020. https://www.bis.org/publ/bisbu ll20.htm (accessed 24 July 2020).
29. https://home.kpmg/xx/en/home/insights/2020/07/covid-19-impact-on-banking-m-and-a-2020.html
30. https://blogs.imf.org/2020/03/31/maintaining-banking-system-safety-amid-the-covid-19- crisis/
31. Airports Council International. The Impact of COVID-19 on the Airport Business, 2020. https://aci.aero/wp-content/uploads/2020/03/200401-COVID19-Economic-Impact-Bulletin-FINAL-1.pdf (accessed 6 Apr 2020).
32. Li, K.; Qin, Y.; Wu, J.; Yan, J. Containing the Virus or Reviving the Economy? Evidence from Individual Expectations During the COVID-19 Epidemic. *SSRN Electron. J.* **2020.**
33. Chinazzi, M.; Davis, J. T.; Ajelli, M. et al. The effect of Travel Restrictions on the Spread of the 2019 Novel Coronavirus (COVID-19) Outbreak. *Science* **2020,** *368* (6489), 395–400.
34. Musselwhite, C.; Avineri, E.; Susilo, Y. Editorial JTH 16 –'e Coronavirus Disease COVID-19 and Implications for Transport and Health. *J. Transp. Health* **2020,** *16*, Article ID 100853.
35. Rodr´ıguez-Morales, A. J.; MacGregor, K.; Kanagarajah, S.; Patel, D.; Schlagenhauf, P. Going Global—Travel and the 2019 Novel Coronavirus. *Travel Med. Infect. Dis.* **2020,** *33*, Article ID 101578.
36. https://www.journals.elsevier.com/journal-of-air-transport-management
37. Ruiz Estrada, M. A.; Khan, A. Globalization and Pandemics: The Case of COVID-19. *SSRN Electron. J.* **2020.**
38. Vidya, C. T.; Prabheesh, K. P. Implications of COVID-19 Pandemic on the Global Trade Networks. *Emerg. Mark. Fin. Trade* **2020,** *56* (10), 2408–2421. http://dx.doi.org/10.1080/1540496X.2020.1785426.
39. Apergis, N.; Apergis, E. Can the COVID-19 Pandemic and Oil Prices Drive the US Partisan Conflict Index? *Energy Res. Lett.* **2020,** *1* (1), 13144. http://dx.doi.org/10.46557/001c.13144.
40. Devpura, N.; Narayan, P. K. Hourly Oil Price Volatility: The Role of COVID-19. *Energy Res. Lett.* **2020,** *1* (2), 13683. http://dx.doi.org/10.46557/001c.13683.

41. Fu, M.; Shen, H. COVID-19 and Corporate Performance in the Energy Industry. *Energy Res. Lett.* **2020,** *1* (1), 12967. http://dx.doi.org/10.46557/001c. 12967.
42. Gil-Alana, L. A.; Monge, M. Crude Oil Prices and COVID-19: Persistence of the Shock. *Energy Res. Lett.* **2020,** *1* (1), 13200. http://dx.doi.org/10.46557/ 001c.13200.
43. Huang, W.; Zheng, Y. COVID-19: Structural Changes in the Relationship Between Investor Sentiment and Crude Oil Futures Price. *Energy Res. Lett.* **2020,** *1* (2), 13685. http://dx.doi.org/10.46557/001c.13685.
44. Prabheesh, K. P.; Garg, B.; Padhan, R. Time-Varying Dependence Between Stock Markets and Oil Prices During COVID-19: The Case of Net Oil-Exporting Countries. *Econ. Bull.* **2020,** *40* (3), 2408–2418. http://www.accessecon.com/Pubs/EB/2020/Volume40/EB-20-V40-I3-P210.pdf.
45. Filis, G. Macro Economy, Stock Market and Oil Prices: Do Meaningful Relationships Exist Among Their Cyclical Fluctuations? *Energy Econ.* **2010,** *32* (4), 877–886. http://dx.doi.org/10.1016/j.eneco.2010.03.010.
46. Garg, B.; Prabheesh, K. P. The Nexus Between the Exchange Rates and Interest Rates: Evidence from BRIICS Economies During the COVID-19 Pandemic. *Stud. Econ. Fin.* **2021.** http://dx.doi.org/10.1108/SEF-09-2020-0387.
47. Zhang, D.; Hu, M.; Ji, Q. Financial Markets Under the Global Pandemic of COVID-19. *Fin. Res. Lett.* **2020,** *36*, 101528.
48. Smith, R. D. Responding to Global Infectious Disease Outbreaks: Lessons from SARS on the Role of Risk Perception, Communication and Management. *Soc. Sci. Med.* **2006,** 63 (12), 3113–3123.
49. Gates, B. Responding to Covid-19—A Once-in-a-Century Pandemic? *New Engl. J. Med.* **2020,** *382* (18).
50. Khan, S. U.; Liu, X.; Khan, I. U.; Liu, C.; Rasheed, M. I. Assessing the Investors' Acceptance of Electronic Stock Trading in a Developing Country: The Mediating Role of Perceived Risk Dimensions. *Info. Resour. Manage. J.* **2020,** *33* (1), 59–82.
51. Fünfgeld, B.; Wang, M. Risk and Time Preference in Consumer Financial Behavior. *SSRN Electron. J.* **2017**. DOI: 10.2139/ssrn.3059481.
52. Olafsson, A.; Pagel, M. The Ostrich in Us: Selective Attention to Financial Accounts, Income, Spending, and Liquidity, NBER Working Paper No. 23945, 2020. DOI: 10.3386/w23945
53. Sumner, A.; Hoy, C.; Ortiz-Juarez, E Estimates of the Impact of COVID-19 on Global Poverty, United Nations University World Institute for Development Economics Research Publication (UNU- WINDER) Working Paper, April, 2020/43, 2020. https://www.wider.unu.edu/sites/default/files/Publications/Working-paper/PDF/wp2020-43.pdf (accessed on: 5 Apr 2020).
54. Wagner, A. F. What the Stock Market Tells Us About The Post-COVID-19 World. *Nat. Human Behav.* **2020,** *4*, 440–440.
55. Ashraf, B. N.; Zheng, C.; Jiang, C.; Qian, N. Capital Regulation, Deposit Insurance and Bank Risk: International Evidence from Normal and Crisis Periods. *Res. Int. Bus. Fin.* **2020,** *52*.
56. Hale, T.; Petherick, A.; Phillips, T.; Webster, S. Variation in Government Responses to COVID-19. Blavatnik School of Government Working Paper 31, 2020.
57. Lou, J.; Shen, X.; Niemeier, D. Are Stay-at-Home Orders More Difficult to Follow for Low-Income Groups? Working Paper, 2002.

58. Stoknes, P.; Rockstr€om, J. Redefining Green Growth within Planetary Boundaries. *Energy Research*; Stoknes, P.; Rockstr€om, J. 2018. Redefining Green. *Soc. Sci.* **2018,** *44.*, 41–49. DOI: 10.1016/j.erss.2018.04. 030.
59. Doherty, M.; Buchy, P.; Standaert, B.; Giaquinto, C.; Cohrs D. P. Vaccine Impact: Benefits for Human Health. *Vaccine* **2016,** *34*, 6707–6714. https://doi.org/10.1016/j.vaccine.2016.10.025.

CHAPTER 9

Impact of COVID-19 on Science and Technology

FATIMA SAQIB[1], MUQEET WAHID[1], IRAM IQBAL[1,2],
ARWA ABDULKREEM AL-HUQAIL[3], AND SAMINA YAQOOB[4]

[1]*Department of Pharmacology, Faculty of Pharmacy,
Bahauddin Zakariya University, Multan, Punjab, Pakistan*

[2]*Drug Testing Laboratory, Health Department, Government of Punjab, Lahore, Pakistan*

[3]*Department of Biology, College of Science,
Princess Nourah bint Abdulrahman University, Riyadh, Saudi Arabia*

[4]*Dr Hasan Murad School of Management (HSM),
University of Management and Technology, Lahore, Pakistan*

ABSTRACT

In a few months, the COVID-19 outbreak had spread globally. The growing number of individuals with this condition presents significant problems to existing health care systems. This pandemic has wreaked havoc. This chapter summarizes current research on using science and computational intelligence (CI) to fight COVID-19 infection. Researchers now evaluate COVID-19 data and derive insights using AI, IoT, deep learning, neural networks, Fuzzy, and machine learning techniques. These measures assist policymakers and frontline workers in preventing the viral spread and controlling epidemics. Researchers advise using AI and IoT to fight the epidemic and follow the government's rules. Since face-to-face healthcare consultations are restricted due to the COVID-19 epidemic, alternative information technologies like

Post-Pandemic Economy, Technology, and Innovation: Global Outlook and Context.
Samina Yaqoob, Arwa Abdulkreem AL-Huqail, and Fakhra Aziz (Eds.)

telemedicine and smartphones are becoming more important. Smartphone and telemedicine technologies have tremendous potential in the present COVID-19 epidemic. It will play a vital part in the future of health medicine, patient referral, consulting, ergonomics, and many more expanded uses of health care as smartphone technology improves.

9.1 INTRODUCTION

COVID-19 has ravaged the world, infecting hundreds of millions, weakening economies, blocking borders, and unleashing destruction on an unimaginable scale, including the healthcare, education, and transportation sectors.[1] Respiratory droplets spread the illness from an infected individual. Severe COVID-19 infections cause pneumonia and multi-organ failure.[2] As COVID-19 instances increase, health professionals and institutions are overloaded. As a result, the healthcare sectors in emerging and rich countries have struggled to cope.

Healthcare services and employees already stretched thin will undoubtedly impact medical research in the short and long terms. A hypothesis, virology (including influenza) comprised less than 2% of total biomedical research. An estimated 10–20% of current biomedical research is devoted to COVID-related problems. Hundreds of millions of dollars have been spent on COVID-19 research.[3] Sharing scientific results and data has never been easier or faster. The crisis has re-emphasized sickness, health, and healthcare and will influence public expenditure in the long term. However, all this hope and dedication has a cost. According to the government-funded medical research body, we will see how the economic downturn affects government's spending on medical research.[4] COVID-19 activities have been given priority over all other research activities. It is uncertain how the economic crisis will affect government's investment in biomedical research. The worldwide crisis of economic makes future medical research funding harder to predict.[5] COVID-19 has already impacted the globe, not just because of the sickness but also the global response to the pandemic.[4] It is vital that medical research does not suffer the same fate as pediatric and developmental urology.

9.2 ARTIFICIAL INTELLIGENCE APPROACHES FOR COVID-19

Artificial intelligence (AI) represents a novel opportunity in the internet and virtual world age. Numerous nations use artificial intelligence to monitor COVID-19 outbreaks, alert healthcare institutions, and limit its spread.[6] We investigated COVID-19 detection and prediction utilizing methods inspired by nature, big data, and artificial intelligence. When a class is underrepresented, or the dataset is small, the accuracy of machine learning may be deceptive.[7] COVID-19 pandemic case screening and diagnosis using AI; use of big data for contact monitoring and case detection; and use of nature-inspired computing (NIC) to improve COVID-19 case detection accuracy.[8]

Technology-driven techniques have boosted demand for breakthroughs and alternative tactics, stretching technology limitations.[9] During the pandemic, technologies like telehealth (STAT 2020), AI,[10] robotics,[11] and drones[12] have increased in importance. Drone and robot technology can help with disinfection, medical supply delivery, surveillance, and early infection detection. Patients and healthcare personnel may get medical assistance from robots.[11] The fast rise of COVID-19 cases needed a large-scale data analysis to create pandemic strategies. A strategic framework based on AI and data-driven apps has been created to detect better, track, and analyze data.[9] AI has been used in infection prediction, medicine, and diagnostic findings because of its ability to operate independently, self-learn to better with fresh data sets, and swiftly draw imperatives.[13] Even a mobile phone network may be useful in epidemic situations.[14]

It is critical to conduct timely monitoring and forecasting of illnesses, particularly those that have the potential to throw the globe into turmoil. For this purpose, BlueDot, a Toronto-based health monitoring firm, successfully reported an anticipated coronavirus epidemic on 31 December 2019, nine days ahead of the WHO's deadline.[15] To seek indications of new illnesses, BlueDot's AI model uses a combination of machine learning (ML) and natural language processing (NLP) technologies. BlueDot was able to follow the progress of SARS-CoV-2 and predict the epidemic ahead of epidemiologists because of this methodology. That is not to argue that no human effort was necessary. While their AI model could anticipate the disease's spread, human interpretation of the algorithm's output remained critical to its operation.[16] Apart from BlueDot, numerous other organizations have embraced artificial intelligence to forecast the risk of new illnesses. For instance, Metabiota, a risk analytics firm launched in 2008, has built an epidemic-monitoring technology to anticipate disease transmission. Metabiota makes its forecasts based on parameters such as the clinical characteristics of the illness, the mortality rate, and the availability of therapy. Additionally, the Epidemic Tracker of Metabiota provides thorough information and up-to-date data on over 120 new diseases.[17]

9.3 COVID-19 AI-BASED DATA SCIENCE MODELING

The global community is doing critical technical research in artificial intelligence and statistics to identify and combat the pandemic. Recently, the Australian Census-based Epidemic Predictor (ACEMod) was modified and calibrated to better simulate the COVID-19 pandemic in Australia. Allam and Jones argue that using artificial intelligence to manage systems and regulate protocols.[18] Researchers in China employed deep learning to forecast COVID-19 infections in infected regions. Data such as death counts, social media awareness, tourist density, and demographics are collected to estimate disease risk in an area. Maghdid and Ghafoor[19] reported using smartphone sensors with AI technology to test for COVID-19 infection. The envisaged AI-enabled protocol examines smartphone sensor data to assess the user's illness.[20] In another study, deep learning was used to diagnose diseases by collecting and analyzing data[21]. For example, videos and photos from smartphones or data from inertial sensors were used to assess human weariness.[22]

Similarly, a smartphone microphone may detect coughing.[23] Even smartphone video may help anticipate sickness.[24] A recent cooperative venture between India and Japan intends to improve human health via smart technology. The organization will develop autonomous systems, robotics, AI, and blockchain technologies to address healthcare challenges.[18,25] Infection risk and danger level in a demographic zone are exactly perceived by the Canadian startup BlueDot (Bluedot 2020). Another company leveraging AI and fitness data to anticipate future coronavirus hotspots in the US is Cotiviti. Using the Susceptible-Infected-Recovered-Dead (SIRD) methodology, an AI model predicted probable infection centers in Hubei, China. Meanwhile, different technologies are being developed to help combat pandemics like the coronavirus.[11,26]

During self-quarantine, Siri, Alexa, and other AI applications might be used to monitor and record body temperature, heart rate, and oxygen saturation.[27] Apple Health Check is a screening and information portal.[28] Alexa's daily check focuses on the elderly, who are digitally assessed for possible COVID-19 symptoms through daily survey replies.[29]

Following the COVID-19 epidemic, several authorities employed infrared temperature scanners to test individuals for fever in various public locations. However, this technology cannot be used without the presence of frontline staff. To reduce frontline worker exposure to possible COVID-19 patients, numerous hospitals, airports, and medical institutions have used cameras equipped with artificial intelligence-based multimodal technologies.[30] These cameras can watch crowds, identify persons with elevated body temperatures, recognize faces, and track movement. Tampa General Hospital in Florida was one of the first institutions to use the technology. The hospital put an AI-enabled camera at its entrance to check all entering patients using a thermal facial scan for excessive body temperatures. Their AI technology utilizes machine learning and video data to determine if someone has COVID-19 symptoms.[30]

9.4 AI FOR CORONAVIRUS TREATMENT

The strength of AI and edge computing is their capacity to analyze enormous amounts of data at breakneck speed while simultaneously increasing efficiency. It facilitates big data analytics, algorithm implementation, and data transfer across edge and cloud.[31]

In pandemic conditions like COVID-19, AI and data science are essential. Google's "Deep Mind" team studied the coronavirus' proteins and genomes (ZD Net).[8,32] These results will help others create medicines and better understand the virus. "BenevolentAI" has been employing AI models to produce medications that may heal complex disorders, like COVID-19. In the early pandemic, the AI module recommended existing medicines that would be beneficial in treating coronavirus illness.[18] The world's supercomputers and cloud computing capabilities are being used to create a coronavirus vaccine.[32] These systems can calculate and simulate solutions significantly quicker than regular computers.[33,34]

Stebbing et al. employed artificial intelligence algorithms to see whether baricitinib, a JAK1/JAK2 inhibitor used to treat rheumatoid arthritis, might halt SARS-CoV-2 infection and minimize virus-induced inflammation.[35] Its combination with remdesivir improves the clinical recovery rate of COVID-19 patients with less serious adverse effects than remdesivir alone.[36] Ge et al. (2021) used machine learning and statistical analysis to discover the PARP1 inhibitor meguparib (CVL218), which inhibits SARS-CoV-2 replication in vitro.[37] With the advancement of artificial intelligence (AI), robots are gaining "*social intelligence*"—the capacity to be socially aware, comprehend emotional cues, and respond in the same way that a real person would. The application of artificial intelligence by a socially intelligent robot emphasizes contact with people.[38]

9.5 PATIENT'S PERSPECTIVE

The COVID-19 pandemic poses substantial clinical concerns. With limited clinical assets, patient severity dictates therapy demands.[21] It is vital to identify mild outpatients early and provide appropriate therapy to optimize the treatment process and reduce mortality. AI can assist in assessing, anticipating, and remediating COVID-19 contaminations and monitoring financial impacts. Most clinical applications of artificial intelligence to the COVID-19 response have focused on clinical imaging diagnosis.[39] The quality of current diagnostic procedures for early illness detection has been questioned. Recently, it was observed that some study uses artificial intelligence to evaluate computed tomography (CT) images, while others utilize clinical data to predict infection progression.[34]

For COVID-19 patients, AI can predict their chances of survival and if they need ICU therapy. Patients with COVID-19 at risk of worsening disease are being identified by specialists at colleges like Stanford and Chicago. These systems have already shown their ability to predict ICU admissions for heart disease patients. An early warning system for acute respiratory distress syndrome (ARDS), one of the severe symptoms linked with the COVID-19, is also being developed by Bayesian Health, a startup based at the John Hopkins University.[40,41] The authors offer an AI system for clinical decision-making based on real-world COVID-19 patient data prediction analysis. A computer algorithm can predict who would get severe symptoms like ARDS. Their approach predicted severe COVID-19 patients with a 70%–80% accuracy.[42]

9.6 DIAGNOSIS USING RADIOLOGY IMAGES

The quick and exact diagnosis of COVID-19 may save lives, slow disease spread, and create extensive data from AI models. Innovative medical treatment options include AI-driven picture analysis. Taking X-ray and computed tomography (CT) images for COVID-19 infection detection and therapy takes a lot of time and effort.[39] In this scenario, AI may aid by changing treatment regimens based on patient feedback. Scientists working on AI applications suggest that it may help radiologists diagnose faster and cheaper than standard coronavirus testing.[10] Doctors may employ X-rays, and CT scans to perform diagnoses. Table 2 summarizes AI uses in COVID-19 CT diagnostic.

All emergency clinics, however, have X-ray (or CT) machines. Using Deep Learning and X-ray pictures, radiologists can diagnose COVID-19. COVID-Net and CoroNet, an artificial intelligence tool, assess COVID-19 symptoms in chest x-rays using data from people with different lung diseases.[43,44] A diagnostic study discovered that an inception migration neural network correctly identified COVID-19 symptoms from CT scans with an accuracy of 89.5%.[39] A deep learning-based early detection approach was developed to identify COVID-19 pneumonia from influenza-A virus pneumonia and sound patients.[21,45]

A 3-D deep learning model proportioned the patient's afflicted regions. The model was 86.7% accurate. Jin et al.[45] created a deep learning algorithm that accurately recognizes coronavirus symptoms in CAP and other lung illnesses. A 3D deep learning framework employing chest CT was built (COV-Net). A deep learning model was presented for Coronavirus detection that uses CT scan data to divide lungs, identify COVID-19, and locate aberrant slices. The research also believes that the AI framework's diagnostic results may be quantified in the first image to overcome the deep neural systems' black box disadvantage.[46] An automated tool was constructed using deep learning to measure the virus's symptoms in the patient's lungs and track its development or treatment. However, Chinese hospitals have installed "AI-assisted" imaging equipment.

9.7 PREDICTION OF A PATIENT'S HEALTH CONDITION

A novel method based on clinical data and blood tests was shown to assist doctors in identifying high-risk patients as early as feasible, improving patient forecasting, and decreasing mortality.[47] Instead, the XGBoost algorithm anticipated mortality risk and particular crucial traits assessed in clinics. Lactate dehydrogenase, lymphocytes, and high-affectability C-receptor protein are three critical clinical markers determining patient mortality. As a positive, the method's three indications match the pathophysiological elements of COVID-19, namely cell injury, immunity, and inflammation.[18,48] A subsidiary of U-Net based on CT imaging data predicted whether or not current COVID-19 patients will need a longer hospital stay.[49] These two methods may assist clinics in better identifying patients who need escalating or long-term care. Finally, although both studies had limited breadth and information, they established critical research paths that may be expanded with clinical data from throughout the globe.

Several AI-powered techniques have helped Korea quickly examine and identify COVID-19 cases in the country. VUNO's Chest X-Ray Image Support Decision Tool may identify patients needing critical care by detecting odd observations in their chest X-ray images. A lung problem is determined by studying the patient's X-ray scans. JLK inspection, an AI-based medical and security solutions firm, has launched another AI platform dubbed AiHub in South Korea. The platform leverages AI and large data from numerous imaging equipment to identify lung diseases. AI has helped speed up the creation of COVID-19 testing kits in Korea. The Korean authorities and the European Union have accepted these testing kits.[50]

9.8 PANDEMIC VS. MOBILE APPS

Since the COVID-19 outbreak began, various smartphone apps have been created, some by state agencies, others by commercial firms. The use of smartphone apps by governments and organizations worldwide is increasing. Mobile Apps may be categorized as informational, self-assessment, or contact tracking apps.[14,51]

204 billion applications were downloaded in 2019, and 3.8 billion people accessed social media in January 2020. Of course, telehealth is perfect for transmittable disease control. Telehealth may aid patients with COVID-19 or those worried about infection with remote evaluation (triage) and management. Telehealth may give easy access to regular treatment without the danger of exposure in a crowded hospital or medical office waiting room for individuals not infected with the COVID-19 virus.[52] iWorkSafe, a mobile app-based intelligent portable healthcare (pHealth) technology, helps enterprises identify COVID-19 infection suspects among workers who require primary care. The iWorkSafe software merges data from the industry's database, mobile device proximity and contact tracking, and user-reported COVID-19 self-test data.[53]

On Android, there is a universal app called Test Yourself Goa. The app uses symptom-checking to assess whether a person is at high risk of COVID-19. After the symptom-checking test, the CDC-approved advice is offered.[54] COVID Symptom Tracker is the only universal app accessible in the App Store and the Play Store. COVID-19 allows users to report symptoms every day. Inputs include age, gender, height, weight, and postal code. The health authorities will also gather user data. COVID Symptom Tracker needs internet connectivity to run and provides no instructional information, according to the preliminary feature evaluation.[55]

9.8.1 MOBILE PHONE APPLICATION AND TECHNOLOGY FOR COVID-19

Mobile phone technology has spread across cities in recent years, linking individuals to larger populations. Smartphone applications (apps) have proven to be an ideal vehicle for communicating with bigger groups. Numerous smartphone applications have been created to educate the public, give medical aid, and, most critically, monitor COVID-19 encounters.[56] Numerous industries, technology, and competent governance have contributed to developing a defensive system against COVID-19. Given the incredible role that technology plays in the battle against COVID-19, it is vital to understand how these advancements act in concert to combat the pandemic.[20] This section discusses the untapped potential of smart technology for pandemic control. Mobile applications have been a prominent approach in the battle against COVID-19. Numerous governments and commercial companies have already adopted COVID-19 impact management apps and platforms, and numerous more are in the process of doing so. Currently, most of these systems rely on various technologies, including Bluetooth, GPS, and GIS (geographic information system) (GIS). Additionally, specific applications have incorporated blockchain technology, a relatively new technology that enables the storing of data in immutable chunks.[20]

9.8.2 APPS FOR EDUCATION

Because these apps are supposed to educate rather than engage, customization is not required. These apps provide up-to-date COVID-19 news, fact sheets, and guidelines.

Due to the COVID-19 viral pandemic, schools, colleges, universities, and other government institutions have been closed. Teachers have been instructing students using e-learning platforms during these trying times.[57] e-learning is a kind of learning that occurs through the internet. It was first used in 1999 at a CBT systems conference. It is sometimes referred to as "virtual" or "online" education. It lets users share reading materials through email, papers, presentations, and webinars via the internet. IT has become an important part of modern education, indicating its importance in the present teaching-learning process.[58] Educators may share study materials and lectures in PowerPoint, PDF, or Word documents with as many students as possible during the lockdown by publishing them on their university websites, sharing them over Whatsapp, or emailing them. WeChat, email sharing of audio-visual movies, and other online teaching platforms like Voov, Zoom, Superstar, g-suite cloud conference, and so on have all been used to provide lectures.[59]

More students are utilizing the learning platform and apps due to COVID-19. Some systems, such as ED-TECH and cloud computing, are already well established and economical to use.[60] e-Learning has shown to be very advantageous during this COVID-19 issue. More students have chosen Ed-tech and other online educational platforms during this continuing epidemic. Vedantu, Unacademy, and Byju's have all provided free access to live classes to allow students to study comfortably from home, and these educational apps have been connected with a significant rise in student enrolment. Additionally, educators on online platforms have begun to provide more live courses. e-Learning was very advantageous during the COVID-19 issue. During this pandemic, an increasing number of pupils are learning using Ed-tech and other online platforms.[61]

9.8.3 SELF-TESTING APPLICATIONS

Using COVID-19 mobile apps, consumers may analyze their health and get COVID-19 instructions/recommendations. A simple series of questions are intended to help persons who seem to have infection symptoms and a preferred illness. It also educates individuals on how the disease spreads and helps them prevent it. The secondary goal is to reduce the number of mild symptom patients visiting hospitals.[14,51]

Numerous systems claim that they spotted COVID-19 early sickness reports utilizing crowdsourcing data and news sources prior to the WHO declaring the outbreak. Automated syndromic surveillance investigates the National Health Service's digital data in search of COVID-19 clusters.[52] While self-quarantine and social isolation are critical in a pandemic, COVID-19 is detected via nasal swabs, saliva test kits, and blood tests. The development of modified COVID-19 and other viral self-testing kits has been lauded. Smartphones equipped with embedded software, hardware, high-performance processing, and connectivity have enabled the viability of several e-health initiatives. COVID-19 users' breathing noises may reveal interesting acoustic signal patterns. Obtaining respiratory data just from breathing sounds obtained by a smartphone's microphone appeals to this goal. Due to increased signal processing and analysis, new deep/machine learning and pattern recognition algorithms may be utilized to classify breathing data into healthy or ill states. They might be utilized as self-test breathing monitoring apps in response to the current global COVID-19 pandemic, allowing users to check their breathing sound pattern routinely.[62]

A Carnegie Mellon University research team has built an automated artificial intelligence system capable of identifying the COVID-19 in a person's voice. After requesting the user's height and weight, the software coughs three times. Following that, a vowel and an alphabet are read aloud, allowing the app to calculate the user's lung capacity by comparing it to the data of thousands of other users, including infected individuals. Following this quick process, the buyer receives a score out of ten. A higher score indicates that the user's attributes are similar to those of COVID-19 sufferers. The researchers emphasize that this is not a diagnostic process and cannot be used instead of laboratory or hospital testing.[63,64] Students have developed similar smartphone applications for voice-based COVID-19 diagnosis at Mumbai's DY Patil Institute of Bio-Technology and Bio-Informatics. Tor Vergata University in Rome is currently evaluating this software. To use the app, just speak into the microphone on the smartphone, and the application will analyze the sound for frequency and noise distortion. The values of the parameters are then compared to those of an average person to determine whether or not a person has COVID-19.[65]

9.8.4 CONTACT-TRACKING APPS

Contact tracing is the technique of finding persons who have been exposed to infectious people. The COVID-19 has a very long incubation time, and there is no widespread testing, making it difficult for authorities to determine the true infection rate.[1] Contact tracing and alerting have been vital throughout the pandemic. Contact tracing and warning alert infected people to self-quarantine or isolate if they display symptoms. Contact tracing also helps track virus dissemination trends in society. Contact-tracking Apps use technologies like Bluetooth, encryption, and API framework. So, contact tracing is the only practical method. The WHO states that contact tracing has three steps:

1. It is detecting those who have had touch with an infected person.
2. Keeping track of their information.
3. Get those people tested ASAP.

Adopting contact tracing may benefit nations in the early and second stages of the COVID-19 pandemic. To avoid future transmission after case identification and isolation, quick tracking and quarantining of contacts are required. In high-transmission zones, these interventions must be implemented and monitored at a scale that is becoming more unrealistic or at least difficult to do by conventional methods.[52] Early digital tracing projects raised privacy issues.

The Chinese government has created a surveillance app called "Health Code" that uses vast data to assess a person's risk. The "CovidSafe" App released by Australia certifies users' fitness and collects data to determine if they have been infected. As the COVID-19 pandemic spreads globally, so will the use of contact-tracking tools. In South Korea, confirmed case contacts were tracked using location, surveillance, and transaction data. In China, the AliPay HealthCode app automatically recognized contacts based on their location and enforced tight quarantine measures by prohibiting transactions for high-risk individuals. These applications capture location data through GPS or cellular networks, proximity data via Bluetooth, or a mix of these.[52]

TraceTogether is a contact tracing program developed by the Singaporean government that employs Bluetooth technology to discover a healthy person's history of exposure to an infected person. If both devices have Bluetooth enabled, an encrypted code is sent between them while closing. As soon as a user of this app is diagnosed with COVID-19, the authorities may look up all the persons who had close touch with the infected user. This program does not utilize GPS to determine a user's position, assuaging concerns about privacy.[66] This app has approximately one million downloads as of 1 April 2020, a Singapore record for an app hosted on a government website.

The National Informatics Centre (NIC) of India's Ministry of Electronics and IT (MeitY) developed a contact-tracking software called Aarogya Setu to reduce COVID-19 spread in India. Any Indian citizen may download this app for free and register using their cell number to access its features. This app asks the user whether they have COVID-19 symptoms or have traveled internationally; if not, they are in the green zone. This software supports 11 Indian languages and is available for iOS and Android.[67] Unlike TraceTogether, this software utilizes GPS and Bluetooth to assess whether a person has been exposed to a prospective COVID-19 patient. If a person in the green zone meets someone in the red zone, this app quickly alerts the former, informing him/her of the rules to follow. This software also enables fast access to vital information.[68] Some nations, including Italy, Australia, and Germany, have shown strong interest in Israel's new contact-tracking program HaMagen. To establish whether an app user has come into touch with a virus-positive person, HaMagen uses GPS technology. According to the Health Ministry, no user's data leaves the phone without their agreement, dispelling concerns about privacy issues around the program. For the app to work, users must record their COVID-19 exposure. 50,000 app users reported self-isolation within the first week of the app's debut.[69]

The real downside of contact tracing is that it is time-consuming and labor-intensive, and it is only successful when done quickly. When patients show signs of COVID-19 infection and test positive for the virus, many of their contacts must be notified and confined as soon as possible to prevent future infections. Public health officials may not do this.[70]

9.8.5 TELEHEALTH

Telehealth and digital care include delivering medical services using information and communication technology (ICT). To reduce expenses while improving treatment, digital care may be seen as a vital instrument that reduces the need for patients to travel and provides remote services. The benefits of telemedicine and digital care cannot be emphasized in times of public health catastrophes like the COVID-19 outbreak.[71] The Internet of Medical Things (IoMT) is a network of medical equipment and software applications linked to healthcare IT systems. Like the IoT, the IoMT has recently seen increased possible applications.[72]

Telemedicine is the use of IoMT technology to monitor patients remotely. Using telemedicine, professionals may assess, diagnose, and treat patients without seeing them in person. Recently, various IoMT tech and telemedicine platforms have increased visitors due to the extremely infectious COVID-19 epidemic. Demand for online consultations has increased dramatically since the COVID-19 epidemic, reports JD Health, an e-commerce platform for healthcare products.[73]

Prior to the practice of social distancing, 74% of patients were unaware of telemedicine as a method of receiving medical treatment from their physician. However, due to the COVID-19 pandemic, telemedicine platforms have increased virtual patient consultants from around 25% to 70%.[74]

It is now possible for physicians to give remote medical expertise through telehealth platforms in the USA. These regulatory changes have resulted in an extraordinary surge in demand for Teledoc Health's telemedicine products.

In response to the spike in demand, its stock price has risen by almost 100% in recent weeks.[75] The Australian Department of Health (2020) urges individuals to use telemedicine to limit their risk of exposure to COVID-19. Similarly, the NHS in the UK offers online consultation in defined regions to minimize GP visits. These projects support the CDC's 2019 proposal to adopt telemedicine triage prior to patient visits to reduce unnecessary visits. These instances show how telemedicine may protect patients and doctors while serving the public.[76] Patients undergoing telemedicine therapy are asked whether they have an internet-enabled device (phone, computer, etc.) with a camera and microphone.[77]

Additionally, telehealth devices such as wearables monitor basic vital indicators (e.g., blood pulse wave, heart rate, and temperature) and provide data that clinicians may use to monitor patients remotely. Telehealth does not preclude an attending physician from referring a confined patient to a higher suitable level of medical care if physical therapy is necessary before referring them to intensive care. Thus, telemedicine and digital care may be a great approach for minimizing the risk of infection among doctors and patients while still delivering treatment.[77]

Telehealth is classified into the following categories.[77]

- ***Asynchronous*** is a data collection, summarization, storage, and distribution for subsequent review by a patient. This includes email, video messaging, and medical record annotations. Licensed medical specialists were accessible hours per day to perform preliminary tests remotely. The Johns Hopkins Corona website and the VG live corona website update in Norway give information on the present state of COVID-19. These sites also include information about the home quarantine, personal safety, and medical assistance.
- ***Telecare*** is comparable to synchronous applications through online conversations utilizing video conference or telephone for patients seeking health advice or reporting problems.
- ***Sensors devices*** such as GPS trackers in remote applications warn users to avoid high-level COVID-19 regions.
- ***Virtual agents*** Chatbots for FAQs, referrals, and linking confined patients to available physicians. WHO has launched a WhatsApp chatbot to deliver up-to-date COVID-19 information and suggestions. A chatbot provides health information to consumers through voice or text chat. [23]
- Augmented and virtual reality systems are useful yet expensive and difficult to deploy.

9.9 COMPUTATIONAL BIOLOGY AND MEDICINES PERSPECTIVE

Computer Biology is a branch of biology that uses data analytics, mathematical modeling, and computational simulation to study biology. Computational biologists assist in the fight against the coronavirus and developing a cure. Disease dynamics are modeling aids in understanding the elements that influence infection transmission and how mediations may control it.[30] Both lungs reveal ground glass and infiltrate following death. Numerous data-driven medication repurposing strategies have been published to identify diseases, conditions, or patient groups that may be treated with currently available pharmaceuticals that are not recognized for this disease.[31]

9.10 PREDICTION OF PROTEIN STRUCTURE AND PHYLOGENETIC ANALYSIS

At the outbreak of the COVID-19 pandemic, the structure of SARS-CoV-2 and its link to other viruses were unclear. In this case, silico techniques aided researchers by providing useful predictions such as viral structural homology modeling.[78] Due to the time required to identify all SARS-CoV-2 viral components using laboratory processes, in silico technology-enabled computer-aided researchers stay ahead of others who relied purely on laboratory data. Numerous in-silico approaches were used in the early stages of the study. They discovered no significant variations in the open reading frame (ORF) 1 ab expression in the envelope, membrane, nucleocapsid, and essential proteases.[79] Baruah et al. analyzed the SARS-CoV-2 accessory proteins 9b and ORF14 and predicted their structures. Their investigation established a connection between it and bat coronavirus.[80] Vandelli et al. predicted the human interactome using genomic analysis of SARS-CoV-2. They accomplished this by calculating the secondary structure of over 2000 coronaviruses and over 100,000 interactions with human proteins.[81]

In-silico approaches have also offered SARS-CoV-2 phylogenetic analysis, which is vital for determining the link of various structures with other viruses. Li et al. found that an MRP pseudo-sequence supertree might reveal more about SARS-CoV-2 evolution than a typical phylogenetic tree based on full-length genomic sequences.[82]

9.11 DRUG DISCOVERY

Aside from assisting in medication development, AI is also being used to find current pharmaceuticals that can be repurposed to treat COVID-19. As part of its AI-powered drug discovery platform, Innoplexus AG identified a combination of the existing medications that may be useful in treating the COVID-19. Their platform discovered that Chroloquine, an antimalaria drug, may work better in combination with Remdesivir (an experimental antiviral originally developed to treat Ebola), Tocilizumab (an immunosuppressive drug), Pegasys (used to treat Hepatitis B and C), or Clarithromycin (used to treat hepatitis B and C) (an antibiotic).[83]

Exscientia, a British startup company, wants to employ its AI medication delivery platform to find a chemical combination that could help treat the COVID-19. Exscientia plans to screen 15000 clinically ready compounds of Calibr chemical library against three critical SARS-CoV-2 viral therapeutic targets.[84] Small-molecule antiviral drugs may influence virus–host interactions. For example, pharmacological target identification based on protein–protein interactome provides a good potential for drug discovery and development.[85,86] Because the SARS-CoV-2 spike RBD directly binds ACE2, neutralizing antibodies and small compounds can disrupt the spike/ACE2 relationship. Several natural substances, such as baicalin, scutellarin, nicotianamine, and glycyrrhizin, may inhibit SARS-CoV-2 attachment and entrance.[87] Nobiletin and neohesperidin that bind to ACE2 can partially prevent ACE2 and RBD binding.[88]

The MIT is working on a "decoy" receptor or protein that could be used to treat COVID-19. Most coronaviruses infect the host by activating ACE2 receptors. The MIT researchers used an AI model trained on ACE2 receptor data.[89] Some research on SARS-Cov2 uses a novel route to create 3C-like protease inhibitors.[37] The models use three types of data: protein crystal structure, cocrystallized ligands, and protein homology model. Generative auto-encoders and generative adversarial networks (GEN)[38] are models for each data type. A reward capacity encompassing medicine, likeness, novelty, and diversity is used to assess potential candidates.[48]

In one such study, 332 interactions have been identified between SARS-CoV-2 proteins and human host proteins, including ACE2, Furin, TEPRSS2, NRP1, eEF1A, etc.[90]

Two inhibitors can potently suppress SARS-CoV-2 infection, one by limiting mRNA translation (Zotatifin) and the other via modulating sigma-2 and sigma-2 receptors (haloperidol). This study also found that the host protein eEFIA inhibitor plitidepsin reduces SARS-CoV-2 infection in vivo.[91] According to another study, 16 putative anticoronavirus medicines (irbesartan, toremifene, camphor, equilin, mesalazine) reduce SARS-CoV-2 infection through pharmacological targets viral–host interactions.

From another study, 16 potential anticoronavirus drugs (Irbesartan, toremifene, camphor, equilin, mesalazine, mercaptopurine, paroxetine, sirolimus, carvedilol, colchicine, dactinomycin, melatonin, quinacrine, eplerenone, emodin, Oxymetholone) were found to inhibit SARS-CoV-2 infection based on drug targets and viral–host interactions through implementing a systemic network medicine platform.[92] Based on computational biophysical studies, toremifene, an authorized selective estrogenic receptor modulator for treating breast cancer, can inhibit MERS-CoV, SARS-CoV, and SARS-CoV-2.[93,94] Beck et al. predicted that atazanavir, remdesivir, efavirenz, ritonavir, and dolutegravir potently suppress the activity of 3CLpro of SARS-CoV-2 with low Kd values using the deep learning-based drug target prediction method.[95]

9.12 DRONE TECHNOLOGY

Drones are unmanned aerial vehicles that autonomously fly in natural and man-made environments. Unmanned aerial vehicles (UAVs) or drones can help battle the Coronavirus epidemic in numerous ways. Drones are also being used by numerous governments, such as China, to contain the Coronavirus spread. Canada, China, and Australia were the first to legalize commercial drones.[96] Drones help authorities and citizens avoid the spread of coronavirus and unauthorized movement during a lockdown. Authorities used drones for medical supplies, monitoring, disinfection, infection screening, and public awareness. Drones can do these functions and even operate in remote areas without human interaction.

9.13 SCREENING OF MASS PUBLIC

Following the COVID-19 outbreak, several Chinese officials pledged to find COVID-19 sufferers as soon as feasible. Drones outfitted with infrared cameras were used to conduct large-scale temperature monitoring in several residential areas.[11] In India, the authorities in New Delhi have used a multipurpose drone to help restrict the spread of the COVID-19 virus. The drone dubbed the "corona combat," is equipped with a thermal camera for screening individuals, a night vision camera for crowd monitoring, a portable medical box for carrying essential medical supplies, a loudspeaker for making announcements, and a disinfectant tank with a capacity of ten liters for sanitizing public spaces. Unlike infrared thermometers, which can only take the temperature of one person at a time, this drone can take the temperature of numerous individuals at the same time.[97]

9.14 DELIVERY

Since the outbreak of COVID-19 in December 2019, people have begun to adopt a new way of life, which involves social withdrawal, based on emerging evidence that the coronavirus enters the body via the respiratory system. This also resulted in the adoption of legislation in many nations requiring people to exercise physical distance, which includes remaining at least 6 feet apart from other people, to avoid contracting the coronavirus.[98] It saw an acceleration in the usage of drones to deliver items in 2020, both in pilot tests and in real-world scenarios. Alphabet's technology company has noticed an increase in demand for drone deliveries in test sites in the United States and Australia, mostly due to clients adhering to social distancing norms.[99] Several countries and regions have been debating new regulatory frameworks in recent years to clear the way for these new drone cargo delivery services, which will be largely operational in the coming years.[98]

In a coronavirus epidemic, drones have been widely used to deliver crucial supplies quickly and safely. The delivery strategy may be grouped into two categories: food/basic requirements and health care facilities, which comprise test samples for laboratories, medications, and PPE kits.[97,100] Drones take test samples from localized/remote places and carry them to the closest testing facility, relieving the healthcare system. This method saves time and reduces the chance of viral propagation. Drones can be used to quickly transfer medicines and supplies between medical facilities or to COVID-19 patients at home (in case of a mild form of the COVID-19). A prospective idea named "lab-on-a-drone" is suited for labs situated in distant areas where delivering diagnostic equipment is challenging. It combines a drone with sample preparation and diagnostic platforms, reducing testing time.[100] A California-based business called "Zipline" has employed drone technology to carry medical supplies to Ghana and Rwanda.[101] The novel coronavirus epidemic has accelerated the healthcare revolution. Ghana was the first to program and deploy unmanned drones to transport medical supplies and COVID-19 samples. This strategy allowed Ghana to respond rapidly to the outbreak and save many lives. This feature can help hospitals and medical professionals cope with the current crisis.[101,102] China used drones to transport loads of medical supplies and packages in virus-infected regions during the COVID-19 epidemic. Helicopters delivered test samples to labs and safely transported medical supplies to COVID-19 patients. Moreover, excluding people from the distribution process decreases coronavirus transmission and saves delivery time.[103] JD.com, a Chinese e-commerce website, has started employing drones for the last-mile transport of crucial goods.

Marut Drones, a Hyderabad-based firm led by IIT alumni, recently released a series of drones to tackle the COVID-19 pandemic. The company's drone armament includes sanitizing, pharmaceutical distribution, thermal analysis, movement monitoring, and crowd observation. The company claims its medical delivery drones can reach 12 kilometers in just 8 minutes, making them 80 times faster than current techniques. Drone-delivered food is also being tested in other underdeveloped countries. For example, in June 2019, Zomato, one of India's largest food-tech businesses, declared a successful test of food delivery by drone, and lately, 13 delivery companies were granted a license to utilize drones for food delivery in India.[104] As shown in Australia, China, and the USA, drones can carry groceries and medical supplies.

9.15 DISINFECTION

Since no cure or vaccine for COVID-19 has been identified, authorities focus on prevention. Because preventing coronavirus infection takes months, governments are easing lockdowns to stabilize the economy. As we prepare to return to routine, it is critical to regularly disinfect high-risk areas such as parks, public transportation, and outdoor markets. Authorities have devised a plan to use agricultural spraying drones to clean high-risk areas quickly. Compared to previous spray approaches, these drones can disinfect a larger area faster.

A person-to-person encounter is one method coronaviruses spread. Identifying the sick individual and the probably infected person due to contact is critical early on. The objective is to do mass screening with little human-to-human contact. In this regard, drone technology has revolutionized symptom-based mass screening. These drones include a temperature sensor to keep visitors out of their houses. They also have a camera to photograph the subject and a GPS to monitor their position. The "Pandemic Drone" device that remotely monitors respiratory problems is used to improve screening accuracy. Originally, pandemic drones were designed to monitor catastrophes and combat zones remotely. The innovative gadget used computer vision and specialized sensors to monitor crowds' respiratory, heart, and temperature rates. An infectious and respiratory disease pandemic drone termed "Draganfly" has been launched in the USA to prevent the worldwide spread of coronavirus. The technology allows for rapid health evaluation of huge areas and big numbers of people daily.[98]

Authorities in several nations, including France, China, Philippines, USA, India, Colombia, Spain, Chile, and the UAE, have utilized them to disinfect public spaces while limiting human-to-human interaction and contact with potentially contaminated surfaces.[98] Drones equipped with spraying capabilities are not novel; the technology has been used to spray herbicides on agricultural fields for years. However, the objective of these spraying drones is to disinfect public places to prevent viral spread, a function extension.[105] The Spanish Military Emergency Unit (UME – Unidad Militar de Emergencia) employed drones to disinfect vast outdoor areas during the pandemic. The drones utilized were DJI's Agras and DroneTools' DRONEHEXA XL.[98]

9.16 SURVEILLANCE AND BROADCAST

Effective pandemic prevention measures like social distance need widespread public acceptance and cooperation. However, keeping people informed about mitigation measures may be challenging, and authorities may be motivated to monitor the population's adherence to lockdown and social distance rules. Drone usage for population control has taken two major forms: voice message transmission and video monitoring.[98]

Drones with speakers have been used in numerous regions across the globe to communicate social separation or lockdown measures. Most nations banned big gatherings and implemented social distancing policies to restrict physical contact. Surveillance is a critical concern for governments, organizations, and communities. Authorities use drones to track people's movements and prevent dangerous social gatherings.[97] In several nations, drones are utilized to broadcast messages and raise public awareness using loudspeakers and digital displays.[106] Using a GPS-enabled drone control system, authorities may easily detect undesired behaviors in crowded areas. MicroMultiCopter, a well-known industrial drone manufacturer based in Shenzhen, China, has launched more than 100 drones around the nation to survey areas and crowds properly. Drones may also be used to disseminate essential information, especially in locations where communication is difficult. The Madrid police utilized a drone with a loudspeaker to alert the public about the state of emergency enacted.[31]

9.17 ROBOTICS

Assisting in various domains, robotics has demonstrated its worth. The technology has shown promise in pharmaceutical distribution, surveillance, patient screening, and disinfection. Robotics in healthcare has shown promising results in reducing COVID-19 escalation. Robots are more successful in treating and diagnosing infections when combined with machine learning algorithms and AI.[107] For example, robots collect data to evaluate individual health reports. Robots have helped in pandemic scenarios like coronavirus by completing repeated operations with a little mistake. The effectiveness of human–robot communication characterizes robot technology.

9.17.1 AUTONOMOUS ROBOT

Autonomous robots are capable of making judgments and acting without human interference. UV sterilization robots are the most commonly deployed autonomous mobile robots at COVID-19. Hospitals, airports, shopping malls, and retailers utilize UV disinfection robots.[108] Aside from that, wheeled autonomous robots visit patient rooms and capture important health information. With manipulators, these robots can even undertake medical therapy. A self-driving autonomous robot can deliver PPE, medicine, equipment, food, and other supplies.

9.17.2 TELEROBOT

Telerobot technology allows robots to be controlled remotely over a wireless network such as the internet. During the COVID-19 pandemic, human-operated telerobots proved safer and more effective technology. The robots are readily sterilizable, making them useful for patient screening and intake. It operates with a surgical software console that a physician may handle. Teleoperated robot arms can also do ultrasound exams.[109] Using telerobots with mobile phone software allows frequent monitoring of blood oxygen levels, pulse, blood pressure, and temperature. Telerobots are also employed in hospitals and communities for secondary healthcare activities, including screening, patient isolation, and rehabilitation. Patients at home are connected to telerobotics-aided telerehabilitation.[110] Using this technique, persons at high risk of infection may stay at home and get remote rehabilitation treatment.

9.17.3 HOSPITAL COLLABORATIVE ROBOT

During the COVID-19 pandemic, social robots were used in several situations.[111] Assistive social robots might be used due to the lockdown and different country-wide measures, such as physical distance and isolation.[112] Consequently, social robots helped reduce the spread of COVID-19 by monitoring and assisting patients and healthcare workers.[113] Furthermore, research shows that isolation and lockdowns significantly damage mental health and welfare,[114] suggesting that social robots might be useful in a pandemic.[115]

Collaborative robots are designed to complement human-operated processes and physically interact with people. Unlike telerobots, collaborative robots can adapt to changing task dynamics. A collaborative robot can collect and evaluate oropharyngeal and nasopharyngeal swabs.[113] These robots can do tests, including swabs, ultrasound scans, and capturing information by listening to organs with a robot stethoscope. Using Smart telecare technology can reduce the danger of frontline employees contracting lethal infections by remotely monitoring, testing, and diagnosing sick patients.[115] Wheeled robots with manipulators may do diagnostic procedures such as swab testing or measuring a patient's temperature, possibly protecting medical professionals from direct contact with the infected.[116] Telecare systems may minimize PPE usage during patient examinations since treating patients while wearing PPE. CloudMinds, a Beijing-based robotics business, sent almost 14 robots to Wuhan to assist. Ginger, a CloudMinds humanoid service robot, helped at the hospital.[117] At the University of Southern Denmark, researchers have created a robot that gathers and stores samples from the neck. Collaborative robots employ augmented reality (AR) technology to instruct and help healthcare staff in different tasks. The COVID-19 pandemic uses robotic task simulators to teach medical personnel complex operations.

9.17.4 SOCIAL ROBOT

COVID-19 is a significant source of disruption for service users. Consumers are forced to live in social isolation due to coordinated global quarantine efforts, with immediate- and long-term negative psychological health repercussions.[118] Social robots can speak and engage with people and their surroundings. These robots are outfitted with various actuators and sensors to interact with people effectively. Social robots are made to look like humans or toys and converse with users. These robots are designed to help isolated people, older people, and those with impairments. Sensors in these robots assess illness symptoms, stress, and other vital indicators. In the COVID-19 pandemic, social robots help individuals through the hospital.[119]

Social robots might play three strategic roles in facilitating physical separation and mitigating the negative effects of isolation. To begin with, to serve as a point of contact for actions requiring human–human interaction, this includes tasks such as delivering and monitoring medications and supplies to patients in hospitals, distributing hand sanitizer and masks in congested areas, assisting physicians with patient assistance through robot avatars, and even socially helpful self-driving ambulances.[120] Second, to function as a precautionary measure to guarantee contagion-free workplaces. This includes monitoring physical separation in public settings and inspections and sanitation of the environment. Third, serve as well-being coaches for confined patients by performing therapeutic and entertainment tasks.[112]

9.18 CONCLUSIONS

Researchers are exploring all options for countering the coronavirus epidemic, and modern technology is one. While technological advancements have aided us in our daily lives, they have also aided in the ongoing struggle against COVID-19. The articles discuss the difficulties of utilizing these algorithms in clinical practice. Also, additional work on developing a benchmark framework to review and look at present methodologies is desired. They accurately identify COVID-19 symptoms in various viral pneumonia but lack transparency and interpretability. The coronavirus pandemic has created a broad range of clinical and cultural challenges that contemporary technology may help address, although few are yet developed enough to be practical.

KEYWORDS

- **COVID-19**
- **telehealth**
- **artificial intelligence**
- **mobile apps**
- **computational biology**
- **Telerobot**

REFERENCE

1. Agbehadji, I. E. et al. Review of Big Data Analytics, Artificial Intelligence and Nature-Inspired Computing Models towards Accurate Detection of COVID-19 Pandemic Cases and Contact Tracing. *Int. J. Environ. Res. Public Health* **2020,** *17* (15), 1–16.
2. Kow, C. S.; Hadi, M. A.; Hasan, S. S. Vitamin D Supplementation in Influenza and Covid-19 Infections Comment on: "Evidence That Vitamin D Supplementation Could Reduce Risk of Influenza and Covid-19 Infections and Deaths". *Nutrients* **2020,** *12* (6), 988.
3. Prudêncio, M.; Costa, J. C. Research Funding After COVID-19. *Nat. Microbiol.* **2020,** *5* (8), 986.
4. Harper, L. et al. The Impact of COVID-19 on Research. *J. Pediatric Urol.* **2020,** *16* (5), 715–716.
5. Doidge, S.; Doyle, J. Australian Universities in the Age of Covid. *Educ. Phil. Theor.* **2020,** 1–7.
6. Sharifi, A.; Ahmadi, M.; Ala, A. The Impact of Artificial Intelligence and Digital Style on Industry and Energy Post-COVID-19 Pandemic. *Environ. Sci. Pollut. Res.* **2021,** *28* (34), 46964–46984.
7. Modgil, S.; Singh, R. K.; Hannibal, C. Artificial Intelligence for Supply Chain Resilience: Learning from Covid-19. *Int. J. Logistics Manage.* **2021.**
8. Piccialli, F. et al. The Role of Artificial Intelligence in Fighting the COVID-19 Pandemic. *Inf. Syst. Front.* **2021,** *23* (6), 1467–1497.
9. Kim, J. et al. Coronavirus Disease—2019 (COVID-19). ChemRxiv, 2020.
10. Browning, L. et al. Digital Pathology and Artificial Intelligence Will Be Key to Supporting Clinical and Academic Cellular Pathology Through COVID-19 and Future Crises: The PathLAKE Consortium Perspective. *J. Clin. Pathol.* **2021,** *74*, 443–447.
11. Jain, R. et al. Robotics and Drone-Based Solution for the Impact of COVID-19 Worldwide Using AI and IoT. *Stud. Syst. Decision Control* **2021,** *324*, 139–156.
12. Vaishya, R. et al. Drones for Fighting COVID-19 Pandemic. *Curr. Med. Res. Pract.* **2021,** *11* (6), 303.
13. Chen, J.; See, K. C. Artificial Intelligence for COVID-19: Rapid Review. *J. Med. Int. Res..* **2020,** *22* (10).
14. Rakshit, S. et al. Mobile Apps for SME Business Sustainability During COVID-19 and Onwards. *J. Bus. Res..* **2021,** *135*, 28–39.
15. Hollister, M. AI Can Help with the COVID-19 Crisis—But the Right Human Input Is Key. *Proc. World Econ. Forum* **2020,** *30*, 1–7.
16. Naudé, W. Artificial Intelligence Against Covid-19: An Early Review. *SSRN Electron. J.* **2021.**
17. Badker, R. et al. Challenges in Reported COVID-19 Data: Best Practices and Recommendations for Future Epidemics. *BMJ Glob. Health.* **2021,** *6* (5), e005542.
18. Rana, A.; Malik, S. A Review of Computational Intelligence Technologies for Tackling Covid-19 Pandemic. *Internet of Things* **2021,** 223–242.
19. Maghdid, H. S.; Ghafoor, K. Z. A Smartphone Enabled Approach to Manage COVID-19 Lockdown and Economic Crisis. *SN Comput. Sci.* **2020,** *1* (5).
20. Maghdid, H. S. et al. Enabling Accurate Indoor Localization for Different Platforms for Smart Cities Using a Transfer Learning Algorithm. *Internet Technol. Lett.* **2022,** *5* (1).

21. Ali, A. M. et al. Diagnosing Covid-19 Lung Inflammation Using Machine Learning Algorithms: A Comparative Study. *Stud. Big Data* **2020,** *80*, 91–105.
22. Karvekar, S.; Abdollahi, M.; Rashedi, E. Smartphone-Based Human Fatigue Level Detection Using Machine Learning Approaches. *Ergonomics* **2021,** *64* (5), 600–612.
23. Pahar, M. et al. COVID-19 Cough Classification Using Machine Learning and Global Smartphone Recordings. *Comput. Biol. Med.* **2021,** *135*.
24. Li, H. L. et al. Pilot Study Using Telemedicine Video Consultation for Vascular Patients' Care During the COVID-19 Period. *Ann. Vasc. Surg.* **2020,** *68*, 76–82.
25. Mashamba-Thompson, T. P.; Crayton, E. D. Blockchain and Artificial Intelligence Technology for Novel Coronavirus Disease-19 Self-Testing. *Diagnostics* **2020,** *10* (4).
26. Vargo, D. et al. Digital Technology Use During COVID-19 Pandemic: A Rapid Review. *Human Behav. Emerg. Technol.* **2021,** *3* (1), 13–24.
27. Wright, J. H.; Caudill, R. Remote Treatment Delivery in Response to the COVID-19 Pandemic. *Psychother. Psychosomat.* **2020,** *89* (3), 130–132.
28. Vidal-Alaball, J. et al. Telemedicine in the Face of the COVID-19 Pandemic. *Atencion Primaria.* **2020,** *52* (6), 418–422.
29. Bokolo Anthony JNR Use of Telemedicine and Virtual Care for Remote Treatment in Response to COVID-19 Pandemic. *J. Med. Syst.* **2020,** *44* (7).
30. Ahuja, A. S.; Reddy, V. P.; Marques, O. Artificial Intelligence and COVID-19: A Multidisciplinary Approach. *Integr. Med. Res.* **2020,** *9* (3), 100434.
31. Jat, D. S.; Singh, C. Artificial Intelligence-Enabled Robotic Drones for COVID-19 Outbreak. In *SpringerBriefs in Applied Sciences and Technology*; 2020; pp 37–46.
32. Raza, K. Artificial Intelligence Against COVID-19: A Meta-Analysis of Current Research, 2020; pp 165–176.
33. Gajjar, N. D.; Dhameliya, T. M.; Shah, G. B. In Search of RdRp and Mpro Inhibitors Against SARS CoV-2: Molecular Docking, Molecular Dynamic Simulations and ADMET Analysis. *J. Mol. Struct.* **2021,** *1239*, 130488.
34. Bullock, J. et al. Mapping the Landscape of Artificial Intelligence Applications against COVID-19. *J. Artif. Intell. Res.* **2020,** *69*, 807–845.
35. Stebbing, J. et al. Mechanism of Baricitinib Supports Artificial Intelligence-Predicted Testing in COVID-19 Patients. *EMBO Mol. Med.* **2020,** *12* (8).
36. Pujari, R. et al. Therapeutic Options for COVID-19: A Review. *Cureus* **2020**.
37. Ge, Y. et al. An Integrative Drug Repositioning Framework Discovered a Potential Therapeutic Agent Targeting COVID-19. *Signal Transduct. Targeted Therap.* **2021,** *6* (1), 165.
38. Zeng, Z.; Chen, P. J.; Lew, A. A. From High-Touch to High-Tech: COVID-19 Drives Robotics Adoption. *Tour. Geogr.* **2020,** *22* (3), 724–734.
39. Maghdid, H. et al. Diagnosing COVID-19 Pneumonia from x-Ray and CT Images Using Deep Learning and Transfer Learning Algorithms, 2021; p 26.
40. Pourhomayoun, M.; Shakibi, M. Predicting Mortality Risk in Patients with COVID-19 Using Machine Learning to Help Medical Decision-Making. *Smart Health.* **2021,** *20*, 100178.
41. Strickland, E. AI May Help Hospitals Decide Which COVID-19 Patients Live or Die—IEEE Spectrum.
42. Jiang, X. et al. Towards an Artificial Intelligence Framework for Data-Driven Prediction of Coronavirus Clinical Severity. *Comput. Mater. Continua* **2020,** *63* (1), 537–551.

43. Gunraj, H.; Wang, L.; Wong, A. COVIDNet-CT: A Tailored Deep Convolutional Neural Network Design for Detection of COVID-19 Cases From Chest CT Images. *Front. Med.* **2020,** *7*.
44. Khan, A. I.; Shah, J. L.; Bhat, M. M. CoroNet: A Deep Neural Network for Detection and Diagnosis of COVID-19 from Chest x-Ray Images. *Comput. Methods Programs Biomed.* **2020,** *196*, 105581.
45. Jin, C. et al. Development and Evaluation of an Artificial Intelligence System for COVID-19 Diagnosis. *Nat. Commun.* **2020,** *11* (1), 1–14.
46. Huang, L. et al. Serial Quantitative Chest Ct Assessment of Covid-19: A Deep Learning Approach. *Radiol.: Cardiothorac. Imag.* **2020,** *2* (2).
47. Yan, L. et al. A Machine Learning-Based Model for Survival Prediction in Patients with Severe COVID-19 Infection. *medRxiv*. **2020,** 2020.02.27.20028027.
48. Kumar, A.; Gupta, P. K.; Srivastava, A. A Review of Modern Technologies for Tackling COVID-19 Pandemic. *Diab. Metabol. Syndrome: Clin. Res. Rev.* **2020,** *14* (4), 569–573.
49. Yue, H. et al. Machine Learning-Based CT Radiomics Method for Predicting Hospital Stay in Patients with Pneumonia Associated with SARS-CoV-2 Infection: A Multicenter Study. *Ann. Transl. Med.* **2020,** *8* (14), 859–859.
50. Kim, P. S. South Korea's Fast Response to Coronavirus Disease: Implications on Public Policy and Public Management Theory. *Public Manag Rev*. **2021,** *23* (12), 1736–1747.
51. Ning, B. et al. A Smartphone-Read Ultrasensitive and Quantitative Saliva Test for COVID-19. *Sci. Adv*. **2021,** *7* (2).
52. Budd, J. et al. Digital Technologies in the Public-Health Response to COVID-19. *Nat. Med.* **2020,** *26* (8), 1183–1192.
53. Shamim Kaiser, M. et al. IWorksafe: Towards Healthy Workplaces During COVID-19 with an Intelligent Phealth App for Industrial Settings. *IEEE Access*. **2021,** *9*, 13814–13828.
54. Morley, J.; Floridi, L. The Limits of Empowerment: How to Reframe the Role of MHealth Tools in the Healthcare Ecosystem. *Sci. Eng. Ethics* **2020,** *26* (3), 1159–1183.
55. Chomutare, T. et al. Features of Mobile Diabetes Applications: Review of the Literature and Analysis of Current Applications Compared against Evidence-Based Guidelines. *J. Med. Internet Res.* **2011,** *13* (3), e65.
56. Lee, B.; Ibrahim, S. A.; Zhang, T. Mobile Apps Leveraged in the COVID-19 Pandemic in East and South-East Asia: Review and Content Analysis. *JMIR mHealth and uHealth*. **2021,** *9* (11).
57. Daniel, S. J. Education and the COVID-19 Pandemic. *Prospects*. **2020,** *49* (1–2), 91–96.
58. Maatuk, A. M. et al. The COVID-19 Pandemic and E-Learning: Challenges and Opportunities from the Perspective of Students and Instructors. *J. Comput. High. Educ.* **2021**.
59. Alqahtani, A. Y.; Rajkhan, A. A. E-Learning Critical Success Factors During the Covid-19 Pandemic: A Comprehensive Analysis of e-Learning Managerial Perspectives. *Educ. Sci*. **2020,** *10* (9), 1–16.
60. Bhardwaj, A. K. et al. E-Learning During COVID-19 Outbreak: Cloud Computing Adoption in Indian Public Universities. *Comput. Mater. Continua* **2020,** *66* (3), 2471–2492.
61. Adeshola, I.; Agoyi, M. Examining Factors Influencing E-Learning Engagement Among University Students during Covid-19 Pandemic: A Mediating Role of "Learning Persistence." *Interact. Learn. Environ.*. **2022,** 1–28.

62. Faezipour, M.; Abuzneid, A. Smartphone-Based Self-Testing of COVID-19 Using Breathing Sounds. *Telemed. e-Health.* **2020,** *26* (10), 1202–1205.
63. Verde, L. et al. Exploring the Use of Artificial Intelligence Techniques to Detect the Presence of Coronavirus Covid-19 Through Speech and Voice Analysis. *IEEE Access.* **2021,** *9*, 65750–65757.
64. Cavallaro, G. et al. Acoustic Voice Analysis in the Covid-19 Era. *Acta Otorhinolaryngol. Italica.* **2021,** *41* (1), 1–5.
65. Kulkarni, P. et al. Utility of Digital Technology in Tackling the COVID-19 Pandemic: A Current Review. *J. Clin. Diagn. Res.* **2020.**
66. Stevens, H.; Haines, M. B. Trace Together: Pandemic Response, Democracy, and Technology. *East Asian Sci. Technol. Soc.* **2020,** *14* (3), 523–532.
67. Jhunjhunwala, A. Role of Telecom Network to Manage COVID-19 in India: Aarogya Setu. *Trans. Indian Natl. Acad. Eng.* **2020,** *5* (2), 157–161.
68. Basu, S. Effective Contact Tracing for COVID-19 Using Mobile Phones: An Ethical Analysis of the Mandatory Use of the Aarogya Setu Application in India. *Cambr. Quart. Healthcare Ethics.* **2021,** *30* (2), 262–271.
69. Wang, D.; Liu, F. Privacy Risk and Preservation in Contact Tracing of COVID-19. *Chance* **2020,** *33* (3), 49–55.
70. Cheng, H. Y. et al. Contact Tracing Assessment of COVID-19 Transmission Dynamics in Taiwan and Risk at Different Exposure Periods before and after Symptom Onset. *JAMA Intern. Med.* **2020,** *180* (9), 1156–1163.
71. Whaibeh, E.; Mahmoud, H.; Naal, H. Telemental Health in the Context of a Pandemic: The COVID-19 Experience. *Curr. Treatment Options Psych.* **2020,** *7* (2), 198–202.
72. Otoom, M. et al. An IoT-Based Framework for Early Identification and Monitoring of COVID-19 Cases. *Biomed. Signal Process. Control.* **2020,** *62*, 102149.
73. Mohd Aman, A. H. et al. IoMT Amid COVID-19 Pandemic: Application, Architecture, Technology, and Security. *J. Netw. Comput. App.* **2021,** *174*, 102886.
74. Saleem, S. M. et al. Virtual Ophthalmology: Telemedicine in a COVID-19 Era. *Am. J. Ophthalmol.* **2020,** *216*, 237–242.
75. Chamola, V. et al. A Comprehensive Review of the COVID-19 Pandemic and the Role of IoT, Drones, AI, Blockchain, and 5G in Managing Its Impact. *IEEE Access.* **2020,** *8*, 90225–90265.
76. Machado, R. A. et al. Social Media and Telemedicine for Oral Diagnosis and Counselling in the COVID-19 Era. *Oral Oncol.* **2020,** *105*, 104685.
77. Anthony Jnr, B. Integrating Telemedicine to Support Digital Health Care for the Management of COVID-19 Pandemic. *Int. J. Healthcare Manage.* **2021,** *14* (1), 280–289.
78. Dong, S. et al. A Guideline for Homology Modeling of the Proteins from Newly Discovered Betacoronavirus, 2019 Novel Coronavirus (2019-nCoV). *J. Med. Virol.* **2020,** *92* (9), 1542–1548.
79. Li, Q.; Peng, W.; Ou, Y. Prediction and Analysis of Key Protein Structures of 2019-NCoV. *Fut. Virol.* **2020,** *15* (6), 349–357.
80. Baruah, C.; Devi, P.; Sharma, D. K. Sequence Analysis and Structure Prediction of SARS-CoV-2 Accessory Proteins 9b and ORF14: Evolutionary Analysis Indicates Close Relatedness to Bat Coronavirus. *BioMed Res. Int.* **2020,** *2020*, 1–13.
81. Vandelli, A. et al. Structural Analysis of SARS-CoV-2 Genome and Predictions of the Human Interactome. *Nucl. Acids Res.* **2020,** *48* (20), 11270–11283.

82. Li, T. et al. Phylogenetic Supertree Reveals Detailed Evolution of SARS-CoV-2. *Sci. Rep*. **2020,** *10* (1), 22366.
83. Monteleone, S. et al. Fighting COVID-19 with Artificial Intelligence. 2022; pp 103–112.
84. Aydinoglu, A. T.; Kushchu, I. Artificial Intelligence and COVID-19. In *Data Science for COVID-19*; Elsevier, 2022; pp 95–112.
85. Zumla, A. et al. Coronaviruses—Drug Discovery and Therapeutic Options. *Nat. Rev. Drug Discov* **2016,** *15* (5), 327–347.
86. Zhu, Z. et al. Arbidol Monotherapy Is Superior to Lopinavir/Ritonavir in Treating COVID-19. *J. Infect*. **2020,** *81* (1), e21–e23.
87. Mei, M.; Tan, X. Current Strategies of Antiviral Drug Discovery for COVID-19. *Front. Mol. Biosci*. **2021,** *8*.
88. Zhou, J.; Huang, J. Current Findings Regarding Natural Components with Potential Anti-2019-NCoV Activity. *Front. Cell Dev. Biol*. **2020,** *8*.
89. Busse, L. W. et al. COVID-19 and the RAAS—A Potential Role for Angiotensin II? *Crit. Care*. **2020,** *24* (1), 136.
90. Gordon, D. E. et al. A SARS-CoV-2 Protein Interaction Map Reveals Targets for Drug Repurposing. *Nature*. **2020,** *583* (7816), 459–468.
91. White, K. M. et al. Plitidepsin Has Potent Preclinical Efficacy Against SARS-CoV-2 by Targeting the Host Protein EEF1A. *Science*. **2021,** *371* (6532), 926–931.
92. Zhou, Y. et al. Network-Based Drug Repurposing for Novel Coronavirus 2019-NCoV/SARS-CoV-2. *Cell Discov*. **2020,** *6* (1), 14.
93. Jeon, S. et al. Identification of Antiviral Drug Candidates Against SARS-CoV-2 from FDA-Approved Drugs. *Antimicrob. Agents Chemotherap*. **2020,** *64* (7).
94. Martin, W. R.; Cheng, F. Repurposing of FDA-Approved Toremifene to Treat COVID-19 by Blocking the Spike Glycoprotein and NSP14 of SARS-CoV-2. *J. Proteome Res*. **2020,** *19* (11), 4670–4677.
95. Beck, B. R. et al. Predicting Commercially Available Antiviral Drugs That May Act on the Novel Coronavirus (SARS-CoV-2) through a Drug-Target Interaction Deep Learning Model. *Comput. Struct. Biotechnol. J*. **2020,** *18*, 784–790.
96. Kumar, A. et al. Drones Combat COVID-19 Epidemic: Innovating and Monitoring Approach. *Stud. Syst Decision Control* **2021,** *322*, 175–188.
97. Khan, H. et al. Smart Technologies Driven Approaches to Tackle COVID-19 Pandemic: A Review. *3 Biotech*. **2021,** *11* (2), 50.
98. Martins, B. O.; Lavallée, C.; Silkoset, A. Drone Use for COVID-19 Related Problems: Techno-Solutionism and Its Societal Implications. *Glob. Policy* **2021,** *12* (5), 603–612.
99. Hwang, J. et al. A Comparative Study on the Motivated Consumer Innovativeness of Drone Food Delivery Services Before and After the Outbreak of COVID-19. *J. Travel Tour. Market*. **2021,** *38* (4), 368–382.
100. Poljak, M.; Šterbenc, A. Use of Drones in Clinical Microbiology and Infectious Diseases: Current Status, Challenges and Barriers. *Clin. Microbiol. Infect*. **2020,** *26* (4), 425–430.
101. Sibiri, H.; Zankawah, S. M.; Prah, D. Coronavirus Diseases 2019 (COVID-19) Response: Highlights of Ghana's Scientific and Technological Innovativeness and Breakthroughs. *Ethics Med. Public Health*. **2020,** *14*, 100537.
102. Ackerman, E.; Strickland, E. Medical Delivery Drones Take Flight in East Africa. *IEEE Spectrum* **2018,** *55* (1), 34–35.

103. Kunovjanek, M.; Wankmüller, C. Containing the COVID-19 Pandemic with Drones—Feasibility of a Drone Enabled Back-up Transport System. *Transp. Policy* **2021,** *106*, 141–152.
104. Gupta, K.; Bansal, S.; Goel, R. Uses of Drones in Fighting COVID-19 Pandemic. In *Proceedings of the 2021 10th International Conference on System Modeling & Advancement in Research Trends (SMART)*; IEEE, December 10, 2021; pp 651–655.
105. Restás, Á.; Szalkai, I.; Óvári, G. Drone Application for Spraying Disinfection Liquid Fighting against the COVID-19 Pandemic—Examining Drone-Related Parameters Influencing Effectiveness. *Drones* **2021,** *5* (3), 58.
106. Mishra, B. et al. Drone-Surveillance for Search and Rescue in Natural Disaster. *Comput. Commun.* **2020,** *156*, 1–10.
107. Vacca, A.; Onishi, H. Drones: Military Weapons, Surveillance or Mapping Tools for Environmental Monitoring? The Need for Legal Framework Is Required. *Transp. Res. Procedia.* **2017,** *25*, 51–62.
108. Ruan, K.; Wu, Z.; Xu, Q. Smart Cleaner: A New Autonomous Indoor Disinfection Robot for Combating the COVID-19 Pandemic. *Robotics.* **2021,** *10* (3), 87.
109. Carriere, J. et al. An Admittance-Controlled Robotic Assistant for Semi-Autonomous Breast Ultrasound Scanning. In *Proceedings of the 2019 International Symposium on Medical Robotics (ISMR)*; IEEE, April 2019; pp 1–7.
110. Tao, R. et al. Modeling and Emulating a Physiotherapist's Role in Robot-Assisted Rehabilitation. *Adv. Intell. Syst.* **2020,** *2* (7), 1900181.
111. Sierra Marín, S. D. et al. Expectations and Perceptions of Healthcare Professionals for Robot Deployment in Hospital Environments During the COVID-19 Pandemic. *Front. Robot. AI* **2021,** *8*.
112. Aymerich-Franch, L. Why It Is Time to Stop Ostracizing Social Robots. *Nat. Mach. Intell.* **2020,** *2* (7), 364–364.
113. Javaid, M. et al. Robotics Applications in COVID-19: A Review. *J. Ind. Integr. Manag.* **2020,** *05* (04), 441–451.
114. Violant-Holz, V. et al. Psychological Health and Physical Activity Levels During the COVID-19 Pandemic: A Systematic Review. *Int. J. Environ. Res. Public Health* **2020,** *17* (24), 9419.
115. Yang, G.-Z. et al. Combating COVID-19—The Role of Robotics in Managing Public Health and Infectious Diseases. *Sci. Robot.* **2020,** *5* (40).
116. Duan, S. et al. A 5G-Powered Robot-Assisted Teleultrasound Diagnostic System in an Intensive Care Unit. *Crit. Care.* **2021,** *25* (1), 134.
117. Mohanty, K. et al. Opportunities of Adopting AI-Powered Robotics to Tackle COVID-19. In *Proceedings of the 2021 International Conference on COMmunication Systems & NETworkS (COMSNETS)*; IEEE, January 5, 2021; pp 703–708.
118. Brooks, S. K. et al. The Psychological Impact of Quarantine and How to Reduce It: Rapid Review of the Evidence. *Lancet* **2020,** *395* (10227), 912–920.
119. Ghafurian, M.; Ellard, C.; Dautenhahn, K. Social Companion Robots to Reduce Isolation: A Perception Change Due to COVID-19. 2021; pp 43–63.
120. Aymerich-Franch, L.; Kishore, S.; Slater, M. When Your Robot Avatar Misbehaves You Are Likely to Apologize: An Exploration of Guilt During Robot Embodiment. *Int. J. Soc. Robot.* **2020,** *12* (1), 217–226.

CHAPTER 10

Travel and Tourism During and Post Pandemic: Issues, Challenges, and Lessons

SADIA JAVED[1], LARAIB SHOUKAT[1], AIMAN ELAHI[1], NAHEED BANO[2], and SAMINA YAQOOB[3]

[1]*Department of Biochemistry, Government College University, Faisalabad, Pakistan*

[2]*Faculty of Veterinary and Animal Sciences, MNS-University of Agriculture, Multan, Pakistan*

[3]*Dr Hasan Murad School of Management (HSM), University of Management and Technology, Lahore, Pakistan*

ABSTRACT

The World Tourism Council (WTC) has warned that the COVID-19 epidemic could result in 50 million unemployed people from employed status worldwide in the tourism and travel sector and is predictable to have the greatest impact in Asia. Social distancing, travel and entry restrictions, and personal protection equipment make it possible to stabilize future crises by controlling the potential demand for tourism. More than 90% of the world's population is affected by international travel bans, public meetings, widespread limitations on public movement, and tourism will be essentially halted in March 2020. This chapter compares COVID-19's consequences to prior pandemics/epidemics and other worldwide catastrophes, as well as how pandemics transform society, tourism, and the economy.

Post-Pandemic Economy, Technology, and Innovation: Global Outlook and Context.
Samina Yaqoob, Arwa Abdulkreem AL-Huqail, and Fakhra Aziz (Eds.)

10.1 INTRODUCTION

Since the Chinese government first notified the World Health Organization (WHO) on December 31, 2019, and then the WHO on March 11, 2020 (WHO, 2020) declared pandemic symptoms. In a short period of time, the COVID-19 virus has never before experienced a global crisis that had a profound effect on our political, social, and economic systems in just a few months.[1,2] In many countries, hospitality and tourism have almost ceased, and international tourism (even domestic tourism in some countries) has come to a standstill. Indeed, air and sea tourism (particularly mega-ship voyages) have been identified as one of the leading causes of the pandemic's rapid and global spread.[3]

In the field of tourism, great attention has been paid to tourism research in terms of actual tourism contribution to society and economy.[4] The increasing prevalence of the novel coronavirus has resulted in a major decline in practically all global travel.[5] Domestic tourism has a significant impact on society, and in addition to its beneficial impacts, it may have a negative impact on the social and economic well-being of residents of tourist areas.[6] The negative impact of incoming tourism may increase during crises and disasters.[7]

The pandemic, which is being triggered by new cases outside of China, is entering an alarming new stage. As governments tighten their restrictions,[8] the world is currently experiencing such a crisis in the form of a new coronavirus pandemic that has spread to 206 countries and territories (April 3, 2019, WHO). While COVID-19 covers the entire globe, it has restricted the spread of travel and borders in many countries and regions.[9]

Urbanization and globalization are accelerating the virus's spread.[10] but tourism plays a significant role in compounding the consequent public health catastrophe. As a result, in the event of a COVID-19 pandemic, it is critical to identify and assess the direction of tourism, accepted risks, and social costs. While various studies have looked at the impact of the crisis (including natural catastrophes) on tourism,[7] less attention has been made to how tourism exacerbates the crisis and harms public interest and well-being. Groups of residents and stakeholders in tourist locations. The effects of the crisis should be seen in the interconnectedness of the businesses and other stakeholders who support our destination. Furthermore, the public and private sectors hold the keys to reacting to the tourism sector's dilemma.[11] Predicting and understanding traveler's behavior is a major challenge for tourism market participants, especially when it comes to plague-like travel.[12]

As signs of a COVID-19 pandemic appear, the number of international tourists skyrocketing has fallen like a rock with a predictable trend of a sharp shift from an annual increase of 3–4% to a 20–30% decline in 2020.[13] The virus has a severe impact on tourism, compelling firms to travel overseas to lay off staff and, at best, temporarily close their operations. The job loss in the tourism sector is estimated to be 50 million jobs worldwide.[14] China was the very first country to be infected with the coronavirus, as well as the first to experience an economic depression. Tourism may be a major negative impact sector.[15] About 70,000 theaters have been closed in mainland China, and most airlines have canceled flights to and from China. NBA News, 2020 reported that the world economy lost about US $40 billion during 2002–2003, China experienced a SARS pandemic, clearly affecting the stock market (NBC News, 2020). The tourism sector accounts for almost 10% of world GDP.[16]

The Travel Council has warned that the COVID-19 pandemic might result in the loss of 50 million jobs worldwide in tourism and tourism, with Asia bearing the brunt of the brunt. The sector could take up to ten months to recover from the outbreak.[16] The virus's spread in Italy and other European countries has prompted widespread alarm among travelers, prospective tourists, and the tourism industry. A study by the World Business Tourism Association (2020) shows that the cancellation and postponement of business meetings is widespread around the world. The European tourism economy has not only collapsed as the coronavirus has spread rapidly around the world, increasing morbidity and mortality. Traditional tourist attractions with constant visitors face losing 90% of their traffic.

Restrictions on international, regional, and local travels have an immediate impact on the national economy, including the tourism system, that is, international tourism, domestic tourism, daily visits, and segments include air travel, sea travel, public transportation, and accommodations, cafes, restaurants, conferences, festivals, meetings, or sporting events. Due to the crisis, international air traffic has slowed sharply, international travel has been banned, borders have been closed and a quarantine has been imposed, and international and domestic tourism has declined sharply in recent weeks. Countries have been trying to repatriate tourists, which is an important outbound market for hundreds of thousands of people around the world FCO (The Foreign & Commonwealth Office).[17]

It should be noted that global tourism has suffered from numerous catastrophes in the past. The September 11 terrorist attacks (2001), the acute respiratory syndrome (SARS) outbreak (2003), the global economic crisis of 2008/2009, and the 2015 Middle East Respiratory Syndrome (MERS) spread were all major causes of riots between 2000 and 2015. None of this has resulted in a long-term reduction in global tourism development, and many have gone unreported; only SARS (−0.4%) and the global economic crisis (−4.0%) have resulted in a worldwide decline.[18,19] This demonstrates that tourism has historically been robust to exogenous shocks. However, there is substantial evidence that the COVID-19 pandemic's impacts and recovery have never been witnessed before. The connection between pandemics and tourism is critical to understanding health security and global transformation.[20]

10.2 TRAVEL TOURISM AS HUMAN RIGHTS

The virtual halt of tourism and tourism activities, as well as the slowing of the overall economy, may have a good influence on the environment at a time when many countries are grappling with climate change. As a result, global consumption of fossil fuels has slowed and oil prices have fallen. The United Nations Basic Principles on Human Rights and the Environment entrench human rights in the natural environment: our human rights are closely related to the environment in which we live. Environmental harm impedes the enjoyment of human rights, and human rights implementation aids in the protection of the environment and the promotion of sustainable development.[21]

In all countries and internationally, the main market for tourism is visiting with the friends and family, which is an important right to cross the culture and the country. When the COVID-19 epidemic broke out, Chinese authorities promptly limited transportation during the lunar vacation in early 2020. This was followed by a slew of measures implemented in other countries, encouraged and implemented at various levels.[22] The impact on consumer protection was a significant result of the COVID-19 problem in the tourism industry. Consumer rights can be regarded as a human right for which the government, commercial enterprises, and other relevant social organizations share responsibilities. Consumer rights have been suspended by government agreement or unilaterally as resorts, airways, and other operators are grappling with the global consequences of global closures in terms of refunds, reparations, and security.[23]

Since the demise of cultural institutions such as theaters and museums in many directions, tourism has eliminated the main reason for tourists to visit, delayed accessibility to sporting events, beaches, and national parks, as well as the closure of nonessential businesses and services visitation points. However, it should be noted that hospitality and the closure of tourist facilities are not uncommon. Countries such as Sweden have taken a slightly different approach to restricting COVID-19 and have allowed such facilities to last longer than commercial ones case elsewhere.[24] Most travelers in Europe and North America cross national boundaries for pleasure, business, or religious reasons. In other situations, this involved the reinstatement of boundaries that had been abolished many years before, such as in Europe's Schengen zone. Many countries have restricted their borders to stateless and nonresidents, including Australia, China, and New Zealand. Conversely, countries such as Vietnam have revoked visas, while other countries, such as Singapore, have denied transit through airports.[22]

10.3 HOW HAVE OUR RIGHTS TO PARTICIPATE IN HOSPITALITY AND TOURISM BEEN AFFECTED BY RESPONSES TO COVID-19?

The outbreak of COVID-19 presents an unprecedented situation in the precarious tourist and hospitality industries. The new extremely contagious coronavirus continues to threaten the industry, creating major concerns about the industry's present and future. Two important issues are: first, the current challenges in the field of hospitality and tourism. Second, it is related to the vital knowledge required by industry.[25] COVID-19 has an impact on all countries and people around the world, causing extraordinary political, economic, and socio-behavioral changes in modern civilization. Consumer impact is related to persons who have severely restricted their right to be tourists in the North. The impact on tourism workers is felt in both the South and the North. Indeed, in more affluent countries, there is no widely used social security network, so the impact on employees is much greater in the first place.[26]

10.4 EFFECT ON AIRLINE INDUSTRY, RESTAURANTS, ACCOMMODATION, CRUISE VISITS, SAFARI, MOUNTAIN HIKING, RELIGIOUS TOURISM (HAJJ UMMRAH)

Religious tourism is considered to be the oldest form of tourism.[27] And it is one of the most important parts of the tourism industry. According to the literature, the basis of religious travel is rooted in religious evolution.[28] This type of tourism provides several social, economic, and other benefits. Although religious tourism is important around the world, there is a need to expand the literature to a wider range as few studies cover this area.[29] Religious tourism is an important part of the tourism business, with 330 million tourists worldwide.[30] and has a positive economic impact on the places visited.[31] Religious tourism not only creates many jobs but also plays an important role in infrastructure development.[29]

Mosques, monasteries, synagogues, as well as other places of worship are considered COVID-19 hotspots.[32] COVID-19 is easily spread from one person to another in certain regions. The number of COVID19 cases has risen dramatically as a result of missionary work in Malaysia and Pakistan. COVID19 has spread from China to the rest of the world, and when the WHO proclaimed a state of health, each country closed its borders to pilgrims, shuttered holy sites, halted visas, and cancelled visas given by several countries to protect their own countries. All religious sites were closed for religious purposes, resulting in a decrease in religious tourism.[29] For example, the Hajj pilgrimage to Mecca is one of the five pillars of Islam established jointly by religious organizations and the state.[33]

In 2020, due to COVID-19, the Saudi government allowed 1000 pilgrims to worship, not two million, and banned pilgrims from other countries to worship in Saudi Arabia[34] Medina, like Mecca, is an important place for Muslims to bury the Holy Prophet Muhammad (PBUH) and is visited by Hajj pilgrims[29] Historians believe that the journey was abolished in 967 AD due to an outbreak of sacrificial disease, and then in 1048 AD due to drought and famine, the pilgrimage ceased. In 1832, thousands of pilgrims from India were killed in an outbreak of the Hubon plague on their way to Hajj. Cholera outbreaks during the 19th century killed thousands of pilgrims during the Hajj.[35]

COVID-19 has wreaked havoc on hospitality firms such as hotels, restaurants, and bars. Restaurants, for example, were compelled to close in early 2020 due to a lockout regulation. Furthermore, in public locations, customers tend to avoid other individuals. Despite this reopening, jurisdiction has offered or ordered a reduction in seating capacity due to a focus on services provided to such businesses or a social exclusion policy. The outlook for future restaurants is bleak. According to experts, more than half of the restaurants will be uninhabitable.[36] Many people have overreacted to COVID-19 by stockpiling or avoiding it to avoid other people. Consumers dislike being served in restaurants and pubs as part of the service. As a result, in such a case, it is critical to explore a variety of elements that can rekindle consumers' desire to visit the restaurant frequently. Location in a restaurant's private room is a significant component in consumers' perceptions and evaluations of restaurants.[37,38] Based on Behavioral Repression System Theory, Infectious Effects,[39] since the beginning of 2020, the international society has been witnessing an unprecedented impact of COVID-19, which the WHO labeled a pandemic in March 12. In terms of imprisonment, hygiene, sanitation, and border restrictions, the world's tourist, tourism, and hospitality sectors are among the worst affected by the pandemic. International arrivals declined by 22% worldwide in the first quarter of 2020 (57% in March alone), with an absolute loss of nearly 67 million international tourists and a revenue loss of approximately US $80 billion.[30] As countries gain confidence in the gradual opening of their businesses and markets from the beginning of June, the duration and intensity of their impact on the market will largely depend on restoring customer confidence[40]

The enormity of the pandemic's social and economic impact, particularly the response of businesses, raises concerns about the sector's readiness for a long-term crisis and overall resilience. In earlier crises and periods of uncertainty in demand, dismissal schemes were regular practice in the hospitality business. Given the unique nature of the current pandemic, several academics.[40,41] As COVID-19 spreads over the world, countries have imposed travel restrictions to avoid new infections. Such restrictions have a direct influence on the volume of international flights operated by these countries, resulting in significant social and economic costs. To gain a quantitative understanding of the problem, Open sky network data were utilized to clarify flight patterns and densities around the world, as well as to examine the relationship between the number of flights, new illnesses, and the economy of Barcelona (unemployment rate).[42]

We discovered that the number of daily flights gradually declined by 64% in the second half of March 2020, following travel restrictions imposed by the United States and Europe. During this period, we observed 51% decrease in the density of the global air network. For new cases of COVID-19, there has been a sudden increase, despite travel restrictions around the world. Finally, the number of temporary workers in the tourism and aviation businesses has increased 4.3 times in a week since Spain decided to close the border.[42] McKinsey and Company (2020) conducted a series of countrywide polls on the influence of pandemic consumer emotions, their purchasing behavior, and motivation show that statistics in most countries show a sharp decline in the expected cost of tourism and hospitality. Of the categories considered, sea travel is considered the safest option (for residents of Germany, the United Kingdom, the United States, France, and Italy). However, vehicle travel is preferable to domestic aircraft. In terms of housing preferences, citizens in many nations appear to favor short-term rentals over hotel/resort accommodations, but their reasoning is unclear.[43]

It is, in fact, an understanding of the unconscious and unconscious stimuli at different levels of the decision-making process, which will accelerate operational recovery and industry sustainability. Historically, the number of visitors during the crisis, which has affected the tourism and housing sectors, and the recovery at night have been faster than incomes. However, the COVID-19 pandemic's unusual circumstances make it impossible for even domestic travelers to analyze tourism decision-making and behavior.[41] A national survey conducted by the Athens-based market research firm Kapa in April (2020) found that 55% of participants at the peak of the COVID-19 outbreak were "ready to return to their daily lives."[44]

10.5 IMPACT OF CORONAVIRUS 2019 ON DIFFERENT COUNTRIES

The tourist business in China is a significant contributor to the country's economy. Chinese tourism is regarded as one of the most popular outbound and inbound travel markets in the world. The revenue from domestic trips in China is the most profitable source of capital. However, the proliferation of the Coronavirus in the country had a significant impact on the tourism economy. This has resulted in a significant decline in the tourism business, both domestically and internationally. The tourism business appears to be experiencing a major crisis, which is also causing a stock market drop in all sectors. Hotels, aeroplanes, and cruise ships were all shut down. As a result of the virus's continued spread, the impact on China's GDP is growing. The COVID-19 raises a global health alert, producing healthcare insecurity and impacting the economic breakdown of activities.[45]

Brazil had more than 500,000 confirmed cases by the beginning of June 2020, making it one of the countries with the largest number of COVID19 infections in the globe. Tourist activities were among the first to be impacted, and given the inherent characteristics of this sector, it will also suffer greatly and for a longer period of time due to people's uncertainty to travel in the post-pandemic period, and as a result, its economic recovery will be slow and gradual. The severity of the economic consequences will be determined by the length of the disruption in activity, the execution of economic measures to sustain the sector, and compensation programmes for individual workers. Because of the sector's relative economic importance, the influence on the sector is expected to vary among countries at the international level. Tourism contributed for 8.1% of Brazilian GDP in 2018, according to the World Travel and Tourism Council (WTTC, 2019).[46]

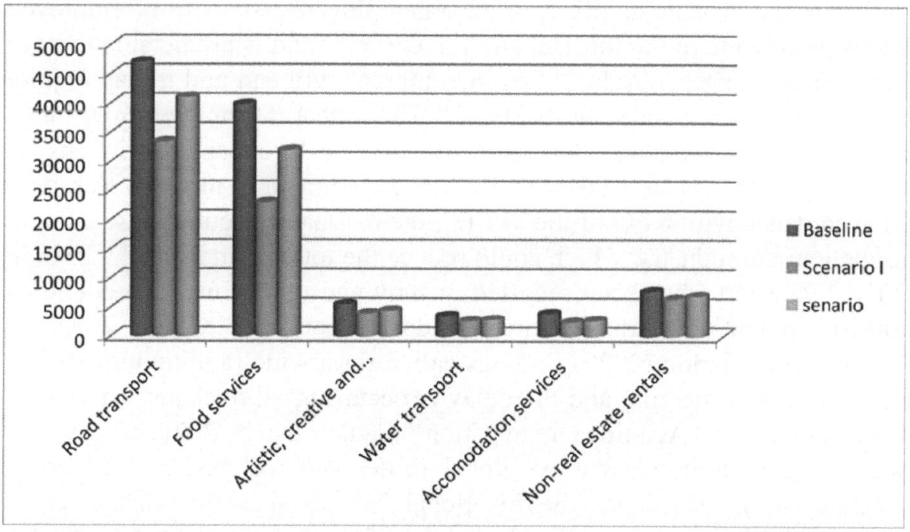

FIGURE 10.1 Economic impact of COVID-19 on tourist activities' GDP in Brazil, Y-axis represents values in $ millions of 2019.[89]

India's hospitality industry is one of the world's largest tourism industries, with more than 2000 hotels and more than 1000 restaurants registered with the Indian Hotel and Restaurant Association's FHRAI (2020) employing millions of people. In India, bookings are being canceled due to congestion and the threat of COVID-19, which could negatively impact the hotel business and jeopardize future employment as it risks losing revenue in 2020 as a cost reduction tool. Recently, there have been few responses from the hotel business group to COVID-19.[47]

Europe is termed as the world's leading tourist destination, with some of Europe's biggest foreign tourist destinations, including Italy, France, and Spain, among the countries most affected by the COVID-19 crisis. In the near future, a large number of tourists from Europe to India could be observed in industry of India. As India's hospitality industry develops, Indian stakeholders require early steps to address the situation.[48]

10.6 COVID19'S NEGATIVE EFFECT ACTIVITIES OF GLOBAL TOURIST

The World Tourism Council (WTTC) has given an alert that the COVID-19 epidemic could lead to fifty million unemployed people from employed status worldwide in the tourism and travel sector and is predictable to have the greatest impact in Asia. When the outbreak will end and it may require ten months for the industry to mend.[49] This effect depends on how much the plague is extended, It has been exacerbated by recent restrictions on travel, such as measures taken by the US government to move to Europe.[14] In accordance with CEO of the WTTC, the coronavirus could pose a threat to the tourism industry, which could reduce the tourism industry by 25% in 2020.[50] The virus has been reported in Italy and other European countries tourists, potential tourists, tourism industry concerns. Global Business Tourism Association (2020) findings called for a wide-ranging termination of the business meeting and the delay is occurring all over the world. The International Civil Aviation Organization[88] predicts that by 2020, coronavirus will US $29.3 billion less in As global air demand declines, so does global air transport income. It was the first global decrease since the financial crisis of 2008–2009 disaster, leading to almost 95% of the projected losses for Asia-Pacific transport companies.[88]

The European tourism economy has not only collapsed as the coronavirus has spread rapidly around the world, increasing morbidity and mortality. 90% of the traffic of traditional tourist destinations with regular traffic will be lost. Tourism in Ireland has been canceled, according to the executive director of the Tourism Authority. The first patients were diagnosed to have Covid. They all traveled from the damaged area of Italy. It should be noted that as the cancelation increases, the anxiety increases, and European tourists spend almost 2 billion euros to the island of Ireland, which is a significant fragment of national earning.[51]

The six-nation rugby tournament between Ireland and Italy has been canceled. Major events, like the St. Patrick's Festival in Dublin, were also missed. With 66% of European tourists visiting Northern Ireland coming through the Republic of Ireland, the tourism industry in Northern Ireland has suffered greatly. The Greek government has ordered all shops except supermarkets, gas stations, bakeries, and pharmacies to be closed from the first week of March to break the chain of the virus. In consequence, the tourist season is being delayed.[52] Airlines in Cyprus have shown their effectiveness, reporting Virgin Atlantic empty flights.

The head of the Cyprus Hotels Association stated that March has almost fallen in a row, and in April there was a considerable silence on bookings.[53] Russia's tourism industry expects to decline about US $100 million in January 2020 because of the Coronavirus COVID-2019 epidemic in China.

On the report of Russian Association of Tour Operators (ATOR), almost 45,000 systematic tourists have arrived from China and plan to travel to Russia in March 2020. Russia has closed its border with China due to the outbreak in the Far East and suspended travel bought by Chinese tourists.[54]

The number of tourists in Egypt has dropped significantly since expansion of Covid in February 2020. It is one of the severe crises to hit India's tourism industry in each geographical area since the declaration of the first Coronavirus infection in Egypt, according to the CII Industrial Chamber in India, has been brought in, out and almost inside, in all vertical areas of tourism—heritage, adventure, recreation, corporations, cruise, MICE, and other segments. The Covid pandemic could hit India's tourism industry hard, especially if the government hangs all visas, costing a lot of money. The entire crisis management of tourism has been hit by hotels, restaurants, travel agencies, tourism activities, destinations, family amusement venues, land, air and sea vehicles. The CII Tourism Committee has announced that it has entered the coronavirus epidemic impact evaluation over US $28 billion in foreign tourism considers for mean of 60–65% from October until March.[55]

With hardly any people traveling these days, A-One Hotels Group of Thailand is implementing a new method of imposing a curfew on its hotels in Bangkok or Pattaya. These filled programs are designed for Thais or inhabitants who would like to quarantine themself for 14 days. Food is brought to the rooms in carriages, and the cutlery, dishes, and bedding used to isolate guests are separated. A particular team will offer daily home care services and assistance to monitor the state of guests in accordance with the quarantine regime. The company's director said he would be rushed to numerous hospitals near the hotel if he became ill and showed signs of Coronavirus during his stay at the hotel. These packages are competitively priced at a 20% discount.[56] This risky plan is the first response to the tasks facing the global hospitality industry.[58]

According to the Wall Street Journal, nine sites sell quarantine proposals for two weeks or 27 days. Guests have to ensure the temperature is examined two times a day for signs of a virus, such as fever. They can order food by using some online food-supplying service or hotel concierge. Some high-end hotels in Hong Kong offer same kind of parcels.

Park Lane Hong Kong offers a fourteen-day package that costs US $2525 and serves three meals a day. Some hotels in Singapore offer low prices for those in necessity of a quarantine regime. In Singapore a Fairmont store has 14-day package and the price is half of the normal of a hotel on daily basis. Meanwhile, Asset World Corp has announced that in Bangkok 5 hotels will be temporarily close from 26 March to 15 April to control the Covid-19 virus epidemic. The five hotels that have been closed are as follows: Bangkok Marriott Hotel Hotel The Surawongse, Le Meridien Bangkok Hotel, DoubleTree by Hilton Sukhumvit Bangkok Hotel, The Okura Prestige Hotel Bangkok, and Bangkok Marriott Marquis Queen's Park.[56]

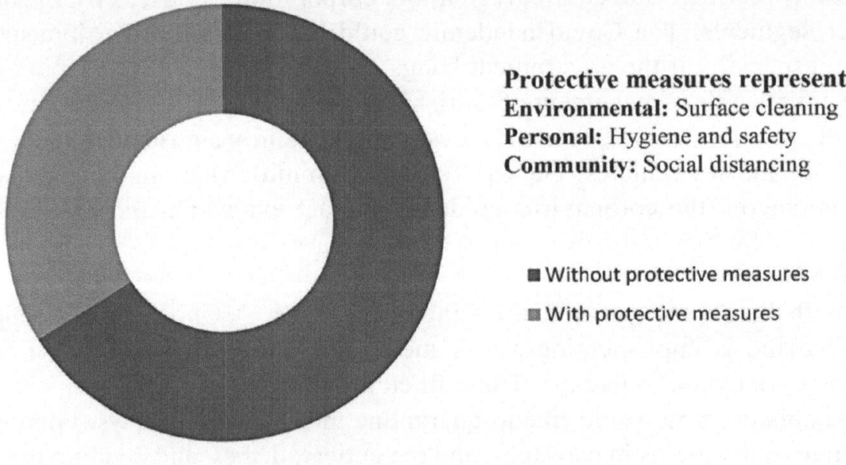

FIGURE 10.3 Comparison of number of cases with and without protective measures.

10.7 TOURISM, PANDEMICS, AND GLOBAL CHANGE

It should have been noted that international tourism has suffered in the past from a variety of disasters. The major rampage of 2000–2015 included the 9/11 attacks (2001), Acute Respiratory Syndrome (SARS) (2003), the 2008 to 2009 global financial catastrophe, and the 2015 Middle East Respiratory Syndrome (MERS) distribution. None of these have been detrimental to global tourism development for a long time, some only to SARS (–0.4%) and the Crisis (–4.0%), which is less important to the global economy, leading to a decline in international influx.[59,60] This is a good thing tourism has shown that the system is resistant to external shockwaves. However, there are many things; the effects and recovery of the Coronavirus pandemic are exceptional. The connection between pandemics and tourism plays an important role in understanding health safety world alteration.[61] No similar thing has happened about the possible impacts of worldwide climate change systems. There is a tendency to assess the effectiveness of the pandemic system and to conduct research in each country is more impactful than at systematic level of experiments and susceptibilities. Various reports have shown the key part of air transportables in speeding up and increasing the spread of Coronavirus and influenza.[62] The core causes for the growing risk of plague in 21st century: mobile global population and rapid growth; population concentration and urbanization fashions; commercial food manufacture in the world price chain; increased consumption of premium food containing meat and developing a global conveyance network that acts as a vector in distribution of pathogenic microorganisms.[63,64] Prevalence of diseases such as SARS, Marburg, Ebola, avian influenza, hantavirus, and zika are the result of anthropogenic effects on environments and biodiversity.[65–67]

Worldwide change consequently comes up with large-scale outbreaks, and epidemic outbreaks are on the rise. It is generally accepted that there were 3 epidemics in the 20th century, called the "Spanish" influenza or flu in 1918 to 1919, the 1957 "Asian" H2N2 flu, and 1968 "Hong Kong" flu. In the 21st century, in 2002 there were 4 plagues already called SARS peaked, in 2009 Avian influenza" , in 2012 MERS peaked, and in 2013 to 2014 Ebola. Outbreaks appear to be exacerbated since 2000 and are strongly linked to global change noted above.[68–70] In 2003, an outbreak of SARS was according to the WHO as a plague, and most cases were reported, there are also case clusters in Canada, China, Taiwan, and Hong Kong. SARS was studied by the tourism situation. Siu and Wong (2004) described complete economic influence appeared like Hong Kong wasn't as difficult as expected, but tourism, travel, and trade were basically plentiful. He had a general assessment of SARS $ 100 billion in worldwide economic costs, US $48 billion in China alone.[71,72] In 2009, swine flu was described as a plague, but it was comparatively less dangerous. However, this swine flu plague killed 284,000 people globally.[73] In 2013 Russi and Smith studied impact of the plague in Mexico on tourism. In five months, it has lost nearly a million overseas visitors, the European market is the slowest to return, with about US $2.8 billion.

One of the key concepts in pandemic research considered travel is crucially important disease reconnaissance and epidemiology.[75,76] It also means recognition to tourism contributes to the spread of disease and its economic consequences due to the NPI.[77] One report in 2020 by Baldwin and Weder di Mauro stated, "The harsh reality is that we have no 21st century tools to fight COVID-19. There is no vaccine or treatment. All we have is the methods that were used to control epidemics in the early 20th century. Those, as we shall see, tend to be very economically disruptive." Due to this, special consideration is on the impact of 1918 to 1919 Spanish flu plague (influenza); it was regarded as one of the dangerous plagues occurred worldwide,[77] in order to understand the potential impact of modern epidemics.[78]

The extent of COVID-19 outburst is quite uncertain, but in early April 2020 The United Nations Office for Economic and Social Affairs (2020) has calculated the restrictions on forecast scenario on a wide range of the world economy is expected to shrink by about 0.9% by 2020 in the second quarter, when the economic activity of many OECD countries lasted until the Middle Ages. It is lower than expected by 2.5%. They warn that they are likely to thwart the efforts of the pandemic; there will be little difference in the execution of 2030's supportable progressive aims in low-income countries. The obvious question it warns that if world leaders should have anticipated a pandemic such as COVID-19, many economic and health organizations, in particular, would be at high risk of increased probability of the scourge of the poisonous world. For example, the World Economic Forum (WEF) was involved in politics and business.

Each year, other global analysts/leaders estimate the crucial risks to the worldwide economy. The first global risk report (WEF 2006) identified symptoms of the epidemic as one of four risk factors. But, the 2020 Global Infectious Disease Risk Report lists the third (just beyond the armaments of massive destruction and unimaginable expansion) and 1/10th of the probable affect. Unexpectedly, this was considered the least interrelated risks. Similarly, as time passes there are warnings of a pandemic due to tourism.[40,41,79]

10.8 A LATEST OPPORTUNITY FOR A MORE VERIFIABLE TOURISM

It is frequently said that the tourism industry is highly resilient and has strong adaptation and recovery from disasters or emergencies. But this time the industry will be under a lot of stress to overcome. There are experts trust that after the disastrous time is over, we'll progressively come back, does not seek to provide a measure of time—at a certain normal level, or not less than in a condition comparatively familiar to the period before crisis.[80] This will confirm the black swan theory. This theory shows, there were unexpected events, such as the crisis, which had a huge social and economic impact as time passed, it becomes rational and seems predictable or explanatory that the case is predictable.[81] According to this school of thoughts, the current crisis will not make a significant difference in tourism industry, at the minimum regards to future planning and management. The usual philosophy will induce instead of a business. It is problematic that the sector is getting repeated warnings of instability (long-term vision's insufficiency), as well as the risk of recurrence due to environment change and worldwide health tragedies.[82]

It would be carelessness to ignore these risks. According to the existing state, there has been call for this stalemate to be used to make major structural changes in the tourism sector, rather than reflecting its sustainability in the sector. It should be noted that in current years, the concept of sustainable tourism has faced serious criticism in research field.[83,84]

In the recent disaster, this is the need of the hour. For instance, Higgins-Desbioles in 2020 reported, one astonishes whether the COVID-19 crisis is truly a heroic catastrophe. If we want to keep away the disastrous consequences of climate change, we need a change in human activity. COVID-19 compels us to consider the uncertainty of tourism industry before the crisis despite returning to the preceding operating framework promptly. This is due to another controversy that started a few years ago, that is called for the overdevelopment of international tourism in order to stop the unconfined (and hence unsupportable) development of tourism and to choose strategies to reduce economic growth, especially in overcrowded areas.[85] Though, unexpectedly and swiftly places that used to suffer from this problem are now facing its Contradictions: "under-tourism." It must be said that this crisis has nothing to do with aging, planned, and voluntary contractions.

FIGURE 10.4 Ways to use COVID-19 as an opportunity to sustain tourism.

Fletcher et al. stated, even if the coronavirus catastrophe finishes in a comparatively short period of time, we will not be able to return to normal levels, especially tourism in the richest part of the global population. Its reason is social disorder; this is because of the environmental damage the sector (including climate change, resource reduction, and pollution) is already unstable. Same authors described, the existing limitations and controls of mobility show how and where people in crisis have the will and the political will. In order to do so, it will be possible to regulate the flow of tourism to a certain extent stability standard, it has been argued many times that this is not possible.[86]

After this catastrophe, travelers will likely decide to move nearer to their living arrangement. Due to increased uncertainty and anxiety, a lot of possible travelers who have experienced an economic downturn and reduced purchasing power due to the health crisis may consider the surrounding area "low risk." In addition, international (long-distance) travel may be restricted. To help in falling overall emissions, this is in line with the concept of promoting more environmentally friendly tourism.[87]

KEYWORDS

- **pandemic**
- **travel**
- **tourism**
- **airlines**
- **hospitality**
- **restaurants**

REFERENCES

1. Carlsson-Szlezak, P.; Reeves, M.; Swartz, P. What Coronavirus Could Mean for the Global Economy. *Harv. Bus. Rev.* **2020,** *3*, 1–10.
2. Fuchs, C. Everyday Life and Everyday Communication in Coronavirus Capitalism. *tripleC: Commun. Capitalism Critique. Open Access J. Glob. Sustain. Inf. Soc.* **2002,** *18* (1), 375–399.
3. Chinazzi, M.; Davis, J. T.; Ajelli, M.; Gioannini, C.; Litvinova, M.; Merler, S. et al. The Effect of Travel Restrictions on the Spread of the 2019 Novel Coronavirus (COVID-19) Outbreak. *Science* **2020,** *368* (6489), 395–400.
4. Lindberg, K.; Johnson, R. L. The Economic Values of Tourism's Social Impacts. *Ann. Tour. Res.* **1997,** *24* (1), 90–116.
5. Estrada, M.; Park, D.; Lee, M. How A Massive Contagious Infectious Diseases Can Affect Tourism, International Trade, Air Transportation, and Electricity Consumption? The Case of 2019 Novel Coronavirus (2019-nCoV) in China (February 19, 2020). Available at SSRN https://papers.ssrn.com/sol3/papers.cfm?abstract_id=3540667 [Accessed on 25 Mar 2020].
6. Jordan, E. J.; Moran, C.; Godwyll, J. M. Does Tourism Really Cause Stress? A Natural Experiment Utilizing ArcGIS Survey123. *Curr. Iss. Tour.* **2021,** *24* (1), 1–15.
7. Qiu, R. T.; Park, J.; Li, S.; Song, H. Social Costs of Tourism During the COVID-19 Pandemic. *Ann. Tour. Res.* **2020,** *84*, 102994.
8. Worldometers. Coronavirus Worldwide Graphs, 2020. https://www.worldometers.info/coronavirus/worldwide-graphs/ (Accessed on 8, Apr 2020).
9. Al Jazeera. Coronavirus: Travel Restrictions, Border Shut Downs by Country. *Al Jazeera and News Agencies*, Mar 20, 2020. https://www.aljazeera.com/news/2020/03/coronavirus-travel-restrictions-border-shutdowns-country-200318091505922.html.
10. Hilsenrath, J. Global Viral Outbreaks Like Coronavirus, Once Rare, Will Become More Common. *Wall Str. J* **2020,** *6*. https://www.wsj.com/articles/viral-outbreaks-once-rare-become-part-of-th e-global-landscape-11583455309.
11. Ritchie, B. Tourism Disaster Planning and Management: From Response and Recovery to Reduction and Readiness. *Curr. Iss. Tour.* **2008,** *11* (4), 315–348.

12. Lee, K. How the Hong Kong Government Lost the Public Trust in SARS: Insights for Government Communication in a Health Crisis. *Public Relat. Rev.* **2009,** *35* (1), 74–76.
13. UNWTO. International tourism arrivals could fall by 20–30% in 2020, 2020. https://www.unwto.org/news/international-tourism-arrivals-could-fall-in-2020?fbclid=IwAR1m54QtKWGn3 RoHIlALy6IsuYYquLsoHU-4Nr3stJFJMclvXadvXdxEhg
14. World Travels and Tourism Council. Impact of pandemic on travel and tourism, 2020.
15. Ayittey, F. K.; Ayittey, M. K.; Chiwero, N. B.; Kamasah, J. S.; Dzuvor, C. Economic Impacts of Wuhan 2019-nCoV on China and the World. *J. Med. Virol.* **2020,** *92* (5), 473–475.
16. World Economic Forum. This Is How Coronavirus Could Affect the Travel and Tourism Industry, 2020. https://www.weforum.org/agenda/2020/03/world-travel-coronavirus-covid19-jobspande mic- tourism-aviation/ (Accessed on 20 Mar 2020).
17. FCO (The Foreign & Commonwealth Office). Foreign Secretary Advises All British Travelers to Return to the UK Now, 2020 https://www.gov.uk/government/news/foreign-secretary-advises-all-british-travellers-to-return-to-the-uk-now (Accessed on 31 Mar 2020).
18. World Bank. Air Transport, Passengers Carried, 2020. https://data.worldbank.org/indicator/is.air.psgr (Accessed on 4 Apr 2020).
19. World Bank. International Tourism, Number of Arrivals, 2020. https://data.worldbank.org/indicator/ST.INT.ARVL (Accessed on 4 Apr 2020).
20. Burkle Jr, F. M. Globalization and Disasters: Issues of Public Health, State Capacity and Political Action. *J. Int. Aff.* **2006,** 241–265.
21. Human Rights Council. Report of the Special Rapporteur on the Issue of Human Rights Obligations Relating to the Enjoyment of a Safe, Clean, Healthy and Sustainable Environment. No. A/HRC/37/59, 2020. www.ohchr.org/Documents/Issues/Environment/SREnvironment/ A_HRC_37_59_EN.pdf (accessed on 27 Mar 2020).
22. Baum, T.; Hai, N. T. T. Hospitality, Tourism, Human Rights and the Impact of COVID-19. *Int. J. Contemp. Hosp. Manag.* **2020**.
23. Murray, W. Airlines and Travel firms Deny Refunds. *The Guardian*, 22 Ap, 2020. www.theguardian.com/world/2020/apr/22/wednesday-briefing-airlines-and-travel-firms-deny refunds (Accessedon 24 Apr 2020).
24. Franks, P. Coronavirus: Are We Underestimating How Many People Have Had It? Sweden Thinks So. *The Conversation*, 23rd April, 2020.
25. Kaushal, V.; Srivastava, S. Hospitality and Tourism Industry Amid COVID-19 Pandemic: Perspectives on Challenges and Learnings from India. *Int. J. Hosp. Manage.* **2021,** *92*, 102707.
26. Baum, T.; Hai, N. T. T. Applying Sustainable Employment Principles in the Tourism Industry: Righting Human Rights Wrongs? *Tour. Recreat. Res.* **2019,** *44* (3), 371–381.
27. Zamani-Farahani, H.; Eid, R. Muslim World: A Study of Tourism & Pilgrimage Among OIC Member States. *Tour. Manag. Perspect.* **2016,** *19*, 144–149.
28. Ayorekire, J.; Obua, J.; Mugizi, F.; Byaruhanga, B. M. Opportunities and Challenges of Religious Tourism Development in Uganda: Policy, Planning and Institutional Perspectives. *Int. J. Religious Tour. Pilgrimage* **2020,** *8* (3).
29. Yasin, R.; Jauhar, J.; Rahim, N. F. A.; Namoco, S.; Bataineh, M. S. E. COVID-19 and Religious Tourism: An Overview of Impacts and Implications. *Int. J. Religious Tour. Pilgrimage* **2020,** *8*, 155–162.

30. UNWTO. Impact Assessment of the COVID-19 Outbreak on International Tourism (May 2020 Update). United Nations World Tourism Organisation, 2020. https://www.unwto.org/impact-assessment-of-the-covid-19-outbreak-on-international-tourism (Accessed on 14 June 2020).
31. Amaro, S.; Antunes, A.; Henriques, C. A Closer Look at Santiago de Compostela's Pilgrims Through the Lens of Motivations. *Tour. Manag.* **2018,** *64*, 271–280.
32. The Star. How Rally at Malaysian Mosque Became COVID-19 Hotspot, 2020. https://www.thestar.com.my/news/regional/2020/03/18/howrally-at-malaysian-mosque-became-COVID-19-hotspot (Accessed on 16 June 2020).
33. Jafari, J.; Scott, N. Muslim World and Its Tourisms. *Ann. Tour. Res.* 2014, *44*, 1–19.
34. CNN. Unprecedented Hajj Begins—with 1000 Pilgrims, Rather Than the Usual 2 Million, 2020. https://edition.cnn.com/travel/article/hajj-2020coronavirus-intl/index.html (Accessed on 19 Aug 2020).
35. Smithsonian. This Pandemic Isn't the First Time the Hajj Has Been Disrupted for Muslims, 2020. https://www.smithsonianmag.com/ history/pandemic-isnt-first-time-hajj-has-been-disruptedmuslims-180974735/ (Accessed on 19 Aug 2020).
36. Severson, K.; Yaffe-Bellany, D. Independent Restaurants Brace for the Unknown. *The New York Times* 2021, p. 21.
37. Hwang, J.; Yoon, S. Y. Where Would You Like to Sit? Understanding Customers' Privacy-Seeking Tendencies and Seating Behaviors to Create Effective Restaurant Environments. *J. Food Serv. Bus. Res.* **2009,** *12* (3), 219–233.i3tUMA.pdf
38. Yim, E. S.; Lee, S.; Kim, W. G. Determinants of a Restaurant Average Meal Price: An Application of the Hedonic Pricing Model. *Int. J. Hosp. Manag.* **2014,** *39*, 11–20.
39. Argo, J. J.; Dahl, D. W.; Morales, A. C. Consumer Contamination: How Consumers React to Products Touched by Others. *J. Market.* **2006,** *70* (2), 81–94.
40. Gossling, S. Global Environmental Consequences of Tourism. *Glob. Environ. Change* **2002,** *12* (4), 283–302. https://doi.org/10.1016/S0959-3780 (02)00044-4
41. Hall, C.M.; Scott, D.; G¨ossling, S. Pandemics, Transformations and Tourism: Be Careful What You Wish For. *Tour. Geogr.* **2020,** *2020*, 1759131. https://doi.org/10.1080/14616688.
42. Suzumura, T.; Kanezashi, H.; Dholakia, M.; Ishii, E.; Napagao, S. A.; Pérez-Arnal, R.; Garcia-Gasulla, D. The Impact of Covid-19 on Flight Networks, 2020. arXiv preprint arXiv:2006.02950.
43. Mckinsey & Company. Global Surveys of Consumer Sentiment During the Coronavirus Crisis. Surveys Per Country, 2020. https://www.mckinsey. com/business-functions/marketing-and-sales/our-insights/global-surveys-of-consumer-sentiment-during-the-coronavirus-crisis (Accessed on 21 June 2020). medium.com/@alanalew/creating-a-better-post-covid-19-world-36b2b3e8a7ae
44. Kapa Research. COVID-19: Life With Coronavirus and the Next Day: April 2020 Nationwide Research. https://kaparesearch.com/wp-content/uploa ds/2020/04/2020.04_Kapa_Covid19.pdf (Accessed on 23 June 2020).
45. Hoque, A.; Shikha, F. A.; Hasanat, M. W.; Arif, I.; Hamid, A. B. A. The Effect of Coronavirus (COVID-19) in the Tourism Industry in China. *Asian J. Multidisc. Stud.* **2020,** *3* (1), 52–58.
46. Škare, M.; Soriano, D. R.; Porada-Rochoń, M. Impact of COVID-19 on the Travel and Tourism Industry. *Technol. Forecast. Soc. Change* **2021,** *163*, 120469.

47. Tourism Breaking News. COVID-19 Impact on Industry, 2020. https://tourismbreakingnews.com/tag/federation-of-associations-in-indiantourism-and-hospitality/
48. Kumar, V. Indian Tourism Industry and COVID-19: Present Scenario. *J. Tour. Hosp. Educ.* **2020,** *10*, 179–185.
49. World Economic Forum. This Is How Coronavirus Could Affect the Travel and Tourism Industry, 2020. https://www.weforum.org/agenda/2020/03/world-travel-coronavirus-covid19-jobspande mic-tourism-aviation/ (Accessed on 20 Mar 2020).
50. BBC News. Virus 'Could Cost Millions of Tourism Jobs'. https://www.bbc.com/news/business-51852505 (Accessed on 27 Mar 2020).
51. BBC News. Coronavirus: 'Extremely Serious' Concerns on Potential Tourism Impact. https://www.bbc.com/news/uk-northern-ireland-51695480 (Accessed on 19, March 2020).
52. Balkan in Sight. Greece Braces for New Coronavirus-Driven Recession, 2020. https://balkaninsight.com/2020/03/18/greece-braces-for-new-coronovirus-driven-recession/ (Accessed on 20 Mar 2020).
53. Tornos News. Cyprus Tourism Hopes Warmer Weather Would End the Coronavirus Crisis, 2020. https://www.tornosnews.gr/en/tourism-businesses/markets/39309-cyprus-tourismhopes
54. Statista. Key Figures on the Impact of Coronavirus (COVID-19) on Russian Inbound Tourism from China in 2020, 2020. https://www.statista.com/statistics/1092398/russia-tourismsector-losses-from-novel-coron avirus-2019ncov/ (Accessed on 24 Mar 2020).
55. The Economic Times. Impact of Coronavirus on Indian Tourism Could Run Into Thousands of Crores of Rupees, 2020. https://economictimes.indiatimes.com/industry/services/travel/impact-of-coronavirus-on-i ndian-tourism-could-run-into-thousands-of-crores-of-rupees/articleshow/74592482.cms?from=mdr (Accessed on 5 Apr 2020).
56. Skift. Coronavirus and the Travel Industry. https://skift.com/coronavirus-andtravel/ (Accessed on 24 Mar 2020).
57. The Wall Street Journal. Do Not Disturb: Hotels Hammered by Coronavirus Offer 14-Day Tornos, 2020
58. The Real Deal. Coming to a Hotel Near You: The US $2,500 Coronavirus Quarantine Package, 2020. https://therealdeal.com/2020/03/19/coming-to-a-hotel-near-you-the-2500-coronavirus-quarantine-package/ (Accessed on 23 March 2020).
59. World Bank. Air Transport, Passengers Carried, 2020. https://data.worldbank.org/indicator/is.air.psgr (accessed 4 Apr 2020).
60. World Bank. International Tourism, Number of Arrivals, 2020. https://data.worldbank.org/indicator/ST.INT.ARVL (accessed on 4 Apr 2020).
61. Burkle, F. M. Jr, Globalization and Disasters: Issues of Public Health, State Capacity and Political Action. *J. Int. Aff.* **2006,** *59* (2), 231–265.
62. Brown, A.; Ahmad, S.; Beck, C.; Nguyen-Van-Tam, J. The Roles of Transportation and Transportation Hubs in the Propagation of Influenza and Coronaviruses: A Systematic Review. *J. Travel Med.* **2016,** *23* (1), tav002. https://doi.org/10.1093/jtm/tav002
63. Pongsiri, M. J.; Roman, J.; Ezenwa, V. O.; Goldberg, T. L.; Koren, H. S.; Newbold, S. C.; Ostfeld, R. S.; Pattanayak, S. K.; Salkeld, D. J. Biodiversity Loss Affects Global Disease Ecology. *BioScience* **2009,** *59* (11), 945–954. https://doi.org/10.1525/bio.2009.59.11.6

64. Labonte, R.; Mohindra, K.; Schrecker, T. The Growing Impact of Globalization for Health and Public Health Practice. *Annu. Rev. Public Health 2011*, *32* (1), 263–283. https://doi.org/10.1146/annurev-publhealth-031210–101225
65. Petersen, E.; Wilson, M. E.; Touch, S.; McCloskey, B.; Mwaba, P.; Bates, M.; Dar, O.; Mattes, F.; Kidd, M.; Ippolito, G.; Azhar, E. I.; Zumla, A. Rapid Spread of Zika Virus in the Americas—Implications for Public Health Preparedness for Mass Gatherings at the 2016 Brazil Olympic Games. *Int. J. Infect. Dis.* **2016,** *44*, 11–15. https://doi.org/10.1016/j.ijid.2016.02.001
66. Schmidt, C.W. Zika in the United States: How Are We Preparing? *Environ. Health Perspect.* **2016,** *124* (9), A157–A165.
67. World Bank. *People, Pathogens and Our Planet: Volume 2 – The Economics of One Health*; World Bank, 2012.
68. Coker, R. J.; Hunter, B. M.; Rudge, J. W.; Liverani, M.; Hanvoravongchai, P. Emerging Infectious Diseases in Southeast Asia: Regional Challenges to Control. *Lancet* **2011,** *377* (9765), 599–609.
69. Greger, M. The Human/Animal Interface: Emergence and Resurgence of Zoonotic Infectious Diseases. *Crit. Rev. Microbiol.* **2007,** *33* (4), 243–299. https://doi.org/10.1080/10408410701647594
70. Wu, T.; Perrings, C.; Kinzig, A.; Collins, J. P.; Minteer, B. A.; Daszak, P. Economic Growth, Urbanization, Globalization, and the Risks of Emerging Infectious Diseases in China: A Review. *Ambio* 2017, *46* (1), 18–29. https://doi.org/ 10.1007/s13280–016–0809–2
71. McKercher, B.; Chon, K. The Over-Reaction to SARS and the Collapse of Asian Tourism. *Ann. Tour. Res.* **2004,** *31* (3), 716–719. https://doi.org/10.1016/j.annals.2003.11.002
72. Siu, A.; Wong, Y. R. Economic Impact of SARS: The Case of Hong Kong. *Asian Econ. Papers* **2004,** *3* (1), 62–83. https://doi.org/10.1162/1535351041747996
73. 74. Viboud, C.; Simonsen, L. Global Mortality of 2009 Pandemic Influenza A H1N1. *Lancet Infect. Dis.* **2012,** *12* (9), 651–653. https://doi.org/10.1016/S1473–3099(12)70152–4
74. Hon, K. L. Severe Respiratory Syndromes: Travel History Matters. *Travel Med. Infect. Dis.* **2013,** *11* (5), 285–287. https://www.internationalsos.com/pandemic-sites/pandemic/home/2019-ncov/ncov-travel-restrictionsflight- operations-and-screeninghttps://doi.org/10.1016/j.tmaid.2013.06.005
75. Khan, K.; Arino, J.; Hu, W.; Raposo, P.; Sears, J.; Calderon, F.; Heidebrecht, C.; Macdonald, M.; Liauw, J.; Chan, A.; Gardam, M. Spread of a Novel Influenza A (H1N1) Virus via Global Airline Transportation. *New Engl. J. Med.* **2009,** *361* (2), 212–214. https://doi.org/10.1056/NEJMc0904559
76. Nicolaides, C.; Avraam, D.; Cueto-Felgueroso, L.; Gonz_alez, M. C.; Juanes, R. Hand-Hygiene Mitigation Strategies Against Global Disease Spreading Through the Air Transportation Network. *Risk Anal.* **2019,** *40* (4), 723–740. https://doi.org/10.1111/risa.13438
77. Holtenius, J.; Gillman, A. The Spanish Flu in Uppsala, Clinical and Epidemiological Impact of the Influenza Pandemic 1918–1919 on a Swedish County. *Infect. Ecol. Epidemiol.* **2014,** *4* (1), Art. 21528. https://doi.org/10.3402/iee.v4.21528
78. Greger, M. The Human/Animal Interface: Emergence and Resurgence of Zoonotic Infectious Diseases. *Crit. Rev. Microbiol.* **2007,** *33* (4), 243–299. https://doi.org/10.1080/10408410701647594

79. Page, S.; Yeoman, I. How VisitScotland Prepared for a Flu Pandemic. *J. Bus. Continuity Emergency Plan.* **2007,** *1* (2), 167–182.
80. Navarro Jurado, E.; Ortega Palomo, G.; Torres Bernier, E. Propuestas de reflexi_on desde el turismo frente al COVID-19. Incertidumbre, impacto y recuperaci_on.Universidad de M_alaga, 2020. http://www.i3t.uma.es/wp-content/uploads/2020/03/Propuestas-Reflexiones-Turismo-Im pactoCOVID_
81. Taleb, N. N. *The Black Swan: The Impact of the Highly Improbable*; Random House, 2007.
82. Jamal, T.; Budke, C. Tourism in a World with Pandemics: Local-Global Responsibility and Action. *J. Tour. Fut.* **2020,** ahead-of-print (ahead-of-print). https://www.emerald.com/insight/content/doi/10.1108/JTF-02–2020–0014/full/pdf. doi: 10.1108/JTF-02–2020–0014
83. Channelview. Cheer, J. M.; Lew, A. A. (Eds.). Tourism Resilience and Sustainability: Adapting to Social, Political and Economic Change, 2017.
84. Hall, C. M.; Prayag, G.; Amore, A. Tourism and Resilience: Individual, Organisational and Destination Perspectives, 2018.
85. Higgins-Desbiolles, F.; Carnicelli, S.; Krolikowski, C.; Wijesinghe, G.; Boluk, K. Degrowing tourism: Rethinking Tourism. *J. Sustain. Tour.* **2019,** *27* (12), 1926–1944. DOI: 10.1080/09669582.2019.1601732
86. Fletcher, R.; Murray Mas, I.; Bl_azquez-Salom, M.; Blanco-Romero, A. Tourism, Degrowth, and the COVID-19 Crisis. *Polit. Ecol. Netw.* **2020,** 24 March 2020. https://politicalecologynetwork.org/2020/03/24/tourism-degrowth-and-the-covid-19-crisi s/.
87. Lew, A. How to Create a Better Post-COVID-19 World. *Medium* 2020, 16 March 2020.
88. IATA. International Air Transport Association: Airlines Financial Monitor January–February 2020. https://www.iata.org/en/iata-repository/publications/economic-reports/airlinesfinancial-monitor---feb-2020/ (Accessed 24 Mar 2020).

Index

H

I

L

M

N

P

Q

R

S

T